A Positive Approach to Autism

of related interest

Autism: An Inside–Out Approach
An Innovative Look at the Mechanics of 'Autism' and its Developmental 'Cousins'
Donna Williams
ISBN 1 85302 387 6

Autism and Sensing
The Unlost Instinct
Donna Williams
ISBN 1 85302 612 3

Through the Eyes of Aliens
A Book About Autistic People
Jasmine Lee O'Neill
ISBN 1 85302 710 3

Discovering My Autism
Apologia Pro Vita Sua (with Apologies to Cardinal Newman)
Edgar Schneider
ISBN 1 85302 724 3

Children with Autism, Second Edition
Diagnosis and Intervention to Meet Their Needs
Colwyn Trevarthen, Kenneth Aitken, Despina Papoudi and Jacqueline Robarts
ISBN 1 85302 555 0

Asperger's Syndrome
A Guide for Parents and Professionals
Tony Attwood
ISBN 1 85302 577 1

Pretending to be Normal
Living with Asperger's Syndrome
Liane Holliday Willey
ISBN 1 85302 749 9

Autism and Play
Jannik Beyer and Lone Gammeltoft
ISBN 1 85302 845 2

Small Steps Forward
Using Games and Activities to Help Your Pre-school Child with Special Needs
Sarah Newman
ISBN 1 85302 643 3

A Positive Approach to Autism

Stella Waterhouse

Foreword by Donna Williams

*Drawings by Chris Redman, based on the original
ideas of Drucilla Bruton*

Jessica Kingsley Publishers
London and Philadelphia

Material from *The Empty Fortress: Infantile Autism and the Birth of the Self* by Bruno Bettelheim, copyright © 1967 Bruno Bettelheim, is reprinted with the permission of the Free Press, a division of Simon & Schuster Inc. The passage from *Taken on Trust* by Terry Waite, © 1993 Terry Waite, is reproduced with the permission of Hodder and Stoughton Ltd. The excerpts from *The Boy Who Couldn't Stop Washing* by Judith Rapoport, Copyright © 1989 Judith L. Rapoport, M.D. is used by permission of Dutton, a division of Penguin Putnam Inc., and Harper Collins Publishers Ltd. Extracts from *Emergence Labelled Autistic* by Temple Grandin and Margaret Scariano are reproduced with the permission of Academic Therapy Publications, Novato, California. The material from *An Evil Cradling* by Brian Keenan, published by Hutchinson, is reproduced with the permission of Random House. The quotation from *Little Boy Lost* by Bronwyn Hocking, was published by Bloomsberg Publishing Ltd. in 1990 and is reproduced with permission. The passages from *Living with Your Hyperactive Child* by Miriam Wood and *A Real Person – Life on the Outside* by Gunilla Gerland are published by Souvenir Press and reproduced with permission.

First published in the United Kingdom in 2000 by
Jessica Kingsley Publishers Ltd,
116 Pentonville Road, London
N1 9JB, England
and
325 Chestnut Street,
Philadelphia PA 19106, USA.

www.jkp.com

© Copyright 2000 Stella Waterhouse
© Foreword Copyright 2000 Donna Williams

Second impression 2001

Library of Congress Cataloging in Publication Data
Waterhouse, Stella, 1950
A positive approach to autism / Stella Waterhouse. p. cm.
Includes bibliographical references and index.
ISBN 1 85302 808 8 (pbk. : alk paper) 1. Autism. I. Title.
RC553.A88W38 1999   99-42605
616.89'82--dc21   CIP

British Library Cataloguing in Publication Data
Waterhouse, Stella
a positive approach to autism
1. Autism 2. Autism in children
I. Title
616.8'982

ISBN 1 85302 808 8 pb

Printed and Bound in Great Britain by
Athenaeum Press, Gateshead, Tyne and Wear

Contents

APPENDICES

For David

Acknowledgements

This is the most important page in the whole book, for it gives me the opportunity to thank all those people who helped and encouraged me along the way.

With love and thanks to David, my parents and to Auntie Pat who gave me support and the encouragement to continue each time I faltered. Thanks too to Vida Sutton and to Cilla Bruton whose original ideas were the basis for the drawings found throughout this book. Many other parents deserve acknowledgement too for they gave unstintingly of their time and our discussions helped shape my ideas; in particular Anne Morton, Shirley Johnson and Mr and Mrs Fox.

Special thanks go to Donna Williams whose ideas, criticisms and – especially – questions constantly challenged my thinking.

I am also extremely grateful to Richard Attfield, Helen Fox, Neil Mitchelhill and their respective families who kindly allowed me to use their writings, and to Isabella Thomas who allowed me to use her son's drawing. The accounts of many other people with autism have also helped in the writing of this book by elucidating the questions, challenging my preconceptions and, like Gunilla Gerland, making me question some of my ideas. Many thanks to those organizations which helped provide information, especially the National Autistic Society and the Autism Research Institute.

I would also like to acknowledge all those who have allowed me to use their work to illuminate the path and thank the many professionals from different fields who so willingly contributed their knowledge and freely shared their ideas. I hope they consider their time well spent. Whilst too many to mention individually I would particularly like to mention Paul Shattock OBE, Paul Whiteley and Sally Goddard Blythe who have answered my questions with unfailing patience. Thanks are also due to Ian Jordan who commented on my ideas and provided the proof I needed of the visual problems; to Norman Healey who, despite the many pressures on his time, read and commented on the parts of the manuscript for me; and to Barbara Jones for her unceasing patience in deciphering and typing my notes. Thanks also to Helen Parry, my editor, and to Caroline Tingay and the many other people who have worked so hard on the production of my book.

I am extremely grateful to the following people and organizations who have given me permission to use the quotes from various books and journals which have enriched the text: Bloomsbury Publishing Ltd, Dr Jules Bemporad and Plenum Publishing Corporation, Clara Claiborne Park, Random House, Macmillan, Dr David Comings, Dr Glenn Doman, Gunilla Gerland and the Hannserik Gonnheim Agency, Paul Shattock and Paul Whiteley, Souvenir Press Ltd, Terry Waite, Lucas Alexander Whiteley, Hodder and Stoughton, Donna Williams, Dr David Horrobin and Medical Hypotheses, Academic Therapy Publications, Fred R. Volkmar. Annabel Stehli, Bernard Rimland, Daniel Goleman, J. Marriage PLD, Helen Irlen and Oliver Sacks.

Foreword

When I met Stella Waterhouse around five years ago I was, on reflection, surprised that a non-autistic 'professional' had ideas about autism which seemed so much closer to an autistic perspective than can be said for many others. Generally, professionals view autism as a collection of symptoms, generally overlooking the place of those symptoms within the autistic system of functioning and so, too, they miss the language of autism and what it is trying to tell the non-autistic world. As one teacher wrote: if you want to understand French you get a native French speaker, if you want to understand Autistic, you approach an Autistic person. Stella's somewhat anthropological approach attempts to use a refreshingly an inside-out approach instead of the usual outside-in one which relies on description of symptoms rather than the experience of those symptoms.

Stella Waterhouse seemed to have stumbled through the obstacles of non-autistic assumption to attempt to see past the symptoms to the systems at work within autism. She looks at these as a key not to suppression and control of autistic symptoms, but to reducing some of their causes; the goal of functioning on its own, not seen as so important on its own but in the context of autistic discomfort. As a person with autism who grew up with the ignorant emphasis on functioning without regard for experiencing one's learned functioning and as someone who hears from too many very sad high functioning 'facades' out there, I welcome Stella's book; it gives hope for some directions through which these people can pick up their developmental pieces. It also gives paths through which those so called 'low functioning' people who didn't, wouldn't or couldn't buy into the production-line learn-to-function theme: they may be able to come forward a little more as 'whole selves'.

Stella takes the loose ends of sensory and perceptual, cognitive, anxiety, self-control and biochemistry problems, tracing them back to the spool from which these seemingly disconnected tangles came from. In this, she has a holistic approach to the understanding of autism, something sadly lacking in most professional literature on the subject.

Donna Williams

Introduction

These children are denied the greatest gift of life – the joy of a relationship with another person.

Dustin Hoffman, after playing the title role in the film 'The Rainman'.

There have always been people suffering from autism, but it was only in 1943 that it was identified as a specific syndrome by Dr Leo Kanner, an American child psychiatrist at Johns Hopkins University (Kanner 1943). He used the Greek word 'autos' (self) to describe the condition, which he then termed 'early infantile autism', because he felt that such children were 'inward looking' and engrossed only in themselves.

In ancient times, people with autism and those with epilepsy may well have been considered 'possessed'. Moving forward to the nineteenth century, we find a description suggestive of a child with autism in Itard's account of *The Wild Boy of Averyon* (Humphrey 1962). It has also been suggested that the central character of Charles Dickens' book *Barnaby Rudge* fits the description of an adult suffering from Asperger's syndrome in many ways (Grove 1988). Indeed, it is quite possible that some of the bizarre and distressed behaviour seen by paying spectators at the Bethlehem Royal Asylum (Bedlam) was that of people with such problems. This speculation is confirmed in part by Dr Bernard Rimland who mentions a very early textbook which describes a five-year-old boy, identifiable as autistic, who was admitted to Bethlehem Asylum in 1799 (Rimland 1964).

Even now, over fifty years later and despite continuing research, the cause or causes of autism have yet to be discovered, for although many theories have been proposed, none appears to fit all cases. However, with the development of more sophisticated brain scanning techniques and co-operation between researchers in different fields it should be possible to acquire an answer in the next decade, perhaps by validating a number of causes.

Autism can range from mild to extremely severe and although estimates vary, studies indicate that the incidence of autism is found in almost one child out of every hundred. It is also known to affect four times more boys than girls and that, in comparison with the rest of the population, sufferers have an increased risk of epilepsy, although the reasons for these factors are as yet unclear.

Even within my lifetime, children suffering from autism have been subjected to some very disturbing 'treatments' involving electric shocks and other questionable practices, which would appear to have evolved out of desperation. These seem to have their origins in earlier ages when such people were subjected to punitive treatment in order to exorcize the devils by which they were thought to be possessed: methods which would have been strongly criticized if the children had been physically handicapped or suffered from other more understandable problems such as Down's syndrome. Perhaps the fact that they received little condemnation merely indicates the levels of confusion and despair surrounding the problem.

These 'treatments' have fortunately given way to more civilized methods, but there are still many conflicting views on effective treatment. To date no one cure has been found, although some people appear to have recovered and the effects of the handicap have been minimized and alleviated for many.

It is a subject, too, in which there still appear to be many sacred cows – theories which are not necessarily proven but which are of long standing. These are often fiercely defended by their advocates if questioned or, worse still, 'challenged'. Currently there are many different groups working on their own theories, who look, sometimes with scant objectivity, at new ideas.

Against this background, the views of parents and sufferers often seem to be disregarded, while potentially valuable ideas do not easily reach across oceans. In a book review in December 1989 of a collection of poems by a Canadian suffering from autism (Eastham 1989), the reviewer had the arrogance to make the following comments: 'The author was almost too intellectually aware of autism to be autistic himself; the description of his world showed more insight and imagination than one imagined in a person with autism' concluding that '...while an interesting collection it did not describe autism as [the reviewer] understood it!'

I have worked closely with both children and adults suffering from autism over a period of several years and am concerned that much of the current literature appears unduly pessimistic. In addition, several fallacies which need to be challenged still surround this handicap. These include the following:

- Many people with autism are uneducable and the majority would be mentally handicapped if they were not autistic.

- They have no feelings and do not want to communicate.

- The problem is caused/made worse by the parents.

While most people believe that the first two ideas are already out of date, I have heard both said within the past few years; not by the general public but by 'professionals'. It is strange that such ideas still linger for, even in the 1970s people recognized that it would be dangerous to assume that a child who had no command of words and little apparent understanding had no feelings.

Unfortunately the idea of 'cold parenting', a common assumption in the 1950s and 1960s, has been reawakened (albeit unintentionally) by some proponents of 'Holding Therapy' for, although shying away from bleak words such as 'cold' or 'frozen', they suggest that the behaviour of parents can 'facilitate' autism.

So after examining the reasons behind the existence of these fallacies and discussing them in some detail, I hope to be able to show that they are indeed misguided. I also intend, if – and only if – the evidence permits, to prove that the converse is in fact true and that:

- The vast majority of people with autism are of potentially normal intelligence and all are educable if provided with the right help.

- They begin life with all the potential for feelings that 'normal' people have and do want to communicate even though they may have difficulties in doing so in a 'normal' understandable manner.

- Most parents are warm and caring people, coping with immense difficulties which are frequently compounded by unthinking attitudes.

Some support for the first two points would seem to come from Sharisa Kochmeister, who has both cerebral palsy and autism and does not speak. At the age of four Sharisa was said to have an IQ of 24 although this had 'dropped' to 10 by the time she had reached twelve. After two years of Facilitated Communication (about which controversial subject more later) she achieved an IQ score of 142 and was able to begin attending classes in a regular high school. She now types independently with any of several familiar facilitators sitting beside her. As she writes in *Dancing In The Rain*:

… I disagree with much of what professionals think they know about autism and people with autism. Most of us are not retarded, we do both have and comprehend feelings, we are capable of both imagination and abstract thinking, and we do experience pain, pleasure, sadness, and joy. While it may seem that we don't understand things, this is not true. The real difficulties occur in speed and style of processing, digesting, and responding to what has been presented. This is largely due to an over abundance of internal communication rather than a lack of it. It is exceedingly difficult to communicate with others when one's time is so taken up with attempts to make sense of a world one finds so confusing. This is the true curse of autism – great ability to absorb coupled with poor ability to process and react. (Stehli 1995, pp.81–86)

So just where does the truth lie? The whole subject is reminiscent of a detective story where there is an abundance of clues, not all of them genuine. Although my aim is clear, it cannot be reached unless I examine each clue, discarding those which are unproven, before attempting to draw the threads together to make a coherent picture which fits the evidence available at present.

Initially I shall look at the criteria used for diagnosis, and then go on to discuss some of the past and present theories surrounding autism and some other disorders which might have some bearing on this search. Background information on some of the terms mentioned is to be found in the Appendices. This book does not claim to be comprehensive but it is, I hope, comprehensible. I make no apology for any omissions from the lists of diagnostic criteria for these are numerous and space is limited. Equally, I do not apologize for the inclusion of some of the less acceptable items in the first chapter, for while it would be easy to select only those ideas with which I agree, all deserve consideration as otherwise my conclusions could be open to doubt and easily (and deservedly) discredited.

I shall also take account of the views, ideas, writings and words of people with autism themselves, for to omit these would nullify any conclusions I might make. It has to be accepted, though, that as I have never had to deal with the difficulties that people with autism face, I obviously see things from a different perspective. This may mean that on some points my ideas and conclusions will differ from those of some of the people concerned but I hope that, whilst there may be many points of disagreement, even the strongest advocates of 'autistic' rights will accept that I am fully supportive of their wish to be treated with respect.

Once all these things have been considered I shall discuss some ideas which might be new to the majority of people and also pose questions which I hope will be answered in the not too distant future. This will then be followed by a look at assessment and a discussion of the various treatments which are available with a bibliography and addresses of relevant organizations at the back.

In the first edition of this book I touched only briefly upon the research into the possible biological causes of autism, feeling that that was best left to those with the facilities for research. While the latter point is still true this edition differs from the original for, as you will see, much of my search through new areas of information threw up clues in relation to the underlying causes which begged for inclusion. These fascinated me, challenging (and altering) some of my previous conclusions by providing further pieces of the jigsaw puzzle and finally enabling me to add greater depth to my hypotheses. I hope they will interest you too.

I should also point out that, while I have tried to ensure that the facts presented here are accurate, any errors or misinterpretations are solely my responsibility.

Finally, and most importantly, I would ask you to suspend any preconceived ideas, so that you can consider what follows with an open mind.

Note: I have used the masculine and feminine singular pronouns interchangeably when referring to a child or an adult.

CHAPTER 1

Investigation

The little things are infinitely the most important.

Sherlock Holmes by Arthur Conan Doyle

Criteria

First, we must look at the various criteria that are used in diagnosing autism. These were initially set out by Kanner (1943) when he listed five common characteristics, which were:

1. The inability to relate to and interact with people from the beginning of life.

2. The inability to communicate with others through language.

3. An obsession with maintaining sameness and resisting change.

4. A preoccupation with objects rather than people.

5. The occasional evidence of good potential for intelligence.

A year later in Vienna, Asperger published a paper which also identified and defined the problem, although he included cases that ranged from the severe (due to organic damage) to the very mild (Asperger 1944). Over the years, Asperger's syndrome has become synonymous with the intelligent and 'near normal' person although it is now being recognized that some people with autism also fall into the 'high functioning' category.

While the main features of the two conditions are similar, there are important differences. People with Asperger's syndrome tend to exhibit special interests or skills, as demonstrated by Stephen Wiltshire's architectural drawings (Wiltshire 1987). Other examples include the ability some have to play music heard only once accurately 'by ear' and by others who demonstrate an excellent grasp of mathematical formulations such as calculations or astronomy. Oddly, though, their movements may be clumsy, in sharp contrast to the children defined by Kanner who are generally extremely well co-ordinated. In addition, it is suggested that people with Asperger's syndrome generally have a higher degree of self-awareness than those with Kanner's syndrome and are therefore more often aware of the impediments posed by their handicap, particularly in the development of social relationships. This awareness may cause anger against and distress about their circumstances, which can lead to depression.

The criteria proposed by Kanner and Asperger have been updated by various authorities since. In 1961 Mildred Creak published a paper that clearly listed nine features which, if observed, would indicate the child was autistic. These were:

1. Gross and sustained impairment of emotional relationships with people. *He is withdrawn, does not make friends and lacks awareness of other people.*

2. Apparent unawareness of the child's own personal identity to a degree inappropriate to his age. *He may remain 'unaware' of his own body even in adulthood.*

3. Pathological preoccupation with particular objects or certain character-istics of them without regard to their accepted functions. *Unlike other children his play is repetitive, for example he may continually spin the wheels on a toy car. He does not demonstrate imaginative play.*

4. Sustained resistance to change in the environment and a striving to maintain or restore that sameness. *He finds changes confusing and frightening.*

5. Abnormal perceptual experiences. *These are not fully understood. The child might be sensitive to light and sound, but can react strangely when hurt, as he apparently ignores pain.*

6. Acute, excessive and illogical anxiety. *He often displays a fear of something most people would regard as perfectly safe, for example some smells and/or physical touch can cause a fearful reaction.*

7. Speech may have been lost, or never acquired, or may have failed to develop beyond an elementary level.

8. Distortion in mobility patterns. *He often moves in an unusual manner, perhaps walking on tiptoe.*

9. A background of serious retardation in which islets of normal, near normal or exceptional intellectual function or skill may appear. *He may have difficulty in doing simple tasks, but be able to play an instrument, draw or do difficult calculations exceptionally well.*

The child's general behaviour may be quite unusual as he can be extremely passive, quiet and lacking in all motivation, or alternatively display signs of frantic hyperactivity.

Since the publication of Creak's criteria, slightly altered lists have been proposed by Gerald O'Gorman (1967) and others. Their ideas were then further condensed and refined by Sir Michael Rutter (1978) and Elizabeth Newson (1977), both of whom have spent many years researching the problems presented by autism. Each of them contracted the criteria to four similar points, covering language and social development, rigidity of thought and resistance to change.

These criteria have been set out in a simplified form by the National Autistic Society (see Useful Addresses at the end of the book) as follows:

1. Difficulty with social relationships.

2. Difficulty with verbal and non-verbal communication.

3. Difficulty in the development of play and imagination.

4. Resistance to change in routine.

These headings are used in conjunction with diagrams which illustrate the various points, such as echolalia (the repetition of words or phrases used by another person), although it is stressed that they are only some of the ways in which autism is displayed.

The criteria miss one point though, for both Rutter and Newson suggested that onset before thirty months was a necessary criterion for autism. This is an interesting point, for while they believed that this is one of the characteristics of 'true autism', there are a growing number of cases where 'autistic features' have been observed in a person who was considered 'normal' until illness struck. Similar features can also appear in accident cases where severe brain damage has occurred. In many of the latter cases the people concerned are classed as brain damaged, although the behaviour they display is typically autistic, in that they are withdrawn and demonstrate obsessive or compulsive behaviours.

Thus in his description of *The Autist Artist*, Sacks (1987, pp. 12–18) refers to 'secondary' autism being caused, at the age of eight, by brain disease (thought to be a type of encephalitis). A similar case was reported in a fourteen-year-old girl after she had suffered from encephalitis for although she had been considered by her parents to be a shy and somewhat anxious child, she attended normal school, related to her peers and did well scholastically. Ten days after the onset of her illness, during which she had a seizure lasting fifteen minutes, she began to display a variety of 'autistic features' which increased as time went on. These included averting her gaze when approached, looking through people, reacting with a pained expression to noise and displaying echolalia and bizarre behaviour. I also know of a young woman who began to display similar autistic features after suffering severe brain injury in a car accident, although she had been 'normal' until the age of twenty-one. While such people may not be truly autistic, they would appear to need similar specialist help in order to progress. Could it also be that the causes of their problems may throw some light upon the cause(s) of 'true' autism?

Interestingly, the World Health Organization and the American Psychiatric Association have also issued similar diagnostic lists in recent years, although the age of onset has altered over the years. While again the behavioural criteria are expanded with concrete examples, an abbreviated version of DSM-IV (Diagnostic and Statistical Manual of Mental Disorders, 1994) for autism now reads:

1. Onset before 3 years.

2. Delayed or abnormal function in at least one of the following areas:

    –   qualitative impairment in social interaction;

    –   qualitative impairment in communication;

    –   restricted repetitive and stereotyped patterns of behaviour, interests and activities.

In contrast, the DSM-IV for Asperger's syndrome makes no mention of age of onset; and although the first two criteria are similar to those of autism, thereafter they differ significantly as can be seen from this abridged version:

1. Qualitative impairment in social interaction.

2. Restricted repetitive and stereotyped patterns of behaviour, interests and activities.

3. Clinically significant impairment in social, occupational, or other important areas of functioning.

4. No clinically significant general delay in language, for example single word used by the age of two, communicative phrases used by the age of three.

5. No clinically significant delay in cognitive development or in the development of age-appropriate self-help skills, adaptive behaviour (other than in social interaction) and curiosity about the environment in childhood.

6. Criteria are not met for other specific pervasive developmental disorder or schizophrenia.

It also points out that people with Asperger's syndrome are likely to suffer from depression in later life, resulting from an awareness on the part of the subject that he or she is different and has difficulty forming relationships.

So can we clarify approximately how many people are affected by autism and Asperger's syndrome? There is some variation in the figures but whilst it is possible that there is a real disparity in the prevalence of such disorders throughout the world it is generally thought that the figures diverge because of variations in the way in which the terms are defined.

Information from the National Autistic Society (1997) suggests that the best estimates are those based on two particular studies. The first, carried out in 1979 in Camberwell by Lorna Wing and Judith Gould, looked at children with an IQ of under 70 who had problems as defined by Kanner. The second was done in Gothenburg in 1993 by Stephan Ehlers and Christopher Gillberg. They looked at children in mainstream schools in order to assess the number of children with Asperger's syndrome and related disorders with IQs of over 70. This latter group seem to include those identified by Sula Wolff in Edinburgh in 1995 who are at the most 'able' end of the spectrum: a group made up of people whose difficulties are very subtle for although their social interaction is impaired they do not have all the other problems normally associated with autism/related disorders and the majority live independent lives.

Thus the results of these two studies cover the whole spectrum of autism. They indicate that 2 people in every 1000 with an IQ under 70 have severe problems whilst approximately 7.1 in 1000 with an IQ over 70 have moderate to mild difficulties associated with Asperger's syndrome and related disorders. This gives a possible prevalence of 9.1 per 1000 people over the whole range of the autistic spectrum which translates into over 500,000 people in Britain. We also find that there is a disparity between the sexes, males being affected far more than females. In autism this ratio is approximately 4:1 but in Asperger's syndrome it rises greatly, reaching a ratio of 9:1.

Returning now to the lists of criteria we find that, although they are coupled with examples, they do not contain comparisons with 'normal' development but rely on qualitative terms which may be difficult to judge, especially when the symptoms are very mild. The first people to be approached by the anxious parents will not be the experienced clinicians but rather the health visitor or doctor, who may in their careers have seen very few children or adults with autism. This lack of knowledge can sometimes lead to problems, as for example when one doctor told his patient that the very fact he could sit and ask if he was autistic meant he couldn't be! As some of the symptoms also occur in other types of handicap, these professionals need clear guidelines to help them make an initial diagnosis.

Fortunately this need has now been addressed in two ways. Simon Baron-Cohen and his colleagues (1992) have developed the Checklist for Autism in Toddlers (CHAT). This is being used to assess young children and can be used by doctors to give an early indication of the problems.

Wing and Gould have also developed a method called the Diagnostic Interview for Social and Communications Disorder (known as Disco). This is helpful in diagnosing new cases at an early stage or in confirming a diagnosis.

It should also identify those children and adults who might previously have been left undiagnosed because their difficulties are subtle. Both these developments offer great hope for early intervention and treatment.

However, before looking at diagnosis or coming to any conclusions it would be useful to consider normal development for this will provide a background to some of the areas I shall detail. Such work fills volumes, but for the purpose of this book I shall only mention those facts which might prove relevant to this investigation.

Development
Birth
The human brain is not fully formed at birth but continues to develop throughout life, the most intense growth occurring during childhood. Children are born with many more neurons than they will retain. These are gradually 'pruned' as the brain eliminates the less well used neural paths and connections, whilst strengthening those which receive most use. New synaptic connections are shaped by our experiences, particularly in childhood, and can form within hours or days. It is interesting to note that the baby's brain has an intimate connection between the visual and auditory systems which will later be lost (Carter 1998).

The healthy baby is born with functioning sensory organs which are of vital importance, for it is through them that he experiences the world. Indeed, as the eighteenth century philosopher Etienne Bonnot de Condillac wrote, 'Nothing is known to us except through our senses'; an idea which formed the basis of Itard's work with the 'wild boy' of Averyon and also underlies the present work done in the Montessori schools.

In the early days of life, the senses of smell, taste and touch are more highly developed than sight or hearing. This is clearly demonstrated in the area of touch, where the baby's sensitivity is such that if tickled in one area the whole of his body will respond by quivering with excitement. This sense is greatest in the regions of the face, finger-tips and thumbs, which all play a large part in his exploration of the world around him.

New facts are now emerging about new-born babies and pain. Whilst premature babies lack the ability to dampen down pain it is now known that new-born babies have a unique pain-signalling mechanism which disappears as they grow older. The sensory nerve fibres that communicate non-harmful touch are very close to the pain-carrying receptors and this leads them to respond less selectively, feeling apparently ordinary stimuli (such as a light touch) as painful. Their sensory nerve cells are also connected to larger areas of skin than that of an adult so they can feel pain over greater areas of the body. Thus the new-born baby has a quicker reaction to pain than an older child. The nerve pathways which carry pain-inhibiting messages from the brain stem to the spinal cord mature later than other parts of the system and may account for the fact that, once triggered, the feeling of pain will last for longer than it would in an adult.

In contrast, although the foetus has been responsive to sounds from the twentieth week, hearing is the least well-developed sense at birth. This is partly because the middle ear still contains amniotic fluid, although the baby will respond to loud noises and low frequency tones (perhaps similar to those of his mother's heartbeat when in the womb) which are particularly effective in soothing him when distressed. It is now also recognized that the infant is more sensitive to high-pitched noises than the older child and his hearing is more prone to damage because of this.

Vision too is not fully developed at birth and, whilst he can see faces perfectly well when they are close to him, he is unable to focus both eyes together and has no depth perception. The colour-sensitive cells in his eyes are not fully developed either and so he cannot distinguish colours properly, seeing the world only in muted colours.

As the child grows, a change occurs. Taste and smell are generally 'relegated' to a secondary role, while the senses of sight and hearing gradually increase in importance. The ability to see will play the greatest part in his exploration of the world, for he uses his eyes not only to explore the environment and avoid hazards, but also to relate to his parents by responding to their facial expressions. Later he will use his vision to recognize the myriad shapes that make up our written language. His hearing too will be of great importance in the learning process, for his parents will talk to him while he is feeding, being dressed or played with, long before he can actually be expected to respond verbally. It is this exposure to speech which forms the basis of his linguistic development in his early years.

The child is at his most receptive in these early years and will actually learn more within the first three years of life than throughout the rest of his life. He does this by listening, observing and exploring, gradually developing his skills through socialization and play.

Development of the young child

Much research has been carried out by various experts into the development of the young child. Perhaps the best known work is that of the renowned Swiss scholar Piaget, who, over a period of many years, did much work on developmental psychology, drawing upon observations of his own children as well as his knowledge of zoology, psychology and philosophy. He proposed the idea that man's psychological development takes place in a particular sequence, each stage of which is dependent on the completion of the previous one so that, even though each child learns at his own pace, the sequence is always the same (Spencer Pulaski 1980).

Whilst Piaget's idea that children learn to think (and develop intelligence) by exploring and doing things for themselves has exerted a strong influence on primary education, researchers generally agree that the transition from one stage to another is a more gradual, continuous process than he recognized and that the ability of most children is in advance of the stages he proposed (see Appendix H).

However, the idea that development follows a particular sequence, with each stage being dependent upon the completion of the previous one, is extremely important: as further research has clearly shown, this pattern also applies to other areas of growth.

The chart shown in Figure 1.1, based on close observation of numerous children over a period of years, was originally developed at the Institutes for the Achievement of Human Potential in Philadelphia by Glenn Doman and colleagues (Doman 1990). It evolved through their work with brain-damaged children and shows the relationship between the development of the young child and the orderly growth of the brain.

While the chart covers physical development there is one other important aspect which also demands attention: emotional intelligence. Although this is a comparatively new area in mainstream science, it provides another aspect of our being which may prove important when exploring autism.

Here I would like to consider Daniel Goleman's 1995 work in which he lists the five different stages of emotional intelligence taken from the work of Salovey. An abridged version of this shows, once again, that each stage is built upon the previous one. Thus we have:

1. *Knowing one's emotions.* Self-awareness – recognising a feeling as it happens. The ability to monitor feelings from moment to moment is crucial to psychological insight and self understanding.

2. *Managing emotions.* Handling feelings so that they are appropriate is an ability that builds on self-awareness.

3. *Motivating oneself.* Marshalling emotions in the service of goal is essential for paying attention, for self motivation and mastery and for creativity. Emotional self-control – delaying gratification, and stifling impulsiveness – underlies accomplishment of every sort.

4. *Recognising emotions in others.* Empathy, another ability that builds on emotional self-awareness, is the fundamental 'people skill'. People who are empathic are more attuned to the subtle social signals that indicate what others need or want.

5. *Handling relationships.* The art of relationships is, in large part, skill in managing emotions in others. These are the abilities that undergird popularity, leadership, and personal effectiveness. (Goleman 1995, p.43)

Simplistically, each aspect of development can be seen as a series of building blocks placed one upon the other. Each has to be carefully placed in the right position if the structure is to prove solid. Successful development is only achieved if each stage is completed correctly and the child's progress will be damaged or hindered if any stage is either missing or incomplete.

Finally I would like to briefly mention the basic personality traits (our character) which psychologists divide into categories, the extremes being the introvert and the extrovert. H.J. Eysenck believed that these factors were probably inherited and as such have a biological basis. He linked these to the way in which the nervous system and particularly the reticular activating system (RAS) (see Appendix B) react to stimuli. He reasoned that extroverts had a strong nervous system in which the RAS inhibits incoming messages while introverts have a weak system which amplifies information. This effectively means that the extrovert is quickly bored by one set of stimuli, liking and seeking variation and novelty. In contrast the introvert is less likely to become bored and as a result is happy with solitary pursuits, his or her own company or that of just a few others. These categories may prove relevant in our search.

This exploration of some of the factors which contribute to the development both of our physical skills and our personalities provides the background upon which I hope we can begin to build a clear picture of the difficulties facing those with autism.

Figure 1.1 The Institutes' Development Profile

	BRAIN STAGE	TIME FRAME	VISUAL COMPETENCE	AUDITORY COMPETENCE	TACTILE COMPETENCE
A	SOPHISTICATED CORTEX	Superior – 36 Months Average – 72 Months Slow – 144 Months	Reading with total understanding *Sophisticated human understanding*	Understanding of complete vocabulary and proper sentences *Sophisticated human understanding*	Tactile identification of objects *Sophisticated human understanding*
B	PRIMITIVE CORTEX	Superior – 18 Months Average – 36 Months Slow – 72 Months	Indentification of visual symbols and letter with experience *Primitive human understanding*	Understanding of 2000 words and simple sentences *Primitive human understanding*	Ability to determine characteristics of objects by tactile means *Primitive human understanding*
C	EARLY CORTEX	Superior – 9 Months Average – 18 Months Slow – 36 Months	Differentiation of similar but unlike simple visual symbols *Early human understanding*	Understanding of 10 to 25 words and two word couplets *Early human understanding*	Tactile differentiation of similar but unlike objects *Early human understanding*
D	INITIAL CORTEX	Superior – 6 Months Average – 12 Months Slow – 24 Months	Convergence of vision resulting in simple depth perception *Initial human understanding*	Understanding of two words of speech *Initial human understanding*	Tactile understanding of the third dimension in objects which appear to be flat *Initial human understanding*
E	MIDBRAIN	Superior – 3.5 Months Average – 7 Months Slow – 14 Months	Appreciation of detail with a configuration *Meaningful appreciation*	Appreciation of meaningful sounds *Meaningful appreciation*	Appreciation of gnostic sensation *Meaningful appreciation*
F	PONS	Superior – 1 Month Average – 2.5 Months Slow – 5 Months	Outline perception *Vital perception*	Vital response to threatening sounds *Vital perception*	Perception of vital sensation *Vital perception*
G	MEDULLA and CORD	Superior – Birth to .5 Average – Birth to 1.0 Slow – Birth to 2.0	Light reflex *Reflex reception*	Startle reflex *Reflex reception*	Babinski reflex *Reflex reception*

(Doman 1990; reproduced with the permission of Glenn Doman)

Figure 1.1 The Institutes' Development Profile (continued)

	MOBILITY	LANGUAGE	MANUAL COMPETENCE
A	Using a leg in a skilled role which is consistent with the dominant hemisphere *Sophisticated human expression*	Complete vocabulary and proper sentence structure *Sophisticated human expression*	Using a hand to write which is consistent with the dominant hemisphere *Sophisticated human expression*
B	Walking and running in complete cross pattern *Primitive human expression*	2000 words of language and short sentences *Primitive human expression*	Bimanual function with one hand in a skilled role *Primitive human expression*
C	Walking with arms freed from the primary balance role *Early human expression*	10 to 25 words of language and two word couplets *Early human expression*	Cortical opposition bilaterally and simultaneously *Early human expression*
D	Walking with arms used in a primary balance role most frequently at or above shoulder height Initial human expression	Two words of speech used spontaneously and meaningfully Initial human expression	Cortical opposition in either hand Initial human expression
E	Creeping on hands and knees, culminating in cross pattern creeping Meaningful response	Creation of meaningful sounds Meaningful response	Prehensile grasp Meaningful response
F	Crawling in the prone position culminating in cross pattern crawling Vital response	Vital crying in response to threats to life Vital response	Vital release Vital response
G	Movement of arms and legs without bodily movement Reflex response	Birth cry and crying Reflex response	Grasp reflex Reflex response

CHAPTER 2

Theories and Ideas

It is a capital mistake to theorise before you have all the evidence. It biases the judgement.

Sherlock Holmes by Arthur Conan Doyle

In this chapter I have selected a limited number of examples which are representative of the various schools of thought. While offering some of the past and current theories for consideration, I will not attempt to discuss them in depth as the reader can gain more information by reading the books referred to.

A variety of theories concerning the cause(s) of autism have been put forward over the years. These theories fall mainly into two groups: those which suggest the cause is psychological and others which support the idea that it has a physical or organic basis. Interestingly, some of these theories overlap into other areas or interweave but, as you will see, even those who broadly agree on one aspect often disagree on others.

Emotional deprivation

First a controversial theory which explained the cause of the condition in psychological terms, stating that it was primarily the child's response to a lack of maternal warmth. This idea appears to have stemmed originally from Kanner and his frequent collaborator Eisenberg when they said that 'emotional refrigeration has been the common lot of autistic children.' Such an extreme statement grasped media and public attention and overshadowed the fact that they continued:

> ...it seems to us equally clear that *this factor,* while important in the development of the syndrome, *is not sufficient in itself* to result in its appearance. There appears to be *some way in which the children are different from the beginning of their extra-uterine existence.* (Kanner and Eisenberg 1956, pp.556–566, my emphasis)

The emphasis placed on 'deprivation' caused much additional distress to parents who were already facing great difficulties in coping with the bewildering and inexplicable behaviour of their handicapped child. Fortunately, that theory remains unsubstantiated and has fallen into disrepute with the passing of time, although the arguments around it have surfaced again over the last few years.

Bruno Bettleheim appeared to reinforce Kanner's theme in his book *The Empty Fortress* (1967) and much of his work has therefore been ignored by those involved with autism, even though he successfully treated several children over a period of time.

His psychoanalytic approach led him to believe that the anxiety demonstrated by the child with autism derived from 'an unremitting fear for his life' which caused mortal anxiety; a thought shared by others. However, there were some apparent contradictions in his work, for in another paragraph he stated: 'Fortunately psychoanalysts are beginning to decry the haunting image of the rejecting mother'. Unfortunately, though, there were other more potent words, which stated that 'a precipitating factor was the parents' wish that the child should not exist'; a comment which, once again, provided rich though inaccurate fodder for the media (Bettleheim 1967, p.69).

The reasons which led to his conviction that the problem was indeed psychological stemmed from his experiences when, at the beginning of the war, he had been imprisoned in a concentration camp. While incarcerated there, he came across people who had effectively withdrawn from the world in order to cope with their intolerable living conditions. The other prisoners nicknamed them 'Muslims' because they appeared to have totally resigned themselves to their fate. They displayed some of the types of behaviour that may be seen amongst people with autism, for they were totally non-communicative and displayed ritualistic behaviour, whilst some replaced the horror of their daily lives with delusions or fantasy. Why was it that all those who suffered so appallingly in these camps did not display such symptoms? Could the reason possibly lie in the 'inner strength' of the person concerned? These questions will be discussed in Chapter 3.

Bettleheim was lucky enough to have influential friends in America who helped secure his release in the early years of the war and he was allowed to emigrate to the United States where he remained for the rest of his life.

Later, while working as a psychiatrist at the Orthogenic School attached to the University of Philadelphia, he observed that several children with autism displayed similar withdrawal and obsessive or ritualistic behaviours. He concluded that such behaviours might have been developed to give 'protection' after traumatic experiences in their early lives which, unfortunately, he linked to a lack of bonding (i.e. the establishment of a relationship between mother and child through which the baby is made to feel secure). This is vital to the child's future emotional health and generally happens naturally for most people, although it can be disrupted by physical separation, illness or, as Bettleheim implied, by the mother's lack of responsiveness to her child. Thus the myth of maternal deprivation as a cause of autism was reinforced.

Three other points were also suggested by Bettleheim, all of which will be discussed in more detail later. These were:

1. The sufferers did in fact interact with others, albeit in a negative rather than a positive way. He felt that their apparent indifference hid an underlying and firmly repressed hatred which he claimed showed in a tremendous anger once their isolation had been penetrated. He further suggested that if the causes of the hatred could be explored and dealt with, 'love' would be found underneath.

2. The breakdown in communication was caused by an overwhelming anxiety which could not be alleviated for the child had given up hope.

3. The child consciously chose not to speak or not to use the word 'I'.

In their book *Autism – New Hope for a Cure* (1983) Niko and Elisabeth Tinbergen agree with Bettleheim and others that the person with autism lives in a state of almost continuous withdrawal, which they also suggest is caused by anxiety. Unfortunately, the Tinbergens also seem to feel that the underlying factor behind the existence of this anxiety is emotional conflict, which they consider to be the result of a gradually developing estrangement between the child and the people around him.

They developed this idea attributing the absence of effective treatment to the fact that it is generally only the child who is seen as the problem and arguing that it is a problem of two people: mother and child. These ideas led them to endorse the theories of Martha Welch and the Holding Therapy she developed, discussed further in Chapter 6.

Welch states that autism is caused by faulty bonding; a statement she supports by saying that children who recover (through holding) show no residual organic pathology; that is, they have no long-term problems in the areas of speech or communication. She then attracts controversy by proposing that the mothers of children with autism lack the normal instincts towards their child prior to treatment! Such comments have, not unnaturally, led to the expression of strong feelings against her treatment, although some parents who have tried her method in their search for a cure feel their child has achieved far more progress than would otherwise have been possible. I must however agree with Anthony when he says: 'I do not think that the traumata which sometimes seem to precipitate a psychosis in childhood are anything greater than normal developmental hazards (sibling birth etc.). It is the predisposition that makes them vulnerable' (Rimland 1964, p.63).

It is important to be aware that, while suggestions of emotional conflict impose further unnecessary and unjustified pressures on parents who are already struggling to understand and cope with their child's difficulties, they can also have a devastating effect on the child with autism. This comes across very clearly in an article by Jim Sinclair in which he says:

> They don't harm the parents nearly as much as they harm the victim when they say a child chooses to be autistic. The results of these assumptions are often subtle, but they're pervasive and pernicious: I am not taken seriously. My credibility is suspect. My understanding of myself is not considered to be valid, and my perceptions of events are not considered to be based in reality. My rationality is questioned because, regardless of intellect, I still appear odd. My ability to make reasonable decisions, based on my own carefully reasoned priorities, is doubted because I don't make the same decisions that people with different priorities would make. I'm accused of being deliberately obtuse because people who understand the things I don't understand can't understand how anyone can possibly not understand them. (*That sentence makes perfect sense. If you have to work a little bit to process it, you may get a slight taste of what it's like to have a language processing problem.*) My greatest difficulties are minimised, and my greatest strengths are invalidated. (Sinclair 1992)

Communication and relationships

It can be surmised from the criteria in Chapter 1 that much current literature and thinking still suggests that the major features of the disability are a combination of a lack of communication and an inability to make social relationships. Is this really so?

In her book *Autistic Children* (1980), Lorna Wing suggests that the sufferers have severe impairments affecting the development of certain kinds of psychological functions, while, as we have already seen, others place much emphasis on 'delayed and deviant language development' and 'impaired social development'.

Although these children are said to be non-communicative and non-interactive, a study carried out in 1984 found that this was not so. It compared the spontaneous communication of children with autism in the pre-linguistic or early stages of speech with 'normal' children at a similar stage. In fact the children with autism displayed more interaction with the investigator, even though their repertoire of communicative skills was far more limited.

In *Nobody Nowhere* (1992), Donna Williams, whose autism was undiagnosed for many years, throws an interesting light on this aspect of the problems for she says:

> Although words are symbols it would be misleading to say that I did not understand symbols. I had a whole system of relating which I considered 'my language'. It was other people who did not understand the symbolism I used, and there was no way I could or was going to tell them what I meant. Everything I did, from holding two fingers together to scrunching up my toes had a meaning, usually to do with reassuring myself that I was in control and no-one could reach me, wherever the hell I was. Sometimes it had to do with telling people how I felt, but it was so subtle it was often unnoticed or simply taken to be some new quirk that 'mad Donna' had thought up. (Williams 1992, p.26)

Three examples of deviant language development which are commonly quoted are echolalia, pronoun reversal and extreme literalness. It is interesting to note that each of these things happens at certain stages during normal child development. Indeed it is only through repetition of both actions and words that children learn the various skills they will need in life. Again, Donna Williams illuminates our understanding as she says:

> As an echolalic child, I did not understand the use of words because I was in too great a state of stress and fearful reaction to hear anything other than patterned sound ... When I later repeated phrases, it was simply because I sensed that some sort of response with sounds was required. Mirroring ... was my way of saying: 'Look, I can relate. I can make that noise too.' (Williams 1992, p.188)

The emphasis placed on pronoun reversal is curious. While many see it as a symptom of deviant development, Bettleheim suggests that the child 'chooses' to transpose the words as a self-protective measure; a total refusal to get involved with the world. However, it must be recognized that such reversal is simply the stage that occurs naturally before the child learns to refer to himself as 'I' or 'me' rather than copying others who call him 'you'. This is a complicated process which most children take in their stride when they are about three years old, so could it be that, rather than a deviance from normal development, it is merely a halting of that perfectly normal process?

Extreme literalness too is found, as all parents know, amongst small children whose vocabulary is limited. It is especially noticeable in three- and four-year-olds and continues until the age of six or seven. It can give rise to misunderstandings and comic situations, of which I will quote only two:

- The small girl who ate very little because her mother had told her to 'eat it all up – it will put hairs on your chest.'

- The young boy, left in the bath while his mother answered the telephone, who shouted, 'Mummy, hurry up, I'm going rusty.'

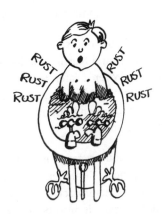

Perhaps this is the point at which to consider one other aspect of language and communication which is frequently found in autism: that of mutism.

First, a very moving passage taken from *Little Boy Lost* (1990) by Bronwen Hocking. This was written by Caroline, a seventeen-year-old (diagnosed as autistic) who had been 'unable to talk' since the age of six. Writing in the third person, as a number of people with autism do, she describes her experiences of living in a silent world thus:

> Caroline wanted to talk so much but it seemed an impossible task. 'Do you think she will ever talk?' was the question that everyone always asked her mother and her teacher, to which they replied, 'There is no reason why she shouldn't. All the apparatus is there. She used to talk when she was a little girl.'
>
> Some people...thought her parents must be deluding themselves and that she had always been silent but she had spoken – she could remember quite clearly the times she had said things to her Mummy. 'Look at the moon,' she said one day, caught by the sudden beauty of it in the daytime sky. She must have been about six years old at the time, lost in her misery, but still responsive to beauty coming unawares from the heavens. She could remember other times when she had tried to say things but had been caught in the black web of her unhappiness and unable to utter a sound. It is very difficult to explain the way in which her fear gripped her vocal cords. It felt as though unseen hands were pressing on her throat struggling to extinguish life itself. Such a little place for the air to come and go, and so very little room for the mysterious life force to exist. That area of her body seemed so vulnerable, so very exposed, that it must be protected at all costs, even the cost of silence itself. It seemed to save valuable air for the process of life itself. There was none to spare for eventual speech, so speech had to go. No one realised that this was one of the fears behind the silence; this sense of tight breathlessness that seemed to suffocate and threaten what little life there was with extinction. (Hocking 1990, pp.56–57)

It is unsurprising then to find that anxiety can affect the use of speech, resulting in muteness, echolalia or repetitive speech. Nothing in autism is ever straightforward, though, for there are stories, told by parents and professionals, of people who are apparently mute who will, on rare occasions, speak extremely clearly, thereby demonstrating their comprehension.

In her book *A Real Person – Life on the Outside* (1997) Gunilla Gerland, who spent her childhood with undiagnosed autism, has a similar description. This, though, dwells not upon fear but rather on a different facet of the problem, for as she says:

The only vestige of this kind (i.e. ritualistic behaviour) was a sort of compulsive clearing of my throat, a sound half-way between clearing my throat and swallowing. I was aware of these sounds – in contrast to the more unconscious sounds I had made when I was small – and I suffered from not being able to stop them. But I did in fact have a reason for them. As I sometimes couldn't speak, and couldn't get a word out, even when inside me I was trying to, by making these little sounds I was able to check that I did in fact still have a voice.

I didn't know why I was sometimes shut off or why I didn't always have an answer when spoken to – I just noticed that it was so. When I didn't succeed in connecting with my nervous system so as to make my voice carry out the order to speak that I given it, it felt as if my voice had disappeared. I was worried that one day I wouldn't have any voice at all, that I wouldn't be able to speak to anyone ever again, so I made that little sound all the time. I did it to reassure myself that my voice was still there. (Gerland 1997, p.174)

Confusing! While fear obviously underlies Caroline's description, Gunilla's problem seems to be simply the 'physical' culmination of some sort of processing problem (something to be discussed in more detail later).

While some children stop speaking after a trauma, I have also heard it said that elective mutism is thought to be associated with a type of depression. These explanations, though, seem to fit neither case. I must therefore echo a question that Rimland asked: 'Does "elective mutism" really represent the child's refusal to speak? One cannot conclude this unless one is willing also to conclude that adult aphasics who are virtually mute until an emergency arises also had 'elected' their disability' (Rimland 1964, p.48).

Jasmine Lee O'Neill is a poet, writer, illustrator and musician who has autism and is herself mute. Although some may disagree with her opinions her book *Through the Eyes of Aliens* (1999) provides some of the answers for, as she says:

Lack of spoken language isn't connected with a malfunction of the brain … There are various reasons for the cases of muteness in autistic people. Some have a motor inability to ever speak. Some speak well until they reach a certain age, then go silent. Some speak regularly with alternating periods of selective mutism. And some have no type of mutism at all.

Selective mutism is when the person chooses whom to talk to, and in which situations. Many times the person talks to family in the home, but won't talk in public, or in unfamiliar surroundings. The stress of strangers being present and a new environment greatly affect how and if the person speaks.

Elective mutism is electing to be silent to everyone. Autistics can have periods of either type which last a lifetime, or several years or weeks. It is quite difficult for the autistic who is selectively mute to find sympathy because outsiders say, 'Well, why can't you speak all the time, then?'

For someone who takes the ease of speaking for granted, it's impossible to explain why. But the autistic person doesn't always plan when he will or won't speak. He isn't trying to be rude by not speaking to another person, nor is he showing his dislike of that person.

In many cases of mutism the child feels too overwhelmed to speak. Speaking involves emotion, and is highly complex. Some autistics fall mute when they feel confused. Sometimes there is a fear of speaking ... (O'Neill 1999, pp.46–47)

A complex area indeed!

The previous quotes lead us neatly on to another interesting aspect of autism. Repeatedly mentioned in the criteria is the lack of imaginative play. Most people would naturally infer from this that such a child would grow into an adult who lacked imagination. This is seemingly, at least in part, contradicted by the writings of people with this condition. How are we to explain the fact that already we have discussed poets and authors with autism and there are others like Temple Grandin, as you will see shortly, who graphically illustrate their writings with imaginative analogies.

This leads me to question the veracity of this observation, for whilst some will say that these are the exceptions which prove the rule such bland explanations do not ring true. Why should such imaginings be surprising? Does the answer instead lie in our shortcomings; our inability to imagine their world?

Whilst toys are often used in a seemingly unimaginative and repetitive manner perhaps we should question whether such children have a hidden wealth of imagery and imaginings. This would certainly seem to be true of some for as Donna Williams, talking about her childhood, says:

People were forever saying that I had no friends. In fact my world was full of them. They were far more magical, reliable, predictable and real than other children and they came with guarantees. It was a world of my own creation. (Williams 1992, p.8)

As Oliver Sacks reminds us, the small child living in a concrete world with no concept of abstract ideas will love and demand stories which use images and symbols to convey a sense of the world. In contrast to many who see 'concreteness' as a deficit which robs a person of some of their humanity, Sacks feels that whilst it can constrict the sufferer (i.e. to very narrow interests) it can conversely be a pathway into imagination, emotions and the spirit.

It is hardly surprising then to find that Sacks considers that 'the autistic imagination is by no means rare' having seen it many times. He also questions whether the skills of 'savants' are merely mechanical and carried out without feeling or understanding, for his observations over many years have led him to believe that such people are 'truly and creatively intelligent' (Sacks 1986, p. 184).

Confusing! Are such people really exceptional or will we find another explanation? It is too early to attempt to answer that, for first we must explore other areas: those theories which place the emphasis on possible physical causes of autism.

Brain damage or dysfunction

Elizabeth Newson (1979) suggested that some infants might have a primary brain dysfunction which interferes with their ability to 'decode' gesture, facial expression, body language or spoken language. She felt that if this were so, the result would be both devastating and progressive as the inability to understand such normal interactions would lead to a failure to respond, thus effectively sabotaging the child's earliest experiences. Messages which make no sense are quite obviously unpleasant and frightening. Newson thought that this would lead the child to withdraw from interaction with others by developing 'cut off' mechanisms to shut out social stimulus and avoid confused interaction: a problem with severe and long-term implications, as his apparent lack of response would initially bewilder and then frustrate his parents.

Rutter, Frith and others agree that the underlying problems stem from the child's inadequate cognitive skills (thought to be due to abnormalities of brain development), which leave him unable to understand the information received by his brain. In *Emergence Labeled Autistic* (1986), Temple Grandin also supports the idea of cognitive difficulties for she has to visualize words and continues to have difficulty in understanding abstract ideas, as do many other people with autism (Grandin and Scariano 1986).

While abstract concepts are difficult for them, people with autism readily understand concrete terms. This can lead them to take metaphorical language literally: a tendency which can have strange consequences and could be potentially distressing to the person concerned. In her book *A Real Person – Life on the Outside* (1997), Gunilla Gerland describes the confusions language caused her.

She had great difficulty in getting on with one of her neighbours, known to her as Aunt Berit. Unfortunately this aunt got a job at Gunilla's school, in charge of the recreation room. As Gunilla says:

Thus in the long run it was difficult to avoid her … One day when she saw me and stopped to chat, I asked her what she was doing there.

'I'm here to keep an eye on you.'

I suppose that was an attempt to joke on her part, but I didn't grasp it. With my concrete way of thinking people meant precisely what they said, I thought it was true that she had come to the school just to teach me some manners. It was a dreadful feeling. I felt persecuted and controlled. Aunt Berit's sharp, watchful and largely disapproving eyes were following me all over the school. She was going to keep an eye on me … it was if she had put a curse on me.

I knew perfectly what 'keep an eye on you' meant. But nonetheless I was uncertain whether the expression might have another meaning, something much more absolute. I saw the image of 'keeping an eye on you' very clearly, but whose eye? Was it the keeper's, or that of the person kept an eye on? As I still didn't know how other people could know about the future or about situations that they weren't present at, I thought the expression perhaps meant her eyes somehow seeing everything. (Gerland 1997, pp.128–129)

Thus a simple 'jokey' statement caused a great deal of worry. Fortunately, the next misunderstanding was easily remedied once the staff understood the problem. It began one day when Jenny anxiously told a member of staff that she was ill. He asked further questions and after a time, once sure she wasn't, he tried to reassure her, to no avail. She was insistent and the conversation continued:

Jenny: I have to go into hospital.

Tom: Why?

Jenny: For an operation.

Tom: What sort of operation?

Jenny: An operation on my heart.

He and other staff were thoroughly puzzled until they found one of their colleagues had told Jenny that she should 'open up her heart to Jesus.'

On a lighter note we find that such problems can sometimes give rise to situations which would be a godsend to a comedy script writer (and which also highlight the inbuilt confusions of the English language). I would just like to reassure those people who feel it is wrong to make a joke about such confusion that no disrespect is intended here. Laughter is often a saving grace for many parents and carers who deal with a constant barrage of questions or seemingly inexplicable behaviours, as indeed it is for any harassed mum with several children under five.

Some 'real life' examples of such confusions are:

- The nine-year-old who tried on a pair of shoes in a shop and then, in response to the salesgirl's encouraging 'let's see you walk up the shop then', promptly, to her mother's horror and embarrassment, proceeded to do exactly what she had been told: climbing up the shoe-stacked shelves at the side of the shop.

- Tim (an independent man), who asked me why someone was away sick. My foolish response was: 'He's a bit under the weather.' Tim walked away, thought for a while and then returned to ask, 'Do you mean he's been standing under the rain?'

- Donna Williams, in her first job as a seamstress, was given the task of sewing buttonholes in fur coats. This she did to perfection, happily and randomly covering the sleeves, fronts, backs and even the collars with buttonholes galore.

- The boy who demonstrated his confusion by becoming very upset when told that the slice of cake he had just been given was 'marble cake'!

This inability to think in abstract terms can also prevent the sufferer from understanding that a change in circumstances should affect his response to a situation. It is difficult for any parent or carer to anticipate all the variations that might occur, things which we often take for granted until they actually happen. It is a combination of problems which seem to underlie the following story (perhaps apocryphal) of one woman who successfully married and had a child. She cared for the baby well, attending carefully to all his needs. Imagine the horror of the other customers in a restaurant when she decided that his nappy needed changing and proceeded to do so – at the table! A perfect motherly response in any other place: well – most other places. Who would have thought to teach her that such things are not done in a restaurant?

This 'concrete' thinking pervades all areas of life. So how do people with autism deal with the difficulties this poses? Gunilla Gerland again 'opens our eyes' when she says:

I desperately wanted to understand and this led to theories: If everything looked in a certain way in the living room – the sun shining in through the curtains, the ashtray on the table with the newspaper beside it – and if Kerstin then came back from school ... I thought that everything had to look exactly the same the next day, for her to come back from school. It quite simply had to be like that. And in fact, it often was ...

People often disturbed my theories. Just when I thought I had grasped the connection between things, someone moved the newspaper and I no longer knew what to think. Would Kerstin not come home now? Couldn't she come home? Ever again? Or didn't I understand anything? In that case was everything I thought also wrong? No it must be that my sister couldn't come home until everything was put right again. The newspaper had to be back in its place – that must be it. (Gerland 1997, pp.26–27)

However, whereas in the previous section such misinterpretations were attributed to deviant linguistic development, here the emphasis shifts to a failure of cognition caused by brain dysfunction.

Do cognitive problems also lie behind another idea which has received a great deal of attention? This is the 'theory of mind' or mind-blindness proposed by Baron-Cohen and colleagues (Baron-Cohen, Leslie and Frith 1985). In simple terms, it means that the person concerned is unable to recognize emotions in others or empathize with other people and will also find it impossible to internalize social rules.

As shown in the list cataloguing the features of emotional intelligence on page 22, the foundation of empathy is self-awareness. Thus being aware of our own feelings and emotions allows us to develop the skill of 'reading' the feelings of others. Much of this is done through the ability to understand non-verbal communication, that is, is conveyed through the tone of voice, facial expression or gesture. An inability to do this, as often found in autism, can result in embarrassing situations as when a person will stare at someone else for a long period of time or go up to a complete stranger and touch their clothing or hair.

This type of problem is mirrored in a condition called dyssemia (from the Greek dys = difficulty and semes = signal) in which the child has great difficulties in interpreting non-verbal signals. It has varied effects, all of which would certainly contribute to or cause a lack of empathy.

Thus people with dyssemia:

- Misinterpret and 'misuse' facial expressions or body language. This is the person who fails to 'pick up' cues from others, that is: doesn't notice that someone else wishes a conversation or telephone call to end; asks intrusive questions; talks about himself or one subject all the time; and ignores attempts to change the topic. (Although to me the two latter points also sound somewhat obsessional.)

- Have a poor sense of personal space. That is, they stand too close to others or encroach on their space.

- Show little awareness of the emotional content of speech (prosody) so that they talk too shrilly or flatly.

Approximately one in ten children is said to have one or more problems in this area, ranging from mild to severe, which will cause ongoing difficulties throughout their lives. Such children seem strange and can leave other people feeling uneasy and uncomfortable. Because of this they are often left out of games by their peers and can (at the extreme end) grow into social isolates. Dyssemia can also often affect academic work as the child misinterprets and misresponds to teachers too.

Stephen Nowicki, a psychologist who studies children's non-verbal abilities, comments:

> Children who can't read or express emotions well feel constantly frustrated. In essence, they don't understand what's going. This kind of communication is a constant sub text of everything you do; you can't stop showing facial expression or posture, or hide your tone of voice. If you make mistakes in what emotional messages you send, you constantly experience that people react to you in funny ways – you get rebuffed and don't know why. If you're thinking you're acting happy but actually seemed too hyper or angry, you find other kids getting angry at you in turn and don't realize why. Such kids end up feeling no sense of control over how other people treat them, that their actions have no impact on what happens to them. It leaves them feeling powerless, depressed and apathetic. (Goleman 1995, p.122)

All three 'symptoms' of dyssemia and their various effects are only too familiar but obviously in autism such difficulties are generally at the extreme end of the scale, causing great distress for those with most self-awareness as they try to make friends and are rebuffed.

While initially it would seem that the 'theory of mind' and the symptoms of dyssemia are purely based on emotional factors I must question if this is actually so in all cases. It is well known that emotional neglect dulls or stunts the development of empathy but could there also be a physical foundation to such skills? Returning to Newson, we find that she provided further support for her theory by observation of babies born with severe visual impairments, who clearly miss out on facial expression and gesture. A baby's ordinary response when an important adult approaches is to crow and gurgle with delight, while his arms and legs wave in all directions. However, because the visually impaired child cannot see the adult, but can hear, he will respond instead by 'stilling', that is, freezing his bodily movements so that the all important sounds can be attended to, and this may initially cause problems for the parents as such behaviour can easily be mistaken for a lack of interest. Thus these problems would surely have an effect on the development of the skills so lacking in people with dyssemia.

Other parallels exist, too, for children without sight are prone to develop stereotypic mannerisms (known as 'blindisms') which are similar to those found amongst children with autism. They may rock backwards and forwards, wave their hands or an object in front of their faces in bright light, tap their eyes or spin an object in their hands. Whether there is any logic behind such mannerisms is hard to determine but we should remember that there may be a reason for apparently bizarre behaviour, as in the case of a man who had gone blind at an early age. For many years afterwards he was observed rubbing his eyes repeatedly with his knuckles, even though he was discouraged from doing so. When someone finally thought to ask him why he rubbed them, he replied that he remembered seeing a bonfire when young and that rubbing recreated the colours within his eyes.

Interestingly, children born with severe hearing impairments also develop certain stereotypic mannerisms (known as 'deafisms'), all of which have a relationship to sound and are again reminiscent of children with autism. These include banging, tapping or making rhythmic sounds. Deaf children, too, often suffer from developmental problems, which include difficulties in interpreting gestures, problems with social relationships and a resulting lack of empathy. Adolescence may then present them with further frustrations which can result in outbursts of aggressive or 'inappropriate' behaviour.

Research has also shown that people who become deaf in later life suffer a variety of problems which are exhibited in the form of anxiety, withdrawal, inappropriate reactions, restlessness and insecurity. These behaviours are similar to those observed in animals who are placed in a situation in which they are deprived of stimulation: deprivation which causes them to become excitable and hyperactive. They may engage in stereotyped behaviour and have disturbed social relations. Such stereotyped behaviour is thought to be an attempt to alleviate the barren situation by self-stimulation, but as it appears common to both humans and animals, one wonders if it could possibly be an instinctive reaction to certain situations.

While many of the problems suffered by children with hearing impairments initially appear similar to those of the child with autism they differ in two main respects. The first is in diagnosis where they show a hearing loss when tested, which is generally associated with a neurological or physical impairment. The second is, at present, in prognosis, as they generally respond well to treatment, learning to use and understand gestures and facial expression. They can also form normal attachments and relationships and learn to play imaginatively with their peers.

If, however, we look at the problems which arise from multi-sensory deprivation (MSD), a somewhat different and very interesting picture begins to emerge. This handicap is perhaps, along with autism, one of the least understood of all. While each child is unique and the degree of auditory and visual loss varies from moderate to total, the only feature they all have in common is some degree of deprivation in their use of both sight and hearing.

In a number of children these are the only two senses which are affected, but for many others the whole 'input' system is damaged although the 'processing' mechanism remains whole. This means that they are not able to rely on their remaining senses of touch, taste and smell to provide alternative information about the environment as these are also damaged to some degree. Unsurprisingly perhaps, some of the children who suffer from MSD were previously diagnosed as autistic, hyperactive, aphasic or even schizophrenic, although in many cases their behaviour was more readily explained by a deeper understanding of the effects of sensory loss.

A clear picture of the difficulties these children encounter and the type of treatment needed is given by McInnes and Treffry in their book *Deaf–Blind Children and Infants* (1982). Some of the complex problems a child may suffer are:

1. He lacks the ability to anticipate future events, which makes each 'normal' experience both new and frightening. Being picked up from the security of the cot, fed or changed, are all circumstances over which he has no control and which are therefore potentially terrifying and stress-inducing.

2. He may have great difficulty in establishing and maintaining relation-ships. As he is unable to hear or see his mother approaching he has no way of responding appropriately and the mother may therefore feel rejected. This may leave him unable to form the emotional bond with the mother which he so badly needs, although a relationship may be developed in time.

3. His environment is limited by his reach and he is unable to learn from his interaction with it as a non-handicapped child would. He demonstrates little motivation to explore as success is almost non-existent and he will even need to be taught how to play. This lack of curiosity then inhibits the child's comprehension as he grows, which causes feelings of frustration. With primary problems of poor vision there will be very little incidental learning. He will not explore because he is not aware that there are things beyond reach waiting to be discovered. Continuing sensory deprivation makes the collection of accurate information about the environment and the people in it difficult, if not impossible, unless help is at hand.

4. The child will have a distorted perception of the world. He will not recognize that his perception is faulty and this will cause severe developmental lags, resulting in apparently bizarre behaviour at times. This is especially noticeable in the low functioning child who may be prone to bang his head, wave his fingers in front of his eyes, rock, or stare at lights. Distortion contributes to lack of comprehension, so that the child is often considered to be retarded. *When retardation does occur, it is not a reflection of the child's ability to process information and draw logical conclusions, but rather a measure of his ability to gather the information in the first*

place – I emphasize this for it is an interesting thought to which I shall return later.

5. He may acquire the habit of disregarding the sounds he can actually hear, so that his hearing appears inconsistent.

The child who is most likely to be misunderstood is the one with some residual vision or hearing, whose handicap may not be very obvious. If encouraged to use his residual senses, he may gradually show some improvement, but in many instances his actions may be judged inappropriate and the resulting mismanagement can cause psychological damage, in addition to his other problems. His continuing lack of success and other people's perceptions of him may cause his frustration level to rise, giving him little opportunity to develop self-esteem. These factors often result in additional or increased inappropriate behaviour(s) which can result in his eventual withdrawal from the world.

An overall view of these problems sometimes results in these children being wrongly diagnosed as emotionally disturbed or mentally handicapped. However, if given the right treatment from an early age, they do respond and can learn a great deal. While it would be unrealistic and unwise to suggest that they will all eventually be able to lead an independent and productive life within the community, even those who continue to need some form of sheltered environment throughout their lives can learn to live happily within the limitations imposed by their handicap.

McInnes and Treffry give an extremely interesting summary of the behaviour of those children who have not had the benefit of intensive intervention in early infancy:

> They tend to develop one of two methods of handling their contact with their environment. One approach is to become hypoactive-like in their behaviour. They withdraw completely from the world about them. Their attempts at spontaneous communication are reduced to almost nil. Often they dislike being touched and spend most of their time in self-stimulating activities or ritualistic play. They are often judged to be profoundly retarded, show little curiosity, and rarely relate in a positive way to visual, auditory, or tactile stimulation.
>
> The second group exhibit hyperactive-like behaviour. They are the erratic butterflies which never light for more than an instant. They often appear to have useful vision: they will pick up a penny from a brown rug and then walk into a wall or coffee table without appearing to see the obstacle. (A description which prompted one woman with autism to say 'that was me'!) Often they don't like to be held or touched, avoid giving eye contact, and refuse to interact with peers or adults. (McInnes and Treffry 1982, p.19)

Perhaps this explains why, as Rimland reminds us, literature on autism has long contained such comments as 'ill focused eyes' or 'functionally blind' while Van Krevelen described a patient with autism as 'blind while seeing, and deaf while hearing' (Rimland 1964, p.96).

'Curiouser and curiouser!' These problems will, I'm sure, seem familiar to many readers and lead me to question the diagnostic criteria. If these children, particularly those in the latter group, are really suffering from MSD the coincidences are overwhelming. Where is the dividing line? How or where do these children fit into the overall picture?

Before attempting to answer these questions we must consider several other interesting facts, perhaps the most fascinating being the one frequently mentioned by the sufferers themselves: abnormal perceptions.

Abnormal perceptions

Berry Brazelton (1993) developed the Neonatal Behavioural Assessment Scale (NBAS) which is used to evaluate the new-born baby within the first few days by assessing the way in which she responds to both human and non-human stimuli. This enables Brazelton to share the baby's behaviour with the parents so that they are aware of her strengths and weaknesses from the beginning and are able to respond in an appropriate manner.

While the Scale assesses many different aspects, one range of tests seems to be particularly relevant here. These are the tests designed to determine whether or not the baby has the ability to shut out disturbing stimuli – a flashing light, a rattle, etc.

Through this work Brazelton identified a group of children who did not respond to stimuli in the expected manner. These were generally premature babies or those who, in some way, had been stressed whilst in the uterus leaving them with a very fragile or 'raw' nervous system.

Normally when negative stimuli are repeated an infant will gradually become accustomed to them and her responsiveness will decrease. However, these more vulnerable children were unable to learn to ignore a stimulus, responding to it over and over and over again in a negative manner. Each stimulus, even when seemingly pleasant (like a cuddle), elicited an action such as frowning, arching away, bringing a hand to their mouths, averting their face, having a bowel movement or crying. Such infants also showed an increase in heart rate and respiration.

There are several possible causes of this hypersensitivity – from the mother's medication to a lack of oxygen or foetal/birth trauma. Brazelton believes that as the trauma wears off the nervous system will adjust and suggests that it should be possible to alleviate any residual problems by careful and sensitive handling. Thus any infant who suffers from a sensory overload when faced with multiple stimuli will tolerate the experiences of being touched or fed or looked at far better when these are done one at a time.

So do children with autism also demonstrate such problems? An educated guess would suggest that this must be so even if there were no apparent problems during pregnancy or birth or if the birth-weight was reasonable. Certainly if a genetic problem underlies autism we should not be surprised to hear mention of the child who was 'different' from birth, as we often do.

Donna Williams' book *Autism – An Inside-Out Approach* (1996) suggests an answer to this. In it she talks about the difficulties she had, even as an adult, in being able to process more than one type of information at a time; a condition which she terms mono processing.

Thus, in contrast to most people who are able to process information from several senses simultaneously, she feels that she and others like her lack this ability and that this causes many problems which dramatically affect their lives. One in particular she terms 'shut down', which means that the overload of information can, at some point, cause her to cease dealing with or responding to any incoming stimuli. This state is also seen in other people with autism and when extreme can lead them to withdraw completely from the world, not just into themselves but occasionally into lengthy periods of sleep.

There is also mention of a contrasting problem, which the author terms 'hyper-connectedness'. This, she suggests, is where information is processed too rapidly, thereby bombarding the person with a series of thoughts which continually lead them away from the reality of the situation. This results in a chaotic response to stimuli whereby one word or sentence can trigger numerous fast-moving images which, when verbalized, may seem random and unconnected. It will be interesting to see just where this fits in.

Creak (1961) included abnormal perceptual experiences in the list of criteria for autism (see Chapter 1). Rimland, also writing in the 1960s, thought such ideas were of great importance too. He discussed their potentially devastating effects, saying: 'There appears to be adequate reason for believing the perceptual abilities of autistic children to be so severely impaired that sensory deprivation psychosis must be considered a real possibility' (Rimland 1964, p.103).

Generally, though, such ideas received little attention until, in the early 1970s, Carl Delacato, working with children with autism, researched the abnormal perceptual experiences in more detail. He felt that these were caused by brain damage, which in turn caused a perceptual dysfunction so that messages to the brain were distorted. He divided these distortions into three categories:

1. **Hyper** – where too much stimulation occurs – thereby magnifying sounds. This is the child who covers his ears at the slightest sound and hears things which most of us do not. Thus falling leaves can sound like

maracas and he may hear conversations of people who are out of sight. This is the child who avoids being touched, whose taste is too effective (so that he will not eat many foods) and whose eyes are oversensitive. The world constantly bombards his senses with stimulation. This leads him to withdraw into his 'own world' in order to escape from the overwhelming reality. Paradoxically, though, he seems unaware of sounds that he makes himself.

2. **Hypo** – where too little stimulation occurs. This leads the child to eat indiscriminately and/or enjoy noisy appliances and loud sounds. In addition he likes strong smells (and may even play with his own faeces). He appears to feel no pain, ignoring cuts and bruises. Delacato observed too that this type of child would often pick at sores or have severely callused areas on his hands, arms, knees or elbows.

3. **White noise** – where messages are garbled or overcome by 'internal' noises. This child lives with a great deal of sensory interference, for 'internal' sounds like his own heartbeat or his digestion interfere with incoming messages. This type of thing was exemplified by one boy who said his ears were noisy inside, making a constant 'shushing' sound. Could this be similar to the experiences of the partially deaf who have the worst of both worlds, hearing enough to be distracted by noise, yet not enough for it to be meaningful, leaving them in a world of auditory 'fuzz'? Or those who have tinnitus?

   He is likely to have a constant taste in his mouth and his body may itch for no apparent reason. He, too, has a range of visual problems. He may often have dilated pupils and will touch, pull, rub or hit his eyes to re-create colours. Such a child will look through people and things but seems to see things situated inside the eye itself. As Delacato describes it: 'He sees as though his eyes weren't turned out to the world, but turned in toward himself. He looks as though he is seeing things that aren't there' (Delacato 1974, p.112).

It is easy to envisage that if these problems were present from birth, children in the first two categories, regardless of birth-weight and circumstances, would not do well in tests on the Neonatal Behavioural Assessment Scale.

Delacato proposed the theory that the stereotyped behaviours demonstrated by these children were symptoms of brain damage and that their responses were a desperate attempt at 'self treatment' and also possibly an attempt to communicate the problem.

He denied that these children were psychotic (another idea which had gained credence in some quarters) and proposed instead that their brain injuries caused severe sensory problems, which left them unable to deal with stimulation from the world outside as most of us would. He also suggested that, by careful observation of the mannerisms, which he termed 'sensoryisms', it would be possible to determine which of the senses was damaged. This idea makes a great deal of sense for these 'sensoryisms' (which for ease I shall refer to as 'sensisms' from now on) are closely akin to the blindisms and deafisms mentioned earlier, all of which seemed to have a direct connection to the sense which was damaged.

Delacato believed that once the problem area had been defined it could be 'normalized' by giving the proper experience and stimulation; and that this would lead to a cessation of the repetitive behaviour, enabling the children to learn to interact with the people around them – something I would certainly confirm from personal experience.

He developed individual treatment programmes for several children, all of whom had been diagnosed as autistic prior to seeing him. These aimed at 'normalizing' the receptive processes in various ways, for instance by using earplugs to block out some sounds for those considered hypersensitive. It is interesting then to find that the majority made much more progress than would generally have been expected.

The implications of these ideas were, unfortunately, given little credence by others until later when a Canadian psychiatrist, Philip Ney, proposed that hypersensitivity to sound might be a cause, rather than merely a symptom, of some types of autism.

This idea has been developed by Gail Gillingham, who feels that the problems of autism are due, not to a disability, but rather to a 'superability' in which the senses are so finely tuned that they make the sufferer acutely aware of things the 'normal' person would not notice. In her paper 'Autism: Disability or Superability' (Gillingham 1991) she proposes that the acute sensations felt by the person with autism lead to a feeling of extreme pain. She suggests that the body deals with this pain by the production of endomorphins which are effective in blocking the pain but coincidentally lead to the suppression of further sensory information, as the child or adult blocks his ears or avoids eye contact or touch.

Others too have now recognized these difficulties. Stephen Edelson, from Portland State University in Oregon, conducted a survey of 1000 people with autism which showed that 65 per cent of them were hypersensitive to sound. Lorna Wing has also acknowledged such problems in her book *Autistic Children* (1980) and, although she does not analyze their significance, she discusses ways of helping the child overcome the very genuine fears which arise from such painful stimuli. Unfortunately, though, there are still many people working with people with autism who disregard the tremendous impact that such disturbances have. I have even heard of one case in which the staff involved misinterpreted the auditory hypersensitivity completely seeing (and 'treating') it as a phobia which it *most definitely* is not.

Delacato's idea of abnormal perceptions is certainly supported by the writings of various sufferers who, from different countries and even continents, have consistently, over many years, detailed their strange 'feelings'. These confirm that they do not receive the correct information from their senses. Many talk of being hypersensitive to sound and touch and having unusual visual perceptions. While this may not apply to all, there is growing evidence to suggest that it is a major and extremely distressing problem for many. Examples may be found in the writings of Temple Grandin, who says she was '...cut off by over-reactions or inconsistent reactions from my five senses', especially sound. Social occasions were extremely distressing as they produced a confusion of startling sensations which she describes:

> ... Thanksgiving or Christmas was even worse. At those times our home bulged with relatives. The clamour of many voices, the different smells – perfume, cigars, damp wool caps or gloves – people moving about at different speeds, going in different directions, the constant noise and confusion, the constant touching, were overwhelming. (Grandin and Scariano 1986, p.19)

She talks about her longing to be touched and hugged but then describes the pain this caused, giving a comical description of 'one very, very overweight aunt' whom she really liked but who 'totally engulfed' her so that she panicked as she felt 'it was like being suffocated by a mountain of marsh-mallows.' Later in the book we find that: 'Small itches and scratches that most people ignored were torture. A scratchy petticoat was like sandpaper rubbing my skin raw. Hair-washing was also awful. When mother scrubbed my hair, my scalp hurt' (Grandin and Scariano 1986, pp.25–26).

More recently Gunilla Gerland also detailed similar weird effects:

> My feeling was special in other areas as well, apart from that of pain. I could never take a shower because I couldn't stand drops of water on my skin. They hurt. They had sharp little points that stabbed me. All forms of washing had to happen in the bath. It was necessary to have as much water around me and all over my body as possible for it to be bearable ...
>
> At eight, I became oversensitive to combs and hairbrushes, and I refused to have my hair done. Suddenly, I couldn't bear the pain that came from having my hair done. It seemed to burn like synthetic fire all over my head and the nape of my neck. In some remarkable way, my actual hair seemed to hurt, a pain I also felt inside my ears. (Gerland 1997, pp.101–102)

Gunilla also had one other strange and highly unpleasant physical feeling affecting her spine rather than her senses, which I have not heard or seen detailed by anyone else. As she says:

All the time I was growing up, I suffered from almost constant shudder down my spine. Periodically, the shuddering grew worse, while at other times it kept relatively quiet so that I was able to live with it. It was like the feeling the moment before you sneeze, only as if it had got stuck and was suspended inside my spinal cord in order to turn into something permanent. The shudder that wasn't really a shudder *must* be released, then ought to be registered on the Richter scale. I so much wanted it to happen, just as your body wants to sneeze when a sneeze is on the way. But the feeling was there to stay, an eternity of eternities. I became slightly used to it, but it was a constant torture, most noticeable when it changed in intensity …

It was like cold steel down my spine. It was hard and fluid at the same time, with metallic fingers lightly drumming and tickling on the outside. Like sharp clips digging into my spine, and lemonade inside. Icy heat and digging fiery cold. It was like the sound of screeching chalk against a blackboard turned into a silent concentration of feeling, then placed at the back of my neck. Placed at the nape of my neck for ever. From there, so metallic, the feeling rang in my ears, radiated out into my arms, clipped itself firmly into my elbows, but never came to end. Never ever came to end. (Gerland 1997, pp.56–57)

Descriptions of abnormal sensory perceptions are also found in *The Sound of a Miracle* (1990) by Annabel Stehli, in which she discusses the various problems which her daughter Georgiana faced, most notably hypersensitivity to sound. She describes how at the age of twelve, Georgiana had called her over to look at a fleck of dandruff under a microscope in which she could see a variety of colours. Her mother could only see a greyish flake and at that point suddenly realized that her daughter could also see exceptionally well: one notable description being of a strand of hair looking like a piece of spaghetti. Pursuing this line of thought, she established that her daughter could see lines, shapes and colours that most of us are unaware of. This led to the idea that perhaps her other senses might also be affected, an idea Georgiana confirmed, commenting that: 'The sound was the only thing that drove me crazy because I was so scared … and sound was going on all the time. It was hard to get away from it. With the other things I could look down or walk away' (Stehli 1990, p.188).

Stehli comments on Delacato's work and feels that her daughter might also have had areas in which she was 'under' or hyposensitive; an idea which will be further discussed later.

Although several other examples are now available, I will conclude with two passages by Darren C. White, who describes his early childhood experiences thus:

... I used to hate small shops because my eyesight used to make them look as if they were even smaller than they actually were ... I was rarely able to hear long sentences because my hearing distorted them. I was sometimes able to hear a word or two at the start ... and then the next lot of words sort of merged into one another and I could not make head or tail of it. I used to like listening to music. My eyes did not play so many tricks ... as before even though on bright days my sight blurred. I was also frightened of the vacuum cleaner, food mixer ... because they sounded about five times louder than they actually were. Life was terrifying ...

Later, at school (second-year infants):

The bus started with a clap of thunder ... and I had my hands in my ears for most of the journey ... When we were going back my ears were making noises sound quieter ... as I could not hear the bus start.

I broke my collarbone falling off a radiator. My eyes were showing a wide windowsill where the radiator was and I sat down, falling off instantly. I didn't feel any pain at all during the time-span between the incident happening and going to sleep. When I woke up I had a dreadful pain ... (White and White 1987, pp.223–229)

In a later unpublished addition to this, White again talks of noises sounding like thunder, which is the reason he doesn't like going to town. He finds touch excruciating, not only when people try to cuddle him but also 'hating it' when people try to make him hold a pencil or do up laces or buttons. Additionally, he says he doesn't like pressing his lips hard on spoons or glass and finds it difficult to see some colours, for example blue, which he describes thus: 'It looked too light and it looked like ice.' (Imagine the sea on a sunny day, it would look frozen over in spite of the sun.)

His final comment in the first article was: 'At last things got better but I thought it happened to everyone and I told no-one.' A common experience I would think, although whether the problems diminished or he simply learned to cope is a moot point.

The abnormal perceptions recounted here will, I am sure, 'ring bells' for the many parents, carers and teachers who are in close contact with people with autism. While they do not have sensory 'impairments' in the usual sense of the word, these problems do impair and reduce their quality of life tremendously.

So we have now explored some of the problems which can affect our five senses. But something is missing, for we also need to explore another sense: that of proprioception, that is, 'body sense', that sense by which we feel, indeed know unquestioningly, that our bodies belong to us. The lack of this is certainly a problem for some people with autism as Creak correctly identified when she incorporated 'an apparent unawareness of the child's personal identity …' in the list of criteria for autism, albeit perhaps the one most difficult to determine.

Body sense is such an automatic, unconscious feeling that some of you may ask whether its inclusion has any relevance here. It is, however, of great significance for, as Donna Williams (1996) confirms, many people with autism not only lack a feeling of what she calls 'body connectedness' but, even worse, can feel that their body is an 'enemy' which 'floods' them with feelings over which they have no control.

Whilst understanding this on an intellectual level some may find, as I did, the emotional implication of such feelings difficult to understand. It became clearer once I read Oliver Sacks' book *The Man Who Mistook His Wife for a Hat* (1986) in which he discusses the difficulties faced by Christina. Although her problems arose from polyneuritus when she was 27 years old rather than in childhood, her description clearly conveys the horrific nature of such problems. Christina had, after admission to hospital for a routine operation, a very disturbing dream (on the day prior to surgery). As he says: 'She was swaying wildly, in her dream, very unsteady on her feet, could hardly feel the ground beneath her, could hardly feel anything in her hands, found them flailing to and fro, kept dropping whatever she picked up.'

Strangely (and tragically) the dream came true and left her in a state in which:

> Standing was impossible – unless she looked down at her feet. She could hold nothing in her hands, and they 'wandered' – unless she kept an eye on them. When she reached out for something, or tried to feed herself, her hands would miss, or overshoot wildly, as if some essential coordination was gone.
>
> She could scarcely even sit up – her body 'gave way'. Her voice was oddly expressionless and slack, her jaw fell open, even her vocal posture was gone.
>
> 'Something awful's happened' she mouthed in a ghostly flat voice. 'I can't feel my body. I feel weird – disembodied.' (Sacks 1986, pp.42–52)

And indeed after a series of tests it was found that she had completely lost all proprioception, that is, she had no sense of her muscles, tendons or joints at all. As she herself described it: 'I feel my body is blind and deaf to itself … it has no sense of itself.'

With much tenacity Christina was eventually able to re-educate herself using her vision to monitor each and every movement until eventually this visual feedback became automatic and enabled her to compensate for her lost body sense. Speech modulation too is proprioceptive and by losing the normal impulses from the vocal organs she also lost the ability to modulate her voice and had to learn to use her ears to compensate for this. Similarly she had problems with posture and facial expression. Thus, although her inner emotions are full, her voice remains somewhat theatrical and her face is rather flat and expressionless unless she uses 'an artificial enhancement of expression'!

Even though she eventually recovered enough to return home and lead a semblance of her former life, major problems still exist for Christina. One is society's lack of understanding, for her disability is not clear and she tends to be treated as either a fraud or a fool. But a second, more major one, lies in the fact that, as Sacks says: 'She has lost, with her sense of proprioception, the fundamental, organic mooring of identity – at least that corporeal identity, or body-ego, which Freud sees as the basis of self' (Sacks 1986, pp.42–52).

This is a story without a happy ending, for Christina will remain this way.

Could some of the strange aspects of autism be explained by this inability to make the correct connections with one's body? It would seem so. The first example of this comes from Gunilla Gerland, and involves a seemingly simple but potentially disastrous difficulty:

> I also had another problem, which required extending my lavatory strategies, though it was a problem I never understood until I was adult. I thought it was the same for everyone. I couldn't feel that I needed to go to the lavatory, so I had to think out when I needed to go. I didn't know other people had a signalling system that warned them at intervals before the need to go became urgent. I had no such system. I felt nothing, nothing, nothing – then it was urgent, then I felt it, and then I had to find a lavatory at once. So I always had to go beforehand and very frequently, so that it could never become that urgent.

Christina had to think about and develop strategies in order to make any movement at all, something shared by a number of people with autism/Asperger's syndrome who find even the simplest movement hard. One example of this (which also indicates comprehension difficulties) again comes from Gunilla who says: 'But when they told me to pick up my feet, to me that meant lifting my whole foot right up and with it my leg, then parading along with my knees raised high. It was horribly hard work' (Gerland 1997, p.120).

This type of problem has often been attributed to some type of motor problem but perhaps proprioception plays a part here too? Could it also explain 'verbal apraxia', a condition in which the person has great difficulty in knowing how to move their lips, tongue and mouth?

Another factor is worthy of comment here, for it too could be caused by a lack of proprioception and certainly reminded me of several people with autism whom I have known. As Gerland says: 'Then the dancing teacher came up to me and said my body was unusually supple. "Like spaghetti" she said.' (Gerland 1997, p.86)

It is confusing then to find that although Sacks believed that Christina had lost the 'the basis of self' and she herself felt that she had lost something essential to her being; her 'pith' as she described it, she still had a rich emotional life. While the latter occurs, albeit often hidden, amongst those with autism the former point suggests that Christina's lack of proprioception is not a totally accurate analogy with autism.

Certainly Jim Sinclair is very clear that his 'core' remains intact despite his problems. Thus he says:

> I have an *interface* problem, not a core processing problem. I can't always keep track of what's happening outside myself, but I'm never out of touch with my core. Even at worst, when I can't focus and I can't find my body and I can't connect to space or time, I still have my own self. That's how I survive and how I keep growing.
>
> I taught myself to read at three, and I had to learn it again at ten, and yet again at seventeen, and at twenty-one, and at twenty-six. The words that it took me twelve years to find have been lost again, and regained, and lost, and still have not come all the way back to where I can be reasonably confident they'll be there when I need them. It wasn't enough to figure out just once how to keep track of my eyes and ears and hands and feet all at the same time; I've lost track of them and had to find them over and over again.
>
> But I *have* found them again. The terror is never complete, and I'm never completely lost in the fog, and I always know that even if it takes forever, I *will* find the connections and put them back together again. I know this because I'm always connected at the core and I never lose track of my own self. This is all I have that I can always count on, all I have that is truly my own. (Sinclair 1992)

It is chilling to realize just how difficult such a life must be. Imagine too just how much time and energy has to be expended simply to maintain one's status quo. Frightening indeed.

Even though not totally accurate, Christina's description gives us some idea of the devastation which may be caused to those people with autism who have never developed a 'body sense' and cannot make the connections that come so naturally to the rest of us. Compound this then with an inability to clearly understand or interpret your emotions and the feeling that your body is an 'enemy' which 'floods' you with uncontrollable feelings. Such difficulties are echoed in a condition called alexithymia, a term used to describe people who 'lack words for their feelings' which is found, albeit infrequently, amongst the general population. So, leaving autism aside for a moment, it would be helpful to explore this further.

This condition has several facets. Such people are unable to correctly recognize and interpret, or to express, either their own or other people's feelings. Most sufferers lack both insight and empathy, the latter being an aspect of the condition which can cause emotional stress/distress to their families – which would seem again to be reminiscent of Baron-Cohen's 'theory of mind'.

They have little ability to distinguish between the different emotions and demonstrate confusion between emotion and bodily sensations so that fear, for instance, is seen merely as a series of physical effects. Thus even when moved by emotion they lack the words to describe it, for they find such experiences confusing and overwhelming and to be avoided. On the rare occasions when they do cry they weep copiously but are unable to explain exactly why, a basic confusion which may lead them to complain of vague medical symptoms when they are really emotionally distressed (a problem called somaticizing).

The combination of these difficulties gives rise to a bland colourless personality who seems to have no 'inner life', devoid of emotions, fantasies or vivid dreams. Thus as Peter Sifneos, the Harvard psychiatrist who originally coined the term alexithymia, says: '...they give the impression of being different, alien beings, having come from an entirely different world, living in the midst of a society which is dominated by feelings' (Goleman 1995, p.51)

Goleman points out that this condition shows how vital feelings are in everyday life, especially when it comes to making those crucial decisions which will deeply affect our lives, for example who to marry or which career to follow, suggesting that 'reason without feeling is blind'. This leads him to postulate that such people lack those intuitive signals that help guide us, that is, they lack gut feeling. He sums up the condition in these words:

> It is not that alexithymics never feel, but that they are unable to know – and especially to put into words – precisely what their feelings are. They are utterly lacking in the fundamental skill of emotional intelligence, self awareness – knowing what we are feeling as emotions roll within us. Alexithymics belie the common-sense notions that it is perfectly self evident what we are feeling: they haven't a clue ... Feelings come to them, when they come at all, as a befuddling bundle of distress; as the patient who cried at the movie put it, they feel awful but can't say exactly which kind of awful it is they feel. (Goleman 1995, p.51)

While the cause of this condition has not been clarified, Sifneos proposes that it could arise from a disconnection between the limbic system and the cortex, particularly the verbal centres.

Certainly alexithymia would seem to parallel the problems of some people with autism – who have no understanding of their 'feelings', sensing them as things which are external and alien. Small wonder that they fear being enveloped and swamped by their emotions. It is hardly surprising then if they try to keep emotion at bay, or see the world as frightening.

Does this underlying lack of self-awareness found in both proprioception and alexithymia explain some of the confusing stories concerning autism and pain? Imagine how you would identify the place that hurts when you feel no connection to that part of your body; or describe how you feel when you neither comprehend the feelings you have, nor even know that they 'belong' to you.

As we should expect by now, though, the picture is somewhat confused for, as previously described, many people with autism do have an inner life even though they may lack a fundamental understanding of their emotions. Perhaps, like those with alexithymia, the apparent lack of imagination simply reflects the fact that they simply do not have adequate means of expression.

The lack of gut feeling, too, is questionable for, although it may not apply to all, some people with autism can sum a person up extremely accurately within moments of meeting them: although whether this is based on an accumulation of previous experiences which are said to be the foundation of our gut feelings or simply a 'sixth sense' is a moot point.

Unfortunately there are still many questions at this stage – and more to come for now we must move on to vision.

Visual perceptual problems

Although hypersensitivity to sound was well catalogued and understandable, Darren White's comments on his apparently 'peculiar' visual perceptions made little sense to me until, in the autumn of 1993, Donna Williams and two of her friends found that they had several problems of a type associated with scotopic sensitivity (Irlen) syndrome.

So what exactly is Irlen syndrome? This is a term used to describe a perceptual dysfunction which can give rise to difficulties in coping with light, glare or black/white contrast. It affects a wide range of the population regardless of the degree of intelligence, including those who have mild reading problems, people with dyslexia, hyperactivity and various developmental delays. When the symptoms are mild the person may cope with and adjust to their problems but when they are more severe the side-effects of poor academic work or work performance often give rise to low self-esteem or behavioural difficulties.

Figure 2.1 shows a variety of ways in which an ordinary page of writing might be perceived by a person who has Irlen syndrome (Irlen 1991). Some people with dyslexia may only ever perceive a printed page with serious distortions but, like Darren, will not realize that others 'see' any differently.

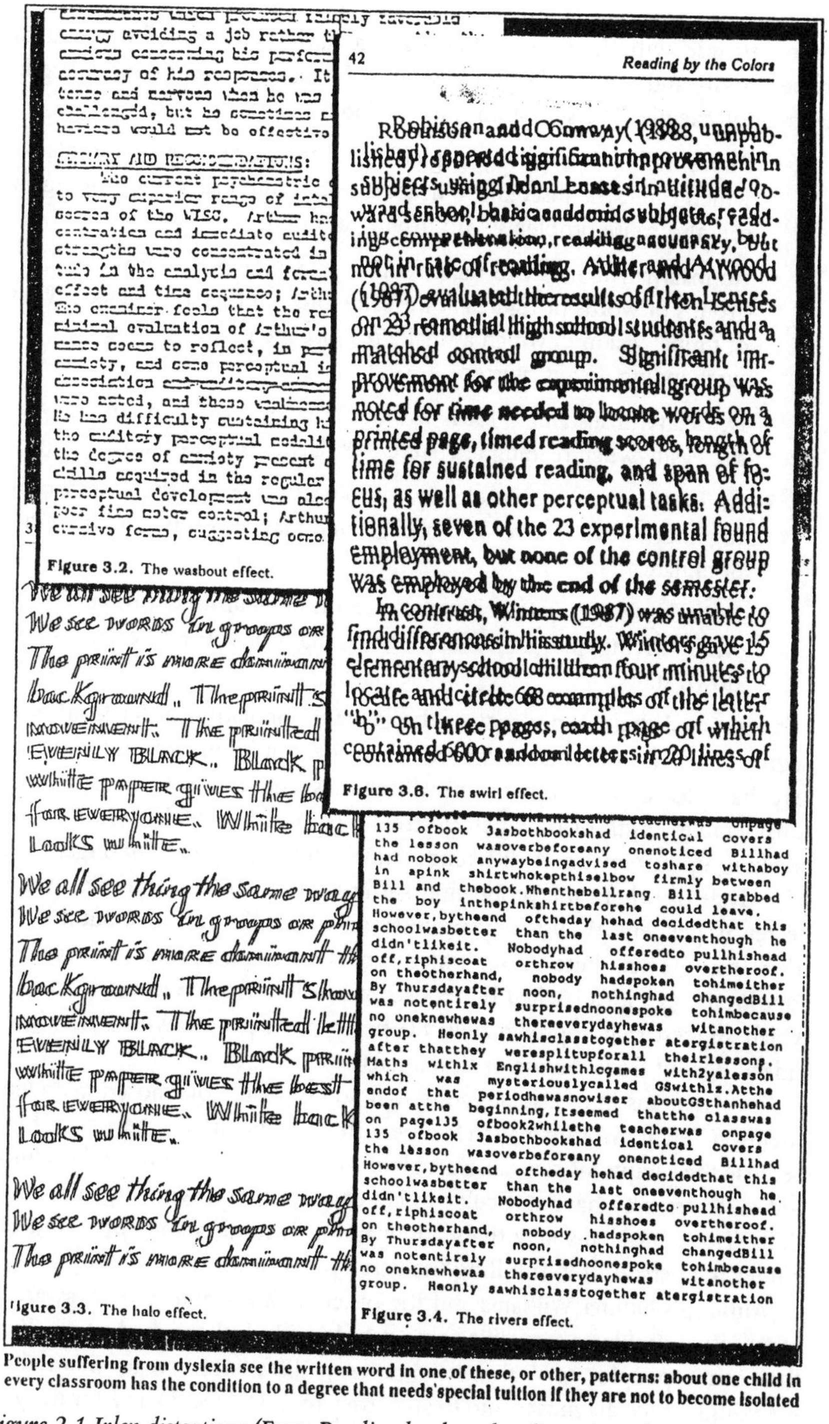
42
Reading by the Colors
Figure 3.2. The washout effect.
Figure 3.6. The swirl effect.
Figure 3.3. The halo effect.
Figure 3.4. The rivers effect.
People suffering from dyslexia see the written word in one of these, or other, patterns: about one child in every classroom has the condition to a degree that needs special tuition if they are not to become isolated

Figure 2.1 Irlen distortions (From Reading by the colors by Helen Irlen, published in 1991 by Avery Press and reproduced with permission)

Many people with Irlen syndrome have a family history of dyslexia or hyperactivity and some will have physical problems such as migraine, allergies or hypoglycaemia. The symptoms may include:

- Photophobia – sensitivity to glare, brightness or fluorescent lights which can cause discomfort, headaches or migraines when reading. It can also cause problems with driving at night.

- An insufficient ability to focus, which deters the person from seeing groups of words or figures at the same time. Difficulties include types of tunnel vision in which a small area of page is clear but the surrounding area is blurred.

- Difficulty in sustaining focus without great effort. The person may tire easily when reading and suffer headaches or eyestrain.

- An inability to see print clearly without distortion so that it may run together or even move. The background may also appear to glare or dominate.

- Poor depth perception, which can result in clumsiness, problems when driving, judging differences in height or width or even walking down stairs.

It is estimated that 15 per cent of the general population suffer from some degree of Irlen syndrome. However, when the condition is mild the person may have learnt to adapt to the difficulties and be able to cope for a considerable length of time before stress sets in or before the writing starts breaking up or moving. A different picture, though, emerges amongst those with dyslexia where the proportion suffering from Irlen syndrome rises to nearer 50 per cent. Whilst some professionals are still sceptical about this, the Irlen Institute has been using tinted lenses to alleviate and correct these conditions – an idea backed by reports of research from Harvard University which suggest that approximately 80 per cent of people with dyslexia do indeed benefit from the use of tinted lenses.

The Irlen Institute also suggests that some people diagnosed as having attention deficit disorder may in fact be suffering from Irlen syndrome. This is because the symptoms can cause problems with reading, writing and spelling; and sufferers may have difficulty in concentrating and with organizational skills. These problems may then culminate in frustration and anger and can hinder the person from fulfilling their true potential.

Although Donna Williams and the others had previously been aware of some visual problems they, like some people with dyslexia, had not realized that other people 'saw' things in a very different way to themselves. Amazingly, once diagnosed and treated, they found that suddenly, for the very first time in their lives, they could actually 'see' other people's faces and the world around them clearly – as she detailed movingly in *Like Color to the Blind* (1996).

Their experiences confirm that some people with autism have great difficulty in forming an image of their surroundings for, rather than seeing or being able to visualize a complete picture, people, objects and surroundings are fragmented, lack depth and are seen a piece at a time. Thus the whole world appears like a broken jigsaw puzzle where even the people who are closest to you may appear frightening. Imagine looking at your mother and seeing only her nose or perceiving her outstretched arms as totally separate from the rest of her body.

These types of experiences were summed up by two friends with autism when, wearing tinted lenses, they met my husband and I. Although we had previously spent a day with them (prior to the lenses), one said that she had never seen me before and knew only that I had dark curly hair, while the other said that the last time we met all he had seen of my husband (quite literally) was 'a bald head, a beard and a belly'! No wonder the world confuses them. Could it also account for the fact that many people with autism will pay particular attention to a distinguishing characteristic and/or like cartoon characters or other two-dimensional images as seen on television – perhaps because the latter make more consistent sense than reality?

How many other people with autism also see in a peculiar way? Certainly Richard Attfield talks of seeing double; whilst we have already heard mention of the difficulties Darren White had, seeing his perspective change and watching things becoming smaller. This is a phenomenon that I have also come across in another man who describes periods of time, since childhood, when he had what he and his family term simply 'the smalls'. Is this similar to Gunilla Gerland who describes her visual problems thus:

> Occasionally I lost all sense of perspective. Something would seem monstrously large if coming towards me at speed, or if I was unprepared. Someone suddenly leaning over me could frighten me enormously. I felt something was falling onto me and that I'd be crushed underneath it. (Gerland 1997, p.27)

Either type of problem would surely make for a lack of co-ordination. So could this account for one aspect of the difference between those who have Asperger's syndrome and the majority of those with autism, many of whom have apparently excellent sight? To take anyone else's sight at face value is foolish, though, without further exploration. Certainly a great number of these people are thought to have no visual problems and yet...? Do they?

We already know that Georgiana Stehli saw 'too well', with everything being magnified, so we have to ask whether those who have no obvious problems actually see in a similarly magnified manner. If so, this too could lead to visual problems, for while longsightedness may magnify things seen in the distance and make it possible for people to carry out delicate manipulative tasks (as many do), it could also prove a major drawback when they look at things which require a wider range of vision as things on the periphery could become unclear or might merge together – an experience akin to tunnel vision.

One particular aspect of these visual problems is interesting not just in terms of autism but rather for the devastating effect it has on other people – the person's inability or dislike of eye contact. A possible cause of this is described, amongst other aspects of the problem, by Nony in an article entitled 'Speculation on light sensitivity':

> As a child I found it difficult to walk in town on a sunny day. My eyes would close. I would have to turn into a darker doorway or cover my eyes to get them open enough to see. The glare of sidewalks and shop windows was too much. I had some difficulty in grassy places but my 'permanent scowl' and closing my eyes took care of it.
>
> As a teenager I decided I wanted sunglasses. The usual grey and green shades I tried on seemed hard to see through. Then I found a different-coloured pair of glasses. The effect was remarkable. I could look around the drugs store and out into the sunny street. I could see distinct shapes of cars and meters and people.
>
> I bought those glasses and kept them for many years. I found that I could walk with my head up and look into the distance. I had always walked with my head down, looking just in front of my feet. I could look directly at things I had only glanced at before. (Nony 1993)

Most interestingly Nony goes on to say:

> I have not heard of anyone looking into physical characteristics of the eyes as possible reasons for eye gaze avoidance or other unusual behaviours. As some others have said, *eye contact was painful* for me. It was not quite like a broken bone or a burn but it can only be described as pain. *Someone looking directly into my eyes felt like an attack.* I needed to protect against it. (Nony 1993, pp.5–6, my emphasis)

Nony queries whether her problems are related to albinism as this ran in her family and further suggests that some people may lack some pigmentation in their eyes. It would be interesting to know if this is a factor.

Knowledge of Irlen syndrome and the 'evidence' from the sufferers themselves would make it seem likely that a high proportion of people with autism could have severe visual difficulties which leave them unable to see in the way in which most of us do. Why then are we still perplexed by the fact that many people with autism do extremely well at tasks in which they are asked to focus on a part of a puzzle rather than the whole whilst conversely having great difficulty with tasks which require observation of the whole? This could be quite 'normal' given what they see. Sadly, though, all too often (and to their detriment), such 'skills' and deficits are seen as a problem of cognition whilst the very real perceptual problems which underlie them remain unrecognized.

Anthony observed that 'the child lives in the world of the young infant set in the twilight of consciousness' (Rimland 1964, p.94). The problems caused by such 'abnormal' visual perceptions would mean that a number of people (the majority?) with autism do indeed inhabit the world of the young infant and throughout their lives have only an infant's vision to illuminate their world. Not twilight, though, simply a dawn in which the sun never fully rises.

Perhaps visual hypersensitivity is the origin of the obsessive need to turn off lights which some people with autism have, for how else can less verbal people make us understand the discomfort and distress they feel when taken into brightly lit places? Does it also contribute to the 'obsessive' need to keep everything in its allotted place? It is hardly surprising to find the usefulness of order is advice given to those who have a visual impairment.

The use of tinted glasses to help with these difficulties is still in its infancy although research is currently under way. Meanwhile Helen Irlen reports that the results with children indicate consistent changes in several areas. This includes a decrease in anxiety, obsessive/compulsive behaviours and self-injurious behaviours with a corresponding increase in eye contact and speech.

Is this type of response common to others? My experience would certainly suggest it is. I was amazed at the high proportion of people with untreated visual perception problems of varying sorts amongst a group with severe 'learning difficulties' at a local Adult Opportunity Centre. Whilst several demonstrated mild 'autistic tendencies' two people had a very pronounced lack of convergence between their eyes and, perhaps unsurprisingly, although not diagnosed as such, they showed very definite 'autistic features'. Both of them had two functioning eyes but, when judged by their actions, their visual perception was very strange. Helen Irlen's findings were upheld when both responded to well to tinted lenses. In both cases these 'held' the wandering eye, allowing it to work more fully in conjunction with the other; this reduced anxiety and increased awareness of and curiosity in things around them.

A friend of mine who has autism started wearing tinted lenses in her late twenties. She has noted far more detailed changes and, although there may be individual variations in the way people respond, I would like to mention some of the more interesting ones here:

- An ability to perceive depth. This enables the person to make more sense of the world giving greater awareness of people and objects. One simple example of the latter is the ability to recognize and cross streams and puddles rather than walking through them. Depth perception can also affect movement, making it easier and less 'staccato'.

- An ability to interpret meaning from behaviour (perhaps because she can accurately see people's expressions for the first time in her life).

- Less need to blink and squint frequently (a technique previously used to slow down or control the light and visual input).

Other far-reaching improvements have arisen from this visual alteration. They include an increased ability to hold thoughts; to conceptualize; better auditory perception; and the 'freedom' to see and hear at the same time.

These, in turn, now allow her to 'process' more than one piece of information at a time with a corresponding reduction in 'shut down'. Thus she can follow a conversation and also converse more easily because each piece of information is no longer erased by the one before. Such changes have given her greater access to her own ideas and feelings and increased her understanding, even of some literal jokes. It has also instigated more genuine self-expression as the need to use stored speech or phrases has decreased. Quite naturally, too, the end result has been a considerable reduction of anxiety and stress.

Obviously, for anyone who has lived with such problems for many years a change of this magnitude takes time. This initially caused a variety of problems which, for a time, were particularly noticeable in her ability to use speech. While some of the results may have been helped or enhanced by a diet and supplement of DMG (dimethylglycine) used to alleviate metabolic problems, such changes are obviously remarkable – particularly in an adult – and bode well for the future.

While not everyone agrees with Helen Irlen's assessment of visual perceptual problems it is increasingly evident that many people do have difficulties which can be corrected by the use of tinted lenses. Arnold Wilkins, a research psychologist, has been looking at the effects of visual stimuli since the early 1970s, initially in terms of the effect on epilepsy. He looked at the underlying reason for such distortions, which he detailed in his book *Visual Stress* (1995). He found that whilst fluorescent lights cause problems (and are a factor in agoraphobia) many people are also very sensitive to the patterns created by stripes – a feature of many different things in modern life from road markings, pages of print and fabric design to television screens. Thus a number of children have more difficulty in coping with print or experience more visual distortions as they get older for generally the books they are then expected to read have smaller print and closer spacing. Such factors create great problems and can contribute to epilepsy and migraine.

During his time with the MRC (Medical Research Council), Wilkins investigated the use of tinted lenses on people with visual perceptual problems and developed a piece of equipment called an Intuitive Colorimeter which enables the correct tints to be selected for each individual. He used the Colorimeter to carry out a double-blind study which proved the effectiveness of tinted lenses for people with this type of visual perceptual problem. Interestingly one woman, discussed in his paper (Wilkins, Milroy and Nimmo-Smith 1992) was unable to read the words 'was' and 'saw' correctly – a problem corrected by the use of a particular hue.

Currently there is some controversy between the Irlen Institute and those using the Colorimeter which is outside the remit of this book. I must however mention that this has even caused confusion about the name that should be given to the condition which was originally called scotopic sensitivity syndrome. It is now known variously as visual perceptual discomfort, Irlen syndrome, Meares–Irlen syndrome or, simply, visual dyslexia.

You will have to wait a little longer for the proof but, regardless of the name and the arguments, it is clear that such visual problems do exist and can cause tremendous problems. For now it is enough to know that these problems can be corrected by the use of tinted lenses and, politics aside, both Irlen lenses and those obtained through the use of the Colorimeter are effective even though it is not yet known exactly how they work.

Auditory problems

These first came to the attention of people working with autism after Annabel Stehli published her book *The Sound of a Miracle* (1990) in which she described the auditory problems her daughter Georgiana had; problems which Georgie later identified as a major factor in her 'autistic' withdrawal and behaviours.

At the age of twelve Georgiana underwent Auditory Integration Treatment which corrected her hypersensitivity to sound and thereby gave her the opportunity to begin to work on and overcome the other problems she faced.

Stehli says that after treatment: 'She told me she was much more comfortable, that she no longer heard street noises three blocks away, or people flushing their toilets at the other end of the building, or the blood rushing through her veins.'

Much became clear as Georgie explained the effect certain sounds had on her:

…When we made soufflés when she was little it was the sound of the electric beater she hadn't been able to stand, although she eventually got used to it. And the noise of the dishes clanking in the sink had disturbed her as well. She hadn't been able to blow out the candles on her birthday cake because the sound of blowing had been so disturbing.

'It sounded like monsters,' she said…

Stehli 'was particularly relieved when it came to light that she'd hit the little boy over the head with the jack-in-a-box simply because of the bink-bink-bink noise of "Pop Goes The Weasel", which he'd insisted on playing repeatedly.'

Georgiana's descriptions continued, enumerating her own breathing, wind, rain, floods and so on, all of which seemed extremely loud and frightening to the young child. She also had difficulty in learning to speak because '…she hadn't liked the sound of voices, and had trouble accurately hearing certain sounds…'

Her mother then realizes that: 'Because there was so much peripheral noise in our house she hadn't been able to think straight.' And as she tellingly comments, 'Georgie had never been crazy – merely crazed!' (Stehli 1990, p.171).

Gunilla Gerland also had auditory problems, for as she says:

> The noise made by mopeds could be heard everywhere in the street, and I couldn't bear it. I was still very sensitive to certain sounds. It was difficult to be on my own and I was so vulnerable out of doors – it was like going around with no skin and always trying to keep everything in place nonetheless. I was raw, and if I let go for a second everything essential to life would threaten to fall out of me.
>
> The boy and the girl used to hang around outside her house, he sitting on his moped, she leaning against the gate. When they saw that the sound of the moped made me react strangely, they started scaring me. They would wait for me to pass them, then suddenly rev the moped. That din made the ground under my feet disappear and I could neither see nor feel the world around me. Up and down were suddenly in the same place and I had no sense of where my feet were. So as not to fall over or explode from inside, I would grab the fence where I was standing, pressing myself against it and holding on hard. I had to feel something that stood still, something anchored, in a world that had suddenly become totally unpredictable … (Gerland 1997, p.130)

Now let us take a closer look at the work of a man who strongly believes that our behaviour is conditioned by the way in which we hear: Guy Bérard. He spent over 25 years developing and honing his technique while successfully treating people who presented with a range of difficulties, from depression through dyslexia and learning difficulties to the more severe problems of autism, whose common link was found in hearing anomalies. His career spanned more than two decades but it did not receive any great publicity until his work with Georgiana Stehli became known.

Unfortunately, Bérard's ideas are considered to be flawed from an audiological point of view and they have therefore been ignored by many audiologists. However, as one audiologist pointed out, this does not mean that all his ideas have little value. Indeed, there is growing evidence that Auditory Integration Training works well with many people with autism. So, a brief discussion of his ideas would be helpful here.

First – to state the obvious: all children learn to speak by mirroring the spoken word and if they do not hear correctly their understanding and pronunciation will be flawed. Bérard found that many children with dyslexia suffer from auditory dyslaterality: that is, they hear sounds of particular frequencies well with one ear whilst hearing them only partially or not at all with the other ear. This obviously results in a slowing of auditory perception as they struggle to make sense of what is said. It can also cause problems of interpretation as letters are lost or their sequence is misheard. No wonder some people with dyslexia think pictorially, using images rather than words. While such difficulties may not prove too problematic at home where parents will often make allowances for the speech difficulties which result, school may become a nightmare as they face an unequal struggle in trying to keep up with their classmates.

People are often less sympathetic towards those who have 'hidden' problems caused by a hearing impairment than to those who are visually impaired; but once this is explained the majority of people will have some empathy for people with the type of difficulties mentioned above. Most too can at least imagine auditory fuzz (possibly similar to tinnitus?) caused by a partial loss of hearing.

Although Bérard's work is now well known within the 'world' of autism, relatively few members of the public have heard of hypersensitivity to sound (hyperacusis). Even now, although some audiologists acknowledge the distressing effects of hyperacusis and understand the magnitude of difficulty it can cause, others, whose training and work has been geared to help those with a hearing loss, demonstrate less awareness of the major impact it can have upon some people's lives.

Much of the recognition of the seriousness of hyperacusis and the problems which arise from it has come, not from autism, but rather from research into tinnitus. Figures now suggest that approximately 45 per cent of people with tinnitus also suffer from hyperacusis, which is thought, in some, to be a contributory factor in the development of the tinnitus.

Although many of us have a particular sound we dislike, such as chalk or a fingernail squeaking on a blackboard, others will find this a strange idea. Even so this condition actually affects a great many people who experience discomfort from everyday sounds that do not bother the majority, for example, people talking, radio or television, traffic noise. It can affect the person's social life as it can lead them to avoid such noises wherever possible, making many mundane tasks such as shopping and travelling difficult. While personal experience suggests that some people may have had unrecognized auditory discomfort throughout their lives, unfortunately hyperacusis is often not recognized until the person develops tinnitus or needs to use a hearing aid. Indeed, it is generally thought to be a late onset problem.

Thus some people may be unaware that they are hypersensitive although they might become increasingly stressed and irritable when exposed to particular noises. Others may realize that certain sounds increase their stress and will go out of their way, often quite literally, to avoid particular situations. Like some of those with visual perceptual problems, such people are often successful at school and in their careers, adapting to the limitations posed by their hyperacusis, though they may appear slightly introverted, preferring their own company or that of a few friends and avoiding certain things such as discos, parties or crowded shops.

Noise pollution has received much attention in recent years, but what happens when this is combined with hyperacusis? That is, what happens when hypersensitive people cannot control the noise in their environment? While some develop physical stress-related disorders or withdraw into themselves others may find themselves increasingly short tempered, becoming involved in arguments which flare up apparently 'without cause' or being more easily provoked into acts of aggression.

The sound made by a crying infant is obviously loud so that it can attract attention and comfort. Could it be, though, that a few instances of child abuse which begin with the seemingly endless cry of a child are then compounded by hypersensitivity? While many such incidents no doubt occur without the added stresses of living with hyperacusis it would be interesting to know how many people are actually affected by this condition. Perhaps we might indeed find that some people's behaviour is conditioned by the things they cannot avoid hearing.

I have mentioned a few of the possible effects, but now let us look at these more closely. To quote from a person with autism here would be to invite that oft-quoted and scornful comment 'anecdote' so it is more helpful to look at the devastating effects that sound can have on an 'ordinary' person. The general lack of awareness of the condition made this hard to find but I did eventually find two examples. The first quote clearly indicates the tremendous distress which can be caused by such problems. It comes from the writer V.S. Naipaul who stated that he was 'immensely happy' when his hearing 'began to degenerate'.

The next quote is more descriptive and closely parallels the potential stresses of the person with autism for, sadly, the author had been living under intolerable conditions which caused tremendous and continuous stress for some considerable time prior to this episode. In his book *An Evil Cradling*

(1992) the former hostage Brian Keenan, having already spent long uncertain months in captivity in Lebanon, describes a tortured period when:

> One night and every night for the rest of our time in that prison the guards hung a small transistor in the passage outside our cell. It was turned up to the limit and tuned to static. The constant buzz and fuzz and crackling screech bored into our heads like a needle. At first we tried to forget it and ignore its pressure but it was useless. The mind was always drawn into it. It seemed to be inside us, recklessly slicing and gouging with a rusty broken scalpel. Every fibre and nerve of the body felt plucked and strained by it. Hour after hour, night after night. It tore at the very membranes of the brain. There was no possibility of rest or sleep. It ate into you, devouring all sense and sensibility.
>
> I tossed and turned, clamped my hands over my ears. Nothing would quell this crazy static. I stuffed balls of paper into my ears. I wrapped my towel around my head, and still the noise was unbearable; how long could I endure this. I rocked, slowly at first then savagely trying to create a rhythm beyond the noise. I tried to sing, I tried to pray but my efforts only added to the torment. I tried sitting on the cold damp floor with the foam mattress wrapped about me but there was no protection from the high-pitched screech. My head was burning inside … It was relentless.
>
> Only in the morning, when the guards prepared breakfast, would the noise be silenced. I walked exhausted to the shower. The luxury of hot water and soap could not refresh me. (Keenan 1992, pp.147–149)

He and John McCarthy requested that the radio be removed or at least turned down: to no avail. He continues:

> That night I slept fitfully, overcome by exhaustion, both physical and mental. On occasions I woke, the noise continually wrenching me out of sleep. Even in that darkness I could feel the whiteness of the walls blinding and burning me. I wondered then as I do even now how noise can affect our perception of colour. The whiteness had become deafening. (Keenan 1992, p.248)

This was a horrifying experience which unfortunately was just one of many suffered during the long years of captivity. It still amazes me that after enduring such conditions they retained their sanity and their humour.

Similarly, noise also had a devastating effect on some of his captors, for as Keenan describes:

> On other occasions, though they loved to watch these movies, whenever music played, particularly Western rock music, Saafi would rock back and forward as I myself had done long ago when I was locked up alone, and

sing Muslim hymns or war-songs to drown out the noise of the pop music
... It was genuinely painful for him. (Keenan 1992, p.248)

Easy to see how sound can be used as a method of torture!

So what are the effects of auditory problems in autism – especially on the child who cannot control his environment or make the problems known? Certainly many have an inability to habituate (cut out unwanted sounds), which must cause tremendous distress. One parent whose son has autism suggests that the effect of this could be comparable to wearing some types of hearing aid which increase the volume of people's voices but also frequently amplifies the background noise which then intrudes constantly, making it difficult to concentrate on the conversation you are having and leaving you 'unable to hear yourself think'!

Worse still, this is compounded by other problems. If Delacato is right, some sufferers are hyposensitive and could therefore suffer problems similar to those with a partial hearing loss. Many more, though, fit into his other category, being acutely hypersensitive to sound. Is this linked to the loudness discomfort level (i.e. the level at which we find it impossible to tolerate sounds)? For the majority of people this would be in the region of 100 decibels, but for some of those with autism this level is totally intolerable and so they 'shut out' particular noises and even some voices (often in the higher range). Certainly one person I know had a loudness discomfort level of just 40 decibels (which roughly equates to low speech sounds, not far above a whisper). Small wonder then that he spent much of his time effectively 'blocking' noise out.

Sometimes too it would seem that the person is able to hear particular frequencies (pitch) which many of us cannot. Two examples of this include the child who heard a 'silent dog whistle' and another who was aware of the noise of the vacuum cleaner inside a house even though he was sitting in a car outside and the doors and windows of both house and car were closed.

It is hardly surprising that they attempt to cope with this by avoiding various situations, covering their ears in order to block out the noise or by becoming extremely distressed or withdrawn. Does this account for the fact that a few people are extremely reluctant to flush the toilet; perhaps because they cannot bear the sound of rushing water?

This acuity of hearing seems common to many people with autism, although why this is so has not, to my knowledge, received much attention. Certainly the result is serious, for those noises to which the person is 'hyper' constantly impinge upon them and render them unable to distinguish between sounds which would normally be relegated to the background and those closer to them. Thus while they would often be able to concentrate upon a single word or two or even a simple sentence, longer sentences could be broken up by intruding background noises and the meaning would easily be lost – as it is if you try to listen to a badly tuned radio.

Questions abound. Are we all born with a particular tolerance level (our 'norm') to which we generally adapt, coping with noise levels we dislike quite adequately under normal conditions only to become more acutely aware of them when ill or stressed? Or are some 'normal' people also born with a high acuity to particular sounds?

We know that when under stress or suffering from migraine some people become less tolerant of sounds which they would normally be able to ignore or cope with and that a magnesium deficiency can, amongst other things, contribute to auditory hypersensitivity. It is interesting to speculate on the part diet might play in the manifestation of this problem. Certainly the inadequate diet of the hostages did nothing for their physical health but perhaps we should also ask if it decreased Brian Keenan's ability to tolerate noise? What is the origin of these auditory anomalies?

Then again one has to ask whether there is actually an undetected physical aspect to these problems. This was certainly the case with one woman who, even though she showed no problems when tested, felt as if her ear had a blockage or hard deposit in it which made cracking noises (which were loud enough to be heard by others) when pressed. After she had massaged it over a period of time the blockage gradually diminished. I wonder if this applies to other people too?

While several factors may be involved in abnormal auditory perception, one which merits consideration comes from the research done by Paul Shattock and his colleagues at the Autism Research Unit in Sunderland. They have now tested approximately 1000 people (late 1997), many of whom developed fairly normally until between 2 and 3 years of age, and have found what they believe are abnormal peptides in over 80 per cent of urine samples taken from people with autism.

Shattock (1991) suggests these may be opioid peptides which, if true, could have some significant effects. One would be to diminish sensory messages, a factor which could account for abnormal perceptions. They would also disrupt the filtration process rendering it ineffective so that the person would be unable to filter out irrelevant stimuli adequately – an explanation for the inability to habituate to sound perhaps? Furthermore, opioid peptides could also interfere with the vestibular system which is concerned with balance, which might explain the extraordinary feats of balance and the ability to spin around without becoming giddy which some are able to perform.

Could these ideas also account for the fact that some people demonstrate a consistent delay in their responses to stimuli? This is particularly noticeable in relation to sound (a delay also found amongst some people with dyslexia), and may account for one intriguing phenomenon: the 'flat' monotonous tones of some people with autism. Proprioception provides one possible explanation for this, while another potential cause is given by Rimland when he clearly describes an incident which occurred to him:

> The incident occurred while I was deeply engrossed in reading. Some time had passed before I became aware that someone had asked me a question and was awaiting a response. My mind was quite blank. I had no idea what I had been asked. I was about to ask that the question be repeated when this suddenly became unnecessary. I could hear the query, phrased in two short but complete sentences, being repeated word for word, the 'sound' coming from within my head. The effect was that of an echo, except that several seconds, perhaps as many as ten, had passed.
>
> The experience was not unfamiliar, though never before had it been so vivid. This experience of what I shall call 'delayed mental audition' was striking in two respects which pertain to the topic of this monograph. First, the question *had been sensed and recorded without interpretation.* I had no idea of what had been said to me until the *second* (internalized) hearing. The usual step whereby incoming stimuli are integrated with the prior content of the brain – are given meaning – was bypassed. This is exactly what I had much earlier postulated for stimuli entering the brain of the autistic child.
>
> The second striking aspect of the event was the nature of the echo-like voice repeating the question. I could identify it as the voice of the person who asked the question, but the sound of the voice was different, in an extremely unique and peculiar way. The voice had a high-pitched, hollow, wooden sound. The inflections were somehow preserved, despite the parrotlike meaninglessness of the vocalization. In short, *the internally experienced voice duplicated precisely and unmistakably the classical manner of speech of the child with early infantile autism.* This was the high-pitched, wooden monotone the autistic child characteristically uses to indicate 'Yes'; the mechanical verbatim repetition of the question – including its inflection – which Kanner has named 'affirmation by repetition'. This was the voice one hears when the child repeats later exactly what he has heard some time before – Kanner's 'delayed echolalia'. This was the 'closed-loop' phenomenon – the stimuli had entered memory and later emerged unchanged. (Rimland 1964, pp.178–179)

Does this also have links with the 'mono' processing already mentioned? Certainly the processing problems and the other clues we have explored suggest that we can now identify several different responses which could arise from such hearing difficulties:

1. The person will hear and respond correctly (particularly to short requests/sentences), albeit often with a slight delay.

2. They may lose the main part of the sentence, hearing only the beginning and end. This can result in an apparently odd reaction as they completely misunderstand what has been said – although they may sometimes attempt to guess, filling in the pieces by looking for additional clues.

3. They will respond after a (very?) lengthy delay, often when the time for that particular response has passed.

4. They may 'shut off' (or 'shut down') and not respond at all.

Although audiologists generally disagree with some of Bérard's methods this does not mean that all his work should be subject to scepticism, as it sometimes is. In one aspect of his work he identified various groups of people as having similar auditory 'profiles'. Thus those who suffered from asthma and some of those with depression showed a great similarity in the placement of the peaks and troughs shown on their audiograms. It is interesting to find that illnesses sometimes thought to be psychological in origin have a physical 'reflection'. It is more fascinating still that those people whose depression was linked to a particular pattern in the hearing test were cured (of their depression) through Auditory Integration Training!

Once again the picture is beginning to look even more muddled. So is there any way of making sense of it? First we must examine a few more matters, the next being dyslexia.

Dyslexia

As you cannot have failed to notice, the word dyslexia has appeared with amazing regularity amongst many of the other difficulties mentioned: so much so that although it is obviously only one facet of those problems the subject deserves a little expansion.

Approximately 10 per cent of the population suffer from dyslexia, with 2 per cent having severe problems. While these can in turn give rise to low self-esteem and other related problems which were previously mentioned, many people with dyslexia such as Duncan Goodhew, Susan Hampshire and Michael Heseltine are 'high achievers' and those like Albert Einstein and Leonardo de Vinci fall into the category of geniuses.

Further details are readily available from a variety of sources so I will only include a brief guide to some of the relevant factors. The first of these you may have guessed, for having read this far you will now be able to anticipate that the ratio of boys to girls with dyslexia is similar to that found in autism.

Bevé Hornsby (1984), who has worked with those with dyslexia, has identified a list of symptoms of dyslexia. Note, though, that she feels that while the first symptom needs to be present for a diagnosis the other factors are very individual and may not be found in all children:

• Reading and writing abilities at variance with obvious intelligence.

- Family history of left-handedness/late reading/poor spelling, etc. May not be able to grasp the basics of punctuation.

- Late developing speech and may have immature speech.

- Left-handed, ambidextrous or late in favouring one side. May also be uncoordinated.

- Little concept of direction. An inability to distinguish left from right, up from down.

- Sequencing problems. May have difficulty in putting things in alphabetical or numerical order.

- May find mathematics extremely hard and/or be late learning to tell the time.

- Spatial ability may be either very poor or excellent.

- Possible auditory and/or visual problems.

Hornsby suggests that some children have a visual dysfunction in which their eyes are unable to converge properly. Thus the eyes see two separate images which do not fuse together. While the majority of people in this situation learn to ignore one image totally, some are not able to do this and either continue to see two images or switch from one image to another. It is hardly surprising then that they have problems with reading and writing and in concentration. While this lack of a fixed reference eye is usually treated by a patch worn over one eye it sounds very similar to the visual perceptual problems already discussed.

An article in the *New York Times* (Blakeslee 1991) discussed another aspect of the problem which was illuminated by research carried out at Harvard University. This indicated that dyslexia was not a malfunction in the way people understand language but rather a brain 'abnormality' which involves vision and possibly also hearing and touch.

While generally no differences have been identified between the eyes of good and bad readers tests now reveal that people with dyslexia have problems in the area of the magno system (see Appendix E) which works more slowly than it should. Thus when shown two images in quick succession people with this condition reported seeing only one image, in contrast to people without such problems who saw both. Only when the process was repeated with the images being shown at a much slower rate were those with dyslexia able to see both images.

When looked at more closely, the magno cells in the visual system were found to be more disorganized and approximately 25 per cent smaller than in people without such problems. This effectively means that the reactions of the person with dyslexia are slower. In related research scientists have now found some evidence to suggest that dyslexia could be an autoimmune disease, acquired prior to or soon after birth, which might damage the magnocellular system. They postulate that the ensuing abnormal sights and sounds might begin to shape the infant's brain in a different way to that of the 'normal' child thus giving rise to the problems later found in dyslexia.

Sandra Blakeslee's article also discussed a similar slowness which was apparent during tests done by Paula Tallal, professor at Rutgers Centre for molecular and behavioural neurosciences. This showed that, like the visual system, the auditory system too had difficulties in processing incoming information. The results indicated that children with dyslexia cannot cope with the speed at which language is usually processed. This causes great difficulty when they hear particular sounds, especially 'ba' and 'da' – something which can be corrected by artificially lengthening the 'b' and 'd' sounds on a computer, making them slower and thereby enabling the child to differentiate between the two.

Hornsby has also identified some auditory problems in dyslexia as having a variety of effects, one of the most common being a tendency to confuse the order of syllables and numbers when they are spoken. She points out that a non-dyslexic person would generally use their right ear to interpret speech and their left for other sounds. Tests have, however, shown that some people with severe dyslexia may prefer to interpret speech sounds only through their left ear or alternatively have no hemispheric preference at all.

Hornsby suggests that the implication of this is that the language area of a person with dyslexia may not be sited mainly in the left hemisphere (as it would normally be) and that the brain therefore tries to use both hemispheres to interpret speech. She feels that this could cause confusion as the connection between the two halves of the brain may become overloaded.

Perhaps it is hardly surprising to find that some brain scans of children with autism have shown results similar to those of people with dyslexia by identifying a defect in the area of the left hemisphere. Or that Georgiana Stehli was dyslexic as well as autistic.

Temple Grandin, too, talks of having a 'visual' mind which makes spatial work such as drawing easy. In contrast she has difficulty in retaining information in her memory if she has to concentrate and perform an action at the same time. Thus in a test which required her to identify the dimensions which differentiated one set of shapes from another she did poorly because she forgot the concept while looking for the answer.

In an article in *The Times* (1999) Anjana Ahuja discussed research from Yale University which identified clear problems in the transmission of messages within the brain. Normally images taken from the eye are sent to the angular gyrus which transforms them into words. From there they should normally be sent on to Wernicke's area where their meaning is interpreted. In those tested the pathway between the angular gyrus and Wernicke's area showed reduced activity and the messages were in fact sent to Broca's area, which deals with speech – a deflection which clearly creates great difficulties for the person when they try to read. While there may be several factors which cause or contribute to dyslexia, PET scans (Carter 1998) clearly demonstrate that there are also other 'faults' in the transmission of messages between Wernicke's area and Broca's area. Normally the two main language areas should work in conjunction with each other but the scans given to people during a complex reading task showed that this was not so in people with dyslexia – the result being a delay between comprehension and speech.

A study (Lewine, Irlen and Orrison 1999) is also under way at the New Mexico Institute Medical Center in conjunction with Helen Irlen to determine the effect of tinted lenses. In this, magnetoencephalography (MEG) is being used to look at visual responses given both with and without tinted lenses. The preliminary results again showed some physical problems. In one test the dyslexic subjects had an abnormal reaction to stimulus so that the neurons continued to fire even after the stimulus was removed: a response which was normalized by the lenses. In the second test the subjects looked at a checkerboard pattern which pulsated at regular intervals. Once again there was a discrepancy between the controls who had no problems in seeing what was shown and those people with dyslexia who saw a variety of visual distortions. Some eventually had a 'white out' in which all the pattern was lost – a problem which was again corrected by the tinted lenses.

There are obviously many facets to this which continue to be explored. Moreover, the next section adds another possible link which may initially seem a little irrelevant, although the reason for its inclusion will soon become clear.

Metabolic disorders and allergies

Before taking a closer look at such problems in relation to autism let us look at the effect allergies have in the general population.

Tuula Tuormaa believes that the majority of allergy sufferers show symptoms from birth although there are some individuals who only begin to demonstrate signs of the problems at a later stage. Amongst many possible causes we find that she suggests a physical or mental reaction to cow's milk. This could be because they are allergic to it and indeed it has been said that there is a correlation between a milk allergy and ear infections, perhaps because the sufferers have an inability to break down the opioid peptides found in milk.

Jeffery Bland, an American-based nutritional biochemist, clarifies the sequence of events (Bland 1983). He suggests that the first factor is a faulty digestive process which allows partially digested proteins to be absorbed into the blood through the intestinal lining. These particles then impair the functioning of the immune system and lead to food allergies/sensitivities and a variety of other effects which will be looked at in greater detail further on.

If an allergic reaction begins very early the child might have some of the following symptoms:

- Colic or nappy rash.
- Various infections affecting the nose or eyes.
- Aches and pains in the head, ears, joints or stomach.
- Prone to head banging or rocking.
- A poor sleeper who is difficult to rouse in the mornings and often irritable on waking.
- Giddy spells or fainting fits.
- Difficult to feed. Frequently thirsty. Still bedwetting later than normal.
- An unhappy baby – often crying for no apparent reason. Rarely smiles. May dislike physical touch.
- Either late in learning to walk or misses some stages.
- Has poor co-ordination and is often clumsy and might be accident prone.
- IQ normal but has difficulty learning to read or write.

Tuormaa suggests that these children fall into three distinct groups the first two of which, while lacking the severity, seem reminiscent of Delacato's description of the different types of autism. Her categories are:

1. Hyperactive and abnormally outgoing. This child is a 'moving disaster' who is hyperactive and impulsive. He has little ability to control his emotions, to respond to affection/correction or to concentrate for any length of time.

2. Withdrawn and underactive. A painfully shy, submissive child who is often fearful, dislikes sudden noises and clings to his mother in strange situations. He may dislike group activities, coping better in a one-to-one situation. He is often a loner, may lack friends and seems to prefer animals to people.

3. A mixture of both so that the symptoms alternate.

The connection to Delacato's ideas is clear, but are there any others? Perhaps here we should look at the work of Allergy-induced Autism (AiA) (see Useful Addresses). This group, which has now changed considerably, originated with a group of parents. They instigated research into the possible link between allergies and autism which has been carried out by Rosemary Waring at

Birmingham University. Many of the children tested come from families whose members have a history of various allergic disorders including asthma, eczema, hay fever and migraine.

The AiA suggest that many of these children develop normally until around eighteen months. They consider that the 'breakdown' into the various behavioural changes associated with autism could merely be the final stage of a slow and almost invisible illness and believe that their children's autism is a result of an intolerance to many foods and/or chemicals. While each child's allergies are different and need individual diagnosis, the main offenders often seem to be gluten (found in wheat and other cereals), cow's milk (casein), sugar and citrus fruits.

The AiA feel that all too often it is only the behavioural changes which are noticed and investigated, while the varied physical symptoms, which may or may not have been evident prior to the onset of the autism, are ignored. The group associate the onset of the 'illness' with these physical changes, some of which are detailed below:

- Diet changes dramatically.
- Intolerance to certain foods whilst craving others. Excessive thirst.
- Pale complexion with red face/ears – which may be especially evident after eating. Dark rings under the eyes.
- Dry skin.
- Sweating excessively (particularly at night).
- Bad catarrh.
- Diarrhoea, bloating, stomach pains.
- Asthma, eczema, or urticaria (nettle rash) which is an allergic reaction produced by the skin to some substance (often food) to which the individual is hypersensitive.
- May run a temperature for no apparent reason.
- Hypoglycaemia.
- Possible petit mal epilepsy. This can also be a manifestation of a metabolic disturbance such as hypoglycaemia.
- Strong tendency to become ambidextrous or even 'change their handedness' at the same time as their behaviour deteriorates.

Research has found that out of the 70 children initially tested (to mid-1995) all had a deficiency of a detoxification enzyme called phenolsulpho-transferase-P which would lead to increased permeability in the gut wall. This effectively means that such children are unable to rid the body of the natural toxins found in food. They will, therefore, have trouble coping with many of their own body chemicals which would normally be broken down and eliminated and so substances such as serotonin, noradrenalin and dopamine can build up in the body. The waste products stay in the body and can have a harmful effect on other important biochemical functions, particularly in the brain.

In addition, although the causes are as yet unclear, Waring observed that 95 per cent of these children also had low levels of plasma sulphate. This is often implicated in allergic reactions and would present problems similar to those caused by a deficient enzyme. Thus such children effectively suffer from a metabolic disease.

It comes as little surprise to find that a lack of phenolsulphotransferase-P is also found in people with migraine whilst low sulphate levels are often found in those with allergies: factors which have led Waring to suggest that any child from a family in which one parent suffers from migraine and the other has low plasma sulphate may inherit a combination of both problems.

Interestingly the lack or malfunction of phenolsulphotransferase-P also leaves the person unable to cope with phenolics. Ber (1983) has collated these into different groups correlating them with various types of problem, from migraine and other physical illnesses to dyslexia and autism. His research suggests that exposure to phenolics can have a detrimental effect on many different bodily functions from the brain to the immune system.

Two of the groups he identified may have particular significance in relation to our search. One is the group containing malvin, which has associations with autism, epilepsy and multiple sclerosis (in which the immune system is affected). The other is that of gallic acid, the most important phenol (found in approximately 70% of foods), which Ber associates with attention problems, dyslexia and hyperactivity. Apparently the elimination of gallic acid is the basis of the well-known Feingold diet. Ber suggests an alternative to this for, as such a restrictive diet could make the child's life miserable, he feels that such intolerances should instead be neutralized through a programme of desensitization.

Whether or not autism arises solely from metabolic disturbances or allergies remains to be seen but much may be learnt from relevant research. At this point I would like to look at 'reactive' hypoglycaemia in more detail, for its potential effects can be wide-ranging. This can be triggered by over-consumption of sugary foods or stimulants such as tobacco or caffeine.

The drop in blood sugar levels and the over- or excessive production of adrenalin can cause the sufferer to have any of the many and varied symptoms mentioned below, a number of which echo those found in the AiA group:

- Pains in muscles and joints.
- Chronic indigestion, nausea, alternating constipation and diarrhoea.

- Excessive thirst. Craving for certain foods.

- Fatigue. Insomnia.

- Hypersensitivity to light and sound.

- Migraines or headaches. Blurred vision, vertigo.

- Poor co-ordination. Cold hands and feet.

- Low blood pressure, palpitations, shaking. Some manifestations of hypoglycaemia may be similar to petit mal seizures while in extreme cases the drop in blood sugar can culminate in a loss of consciousness and occasionally in a seizure in which the limbs twitch noticeably.

- Hyper/hypo ventilation. Intolerance (and build-up) of heat and/or excessive sweating.

The intolerance of heat is of particular interest for, in her account of living with diabetes, Teresa McLean (1985, p.xv) describes one of the bizarre hazards of hypoglycaemia. Thus on one occasion when working as a teacher she actually started to take her clothes off in front of her class. Certainly during an attack one's body seems to become very hot and sweaty, regardless of the temperature outside, whilst clothing (particularly around the waist) starts to feel much tighter and constricting than it actually is. Whilst hypersensitivity no doubt accounts for the apparent dislike of some clothing perhaps hypoglycaemia explains why some people with autism will occasionally strip their clothes off unexpectedly?

It is thought that lack of blood sugar causes the normal rational brain to shut down, leaving the primitive 'instinctive' brain in control. This may account for the fact that sufferers can also demonstrate some of the following personality changes:

- Depression, irritability, lack of concentration.

- Mental confusion. Nervousness, constant worrying.

- Outbursts of aggression – verbal and/or physical.

According to Tuormaa, hypoglycaemia affects more women than men while an age of onset is generally between 30 and 40. However, I would question the latter, as I am aware of several children and adolescents who are affected by it.

Donna Williams suffered from hypoglycaemia which seemed to be exacerbated by excitement. This creates a vicious circle, as the drop in blood sugar causes the body to respond with a further release of adrenaline, which leads to increased stimulation. Once the hypoglycaemia was remedied through diet, her mood swings stabilized so that she became quieter and calmer, which in turn increased her ability to socialize with others. However, it must not be overlooked that she also said that her 'deep rooted emotional insecurity and

the social-communication problems which arose from it still remained'
(Williams 1992).

Since then she has found that she is allergic to many phenolics and
treatment for these, combined with other factors, have had a dramatic effect on
her, so much so that some of the latter problems no longer exist.

However, there is another condition which needs inclusion for it may prove
to be more important than hypoglycaemia. Candida albicans (thrush) is a
fungal infection which is worthy of note for it is found not only in the general
population but also amongst a considerable number of people with autism
and, as such, is thought to be implicated in some 'autistic' symptoms.

It can develop for a variety of reasons, one being the repeated use of
antibiotics which can themselves cause problems as they kill off both the bad
and the good bacteria needed to keep the digestive system functioning
correctly which can contribute to a leaky gut (see Appendix A).

This condition takes on greater significance once we correlate it with the
research findings of abnormal compounds in over 80 per cent of urine samples
taken from people with autism. Shattock suggests that these abnormal
compounds are there because of an incomplete breakdown of proteins (gluten
and casein) probably due to a leaky gut. If they are indeed abnormal peptides
these findings will be of great importance because their presence can,
depending on their type, affect the biochemistry of the brain as indicated in
Figure 2.2. This could alter the mind, mood, memory or behaviour and also
impair the immune system.

Shattock and Savery (1997) suggest the possibility that people in whom
autism develops at an early stage are most likely to be intolerant of casein
whilst those whose problems start later are more affected by gluten. They also
propose that coeliac disease may underlie the autism in 3 to 4 per cent of cases.
Does another clue lie in the fact that gluten used to be omitted from
commercially produced infant foods and so was not generally introduced into
the diet until the child was approximately 18 months old?

Figure 2.3 demonstrates the various ways in which peptides could get into
the brain. It shows how food is broken down in the gut where peptides
(represented by the black dots) occur as intermediate compounds before being
broken down into amino acids.

In healthy individuals (diagram (a)) a proportion of these peptides cross the
intact gut wall to the blood stream. A small percentage of these may then enter
the brain through the blood brain barrier. This will give an increase in opioid
activity but, as the level of peptides is relatively small, the effect on the brain
would be negligible.

The authors suggest that a number of people could have increased levels of
peptides in their guts as shown in diagram (b). These could result in increased
quantities reaching the central nervous system and lead to clinically significant

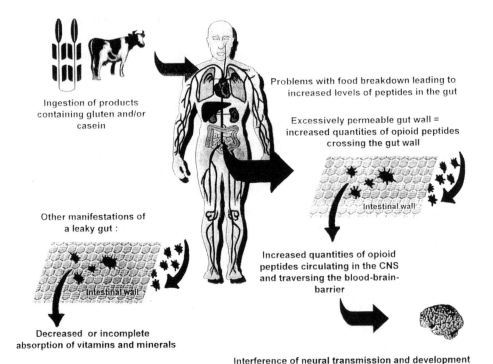

Ingestion of products containing gluten and/or casein

Problems with food breakdown leading to increased levels of peptides in the gut

Excessively permeable gut wall = increased quantities of opioid peptides crossing the gut wall

Intestinal wall

Other manifestations of a leaky gut :

Intestinal wall

Increased quantities of opioid peptides circulating in the CNS and traversing the blood-brain-barrier

Decreased or incomplete absorption of vitamins and minerals

Interference of neural transmission and development = symptoms of autism ?

Figure 2.2 Theoretical view of autism as a metabolic disorder (Shattock and Savery 1997; reproduced with permission)

consequences. This increase could be accounted for by any one of the following:

1. The inheritance of deficiencies of the required endopeptidase enzymes.

2. A shortage of cofactors such as vitamins and minerals.

3. An inappropriate pH level in the relevant area of the gut.

Next we come to diagram (c) which shows the effect of leaky gut. This lets far more peptides through into the brain than normal with the potentially devastating effects already mentioned.

Shattock and Savery also speculate that illness such as encephalitis or meningitis could damage the blood brain barrier which would render it less effective than normal thereby allowing any opioid peptides in the bloodstream easy access to the brain as shown in diagram (d).

Fortunately, it seems from the ongoing work in several places that many of the problems of autism can currently be ameliorated by treatment for the digestive problems.

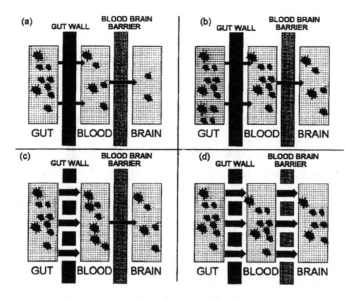

Figure 2.3 Blood brain barrier (Shattock and Savery 1997; reproduced with permission)

This idea is further supported by the latest 'breakthrough' in treatment which is currently attracting much attention. Although there seems to be some argument about who actually first recognized the significance of the developments which took place, the story began with Victoria Beck whose young son Parker has autism.

He was non-verbal and non-responsive, not toilet trained, hardly slept and lacked the ability to concentrate. In addition, he also suffered from stomach problems. An endoscopy was administered in order to determine the cause of the stomach problems. To Mrs Beck's surprise she found that within days of this test Parker began to show remarkable signs of recovery from some of the problems associated with the autism. Thus he became calmer, began sleeping through the night, made more eye contact and also lost the facial tics that he had had for two years. Three weeks later he began to say phrases and within a few weeks he was potty trained.

Mr and Mrs Beck found that secretin, a hormone which stimulates the pancreas to produce enzymes, had been used in the test. The hospital refused to give more than one dose, as it was not licensed for such treatment; but eventually the Becks persuaded a doctor to treat Parker with secretin.

Secretin has now been tried with both children and adults to great effect. While the latest information posted on the Internet suggests that the success rate is in the region of 70–75 per cent, comments from one clinician using this treatment suggest that:

- Those people who responded best were those with gut problems, food allergies, candida, dysbiosis, etc.

- Age was not a factor.

The potential efficacy of secretin seems to have links with the work of Bland. He has spent many years doing research into the effects of diet and nutrition on health and has found that a considerable number of people lack some of the enzymes needed for a healthy digestive system. In his booklet *Digestive Enzymes* (1983, p.13) he also cites some of the research findings, one of which in particular seemed very relevant, for people with a gluten allergy had their symptoms eliminated by digestive enzymes such as pancreatin.

However, before jumping to any conclusions we should also consider some other disorders which may be related to autism, starting with attention deficit/hyperactivity disorder.

Attention deficit hyperactivity disorder

It is interesting to note that metabolic disorders and allergies can also cause or contribute to hyperactivity, a common factor in attention deficit hyperactivity disorder (ADHD). Generally the problems are characterized by impulsiveness, inattention, disorganization and social skills deficits. While some sufferers are hyperactive others have been found to be hypoactive and, although they have all the symptoms of ADHD, they are also listless and appear depressed.

It is strange to find that it is very often girls who are found to be quiet and withdrawn, having difficulty in attending to their work but lacking the (hyper) motor activity of their male peers. Occasionally this has even led to the 'query' diagnosis of autism, although they would perhaps be more accurately classified as having attention deficit disorder (without the hyperactivity).

While attention deficit disorder by itself generally has a ratio of 1:1, hyperactive behaviour affects 3 or 4 times more boys than girls. It is to be found in approximately 3 to 5 per cent of the population, although figures vary between Britain and the United States where ADHD has generally received greater recognition and is thought to affect nearly 6.5 per cent. Many hyperactive children have parents, often fathers, who also suffer from a degree of hyperactivity and, quite frequently, other relatives appear to suffer from any of a range of allergies.

Hyperactivity itself is a condition which warrants attention for it is often observed in people with autism or those with a mental handicap (and has also been cited as a possible cause of delinquency). An interesting book on the subject called *Living with a Hyperactive Child* (1984) by Miriam Wood gives a number of case histories, including that of her own daughter. These suggest that the children fall into two groups, for some initially appear to be calm and placid, in sharp contrast to others who are, from the onset, extremely 'irritable' and easily upset.

The latter type of child is constantly restless, may have feeding problems, dislike being touched or held and as he grows his behaviour becomes extremely hyperactive whilst at around the age of two the formerly quiet child may begin to display a variety of 'hyperactive' features which can get worse as he gets older. Paradoxically this 'hyper' activity often stems from an *under*active nervous system: an idea which will be discussed more fully later on.

Some of the main features of the problem appear to be:

- An inability to concentrate for any length of time.

- Huge amounts of energy which sustain him in constant motion throughout the day and most of the night.

- Speech problems, for example talking incessantly with little regard for others or, in contrast, an inability to communicate properly with others.

- A quick temper showing anger and aggression or alternatively becoming weepy and/or depressed easily.

- Disturbed sleep patterns.

- Prone to metabolic problems and/or allergies.

- Totally oblivious to parental influence.

It was interesting to see that several sufferers of ADHD who appeared on a television 'chat show' in 1996 seemed very unresponsive to light – blinking far less than normal. While it is possible that, for some, this stemmed from their use of medication, could it be linked to a damaged nervous system? Do many ADHD sufferers have visual perceptual problems?

Hyperactivity can lead to a variety of problems which are extremely difficult for parents to cope with. In his search for incessant stimulation, the child may, much to his parents' consternation and distress, disappear frequently, turning up in other houses or even several miles away; although he will generally go to places he already knows and likes. The psychological view of this can cause further distress, as parents may mistakenly be led to think that their child is actually running away from them rather than, as is the reality, attempting to satisfy his overriding need for excitement.

This same 'need' may also lead him to rip or draw on wallpaper or books, attempt to climb curtains, break ornaments and generally create havoc. He may be unable to understand the consequences of his actions and this can inhibit him from learning the concept of danger, leaving him 'accident prone' as he continually acts before he thinks.

As he grows older problems may arise at school for he can be very disruptive in the classroom, irritating both classmates and teachers. Learning may become increasingly difficult as his butterfly behaviour never allows him to light upon subjects for any length of time.

Wood gives several highly descriptive accounts of the problems which the families of such children encounter. In one she says a mother shuddered as she described her son's return from school each day in brief but graphic detail: 'He returned home each day like a lion refreshed and roared about the house, jumping up and climbing trees and tormenting his brothers and sister' (Wood 1984, p.117).

She also describes the interesting way in which her daughter Tanya, who had problems from birth, learnt to walk – in total contrast to 'normal' development:

> As Tanya neared her first birthday she had not yet learned to crawl in the conventional way, but if held by me at one end of the room would run when released and crash into her father's arms at the other end ... When she reached fourteen months I took her for a short visit to her grandparents in Wales; suddenly one day she stood up and walked from one room to another with no trouble at all. On returning home, she went down on her knees and crawled everywhere for about a week and then began to walk again ... Tanya just had to be different – running first, walking next and learning to crawl last! (Wood 1984, p.28)

Many people assume that the hyperactive child is 'a naughty, spoilt, disobedient brat' who is out of control simply because the parents are 'too soft' and that the problem could be solved by a 'good hiding'. While the behaviours are difficult enough to cope with, the family may also face increasing isolation as relatives and friends gradually cease to visit or invite them out.

It is worth noting, though, that some of these children have particular food allergies and will show a marked change in behaviour within a very short space of time if they eat the 'wrong' food. They can quickly turn from a quiet, placid and 'eager to please' child into one who displays all the symptoms mentioned above and is totally oblivious to parental influence.

Most of the parents mentioned in Wood's book had great difficulty in getting helpful medical advice, for not only were the causes seen to be the result of 'faulty' or lax parenting, but the problems were often not visible at the time of their appointment with the doctor, who then labelled the mother neurotic!

Indeed, the controversy which was apparent then still surrounds the causes, as a QED programme 'Little Monsters' showed. This discussed the work of Superintendent Peter Bennett with young 'hyperactive' delinquents whose offending pattern was dramatically changed by their diet.
While other research done at Great Ormond Street Hospital detected a definite link between hyperactivity and food and/or food additives, there are still people who refute that any link exists. They continue to see it solely as an emotional problem which can be solved by altering the way in which the parents handle the child – in addition to the possible use of medication if the problems are severe. How, though, does the psychological approach explain the fact that many of the children in Wood's book showed considerable improvement once placed on a diet, as did those on the QED programme?

Although the argument will no doubt continue for some time, the sceptics should not ignore, as discussed in 'Little Monsters', Danish results from a study into hyperactive children using Positron Emission Tomography (a PET scan), which enables researchers to look at and compare the workings of the brain. These clearly showed that such problems are not 'all in the mind', for some of the children tested had definite neurological 'differences' which were indicated by a decrease in the blood flowing to the striatum, the part of the brain that controls the input of stimuli; a factor which must surely have long-term consequences.

Could such findings have any links with a leaky gut? Is it merely coincidental that one of the many causes of this condition is the ingestion of allergenic foods? And that amongst the consequences of this we find not only deficiencies in the supply of nutrients to the brain, but also toxicity in the body which is thought to affect the blood supply to the brain. If indeed the food allergies are in some way implicated in this we should ask whether the diet similar to that which made such a difference to the behaviour of the children in the programme would be able to alter or reverse this neurological phenomenon?

Unfortunately the children shown on QED were not able to have such brain scans so it is not known whether the blood flow to their brains was affected in a similar way, although it would seem highly likely. It would also seem that scanning the brain like this could provide vital information both in relation to diagnosis and when assessing the efficacy of treatment.

I find it sad that while a child who has a potentially 'brain damaging' illness would have easy access to such scans, such assessment is not readily available to those with hyperactivity. Surely it is incumbent upon all doctors involved with these children to eliminate the possibility of neurological problems before determining the treatment, for any child in whom they exist cannot be treated solely on behavioural lines. While financial constraints may have to be taken into account, accurate assessment at an early age will prove to be more cost-effective in the long term. Given the high proportion of people with ADHD amongst the prison population it would seem highly likely that without effective treatment such problems have a cumulative effect, thereby leaving the adult with more problems than the child: something which eventually affects us all.

At this point it would be helpful to consider just what the long-term effects of a decrease in the blood flow to the striatum could be. One would assume that some atrophy would take place in the growing brain but I was unable to find any studies on children (although they may exist) so cannot deny or confirm this supposition. I did, though, find one done on a group of adults in the 50–80 age range whose blood flow to the brain was decreased by a 50 per cent blockage of the arteries. The study (Russell 1979) showed that once the blockages were removed there was a significant decrease in anxiety, nervousness, suspicion, distress and disorientation with a corresponding increase in verbal comprehension and perceptual organization.

It is interesting then to note that Bernard Rimland said in 1964: 'The fact that autistic children are severely impaired but not completely blocked in their integration of ideas is not inconsistent with the hypothesis that a vital part of the brain may be receiving an insufficient supply of blood' (Rimland 1964, p.131).

Indeed, brain scans done on people with autism (George *et al.* 1992) now show that this is in fact the case for some, thereby confirming Rimland's hypothesis.

I would now like to return to Wood's book to mention two seemingly relevant points. The first is the fact that many of the children in it did respond to dietary treatment which, in several cases, totally changed their lives whilst one child showed improved greatly when given digestive enzymes.

The second is to quote from one of the most noteworthy descriptions in it. This was of Jeremy, whose father was obsessional and had been diagnosed as suffering from manic depression. Jeremy had a normal birth even though labour was protracted, but after returning from hospital with his mother he screamed a great deal, had colic and slept very little, twitching in his sleep and waking at the slightest sound. He seemed very tense, rejected his mother and often screamed as if in severe pain:

> As he grew older he did not smile as other children seemed to do, but he was my first child so I didn't realise that he was much different from other babies ... I used to drive him around in the car to stop him crying as it seemed to soothe him.

As a toddler he was in perpetual motion, stripping wallpaper and touching everything in sight. He seemed to grizzle continuously and:

> He never played with toys as did other children of his age but rather had an obsession with wheels and would sit quietly for long periods watching a wheel go round. He spoke little until two years of age when he suddenly came out with quite a complicated sentence.

His mother had noticed that, from an early age, Jeremy became much worse after eating sweets or 'instant whips' and so cut them out of his diet before he was three years old. Later, reading an article about food which suggested that some children might be hypersensitive to artificial colourings, flavourings and preservatives, she was sufficiently impressed to try it and: 'Within three days he slept through the night, his nightmares stopped, his aggression diminished, he smiled at me and let me hold him. His whole personality changed ...' (Wood 1984, pp.157–158).

The coincidences are of course obvious and lead to further questions, especially when one considers that Jeremy's obsessive behaviour was similar to some of the early symptoms of autism. Puzzling indeed.

Before moving on I would like to clarify one point concerning the term 'allergy'. I have heard it said that people can only be considered to be allergic if they have an immediate physical reaction, that is, they come out in a rash, become asthmatic, etc. This has led to some professionals disregarding the possible link between behavioural problems and allergies. Obviously even if the reaction is unusual, in that it takes a behavioural rather than a physical form (like head banging for instance), when it occurs shortly after consumption of a particular food (and on several occasions) then the child is likely to be allergic to that particular substance.

However, many children do not initially demonstrate any specific reaction to a particular substance for the problems arise from an intolerance which builds up gradually. While the symptoms may take quite a long time to develop it is important to recognize that even with such a time lapse the presenting problem may still be symptomatic of a reaction to a particular food: a possibility which should always be explored rather than dismissed without investigation as it so often seems to be.

Anxiety

Anyone who has lived or worked with people with autism must be aware of their constant anxiety, which is increasingly being mentioned by the sufferers themselves – like Temple Grandin, who needs continuing medication to help suppress the high level of anxiety she suffers from, in order that she can lead a relatively normal life. Conversations with parents, more verbal sufferers and carers give further support to the idea that this is a major problem and also to the fact that as the anxiety lessens there is a corresponding increase in the ability to develop social interaction, use language and take risks.

David Waterhouse, an experienced professional who spent many years working with both mentally ill clients and adults with autism, states that:

> The features of the handicap include severe 'in-built' anxiety leading to insecurity, problems with communication which prevent the development of 'normal' social relationships and behaviour which is often in-appropriate to age … Many people with autism are apparently withdrawn and self-absorbed, experiencing difficulty in making sense of the information they hear, see or feel and are therefore unable to understand or communicate freely with others. Whilst appearing apparently normal and often physically attractive, their inappropriate or disturbed behaviour clearly reflects the insecurity and bewilderment they experience in the confusing world in which they live.

The idea of anxiety and fear perplexed Clara Claiborne Park, whose daughter, Jessy (known as Ellie in the original book), suffers from autism. In her book *The Siege* (1982) she discusses the problem as she attempts to find the underlying cause of her daughter's difficulties:

> Hesitation, caution, unwillingness to interact with the physical world. These sound like the shapes of fear and perhaps they were. Yet she did not seem afraid. It was as if she had found a way to make the fear unnecessary. She did not have to be afraid; she had found a way to protect herself from the challenges of her environment. Ignore them and you will not have to avoid them. If something is there to push, do not push it. Do not pull, twist, open, lift, balance, kick, climb, throw. Attempt nothing. Then there will be no failure and you can remain serene. This was not fear in any recognisable form. If there was fear, it lay so deep it never showed itself. (Park 1982, p.54)

Later Park concludes that fear cannot be the key, for she feels that Jessy lacks the imagination to anticipate, which she believes is an ingredient of both fear and anxiety. Perhaps it is for this very reason that so many others seem to have overlooked this aspect of the problem too. Could it be, though, that her first words are true: that Jessy has indeed buried her fears so deeply that they are unrecognizable; protected herself so securely by withdrawal that her anxiety is not usually 'allowed' to impinge on her daily life? Could she actually be 'paralyzed by fear'? Experience leads me to agree with Waterhouse that people with autism are far more anxious than those of us who are considered 'normal'; a feeling which comes across very strongly (and repeatedly) in the accounts of the sufferers over the years.

Thus a young man, originally diagnosed by Kanner when he was five, described his childhood to Jules Bemporad, a psychiatrist, at the age of thirty-one. As Bemporad recalls:

> According to Jerry his childhood experiences could be summarised as consisting of two predominant states: confusion and terror. The recurrent theme that ran through all of Jerry's recollections was of living in a frightening world presenting painful stimuli that could not be mastered. Noises were unbearably loud, smells over-powering. Nothing seemed constant; everything was unpredictable and strange ... Dogs were remembered as eerie and terrifying. He was also frightened of other children, fearing that they might hurt him in some way. He could never predict or understand their behaviour. The classroom was total confusion and he felt he would 'go to pieces'. This contrasted with liking to 'go to the grocery store ... and spinning objects'. (Bemporad 1979, p.192)

Then we have Tony who says:

> I was afraid of everything! I was terrified to go in the water swimming, [and of] loud noises; in the dark I had severe repetitive nightmares and occasionally hearing electronic noises with nightmares. I would wake up so terrified and disorientated ... I was afraid of simple things such as going into the shower, getting my nails clipped ... (Volkmar and Cohen 1985, p.49)

Donna Williams also talks of being afraid, not simply because of her abnormal sensory perceptions but of other things too, for she feared the dark and was so frightened of sleeping that for many years she counteracted the fear by sleeping with her eyes open. She sums up her feelings by talking of a repetitive dream which she had had since before her grandfather died (when she was five):

> I was walking alone through a bareness, surrounded by hills. Suddenly I heard a roaring sound, and huge ocean waves came gushing fearsomely over the hills from all around me, covering me instantly without warning. I held on desperately to a pole which had been in the middle of the barren land where I had been standing. I closed my eyes tight. I could not breathe. I felt the crushing feeling and immensity of the ocean which had swallowed me up. In the tide going out, the ocean gushed back over the

hills as instantly as it had come. I clung terrified to the pole, too afraid to move. I think that's how my real self experienced emotion for most of my life. (Williams 1992, pp.161–162)

Waterhouse also suggests that one of the possible causes of such anxiety may be an inherent vulnerability. This idea is supported by research done by Kagan and colleagues (Kagan, Reznick and Snidman 1988) of Harvard University, who states that the seeds of shyness are sown early in childhood and may even be inherited through the genes. An article on his research in the *Daily Telegraph* on 20 March 1991 pointed out that the babies in this group had a faster heart rate and a more excitable nervous system, while even the pattern of brain waves was unusual compared to those of more extrovert children. These infants have great difficulty in coping with new experiences or situations, which they actually find painful and which give rise to a number of physical reactions such as a rise in blood pressure and dilated pupils.

Further studies found that about 15 to 20 per cent of children seem to have been born with an in-built fragility that makes them over-react to even mild stress, leaving them oversensitive and fearful. Being extremely shy they are reluctant to meet new people, join in social situations, go to new places or even try new foods. At twenty-one months of age such toddlers were reluctant to play with other children and their hearts raced with anxiety whilst they watched from the sidelines.

These children can suffer from intense but unrealistic fears and may have nightmares. A follow-up study, some years later, found that, although one child became more withdrawn after the death of a parent when she was four, all the others were growing up 'normally' with many having an artistic or intellectual bent. However, such children frequently take their fears into adulthood, growing into shy and timid adults and having more worries, guilt and stress-related health problems than their peers. These descriptions seem to echo Brazelton's mention of children who are unable to shut out stimuli and/or those with increased levels of opioid peptides – but is there a connection?

To confuse the issue still further we find that very young babies with low levels of serotonin slept less and were more restless than others of the same age. As infants they were also less emotionally stable, cried more, were less cuddly and not as easily consoled as other children. It is said that low serotonin decreases the level of opioid peptides so perhaps there are at least two different problems here. It would certainly seem so, although to jump to any conclusions at this point would be premature for some 'evidence' still needs sifting.

The research may still bring us closer to some answers for, as the work of Kagan and of Brazelton demonstrates, it is no longer far-fetched to suppose that some children may be inherently fragile and more susceptible to external stimuli during their formative years.

An article in *Woman's Day Magazine* (Pascoe 1991) discussed another aspect of the problem being researched by the neurologist Paul Millard Hardy of the New England Medical Center, who believes that autism in adults is related to panic disorders and phobias. These appear to be inherited and affect between 2 and 4 per cent of the population.

He first came into contact with children with autism in the late 1970s, while working in a school for children who were 'mentally retarded'. Having observed the self-mutilation of some of them, he felt there had to be a neurological basis for their behaviour. He further observed that two hundred patients with autism suffered from physical reactions – raised blood pressure, accelerated heart beat and sweating – similar to people suffering great stress.

Interestingly, this contradicts another study which found indications of 'low anxiety' as evidenced solely by the heart rate. Could the contradiction be explained by a difference in testing methods and the number of physical factors which were considered? Were physiological abnormalities taken into account? I certainly know one person with autism whose heart rate never alters even after much exertion, some who register a lower than normal temperature at all times and others who do not react to various medications as most people might. Alternatively, as Park suggested, could some of the people tested have been so protected by their isolation that fear had become unnecessary?

Hardy believes that such children are 'encased in fear' and feels that anxiety may explain why some children have started to speak but then either lose the ability or stop at an inappropriate stage, as with those who remain echolalic, which from the comments of Caroline and Jasmine Lee O'Neill would certainly seem to be true of some. He feels it could also be the reason why they 'acquire' retardation, as tremendous anxiety hinders them from learning in a 'normal' manner.

It has long been known that fear can have a devastating effect, for it is the only emotion which can arouse a reflex reaction which initially inhibits motion. In *The Expression of Emotion in Man and Animals* (1904), which is now seen as partially inaccurate, Charles Darwin reliably catalogues some reactions to fear, which include an increased heart rate and hurried breathing, paleness of skin, cold sweat, trembling, dryness of mouth, a lowering of the head, bending of the knees and crouching. Since Darwin's time further research has added to our knowledge and we now know that constant or continual stress can deplete the immune system leaving the person far less resistant to illness or disease.

It is interesting to find that by following the theory of anxiety through to its logical conclusion, Hardy found that drugs used for panic disorders proved more effective for many of the sufferers than the heavy doses of tranquilizers which were often prescribed.

While it is not the purpose of this book to endorse any particular type of 'treatment', many places for both children and adults primarily aim (by various methods about which I shall say more later) to alleviate anxiety. The Higashi School is one example. The late Dr Kitahara, who founded the school, disagreed with the belief that 'two thirds of children with autism are also mentally retarded'. She believed that autism was a separate condition and, like Hardy, felt that the child or adult with autism had the ability to learn but was 'blocked' from learning by 'fear'.

Shader of Tufts University School of Medicine has also investigated the theory (Pascoe 1991). He uses it to explain the often bizarre or distressing behaviour of the person with autism, who may demonstrate great physical activity of a particular (and peculiar) kind, for example jumping excitedly on the spot, or banging his head when agitated. Shader explains that a comforting effect can be achieved through both strenuous effort and self-mutilation for: 'any process involving activity, excitement or great pain involves the release of endomorphins (endorphins) in the brain. It is the release of these which calms people down.'

In his article *A Neurochemical Theory of Autism* (1979), Jaak Panksepp proposed that there were similarities between the symptoms of autism and narcotic addition. His idea is that during pregnancy the foetus is kept happy by high endorphin levels which are later replaced by shorter-acting enkephalins. If normal development was disrupted this change would not take place and thus the person with autism would continue to have a high level of endorphins which would keep him on a 'high'. This could prevent the brain from developing appropriate responses and also account for the heightened sensory perceptions: an idea which might provide a link with those children who are born with a fragile nervous system.

Shattock's work also seems to substantiate Panksepp's theory. He suggests that the biological impairments underlying autism may be related to abnormal levels of peptides, particularly but not exclusively, those with an opioid action (such as beta-endorphin) which, in addition to regulating the immune system, have an effect on perception, mood and pain.

Thus an increased level of opioids could give a variety of effects such as:

- no desire for social companionship;
- decreased sensitivity to pain;
- lack of 'normal' motivation;
- potentially 'explosive' behaviour – a very small stimulus may trigger a large exaggerated response;
- stereotyped behaviours;
- 'odd' physical movements – involving a part of the body (head, mouth, etc.) or the whole (rocking).

Stereotyped behaviours are found in autism and are often referred to as 'self-stimulatory', the implication being that they are 'performed' in order to give pleasure as such behaviours are accompanied by an increase in opioid levels. Opioid peptides can actually alter the balance of dopamine (which is connected to such stereotypes) and affect the serotonin levels.

Shattock suggests that the sequence could in fact be interpreted in a slightly different way since animals under stress (as when restrained from free movement by a cage) also engage in such stereotyped behaviours. He postulates that it is the stress which causes the levels of opioids to increase and that this then results in stereotypical behaviour. Thus it seems, if my interpretation is correct, that some biological factors also give support to the idea that anxiety and stress may play a role in autism. These ideas introduce another element of confusion for we now have several different ways in which to account for the abnormal levels of these opioids – all of which seem highly plausible and, even more confusingly, each seems to correlate to other factors.

Apart from the stereotypical movements, an animal under stress will become over-anxious, withdrawn and may totally ignore all external sights and sounds or panic at the slightest noise: behaviours similar to those that Bettleheim noticed amongst the concentration camp prisoners. Such animal experiments obviously lent support to the idea that the cause of the problem for a person with autism is anxiety-related. Interestingly, this coincides with the feeling of many parents and professionals who increasingly disagree with the idea that communication is a major factor, as time and again they are faced with overwhelming evidence of anxiety. Could the common denominator between the concentration camp victims and people with autism be anxiety or fear? Certainly in support of such ideas we find that once ways have been found to alleviate the overwhelming anxiety that the majority of sufferers feel, social relationships, communication and other problems begin to improve.

However, before analyzing these factors let me add the results of two other animal experiments which might be relevant to this search. In the first, although stress caused a depletion of dopamine in the frontal lobes this did not happen when the subject was able to exert some control over the stress factors. When this was not possible the affected animals effectively lost their memory regarding previously learnt tasks and then had great difficulty in relearning those tasks.

The second found that isolation also decreases dopamine in the frontal lobes whilst conversely increasing it in other parts such as the striatum. This was linked to a variety of difficulties from increased tension and irritability to learning problems, a poor memory, increased vocalizations, compulsion, aggression and hyperactivity.

Are there any links here with children who suffer from severe multi-sensory deprivation or autism? First the stress factor, which I believe links in with the abnormal sensory perceptions over which they have no control. Then, too, people with autism are not 'isolated' from their fellow man in the normal sense. It is the problems they have that drive them towards isolation and it would therefore hardly be surprising if some were found to have similarly unusual levels of dopamine.

In this context it may also be worth considering whether some children also display autistic features after repeated ear infections which may cut them off from the world, even if only for a short time. It is easy to see that normal development interspersed with several periods of sudden isolation in the first few years of life would cause great stress. If this and the isolation it causes affect the levels of dopamine as shown in the experiments, then even in the absence of severe perceptual or processing problems, surely it would be no surprise to find a child who loses previously obtained milestones and has great difficulties in regaining them.

Summary

The theory of anxiety as a cause of autism is not new, although the problems which give rise to it have been and continue to be strongly debated. Generally they are attributed to either psychological or physical problems although Bender, writing in the 1960s, contrived to 'bridge the gap'. She felt that autism was not an inborn impairment of the central nervous system but rather a defensive reaction to such an impairment, suggesting that the child withdrew in order to protect himself from the disorganization and anxiety which arose from an impairment '...in their genes, brains, perceptual organs or social relationships' (Bender 1959, pp.81–86).

Thus in the late 1950s and into the 1960s various theories were put forward, many based on the acknowledgment of autism as a defence mechanism which protected the child against anxiety. Those who believed in the psychological approach suggested that the anxiety arose because the child felt that the conditions surrounding his life were utterly destructive. In contrast others who believed that the problem was a physical one cited 'faulty' genes, brain damage, problems of perception, or an organic deficiency which developed from the child's inability to engage in abstract thinking. Some of these ideas have been researched or developed further over the years, as you will see in Chapter 3.

Before moving on, though, we need to take a look at other conditions which may prove relevant. For many people, 'single-mindedness', or a touch of obsessiveness, can be the key to a highly successful (and often extremely profitable) career. Which of us does not know of someone with a tendency to throw themselves wholeheartedly into a job or hobby – perhaps become slightly predictable (or even boring!?) in their conversation? Struggling to finish this book I certainly have a sneaking suspicion that friends might view me in that way! There is, however, a far more serious side to such a coin, as discussed in the next section.

Obsessive compulsive disorder

This is a well documented but, until recently, relatively 'hidden' disorder which occurs in both adults and children. It causes sufferers to become extremely isolated from 'normal' life, which gradually disintegrates around them. Obsessive compulsive disorder (OCD) is a problem which has existed for centuries, as demonstrated by the fact that one particular form of the syndrome, deep religious fervour, has long been acknowledged by both the Jewish faith and the Catholic church.

The reasons for its inclusion are twofold. Firstly, it is a problem which may perhaps stem from anxiety, whilst, secondly, the sufferers produce a variety of bizarre behaviours and mannerisms which are extremely similar to those seen in autism. Coincidentally it also affects more males than females during childhood although this pattern changes later, for if the onset is in adulthood both sexes are affected equally. The external 'symptoms' appear to vary according to the age of the person, so that the problems of the child are different from those of the adult.

It is now estimated that OCD could affect four to five million people in the USA and possibly one and a half million people in Britain; people who are otherwise normal. They are often too ashamed to admit to their problems and, for long periods of time, may manage to observe their obsessions in secret as they do not wish to be thought 'crazy'.

'Obsession' comes from the Latin word *obsidere*, which means to besiege. It begins suddenly and is usually recognized as a problem from the outset, for it consists of a repeated and persistent intrusion of an obsession which occurs against the person's will and gradually comes to tyrannize his daily life. It may take the form of an endless repetition of thoughts or emotive ideas, or the sufferer may feel 'coerced' to compulsively repeat senseless rituals, over which he has no control (although some sufferers are able to lead apparently 'normal' lives, limiting such behaviours to their 'free' time).

The problem, thought to affect approximately 3 per cent of the population to varying degrees, appears to cease quite naturally at times so that the person concerned may occasionally have periods of remission. The behaviour is quite different from the superstitions, routines and habits that most people have, for these can be altered if necessary, whereas efforts to resist an obsession can lead to further anxiety and conversely an increase in the ritualistic behaviour.

The diagnostic criteria laid down in the American Psychiatric Association's manual are surprisingly familiar because they include:

1. Problems with personal or school/working life.

2. A restricted ability to express warm/tender emotions.

3. An insistence that others submit to the person's way of doing things – without any awareness of how this makes others feel.

4. A preoccupation with details, rules, lists to the extent that the major point of the activity is lost. Perfectionism that interferes with the overall ability to see the needs of a situation.

5. Indecision – perhaps because of great fear of making a mistake?

Several reasons are given as to the cause of obsessive-compulsive disorder. It is thought that it may be hereditary for it appears to run in families and, amongst any large group of obsessional people, similar traits are to be found in approximately one-third of the parents and one-fifth of siblings. Another theory suggests that it stems from anxiety caused by some type of conflict, an example of which might be between the moral standards of the person involved and his underlying urges. Certainly several people identify a feeling of great anxiety before each 'attack' and some describe a release of tension once their 'ritual' has been completed.

In her book *The Boy Who Couldn't Stop Washing* (1990), Rapoport quotes some sufferers who comment that the onset of the problem appeared after some form of traumatic incident. One seven-year-old had a slightly older cousin who died suddenly in what seemed to him a mysterious way. As an adult he now says:

It was also, as I think about it, concurrent with my first memories of ritualizing. I don't know whether there was a sort of symbiosis between the rituals and my cousin's death, but it would not surprise me ... (Rapoport 1990, p.51)

Additionally she talks of the fourteen-year-old who says:

I wish I could go back in time to where it first began because now it seems so out of control. What was once myself and my rituals is now my rituals first, and then myself. What distresses me the most is that I know they are unnecessary and unreal, however, I still do them.

I've really lost touch with myself and that's really frightening ... I have so many goals and dreams ... but I know I will never accomplish them ... I feel like I'm in a labyrinth from which I cannot escape. (Rapoport 1990, p.76)

One of the most notable figures to have suffered from this was apparently Dr Johnson, whose friend Miss Reynolds gave a vivid description of some of his 'peculiarities':

On entering Sir Joshua's house with poor Mrs Williams, a blind lady who lived with him, he would quit her hand, or else whirl her about on the steps as he whirled and twisted about to perform his gesticulations; and as soon as he had finished, he would give a sudden spring and make an extensive stride over the threshold, as if he were trying for a wager how far he could stride. (quoted in Birnbeck Hill 1966, p.273)

The ritual was repeated at the threshold of every doorway. He also touched every post along a street and avoided the cracks of the paving stones, taking, as Boswell said:

...anxious care to go in or out at a door or passage, by a certain number of steps from a certain point, or at least so as that either his right or left foot (I am not sure which), should constantly make the first actual movement. (Boswell 1969, p.342)

In the rich or famous such behaviour was often tolerated as the 'eccentricity of genius', but poorer folk displaying similar problems would no doubt have been described as 'totally mad' and may well have ended their lives in some form of confinement.

Intriguingly, Rapoport's book also contains a description of a young patient who displayed symptoms from an early age and whose father suffers from OCD:

He was excitable and had a low concentration span – taking 15 minutes to put a pair of socks on. He was resistant to change and new experiences and at two would have a tantrum if an object was not in its 'proper' place. He was obsessed with counting, serialising and asking repetitive questions.

Play consisted of jumping up and down in front of a toy, flapping his arms as if excited, while contracting and relaxing his muscles. He grunted and contorted his face as if exerting great effort. When the jumping stopped, he put his arms together and wiggled his fingers just above eye level. Diversionary tactics had no effect. This behaviour grew in intensity until he was spending up to five hours a day 'playing' in this way.

The comparison with autism is unavoidable and the similarity of the 'symptoms' cannot be ignored. However, the picture is then clouded with confusion by the fact that the same child at the age of four:

> ...had many healthy positive attributes – evident intelligence, language skills which were consistently improving, and the ability to express a wide range of feelings – joy, sadness etc. He was also affectionate and showed a strong need to please his parents, especially his mother. (Rapoport 1990, p.29)

After an initial tentative diagnosis of 'possible hyperactivity and/or prone to attention deficit disorder', he was then diagnosed as 'schizophrenic' and eventually, after much parental distress, as having OCD. While the parents recount many positive features, his obsessional behaviour was obviously becoming extremely time-consuming.

It seems logical to surmise that if he had not received treatment his behaviour would have led him to become increasingly isolated and, because the age of onset was so early, his social skills, language, cognition and ability to learn would all have gradually been slowed or even halted.

If so, one must query whether the final diagnosis would have been different if his father had not suffered from similar symptoms or if a different 'expert' had been consulted. Was he in fact actually suffering from autism? Is age is a determining factor? One would surely expect the problems to be worse if the symptoms appear during the early stages of the child's development. In contrast I know two people who have been diagnosed with autism, although in the opinion of several people besides myself, their symptoms are actually those of OCD with the onset being, at the ages of seven and ten, clearly linked to trauma.

I have already mentioned the fact that the symptoms vary at different times in a person's life, detailing some of those seen in a young child. Although Rapoport roughly divides the symptoms into categories, there are no really clear dividing lines between the symptoms of the older child and the adult for they overlap to show a progression of problems throughout the ages. I include a few of the most common ones here:

- The child between the ages of six and twelve years may: avoid picking things up with his hands; carry out bizarre rituals, for example repeatedly crouching to touch the ground or ripping toilet paper into small pieces; wash his hands many times a day; have difficulty walking through a doorway or gate; spin around several times before entering a room.

- The adolescent may: have difficulty in walking through doorways; repeatedly wash his hands or shower himself; count things or repeat certain actions a particular number of times; check that things have been done properly, returning to recheck many times; repeatedly read, write or say particular words; have obsessive thoughts about unacceptable behaviours.

- The adult may: wash, count, clean the house or a room or repeatedly check things. Alternatively he may 'ruminate'; that is have unrealistic and repetitive thoughts either about a particular subject or about various unacceptable behaviours, for example constantly worrying that he has knocked someone over on a car journey or even killed someone.

Initially viewing obsessiveness from the viewpoint of autism suggests a different perspective for as Donna Williams says: 'Ian and I had both always revelled in our compulsions and obsessions, defining them as who we were, as our personalities.'

She describes how they had rituals for every single facet of their lives. Eating, sleeping, bathing and reading were all dominated by ritual as, most sadly, were their speech, stance, movements and facial expressions. To quote again: 'Ritual and compulsion didn't dominate our lives because it *was* our lives' (Williams 1996, pp. 84–85).

It was only later that, like Rapoport's patient, they discovered that the rituals were robbing them of their real identities: their individuality; their lives. This shows only too clearly how much obsessions and compulsions are part of autism.

PET scans have been used to research the problems of OCD and results show that some people with obsessive or compulsive behaviour have an unusually high level of activity in the prefrontal lobes and abnormalities in the basal ganglia. Interestingly, similar abnormalities have been found in people suffering brain damage as a result of some types of encephalitis and also in some people with Tourette's syndrome. There have been many reports which document a relationship between compulsions and Tourette's syndrome which Rapoport believes are two sides of the same coin. Does autism also have a place in the puzzle? Before we can attempt to answer that we must of course make another diversion to discuss Tourette's syndrome.

Tourette's syndrome (TS)

Previously thought to be a very rare condition this complex behavioural disorder actually affects approximately 1 per cent of male children, with the symptoms starting before the age of 21 and often persisting throughout adulthood.

In his book *Tourette Syndrome and Human Behaviour* (1981), David Comings discusses the many factors involved in TS. Often preceded in the early years by learning difficulties, perceptual and co-ordination problems this disorder is mainly characterized by multiple motor and/or vocal tics which occur, usually in bouts, many times a day. Examples of motor tics could include blinking, grimacing or head jerking while the vocal problems might include spitting, barking, humming, squeaking, throat clearing and other noises. The most commonly known feature of the problem, coprolalia (i.e. compulsive swearing), actually occurs in fewer than one-third of the sufferers and does not need to be present for a diagnosis to be made.

Although the sufferer can often suppress the tics for short periods of time, to fulfil the diagnostic criteria they must occur nearly every day or for a period of more than one year. Tics can wax and wane, frequently becoming worse when the person is under stress as during periods of change, emotional upheavals, exams or even the Christmas holidays. Conversely an improvement will often be seen when things are going well and the person is able to relax, as during summer holidays.

Once again coincidence (?!!) rears its head as we find the 3 or 4:1 ratio between males and females. Further research and detailed family histories tend to indicate that TS has close links with several other disorders including OCD and ADHD.

Thus Tourette's sufferers can also have any of a wide range of difficulties including symptoms of ADHD, speech problems, obsessions, compulsions, intolerance of stress, dyslexia and phobias. Some other miscellaneous features which are often associated with Tourette's syndrome include physical problems such as allergies, migraines and colic. The person may demonstrate oppositional behaviour, that is, have difficulty accepting directions or continue to do something when asked to cease. He may also have an intolerance of heat, a low tolerance of stress, a fear of intimacy, self-induced lesions, speech and sequencing problems. Slight visual abnormalities have also been found in many sufferers, the shape of the visual field being stepped rather than circular.

The hereditary perspective has come under investigation with two particularly interesting results. The first showed that both the parents of people with TS and ADHD (regardless of whether or not they themselves demonstrated any symptoms) had low levels of blood serotonin and tryptophan levels. Second, a small study showed that in seven out of nine families both parents also had abnormalities of the visual field.

Comings also suggests that people with low serotonin levels would generally be more susceptible to addictive behaviours with drugs, alcohol or food than other people. While the factors involved in this are many, it happens partially because such things help to increase their serotonin levels.

At the time Comings wrote his book research indicated that TS was inherited as a semi-dominant, semi-recessive trait which means that, in the majority of cases, both parents carry a single mutant gene. He termed this the *Gts* gene, that is, that most clearly linked to Tourette's syndrome so that, unfortunately, the child then inherits two genes which combine to produce Tourette's syndrome. Comings suggested that while some people with a single *Gts* gene would not be affected in any way others might display any of the symptoms from the wide spectrum of behaviours connected to TS.

It is confusing, though, to find that Comings identifies obsessions and compulsions as the most frequent behavioural manifestation of the problems and says that such behaviours may be present *without* tics – particularly in women carrying the *Gts* gene.

He offers a brief outline of the way in which this syndrome could develop, as shown in Figure 2.4 which also gives an indication of some of the different problems that he suggests may arise from this gene.

Figure 2.4 shows some of the symptoms associated with damage or impairment in the frontal lobes, but other difficulties could include:

- Echolalia.

- Echopraxia – (copied movements).

- An impairment of the person's emotional life.

- Problems with complex arithmetic or in coping with more than one instruction at a time.

- Perseveration – an inability to change course so that a particular action may be repeated over and over again.

- Uncontrolled response to stimuli – inability to concentrate on a particular task as constantly reacts to the latest sensory input even if it is irrelevant.

The latter two points of perseveration and an uncontrolled response to stimuli initially sound contradictory but of course are not because they occur at different times. Perseveration is also found amongst people with autism/ Asperger's syndrome who certainly get stuck on one activity and many of those with OCD who compulsively repeat the same action seemingly interminably. Could it also apply to speech – for there are many people with

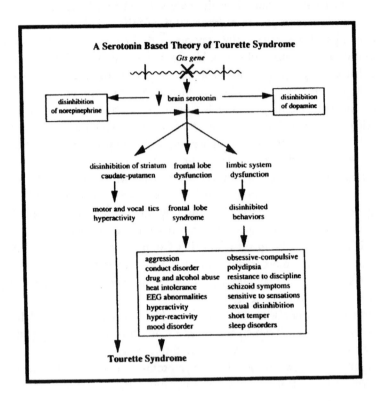

Figure 2.4 A serotonin-based theory of Tourette's syndrome (Comings 1981, p.461; reproduced with permission)

autism who do not just stick to one subject but who rather repeat the same sentence or phrase ad nauseum?

In his book, Comings also discusses the fact that various studies lent support to the idea that the *Gts* gene stems from a genetic defect in the enzyme tryptophan oxygenase. This gene has been isolated in humans and was found to be located on the long arm of chromosome 4 at band q31. If this enzyme is defective it could lead to several other problems as it affects various neurotransmitters.

He also gives a possible explanation for the increased levels of serotonin found amongst some people with autism by suggesting that it could result from a genetic mutation which leads to a reduced level of tryptophan oxygenase. He further postulated that the fundamental problem of autism could be a dysregulation of serotonin and proposed that the causes of autism could be divided into three different groups:

1. Increased serotonin due to:

    (i) a mutation causing too little tryptophan oxygenase;

    (ii) mutations of other genes.

2. Too little serotonin due to:

    (i) mutations causing an increase in tryptophan oxygenase (the *Gts* gene);

    (ii) mutations of other genes.

3. Normal serotonin levels – the problems then arise from other mutations and environmental factors.

Linking the different factors together led Comings to make two other suggestions which may also have some bearing on the outcome of this quest:

1. A significant proportion of the population carries this gene.

2. A percentage of people suffering from ADHD, OCD, phobias, etc. may have such problems because they are carrying the *Gts* gene.

One other, possibly important, point made in a later paper by Comings (1993, p.129) was the suspicion that a major genetic defect was of tryptophan oxygenase in the liver rather than the brain. This led him to suggest that the alterations in the serotonin metabolism in the central nervous system might actually reflect changes in the liver.

Since his book was published, research has continued and Comings now suggests that although Tourette's syndrome, ADHD and autism, etc. are all genetically related they probably stem not from one gene but rather from a number of different genes, some of which are shared. Details of the others which he considers significant (all being connected to abnormalities of dopamine) are to be found in Appendix J.

Thus whilst earlier he effectively argued the case for tryptophan oxygenase he now believes that it is only one of several genes which are implicated in this range of disorders and that these disorders are polygenic, that is, they are caused by the cumulative effects of several or even many mutant genes. This would mean that although both parents have one or more mutant genes they only cause TS, ADHD or autism when a particular combination of these are inherited by the child.

Comings further suggests that TS and ADHD are fundamentally the same genetic disorder, for when three particular genes (see Appendix J) are found together two of the most significant effects are ADHD and tics: an idea which leads him to postulate that it is the balance between particular genes which determines the type of disorder which develops.

Now, however, I would like to take a brief look at one condition which is included because it has occasionally been confused with autism.

Schizophrenia

This is considered to be a mental illness which results in the sufferer losing touch with reality, frequently remaining oblivious to the fact that he is actually ill. Although it can occur in childhood, onset generally begins between the ages of 16 and 25/30 and, in contrast to the other disorders, the incidence between the sexes is equal.

As in Tourette's syndrome some sufferers have a history of developmental delay, withdrawal, 'conduct disorder', dyslexia, learning difficulties and/or poor motor development, including some involuntary movements.

While the social withdrawal of sufferers may have contributed to confusion between schizophrenia and autism, most similarities occur, not in the diagnostic criteria, but rather in various factors which, it is thought, might underlie the problems. These include abnormalities of dopamine, serotonin and, in some cases, an altered blood flow in the brain. There is also speculation at present on the implications of abnormal intestinal permeability, reduced levels of various nutrients, opiod peptides and food intolerances such as wheat and/or milk.

The differences are clearly identified in the first point of DSM-III; although interestingly both (a) and (b) can also found in some people who suffer from Tourette's Syndrome. In abbreviated form, the criteria are:

1) At least one of the following:

    a) bizarre delusions i.e. being controlled by outside forces or delusions of grandeur or persecution

    b) hearing voices

    c) incoherent speech or a marked decrease in spontaneous conversation

    d) illogical thinking.

2) Deterioration of previous functioning.

3) The presence of these problems for at least six months. (American Psychiatric Association 1987)

Thus it would seem that, regardless of the confusions, this condition and autism are clearly different: a point highlighted by Bernard Rimland when he wrote that the major difference between the two was that 'the schizophrenic child seems *disorientated and confused* whereas the autistic child is *unorientated and aloof*' (my emphasis) (Rimland 1964, p.167).

Co-occurrence with autism

Although not solely causes of autism, the following conditions may co-occur with it or perhaps exacerbate it and for this reason they merit inclusion.

Further details can be obtained from the relevant organizations (see Useful Addresses).

Fragile X chromosome

Views on the relevance of the damaged fragile X chromosome in autism vary, perhaps because of differing ideas about the core problems of autism. Thus while one study (Fisch 1992) suggested that fragile X was linked with mental retardation but not specifically to autism, another (Reiss and Freund 1992) found that fragile X males manifested some 'autistic' symptoms or behaviours. These included lack of social play, communication difficulties, repetitive motor behaviour plus a tendency to mouth or smell objects and hyper-sensitivity to sound.

It is also interesting to note that otherwise 'normal' females who carry and transmit the fragile X chromosome often seem to suffer from a variety of symptoms ranging from depression to anxiety and/or obsessive-compulsive disorder.

Tuberous sclerosis (epiloia or Bourneville's disease)

This derives its name from tuber-like growths on the brain which harden and calcify with age. While it is thought to be mainly a hereditary disease, in some cases it seems to occur 'out of the blue'. It is a strange condition for it affects people in different ways and to varying degrees of severity. Over 50 per cent of people with it are intellectually normal and may even be totally unaffected by it, while others will have mild or even severe learning difficulties, although in all cases life expectancy is thought to be normal.

There are a number of different signs of this disease, although not all are necessary for diagnosis. If, however, your child has a combination of those shown below it will be worthwhile consulting your doctor for further advice:

PHYSICAL SYMPTOMS

- White (depigmented) patches on the skin – especially the limbs and body – which may be apparent at birth and also red or brown 'birthmarks' on the face (although both of these can also occur with other conditions).

- Epilepsy, which often starts in childhood, although as the child grows older the seizures may change or even stop altogether.

- A facial rash across the nose and cheeks during adolescence, sometimes mistaken for acne. This starts as red pin-point spots but the redness may fade later and the spots will seem more like bumps.

- During adolescence, or even into adulthood, small nodules of skin may form around the finger or toe nails. This may occasionally be the only external sign of the condition.
- Teeth may be pitted in numerous places.

Tuberous sclerosis can also affect some internal organs such as the heart or gut.

Rubella (German measles)

When contracted during pregnancy, rubella infects the foetus as well; the infection may continue for an extended period, sometimes even after birth. If it occurs during the first three months of pregnancy the risk of rubella-associated defects is greatly increased and the eyes, ears, heart, central nervous system and the brain will be particularly susceptible to damage. The rubella child may suffer from a combination of problems, one of which is multi-sensory deprivation. He may also suffer from:

- Unusual sleep patterns;
- Feeding difficulties – particularly in chewing and swallowing solids;
- Hyperactivity;
- Sensory damage which causes a low toleration of tactile sensations.

It has been said that only those rubella children who suffer deafness will appear autistic, but I would question if this is always so as the one person I know whose mother had rubella and who himself now suffers from autism is extremely hypersensitive to sound.

Rett's disease

This was first identified in 1966 by Andreas Rett in Vienna. Although found in a few males it mainly affects females, who are also often diagnosed as having autism. It probably occurs in more than 1 in 12,000 female births and is thought to be a genetic disorder involving a new mutation of the X chromosome. The onset is usually between nine and eighteen months, although it may occasionally be recognized earlier. The major difference between the two conditions is that a child with Rett's disease may suffer from some of the numerous and often severe physical symptoms not normally associated with autism (excluding epilepsy which is common to both). The signs of Rett's disease are shown below.

PHYSICAL SYMPTOMS

- Slowing of head growth with age.
- Increased spasticity/decreased mobility with age.
- Loss of purposeful hand use.

- Muscle wasting.
- Poor circulation of lower limbs.
- Small feet.
- Unsteady stiff-legged gait (only half the sufferers achieve full mobility).
- Scoliosis – curvature of the spine.
- Epilepsy – 75 per cent may suffer with some form of seizure during their lives.

DEVELOPMENTAL SIGNS

- Loss of previously acquired skills after normal development and/or regression of social development.
- Repetitive hand movements, which may include wringing, patting, clapping.
- Learning difficulties.
- Hyperventilation and/or holding breath and/or air swallowing. Grimacing, mouthing, grinding of teeth.
- Spontaneous vocalizations/laughter.

Landau Kleffner syndrome (LKS)

This rare form of childhood epilepsy generally develops between the ages of three and eight. It may develop slowly over a period of months or suddenly appear overnight. It results in severe language disorder which, when occurring in very young children who have not yet learnt to talk, may be mistaken for a developmental disorder, autism or deafness.

PHYSICAL SYMPTOMS

- Abnormal electrical activity in one or both temporal lobes – responsible for processing language amongst other functions. (This can be identified through a sleeping EEG as it does not always show up if the EEG is done while the person is awake.)
- Approximately two-thirds of these children have seizures.
- Temporary neurological problems leading to:
  - loss of bladder and bowel control;
  - visual disturbances when the child cannot understand what he sees and might have difficulty in recognizing familiar objects such as people, clothes, etc.

DEVELOPMENT AND BEHAVIOURAL SIGNS

- Lack of comprehension – the child may become unable to recognize his own name.
- Difficulty in recognizing environmental sounds, for example the telephone ringing. May appear deaf.
- The ability to speak is often seriously affected and some children may completely lose their speech.
- Hyperactivity and/or lack of attention.
- Irritability and depression.
- 'Autistic'-like behaviours including:
  - avoidance of eye contact – very common;
  - avoidance of contact with others;
  - very disturbed sleep;
  - extreme fussiness over food;
  - attacks of rage or aggression;
  - insensitivity to pain;
  - bizarre, inappropriate or repetitive play.

While surgery has proved successful for some, LKS can also be treated by the administration of corticosteroids (hormones produced by the adrenal glands). This will normalize the EEG but if aphasia has been present for more than a year it may, unfortunately, be unresponsive to treatment.

Epilepsy

Epilepsy is defined as a liability to recurrent seizures which arise from an abnormal discharge of neurons in the brain. It demands attention for it occurs more frequently amongst those with autism and those who are 'mentally handicapped' than in the general population.

I shall not attempt to discuss the various types of epilepsy for these are well documented in specialized books. However, I would like to mention some thoughts which occurred to me whilst researching this book.

It has been suggested that some children also 'become' autistic or begin to display 'autistic features' after a series of seizures. As repeated seizures can cause a loss of memory one must again ask whether, at an early age, periods of normal development interspersed with several periods of sudden memory loss in which one loses previous skills and achievements could be a reason for the onset of 'autisms'.

Although figures vary it is thought that, in contrast to 0.5 per cent of the general population, a much higher figure of approximately 25–35 per cent of the 'autistic' population suffer from epilepsy. Whilst this sounds exceptionally high it is interesting to find that 25 per cent of those with untreated phenylketonuria also suffer from epilepsy. Is there any correlation between these facts? Certainly if some of the problems of autism similarly stem from a metabolic disorder which affects the central nervous system then a high proportion would not be unlikely.

This also has links with the idea that food may play a part in making some children with autism susceptible to seizures. Milk allergy has been implicated in seizures in very young children as it can lead to a deficiency of Vitamin B6. Gluten related/induced seizures have also been recorded and dietary research suggests that diets which exclude casein (milk) and gluten are associated with a reduction in seizures (Shattock 1991). As some of these children may have an immature nervous system and many have underlying problems which leave them intolerant of certain groups of foods, it would be helpful to assess each individual for allergies/food intolerances.

Then too we find that about 4 per cent of 'ordinary' patients with epilepsy have seizures which can be induced by visual stimulation – many having seizures only in response to visual 'triggers', whether these be patterns or television. Whilst the numbers of people with autism who also suffer from visual problems have not as yet been clearly identified an educated guess, in line with the survey carried out by The Geneva Centre (see Useful Addresses), would suggest that visual problems could affect as many as 80 per cent.

An article in *The Times* on 19 August 1997 stated that an American study from the Centres for Disease Control found 34 different side-effects linked to the two triple vaccines DPT and the MMR, with seizures being the most common. The article linked this to a study by the UK Public Health Laboratory, which demonstrated that children given the MMR vaccine were three times more likely to suffer from convulsions than those who didn't have it whilst two-thirds of such seizures were due solely to the measles component.

While many children have a short period of seizures in childhood which cease as they grow, it would be interesting to know whether perhaps the additional problems of autism can increase their susceptibility to vaccines, thereby leaving them with lifelong problems of epilepsy which a more robust child would outgrow.

Finally we should consider one other factor which may at times be mistaken for some form of epilepsy. This is the fact that some people react badly to a gradual build-up of information and stimulation, an 'overload' of which eventually culminates in one of two types of behaviour both of which could be considered indicative of some form of seizure.

In one there is a sudden 'explosion' of hyperactive or bizarre behaviour, whilst in the other this information overload may cause a 'systems shutdown', in which the person ceases to function. The latter can affect people to different degrees but in extreme cases can cause the person to withdraw totally, neither eating nor drinking and perhaps sleeping for lengthy periods.

Taking all these facts into consideration is it any surprise to find such a high proportion of epilepsy amongst this group?

Vaccinations

While separate vaccinations have been available since the Second World War the combined vaccination against measles, mumps and rubella was the only introduced to Britain in 1988. Although anecdotal evidence has long associated vaccinations with several disorders it is only more recently that questions have been asked publicly about its possible side-effects.

In an article in The *Sunday Telegraph* on 24 November 1996 we find that the growing evidence of a link between autism and vaccination had increased the pressure on the Department of Health to fund a research programme into whether childhood vaccines were safe (MacDonald 1996). Further on we are told that there are some 200 cases of 'atypical' autism (a figure which has since risen greatly), in which development was normal until after vaccination at which point the children developed various problems – strange habits such as eating wallpaper, plaster or even dirt off the floor; sleeping problems; ceasing to talk etc.

It had previously been postulated that the MMR vaccine, particularly the measles part, causes encephalitis (swelling of the brain) which could trigger autism, perhaps by damaging the blood brain barrier. While this has not been proven, a report by Wakefield and others in February 1998 gave support to such fears for, although currently much disputed, it provided the following facts:

- Of 12 children initially referred to the paediatric gastroenterology unit all had a history of normal development followed by diarrhoea, abdominal pain, behavioural problems and a loss of acquired skills including language. None had any neurological abnormalities. Subsequent investigation found that all of them had intestinal abnormalities ranging from ulceration to a new form of intestinal disorder (which affected 7 of them) named ileal-lymphoid-nodular hyperplasia. This produces lumpy swellings of lymph nodes in the intestine, patchy recurring inflammation and constipation.

- In eight cases either the parents or the child's doctor had made a link between the deterioration and the MMR vaccine, the average interval between the two events being 6.3 days. One child's development slowed after he received the measles vaccination and his behaviour then deteriorated strikingly after he received the MMR vaccine at four-and-a-half years of age whilst another child who had the vaccine at 16 months developed recurrent otitis media at 18 months. This proved to be resistant to antibiotics and coincided with behavioural symptoms which included a lack of play and disinterest in his sibling.

- At the time of writing forty-seven other children had been tested of whom forty-six also had ileal-lymphoid-nodular hyperplasia with, unsurprisingly, many others waiting to be tested.

The report did not prove an association between the MMR vaccine and the gut disease but a link does now seem to have been clearly established between the intestinal disease itself and autism – for once the physical symptoms have been treated the signs of disturbance often abate.

Although continuing virological studies may eventually resolve this, another study done in Finland (Peltola, Patja and Leinikki 1998) would seem to indicate that no link exists. This study began in 1982 and ran for approximately 14 years during which time some three million doses of vaccine were given. The researchers found that 31 children developed various problems after the vaccine, ranging from fever (in 28) to seizures (in 5) with the most common intestinal problem being diarrhoea, often with vomiting – but no autism.

Does the Finnish study alleviate the fears? Not so. Many families are not convinced and, having formed an association called JABS (see Useful Addresses), have looked at the reaction to such vaccines throughout the world finding, for instance, that some people in other countries have reservations about its use whilst Japan has actually stopped giving the combined vaccine (which should surely give us pause for thought).

JABS would like to see further investigation of the subject, as would I. One doubt arises from the fact that although 31 children developed side-effects the authors of the Finnish study also reported that 'No child developed autistic-spectrum disorder.' Even allowing for problems with translation, given that the incidence of autism is said to be 91 in 1000 (over the broad spectrum of ability), this statement would seem unlikely unless the incidence rate varies in different countries – something which is currently unclear.

Then too we have the fact that autism is thought to be a genetic disorder. Given the lifelong problems of autism it would seem foolish to ignore the fact that some genetic problems result, not initially in a particular disorder, but rather, like some cancers, in a susceptibility to that disorder which will then only develop if certain conditions are 'fulfilled'. Surely in the interests of all it behoves us to see if there is any common thread among the children who are said to have developed autism after being vaccinated?

Initially many people chose to ignore the fact that Wakefield did not suggest that the vaccination should be stopped but rather that it should be given in single doses to lessen the chance of overloading fragile immune systems. As he pointed out, a child would not normally have all three illnesses at the same time.

This seems a perfectly logical suggestion but it is advice which is being hotly disputed in Britain by the Department of Health, the World Health Organization and others (March 1998) even though single doses of the various vaccines could then have been made available. Since then, the licence for the single measles vaccine has been withdrawn (July 1998).

The most charitable explanation for such a heavy-handed approach is that the authorities fear that many families will refuse to have their children vaccinated at all, thereby creating an epidemic. If so, this is an idea which seems to credit parents with very little sense and may, in fact, have the opposite effect to the one hoped for as many parents will prefer to make their own decisions and some are more likely to forgo the vaccine altogether if they are not allowed to have it in three single doses.

A booklet on post-vaccination syndrome (PVS) (1997) written by Tinus Smits, a homeopath who works in the Netherlands, gives further information on this subject. She has studied PVS for a long time whilst treating children and adults with a range of symptoms all of which were linked to vaccines of one sort or another.

Smits divides the symptoms of PVS into two categories – acute and chronic – of which I shall only catalogue a few which seem potentially relevant to autism. Thus symptoms of the acute syndrome (which generally occurs a short time after the vaccine and can lead to a chronic condition) included fever, convulsions and meningitis/encephalitis. Amongst those found in the chronic cases were squinting, loss of eye contact, co-ordination problems, inflammation of the middle ear, allergies, excessive thirst, diarrhoea/constipation, disturbed sleep, lack of concentration, memory loss, disrupted development and behavioural problems.

Citing several cases in support of her arguments Smits makes it very clear that although the child may display no apparently direct or acute reaction, vaccination can still be the cause of chronic complaints which may only become apparent:

1. after some weeks have elapsed;

2. as the result of a cumulative effect of several vaccines;

3. once the child begins to mix with others at nursery school (and is therefore more exposed to germs and infections).

This leads her to make several recommendations amongst which are four which seem particularly relevant (Smits 1997, p.20):

- Vaccinations should be given later when the child's immune system is stronger; in support of which she cites Japan, where, by delaying the whooping cough vaccine until the age of two, they have almost obliterated cot deaths.

- Vaccines should be administered separately where possible.

- There should be longer intervals between vaccinations.

- The child's reactions after vaccines should be recorded carefully and kept.

Smits says that the symptoms of PVS can be alleviated by homeopathic treatment. It will be interesting to know just what effect this treatment would have on people with autism and the new bowel disease. She also suggests that it would be beneficial to carry out a study into the benefits of taking preventive (homeopathic) measures before each vaccine is given.

Whilst there are some people who still scorn homeopathy and may think Smits' ideas are far-fetched, it would seem eminently sensible to carry out some research into the efficacy of such ideas as they could potentially be of great benefit to many people.

If there were indeed a link between the MMR vaccine and autism we should expect to have seen a rise in the incidence of the problem since 1988. Unfortunately, although anecdotal evidence from people concerned with education suggests that this is so, published evidence is inadequate and this cannot be verified.

Although one leading expert, Christopher Gillberg of the Child Neuropsychiatry Clinic University of Gothenburg, Sweden, believes that there has been a rise, he relates this to figures collated in the 1960s – which does not really help clarify the situation. It is interesting, though, to note that he suggests that the reasons behind this rise could be twofold. First is a better awareness of the problems which has led to more cases being reported, whilst second is the fact that he also feels that there has been a genuine rise in prevalence over the years.

I would like to conclude this section with two points:

1. It is of great importance to note that treating the symptoms of ileal-lymphoid-nodular hyperplasia does diminish the behavioural difficulties.

2. Until all the questions are fully researched and the answers found to justify or allay parental fears I do not believe that we know enough to state so categorically that the combined vaccine should be given to all.

Possible causes of autism

Much research is currently going on in different areas throughout the world and various theories have been postulated as to the cause(s) of autism, some of which we have already explored. To include everything would be impossible so I have limited this selection to a few interesting developments which give an indication of the wide area of research covered; some of which have already been discussed. Those who have an interest in this can obtain more information from the Autism Research Review International which keeps readers up to date with new developments.

- Often significantly smaller brainstem than that of other people (Hashimoto, Tatamax and Miyazaki 1992). This would seen to link in with cerebellar abnormalities found in other studies (Corchesne *et al.* 1994)

- Increased central conduction times (CCTs) (McClelland, Eyre and Watson 1992) – that is, messages are passed more slowly than would have been expected in children over 14 years old. This indicates problems within the brainstem and a possible defect in myelination (Singh *et al.* 1993).

- Damage in the area of the limbic system during the development of the embryo (Bauman and Kemper 1985).

- Decreased blood flow in several parts of the brain, for example right, left and mid-frontal lobes (Doyle, Haynes, Giddeon, King and Dempsey 1979).

- Tryptophan depletion – reduced levels of this amino acid resulted in a worsening of symptoms in several people with autism (McDougle *et al.* 1993; Cook and Leventhal 1996).

- Serotonin abnormalities which could in some cases have a link with the tryptophan depletion mentioned above.

- Possible gene linkage – HRAS located on chromosome 11 (Herault, Perrot and Barthelemy 1992) and also chromosome 15.

- Links to fragile X syndrome.

- Possible link to pernicious anaemia – an autoimmune disorder resulting in an inability of the body to absorb Vitamin B12 leading to anaemia, that is, a reduction of haemoglobin in the blood.

- Abnormal compounds in the urine (opioid peptides?) which might cause abnormal sensory perceptions.

- Abnormal reactions within the immune system (Menage, Thibault and Barthelemy 1992).

- Allergies which are linked to the onset of problems.

- Abnormal sensory perceptions.

- Vaccines?

- The most recent world-wide research published in March 1998 (Bailey *et al.* 1998) has now identified some chromosomes which may be involved in the development of autism or in a susceptibility to it. So far two significant regions have been identified: the first in the region of chromosome 7 and somewhat weaker evidence for the involvement of chromosome 16. Research is ongoing but it is currently thought that multiple genes in different combinations may be involved in these problems.

- The fact that those treated with secretin are showing positive results also indicates that the digestive system may be implicated in the problems. Rimland considers that secretin is potentially an extremely important development in helping autism and has called for further research so perhaps we can look forward to finding some answers in the not-too-distant future.

It is intriguing, too, to find that Rimland wrote that: 'Continued study of the reticular formation will provide major advances in our understanding of the mechanisms which underlie behaviour' (Rimland 1964, p.219). Another area for research perhaps?

General points

I would now like to mention one hereditary problem which used to result in mental retardation – phenylketonuria (PKU). This genetic defect leaves the body unable to metabolize the amino acid phenylalanine which, if unrecognized and untreated, then accumulates in the body causing mental retardation from early childhood onwards.

While the untreated child with PKU appears to develop normally at first there is often a general irritability and/or vomiting and early childhood convulsions may also appear. Physical symptoms can include widely spaced incisor teeth, bone calcification and slow growth. Later on, 25 per cent of sufferers will develop epilepsy and a majority will have abnormal EEGs. Some have shown signs similar to those found in cerebral palsy with contractions or hypertonia of the limbs. The central nervous system does not complete its maturation process and there may be defective myelination, or degeneration of grey and white matter.

Such children are characterized by being exceptionally fair-skinned and blonde (the result of a lack of melanin) as shown in Figure 2.5. In addition they also have low brain tryptophan and serotonin levels and some demonstrate behaviour similar to those with attention deficit hyperactivity disorders whilst others have physical mannerisms like tics.

It is also interesting to note that phenylalanine is a phenolic. Ber (1983) suggests that there is a possibility that some people have a mild form of this disease: mild enough to be unrecognized but which predisposes them to other illnesses. While everyone is said to have some mutant genes it is known that one person in every 50 has an abnormal gene which, when combined with another from their partner, can lead to some of their offspring having PKU. Could just one gene lead to the problems postulated by Ber? Does this have any connection to the fact that there is a particular group of children who are classed as hyperactive who also share the characteristic of being 'very fair-skinned and blonde'? Once again there are more questions than answers.

Before it was identified and early detection and treatment became possible, such a condition condemned many a person to lifelong problems, rendering them unable to fulfil their potential. While it seems strange that such an apparently basic factor as an inability to deal with a particular amino acid could cause such a devastating condition it indicates that some apparently complicated problems may stem from something which, once identified, seems quite simple. I wonder if some of the problems associated with autism will eventually prove to stem from similar (comparatively simple) causes?

NORMAL

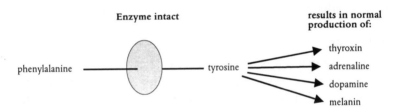

IN PHENYLKETONURIA

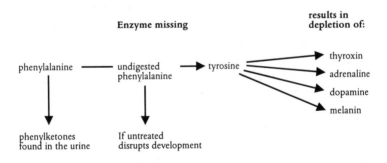

Figure 2.5 Phenylalanine metabolism in children without (above) and with (below) PKU

Sex differences

One final section now. I thought it might also be interesting to explore the possible underlying causes for the differences between the sexes, that is, why males seem to be far more vulnerable to a wide range of disorders than females, particularly in early life. So far I have come across several suggestions which I offer in no particular order:

1. It has long been thought that males are more vulnerable than females during pregnancy and birth. Certainly it is now known that a potential male embryo develops faster than a female and that he is then potentially susceptible to interference from his mother's increasing hormone levels.

2. Males also have approximately 50 per cent less serotonin than females although the level increases in later life. It has been postulated that this obviously leaves them more vulnerable if any other factors reduce the serotonin levels further – which seems logical.

3. The calcium metabolism needed by the nervous system is far less likely to malfunction in females while there are also links between the mother's Vitamin C levels and 'mental abnormality' in the child.

4. Testosterone is obviously another candidate, male monkeys fed low levels of tryptophan demonstrated a corresponding increase in both motor activity and aggressive behaviours although increased levels of tryptophan did not either inhibit or greatly increase the normal levels of aggression. These tests had little effect on the females and the differences were therefore postulated to be the effect of testosterone on aggression.

5. Next is an idea from a study of depression in humans in which the ratio of tryptophan to other neutral amino acids was determined. The level of leucine was found to be significantly higher in males than it was in females. This amino acid competes with tryptophan for entry to the brain and it was postulated that higher levels would disrupt the process, reducing the brain serotonin more and producing more severe symptoms in males with low serotonin levels.

6. Essential fatty acids (EFAs) may also play a part, for some researchers feel that hyperactive children may:

   • have a shortage of these essential fatty acids;

   • have a deficiency of a particular enzyme which is involved in producing prostaglandins;

   • be vulnerable to various external factors which could disrupt the process.

7. Linguistically, girls generally make more sounds than boys, uttering words and sentences earlier and having a larger vocabulary by the age of two. By the age of six boys are usually better at visual spatial skills, which are thought to be located in the right hemisphere. In contrast girls have less specialization because of a greater overlap between the two hemispheres.

    This overlap demonstrates its effect when damage occurs to either hemisphere, for men generally show greater deterioration in the specific skills associated with that area than women do. This links in with research from Johns Hopkins University (*Daily Mail* 18 May 1996). This showed that whilst men have larger brains, women have more grey matter in the areas associated with verbal ability, using both sides of the brain for language in contrast to men who use only the left side. Presumably, then, males would have more difficulty in compensating for damage than females would – but whether this has any bearing on the problems of autism remains to be seen.

8. Early research indicated that many children with autism are first-born. Rimland suggested that biological research into the differences between the first-born and other siblings would be useful and might produce some interesting ideas on possible hypotheses (in addition to a frequently longer period of labour). As time became limited I have, to date, been unable to find out whether this is still a factor or whether any such research has been undertaken.

9. Next, left-handedness, which is included not simply because it affects more males than females but also because of its other connections. Left-handedness is accompanied by increased rates of allergies, autism, depression and migraine amongst other disorders. Nevertheless, left-handers are extremely talented – famous left-handers include Michelangelo, Picasso and Charlie Chaplin.

    Left-handedness is also associated with problems at birth and accounts for a staggering 54 per cent of premature babies. This returns us to the idea of testosterone. In his book *The Left Hander Syndrome* (1992) Stanley Coren suggests that some left-handedness is caused by the presence of too much testosterone in the amniotic fluid surrounding the foetus. The reason for his suggestion is that testosterone retards the development of the left hemisphere (which controls the right hand). He feels that an excess could therefore result in the right hemisphere becoming dominant (Coren 1992, pp.188–189).

    This hypothesis could perhaps explain why left-handed people have a greater risk of allergies and other illnesses, since testosterone also slows the growth of the thymus (which produces white blood cells and is therefore involved in our immune responses) and could, in addition, account for the higher incidence amongst males who are exposed to more testosterone *in utero*.

10. One of the latest theories comes from David Skuse of the Institute of Child Health in London who suggests that genetics play a large part. He hypothesizes that this involves the inheritance of the X chromosome and also a mechanism called imprinting, in which genes can be 'switched' on or off; a device which he feels could explain the fact that women generally have greater 'social intuition'.

    His ideas resulted from research into a rare condition called Turner's syndrome in which affected girls have only one X chromosome instead of two. Skuse found evidence to suggest that the social intuition gene was turned off when passed on from the mother but turned on when passed on by the father.

    This research has led him to suggest that a similar process may exist in autism and Asperger's syndrome. Thus boys would be at greater risk because they receive their single X chromosome from their mothers whilst girls are usually protected by their second X chromosome, inherited from their father, with its 'activated' social intuition gene.

11. There would also seem to be another possibility linked to the X chromosome. Whilst it may not apply to everyone with these disorders it is that another gene such as that which governs monoamine oxidase (MAO) (see Appendix B) could be involved.

    I suggest monoamine oxidase for two reasons. First, it has already been identified as a factor in some inherited problems such as ADHD, depression and schizophrenia. Second, we find that, apart from its effect on serotonin, adrenaline and dopamine, low levels of MAO are involved in food intolerance. They can interact badly with foods, drinks or drugs containing tyramine – for example certain cheeses, yoghurt, chocolate and wine – and can cause headaches, migraine or high blood pressure.

    Certainly if the X chromosome were involved there would be two specific effects. One would be that, as males receive only one X gene, the ratio of affected males would be higher than that of females – the woman being a carrier perhaps? Second, any female who received two faulty X genes would probably have severe problems – which certainly happens in some cases.

    Could it be that, where one of these disorders stems from a cluster of genes, a particular gene on the X chromosome might play a part, not necessarily in determining which disorder occurs, but merely in making the male more vulnerable than the female?

Summary

We have now explored several of the many different theories surrounding autism. Some of these seem to link together whilst others appear to be in opposition to each other. We have also considered some of the facts which are gradually coming to light as sufferers talk or write about their experiences, leaving some confusion. If, however, we look at the findings so far, the situation can be clarified by dividing them into two categories.

Facts

1. The brain, central nervous system, body and emotions all develop according to a set pattern. This development will be halted or weakened if parts of the pattern are incomplete or if the brain does not receive the correct nutrition.

2. The body cannot function properly unless the brain receives and relays messages correctly.

3. The senses which are most developed at birth are those of smell and taste. The other senses need time to develop fully.

4. Extreme stress can cause withdrawal and stereotyped or other disturbed behaviours. It can deplete the immune system and cause a variety of physical and mental problems, inhibiting language, learning and emotional development.

5. 'Autistic' behaviours are similar to those demonstrated by people who have visual handicaps or impaired hearing and especially those who suffer from multi-sensory deprivation.

6. People with obsessive-compulsive disorder and Tourette's syndrome also suffer from some symptoms which are extraordinarily like those of autism. All three disorders have a similar disparity in the ratio of boys to girls.

7. The onset of 'obsessive-compulsive' features can occur at different ages.

8. At present there appear to be several identifiable problems which can contribute to or have a connection with autism:

   - rubella during pregnancy;
   - cerebellar abnormalities;
   - brain damage or an illness such as meningitis after birth;
   - peptide abnormalities;
   - possible vaccine damage associated with the MMR vaccine.

9. One major problem connected with autism and Asperger's syndrome is disturbed perception. This can cause extreme stress.

At this point some people will no doubt mutter the word 'anecdote'; a charge often levelled at those with autism when they describe their experiences. This has always seemed very strange to me. Indeed if I were to visit the doctor and describe my symptoms only to be fobbed off like that I would have good reason to complain. It is naive to say that this 'anecdotal' evidence cannot be confirmed. Of course it can. One cannot continue to discount as coincidence the fact that similar things are being described by (non-communicative!) people from many different parts of the world. Just because people have difficulties in communicating and sometimes in co-operating does not mean that their 'evidence' can be ignored. Perhaps all we need to do is sharpen our powers of observation and put aside our scepticism!?

Suppositions

1. The onset of autism occurs prior to thirty months.

2. Autism can be caused by:

   • emotional disturbance;

   • the mother's stress prior to the child's birth;

   • inherent fragility.

3. The major symptoms of autism are:

   • anxiety;

   • delayed/deviant language development;

   • impaired social development;

   • cognitive problems.

4. Anxiety/stress is caused by:

   • emotional conflict;

   • cognitive problems.

You may query the list and wonder why, for example, delayed and deviant language development comes under suppositions when it is clearly demonstrated by the sufferers. Remember though that we have not yet clarified whether this should be classed as a major problem, although the next chapter will study such points in greater detail.

CHAPTER 3

Analysis and Discussion

'I should have more faith' he said; 'I ought to know by this time that when a fact appears to be opposed to a long train of deductions it invariably proves capable of bearing some other interpretation.'

Sherlock Holmes by Arthur Conan Doyle

The summary in the last chapter listed the theories which I consider to be of importance, but we are left with a certain amount of conflict and apparent paradox for the only common thread which seems to run throughout is anxiety. So, how do we begin to sort out the puzzle? Perhaps if the various points are considered in turn they will enable us to approach and consider the problem from a fresh viewpoint.

Emotional deprivation

At the beginning of Chapter 2 several controversial theories were discussed, which suggested that lack of maternal warmth and emotional 'refrigeration' could be formative factors in the development of a child with autism.

So what exactly does happen to deprived babies? Studies from the late 1940s show that extreme neglect causes severe emotional deprivation. While the deprived baby who receives only minimal stimulation from its carer may actually lose the will to live – a condition known as marasmus – those who survive are abnormal in several areas. They fail to form relationships with other people; they do not respond to physical cues (i.e. do not greet a smile with smile); and they may have problems with intelligence, behaviour, language and motor co-ordination. However, they do not generally suffer from autism.

In 1951 John Bowlby published a report on Maternal Care and Mental Health. He called the emotional relationship (the bonding process) between baby and carer an 'attachment' and concluded that the institutionalized children he had studied failed to 'attach'. Thus they lacked the foundations on which to develop 'normal' social relationships.

If a lack of bonding in itself was truly the underlying cause of autism, then it would surely follow that a higher proportion of children with this condition would be found amongst babies who spent their early months in the old style Children's Homes, where staff changed frequently, than in the general population. This is, however, not so.

Prior to working with adults with autism, I spent ten years working with emotionally disturbed adolescent boys, who would previously have been termed 'maladjusted'. The majority of them had been through various 'traumatic' experiences at an early age and many, for a variety of reasons, had missed the vital bonding process between mother and baby. The outcome of their experiences, as recorded and analysed by many experts, was emotional disturbance, not autism.

The problems such children face can be divided into four different types. Barbara Docker Drysdale, a psychotherapist who devoted much of her life to the treatment of emotionally disturbed children, described their problems clearly (Docker Drysdale 1993).

She used the term 'frozen' to describe the most disturbed of these children, choosing this expression rather than the previously used term 'affectionless' since she felt it implied hope, for 'a thaw can follow frost'. The frozen child presents a complex and puzzling picture which can briefly be described thus:

> He has a kind of charm, is apparently extremely friendly and seems to make contact very quickly although, on consideration, this is always on a superficial level. He is usually clean, tidy and healthy and does not appear anxious or shy. He is frequently generous and may be kind to one particular child whom he will protect. In contrast he may, for no apparent reason, rapidly become hostile and fly into a panic rage, during which he is verbally abusive and destroys anything within reach.
>
> He lives only in the present, never thinking of the past or future and will steal and lie without any sign of remorse. At times he may attack or be cruel to the child he normally protects.

Such behaviours, if untreated, make the child the forerunner of the 'cold' adult psychopath so beloved by the movies and so menacing to the general population.

Second is the 'archipelago' child who has 'islets' of functioning and fluctuates between being gentle, pleasant and concerned or, in stark contrast, being wildly out of control, panicking or being aggressive or destructive. He is less difficult to help than the frozen child for in his calmer moments he is aware that he needs help.

Then there are two groups of children who have begun to bond with their mother but for whom the process has been disrupted at an early age leading to slightly different problems. Thus in the third group we have the child who develops a 'false self', hiding (protecting) his real self behind a camouflage which may be based on a person he knows. This is the child who, without help, will act his way through life. Initially this façade may be quite successful but his relationships with others may gradually fail for the foundations are damaged and those who know him well will come to realize that something vital is missing as his real self remains hidden.

Finally, the fourth category is the 'caretaker' self – a state which can develop when the child has had to begin 'looking after himself' at too early an age.

There is also a difference between those for whom bonding has proved unsuccessful and those whose disturbance started at a later date. The following tale graphically illustrates the effects of trauma on a young child who had already successfully completed the bonding process.

This was shown in one of the saddest films I have ever seen. The film, called quite simply 'John', followed the disintegration of a small child, some two years old, whose mother was hospitalized prior to the birth of her second baby. His father had to hold down a job and so placed John in a nursery during the days.

The researcher filmed and recorded his initial bewilderment as his father first left him; his grief, which went uncomforted in the hustle and bustle of the nursery day; and then his gradual withdrawal from the world. Although aware of the change in his son, the father had no alternative but to leave him so that when his mother eventually returned she found a withdrawn, rejecting and uncomprehending child. John was not autistic but was to need many years of psychotherapy before he was able to resume a normal life. This film made a great impact and I remember being angered, as were many others, by the fact that a researcher who was obviously aware of the probable consequences could so coldly catalogue a child's distress without responding, even when he approached her.

Next we should consider the story of Kaspar Hauser (Tradowsky 1997), a young man who suddenly appeared in Nuremberg in 1828. It is interesting because he could speak only a few words, moved his feet clumsily as if he didn't know how to walk and seemed unable to comprehend anything. It gradually became apparent that he had been kept in a dark cellar from early childhood until he was nearly seventeen with only a rocking horse for company and without ever seeing his 'keeper' who fed him on bread and water. It was rumoured that he was in fact a member of the royal family who had been treated in this awful manner because he had seemed to be slightly retarded; a rumour which gained credibility after two assassination attempts, the second of which succeeded.

We shall never know the exact age at which Kaspar was incarcerated but can guess that this only happened after his problems became obvious; perhaps as a toddler. While Kaspar did not necessarily suffer from a lack of bonding, he was obviously grossly maltreated, his treatment being described by a famous lawyer of the time, Anselm von Feuerbach, as a 'crime on the soul of man'. However, even though he was stunted both physically and emotionally, there was no suggestion that this treatment resulted in autism, as once out of captivity and living amongst people who treated him kindly, he quickly learnt in his short life not only to write and draw, but also to speak and relate to other people.

So, several different pictures have now emerged from these descriptions, none of which coincides with the problems of autism, for although such children have a stunted emotional growth even where learning difficulties and withdrawal also develop, they lack the main characteristics of autism.

Thus we have those children for whom the bonding process has been unsuccessful, who learn to keep other people and reality at bay by a sequence of coping mechanisms which include the – frequently delinquent – behaviours mentioned previously. On the other hand, the child who has bonded, even partially, with his mother suffers from different problems when the process is interrupted or brought to a premature end.

Such disruption can be brought about by many different things, often outside the parents' control, such as illness which necessitates hospitalization for mother or child. These problems will cause the child to become anxious and he will initially look for reassurance. If this is not available he will then become withdrawn, development may be slowed and he may regress to former behaviour, for example wetting the bed or his trousers. The degree of this withdrawal and of any regression will be very individual and determined by a number of factors, including the child's age at the onset of the problem, the duration of the separation or other difficulties and the child's relationship with other members of the family.

Returning now to the Tinbergen ideas (Tinbergen and Tinbergen 1983), I would agree that autism is anxiety related, but feel strongly that their supposition 'that the desire to withdraw is created by emotional conflict' is inaccurate. They do not attach any blame for the situation and, indeed, cite some environmental factors, beyond the parents' control, as possible causes. However, the emphasis placed on the mother's involvement in the treatment process, the term 'faulty bonding' and Welch's comment on a 'lack of normal instincts', appear to return us once more to the idea that some form of 'emotional deprivation' plays a part in creating the condition.

Such ideas can be devastating to parents and therefore warrant further consideration. Is the term 'faulty' being used to imply a lack of bonding or interrupted bonding? As previously discussed, although there may be some similarities, the main features associated with autism are missing.

This, of course, raises some queries regarding diagnosis, for some of the children with autism who have recovered through 'holding' do not seem to have had these problems either. Three questions need answering:

1. Are we talking about the same problems – are those children who recover through 'holding' actually autistic? I can almost hear the comments of those people who agree with Welch or who have seen their child improve through her methods. They may feel that this is a leading question which has often been asked (and answered) by those experts who feel improvements are not possible and are, in their eyes, 'blinkered'. Still, if we wish to determine the facts we cannot shy away from asking questions, however unpalatable. It is important to remain open-minded for while there is, at present, no reason to disbelieve the improvements, the questions cannot be ignored, as the answers may further our quest.

2. If so, what are the factors in the treatment which cause their recovery?

3. Why do children who have recovered through holding show no signs of the 'mental' or 'developmental' problems it is believed they suffer from?

Perhaps some of the answers will become clear as this book progresses. However, one other question is appropriate here. Could disrupted bonding provide an explanation for one aspect of behaviour which puzzled many people, myself included, when first reading *Nobody Nowhere*?

This was in Donna Williams' use of different characters such as Willie and Carol whom she 'became' at certain times in particular situations. I have heard people talk about Multiple Personality Disorder (MPD) in reference to this: a disorder generally associated with child abuse. While its existence is now doubted by many professionals, it could have provided a possible explanation for these characters, although it was one which, knowing Donna, I never felt entirely happy with. Indeed, some people have used this fact along with others to cast doubt on whether she actually had autism as a child; one suggestion apparently being that she only developed such problems as a young adult. While admittedly, once past the echolalic stage, she was probably extremely adept at putting on a 'sociable face', reading her books shows that such ideas are absolutely unfounded and could only have been proposed by those who have scant knowledge of autism.

That aside, I found that reading her book *Like Color to the Blind* (1996) threw further light on this, for other people in it like Ian and Lucy also had a variety of characters which they 'hid behind' – characters which seemed to be triggered automatically, with no conscious volition, by certain situations.

Are such complex charades only found amongst the more verbal group – or do less/non-verbal sufferers also imitate others? It would certainly seem so when we read Jean Jasinski's description of her son:

> Jason was very astute at learning appropriate dialogue for specific situations from his older sister. For instance, if he was standing in line, he would say 'I was first' but he didn't reinforce those words with any actions…
>
> Jason's play skills were limited. His favourite play things were toys that came from TV shows or videos, and his play consisted mostly of repeating the dialogue and reenacting situations from the shows. He fooled one psychologist with this behaviour; she ruled out autism as a possible diagnosis because Jason had arranged the Fisher Price Little People in the doll house like a family and acted out appropriate scenes. What she did not realize was that Fisher Price made Little People videos – that Jason was simply echoing the video. (Stehli 1995, p.3)

Could this explain why some people with autism sometimes use delayed echolalia or someone else's phrasing in a different tone of voice to their own?

I do not believe that this facet of autism fits into the category of Multiple Personality Disorder (assuming it does exist). Whilst this is an aspect of autism which is, as yet, little documented, I would tentatively surmise that although a disrupted bonding process and the development of a 'false self' (which could easily occur if the problems of autism overtook the child at an early age) might apply to some people, yet another explanation is more apposite.

It seems to me that this is a 'coping strategy' which, when it begins early, develops in a similar manner to echolalia. In some cases too the storing of such information may be the natural product of a fantastic memory. Add to this Donna Williams' comment that she initially repeated phrases because: '… I sensed that some sort of response with sounds was required. Mirroring … was my way of saying "Look, I can relate. I can make that noise too"' (Williams 1992, p.26).

Perhaps it was this 'requirement' that led Jason to fool the psychologist with his Fisher Price 'Little People' dialogue and actions.

Thus we find the development of a complex and complicated system which becomes more sophisticated over the years, giving a 'bank of stored information' which is, for some, retrieved automatically to deal with certain situations. Generally this repertoire consists of words and phrases gleaned from family, strangers and television, video or radio characters which can be trotted out 'on demand' when the occasion arises; allowing 'someone else' to cope with the situation.

So, in contrast to the disturbed child whose 'false persona' originates from a disrupted bonding I would suggest that the person with autism generally develops such strategies in order to cope with their daily lives: an idea which would seem to be supported by Gunilla Gerland who, in contrast to those whose reactions become automatic, describes a period when she consciously imitated others (something she no longer finds necessary). As she says:

> I tried imitating other people. Now that I was with people more, I had to be someone. People asked me what I wanted, what I thought. I took features from people I met and added them to me. I often took features from people who seemed very self confident. I did this immensely skilfully. I became a chameleon – if I adopted Karin's way of sighing as she spoke, I could use it with everyone except Karin, and if I adopted Maria's taste in music, then I didn't talk about music with Maria. I was an empty jar that could be filled with anything. People's behaviour simply fell into the jar and I used it to try to feel myself someone, like a real person. I developed this strategy in order to be able to relate to people. If you were no-one, you couldn't relate – you had to be someone. The people I met didn't know each other, and I met them separately as I had such difficulty mixing in groups. This was also a prerequisite for my theft of personality features to be able to function. (Gerland and Tate 1997, p.209)

Jasmine Lee O'Neill describes something similar when she says:

> Their true personalities, which are noticeable autistic, are repressed because they irritate or disturb or annoy or confound others. So the autistic person mimics others to try to fit in, just so the awful pain of being made fun of stops.

She then points out that: 'As an autistic person grows older, her real personality can get buried beneath the ones that are more sociably acceptable. This is harmful and forms scars' (O'Neill 1999, p.66).

While, as will become clear, Jasmine O'Neill and I probably see the 'true personality' somewhat differently I would certainly agree that some people do appear to be 'submerged' by such characters; to have 'lost touch' with their real selves! Strange then to think that this type of 'veneer' is exactly what some schools and centres try to achieve.

It is time now, though, to move on and look at the possible physical aspects of the problem.

Developmental problems: brain damage or dysfunction?

We have already discussed 'normal' child development and found that it takes place in various stages, each of which must be completed satisfactorily before the child can move to the next stage. We must now examine the clues in the light of this knowledge.

Autism is described in more recent literature as a developmental handicap (as opposed to the former description of 'mental' handicap). It is often assumed that it exists from birth, although the symptoms are often not recognized until the child's second or third year, but whether this is true or not remains to be seen. The word developmental is also used where other problems such as dyslexia are concerned, although research now shows that the difficulties which appear when the child starts to read and write are merely an external indicator of fundamental internal problems.

In autism, there is continued emphasis on 'delayed and deviant language development' and 'impaired social development'. While such problems obviously have a devastating effect, I must question whether the importance attributed to them has diverted our attention from more fundamental ones. Certainly other (lesser?) problems like the odd behaviour and mannerisms do often occur prior to these developmental difficulties.

Development is defined as 'the act or process of growing, progressing or developing or the product or result of developing'. This would indicate that problems in this area are the 'result of' rather than 'the' fundamental or underlying difficulty. Should they therefore be considered as secondary problems rather than the primary one? While the child's failure to speak, for instance, is often seen as an inability to express himself, it is in truth often either an inability to receive information or the reception of incorrect information. This is similar to the child born with a severe hearing impairment who only acquires speech with extreme difficulty. There need be nothing wrong with his speech mechanism for the problem clearly lies in a failure of sensory reception and is not a failure of output.

Any approach which places great emphasis on the developmental issues can mislead, for it tends to imply that they are of primary importance. This is reminiscent of work done with brain-damaged children in the United States in the 1950s and 1960s. Initially, if a child's limb did not function in the correct manner, the treatment was to give physiotherapy or various physical aids in the belief that exercise and support would develop or strengthen the limb. It was only after many years when more improvements took place with 'untreated' children than with those in treatment that the professionals began to question their approach.

This led them to a 'discovery' that today seems commonplace, but which at that time was a giant leap in understanding; this is that all motor ability (movement or reaction) is based on sensory intake. The discovery enabled them to take a fresh look at their approach and develop ways of treating the brain where the difficulties originated. Thus, when language is looked at in developmental terms it can be identified as the result of intelligent thought – not the creator of it! This is an idea clearly supported by work with children who are born deaf and in whom thought occurs without speech.

Let us consider the way in which the brain works. Before a baby or child can respond to external stimuli through social development or language the brain has to receive the correct stimuli. However, if the stimuli are blocked or distorted the result will be a failure to 'interpret' expression, gesture or speech; a failure which will in turn lead to an inability to respond in a 'normal' manner and disrupt the basis of learning. This encompasses Newson's theory of a brain dysfunction or malfunction, which could easily be a major factor in causing any input to be blocked or distorted, as shown in Figure 3.1.

External world	Brain dysfunction	Physical response
Input of stimuli, mother's smile, voice, etc.	Message blocked, incomplete or distorted	No response or a distorted response

Figure 3.1 Stimuli blocked or distorted as a result of brain dysfunction

Thus for a person like Darren White, who does not see what others assume he sees, confusion reigns – and, unsurprisingly, results in fear and anxiety. Perhaps the nearest most of us ever come to this feeling is when lost in a thick fog which baffles and confuses. Our eyes still see, but what they see bears no relation to reality; our ears still hear, but can no longer discern which sounds are close and which are distant, for everything appears unnatural and distorted.

Only one conclusion can be drawn from this. The developmental problems which are demonstrated by difficulties in making social relationships and communicating, while giving a clear indication of underlying difficulties, are not fundamental and must therefore be considered secondary symptoms: a conclusion which gives a different emphasis to some of the current theories. Could it be that some of the problems of diagnosis stem not solely from the changing face of autism as the child grows older, but rather from the fact that some of the diagnostic criteria are encouraging us to look in the wrong direction?

In many disorders and illnesses the answer is clear-cut as a particular cause gives a specific effect; for example, a hearing impairment hampers speech.

Unfortunately in autism, the picture is clouded by a multitude of symptoms and ideas. If only the area or type of brain malfunction or abnormality or damage could be defined more clearly, perhaps it might illuminate the fundamental problem(s) underlying autism.

Uta Frith (1989) attempts to answer these questions by propounding and expanding on the idea that the underlying problem is a cognitive one in which the child is unable to understand the meaning of the information he receives. Strangely, though, more recent diagnostic criteria, which cover the 'secondary' problems of language and social development so clearly, omit cognition. Is that because it is too difficult to demonstrate, obscured by other factors, or because some experts disagree with the theory? Perhaps we should examine the idea in more depth.

While accepting the fact that the inability to understand information presents the sufferer with huge problems, we again need to clarify whether this is the fundamental or underlying cause. Let us start by defining exactly what is meant by cognition. According to the dictionary it means: 'the mental act or process by which knowledge is acquired, including perception and reasoning' or 'the knowledge that arises from this process'.

The use of reasoning is a skill which is acquired at a later stage of life when the child has the 'background' knowledge to allow such processes to take place. This has been well catalogued and cannot therefore fulfil the term 'fundamental'. We know that, as has long been recognized, our perceptual experiences form the foundation upon which the conceptual system is built and they must therefore play a fundamental part in our development. While I have no intention of lecturing the reader in semantics, another definition might be helpful at this stage.

Perception is defined as: 'the process by which an organism collects, interprets and comprehends information from the external world by means of the senses.' Thus information is collected by the senses and then interpreted by the brain, which demonstrates its understanding by triggering a response of some kind such as smiling, crying or moving. Cognition has been defined by Frith as the cause of the problems: an idea seemingly endorsed by the sufferers' inability to interpret gestures or understand abstract ideas, all of which could certainly fit in with the idea of a brain dysfunction. So, so far so good.

However, there is one major omission in this theory, for it takes no account of the vital clue which is repeatedly given by the sufferers – that of their abnormal sensory experiences and perceptions. Surely if problems exist during the reception of information – as we know they do – they must lead to further problems of interpretation and comprehension. This might explain the inability to deal with more than one piece of information at a time ('mono' processing problems) and Rimland's 'delayed mental audition'. The way in which this might happen is demonstrated in Figure 3.2 – which, unsurprisingly, is similar to Figure 3.1.

External world	Senses (problems due to ASP)	Brain	Physical response
Information	Information distorted	Interpretation unclear. Comprehension sketchy or missing	No response or a distorted response

Figure 3.2 Information distorted as a result of abnormal sensory perceptions

Thus while I would agree that cognition is one of the major problems of autism it does not underlie the difficulties such people have. Indeed as all the evidence to date suggests that the problem stems from problems in the reception of information, rather than at the later stages of interpretation and comprehension, the word itself has a tendency to mislead. Comprehension, as the culmination of both reception and interpretation, must clearly be classed as a secondary, developmental stage, whilst perception is one of the primary problems.

Perception was, of course, mentioned by Creak in her criteria, although its significance was and has been generally missed except by a few people. Ornitz, Guthrie and Farley (1977) summed up its importance by suggesting that, in line with the diagram, distorted sensory input would become distorted information which in turn was the foundation of deviant language and social communication. While Newson sees the basic problems as an inability to 'decode' physical and facial gestures and verbal messages she expands the idea by suggesting that this would make life so frightening that it would be dealt with by withdrawal and the production of 'cut-off' mechanisms – an idea with which I would entirely agree.

Finally we must also consider Simon Baron-Cohen's 'theory of mind' – that is, the lack of empathy which seems to contain aspects of alexithymia and dyssemia. Salovey's definition of emotional intelligence shows that there are several separate stages which must be achieved prior to reaching empathy: from self-awareness, to an ability to handle one's own feelings, to self-motivation. We have already found that many people with autism lack proprioception and may have little awareness of (and/or an inability to express) their own feelings. If they lack such basic building blocks as these, how can we expect them to reach and achieve any level of empathy? Once again it seems to me that the 'theory of mind' falls into the secondary category which arises from a disruption of more fundamental factors.

So let us now look at perception in more detail.

Abnormal sensory perceptions

In the 1960s Delacato's work seemed revolutionary to many, but unfortunately in spite of, or perhaps because of, this it was largely ignored and its significance missed. Only now have we reached a stage where, hopefully, its worth can be recognized and his ideas used beneficially (Delacato 1974).

Delacato was, as many of us are, initially bewildered by the varied reactions amongst the children he observed. However, in contrast to many people nowadays who consider that any under-reaction is merely the child's way of coping with hypersensitivity, he gradually came to the conclusion mentioned earlier, that the reactions were different because the problems were different; an idea which needs further consideration.

He spent a great deal of time observing children with autism and while I would not wish to contradict his findings, I have already shown that some facts can be misleading. Therefore I must ask whether his theory of three different problems is correct. If so, can it be supported by the 'evidence'? Let us look at each in turn.

Hypersensitivity

Those sufferers who have been able to share their experiences have talked about being hypersensitive to sound, sight and touch, which certainly verifies the first part of his assumption – as does personal observation and a survey by the Geneva Centre. This is further endorsed by Creak's observations on sensitivity to light and sound. These problems, as we have seen, may well provide the explanation for another of Creak's criteria: 'acute, excessive and illogical anxiety' as demonstrated by 'apparently illogical' fears; for with the knowledge we are gaining, such fears are fast beginning to seem perfectly logical.

Hypersensitivity could also contribute to the problem of 'food fads', for many sufferers are quite happy to have a restricted diet and may protest strongly if other foods are introduced. This previously puzzling behaviour becomes quite understandable when one realizes that, as Georgiana Stehli verified, they do not experience tastes in the way most people do – so that they may thoroughly enjoy foods which are generally considered to be quite bland, while relatively mild tastes could seem unbearably strong.

Delacato suggests that the demonstration of some behaviours is indicative of the area and degree of the problem. Thus the child who puts his fingers in his ears or covers them with his hands when a noise occurs, for instance, is likely to be hearing the noise at a greater volume than most people would:

which could indicate that some of his bizarre behaviours are in fact sensisms. If true, this information is of great value in identifying the problem area(s) and should enable the correct treatment to be given.

Now let us examine hypersensitivity a little further in relation to 'autistic' behaviour. Place yourself for a moment inside the mind of an infant suffering from autism, whose sensory perceptions are exaggerated and distorted. You are tiny and dependent on others for all your physical needs.

Your mother appears suddenly and picks you up to wash you. You suddenly become aware of a variety of strong and overpowering smells; a confusion of perfume, hairspray, soap and even her breath as she talks to you. Some of these smells are extremely unpleasant! Her touch causes great discomfort. She looks at you and talks to you. The sponge feels unpleasant. You are overwhelmed by and cannot cope with so many sensations at once. You react automatically by crying or struggling, fighting to the best of your ability in an attempt to 'get away'. She does not, cannot, understand. Thus the bonding process which should bring security and comfort is disrupted and she feels rejected.

Some sounds are magnified! Later you may cover your ears to block them out but for now you can only cry as 'they' [the parents] listen to the radio or turn the vacuum or the mixer on. Even as you get older the sounds they make and those that happen outside the home are still frightening. Your eyes do not develop past a certain stage and thus they play tricks on you so that things, both people and objects, are not always what they seem. You could make more sense of faces if the people came close, but then ... the smell! Your father's clothes smell of dogs and smoke. He breathes smoke and toothpaste over you when he speaks. Touch hurts you. Shops are a horrifying confusion of smells, sounds, fluorescent lights which make your head hurt – and people. People everywhere. Someone (a blur) suddenly appears in front of you and touches you unexpectedly. It's frightening! So you continue to shy away! Similar feelings are described with clarity by Georgiana Stehli who explains:

> People would bug me, I could hear them breathing and their stomachs growling across the room. Their voices were so high-pitched they got on my nerves. Sometimes a teacher would get too close and it really bugged me. Let's face it, nine out of ten people have halitosis. And their bodies smell too. (Pascoe 1991)

You never know what awful thing may happen next. You are unable to tell anyone how you feel. The only options open to you are to withdraw, shutting out sound and sight, hoping against hope that people will not touch you, or to panic and scream. You cling to things which are familiar because you understand them and feel safe with them, but you are terrified by new experiences (and protest strongly if they are forced on you) because you do not know what new horrors they may bring. You may even learn that behaving 'inappropriately' by screaming, kicking or biting achieves peace as the adults withdraw their demands.

You might feel less anxious as you rock back and forth (which of us has not, in childhood, obtained comfort from a swing?), bounce up and down or, as you get older, spin objects around. In *Emergence Labeled Autistic* (1986) Temple Grandin discusses the fact that spinning was a favourite activity which made her feel powerful and in control of things. When she was preoccupied with the movement of spinning herself or an object she saw and heard nothing else. People around were transparent. It was as if she were deaf; even loud noises did not startle her. It is interesting also to note from her comments in *Communication* that a mute child will often start making speech-like sounds while on a swing, whereas spinning around in a chair has been found to reduce hyperactivity, perhaps because the action causes an increase of endorphins (Grandin 1989).

The difficulties caused by abnormal sensory perceptions are so overwhelming that it is easy to see how they cause lifelong problems of comprehension. The child with extremely acute senses withdraws, shutting out the world and effectively making himself deaf and blind: which is why Georgiana only began to learn to speak clearly when she attended a school where lessons were conducted against a background of silence.

It is relevant here to quote from *The Sound of a Miracle* (1990), in which Annabel Stehli discusses her first visit to the Swiss psychologist Cecile Waurin:

> 'But when there is so much wrong with Georgie,' I said, 'why is this one symptom of abnormal hearing so important?'
> 'Because it is the key,' she said.
> 'The key to what?'
> 'The key to her recovery.'
> Dr Waurin explained that she had personally witnessed the recovery of many children as a result of having their hearing corrected, and that once this symptom was relieved, they were able to concentrate, learn and slough off their remaining inappropriate behaviour because basic communication became enjoyable for the first time in their lives. (Stehli 1990, p.154)

If we now return to consider the comments of the sufferers, some of the confusion and anomalies become understandable as, for instance, when Darren White talks of the bus 'sounding like thunder', which is indicative of hypersensitivity, but then says that on the return journey he 'did not hear it start'. It is perfectly feasible to suggest that Darren was indeed hypersensitive and that the reason for his lack of hearing on the return journey was simply, as Temple Grandin explained, because by then his defence mechanisms were effectively blocking the sound out.

Perhaps his reaction to some colours was because he found them glaring or overbright; which again suggests hypersensitivity. It is also possible that Darren's eyes, like those of the young child, did not work properly in conjunction with each other and that he therefore could not clearly focus on the object he was looking at – a very frightening experience.

There was also the accident in which he broke his collar-bone, but showed no reaction for several hours. Several possible explanations exist, some arising from the fundamental laws of biology. The body's response to pain is the production of endorphins which block the pain. If autism is indeed stress-related it is not far-fetched to suggest that some people may already have higher than normal levels of adrenaline which also functions as a pain killer. Then too we have the lack of body sense (proprioception) and/or symptoms of alexithymia, the effects of which have already been discussed.

Next we have the fact that the internal parts of the body are not endowed with the power of feeling pain due to sudden injury. Indeed bone, muscle and tendon are very insensitive and the ends of a broken bone may be scraped together without causing severe pain, although once the area surrounding the bone has become inflamed it will rapidly produce an excruciating, throbbing pain: a factor recognized with young children in whom fractures of the upper arm can sometimes remain undetected for several hours. It might therefore have been possible for some time to have elapsed before the blood vessels around the bone had pressed upon the nerves sufficiently to cause Darren pain of such severity that he complained.

Another theory arises from Bettleheim. He considered that the child, having withdrawn into himself, should logically be more sensitive to internal pain, but can often ignore quite serious pain because he is concentrating so hard on maintaining his defence system that he is able to exclude all stimuli regardless of its origin.

In support of his idea Bettleheim quoted several children who displayed similar behaviour when ill or injured, including one girl who was able to understand and respond through the use of speech but who, when suffering from appendicitis, neither showed pain nor responded when asked if something was wrong. It was only when she became comatose that an emergency exploratory operation uncovered a ruptured appendix, at least two days old. Similarly, I too knew one boy who amazed the staff at a casualty department because he agitatedly jumped up and down without apparent discomfort on an ankle which they eventually found to be sprained.

Conversely, it is interesting to note that Bettleheim also mentions the fact that once the child has gained a degree of trust, she often becomes so hypersensitive that she might complain about a pain, in a tooth for instance, long before any cavity can be found. Confusing indeed!

Certainly all the explanations above are plausible, although without more detailed investigation and knowledge of Darren we cannot reach any definitive conclusion except to acknowledge that it is possible that several of these things combined to enable him to carry on as normal despite his injury.

Apparently strange reactions to both touch and pain are the norm for many people with autism, as Gunilla Gerland explains:

> I had no inkling of the effect I had on other people, but they were provoked by my unmoved exterior. I was slapped and shaken, pushed by both my sister and the teachers, but I no longer felt any pain at all. In fact, my insensitivity to pain was by now as good as total. Until then I had just been insensitive to certain pains, but now nothing hurt at all. And yet I felt – my actual feelings were not shut off – because when I was aware that I had injured myself somewhere, I could sense something, a non-pain, which branched out into my body from the place where the injury was. But the fact was, it didn't hurt.
>
> On the other hand, one thing that was still very difficult to endure was light touches, the kind that went no more than skin deep. Everything else I hardly registered at all. (Gerland 1997, p.157)

Such accounts show that, without doubt, the effects of pain may not provoke the same response in a person with autism as they do in other people. The idea that light touch can hurt acutely, though, something which also affected Temple Grandin, may initially seem confusing, until we find that pain caused by injury to the skin is felt via a separate sense quite distinct from that of touch.

How then can we explain the fact that there are some hypersensitive people who hit or slap themselves? Initially I thought that some of this behaviour, especially in adults, had simply been learned over the years: a theory which appeared to be substantiated by one woman I knew. I had to query whether the explanation lay in her anxiety to be on her own, for in the past exclusion for 'bad' behaviour was her only means of escape (and respite) from the noisy hospital ward where she lived for several years.

Further observation, though, revealed that this type of self-abuse affected several hypersensitive people from different backgrounds who often hit or slapped their heads, or even their ears. Some people who suffer from severe and prolonged migraines try to ease the pain by hitting or banging their heads, which is generally a futile exercise, even though the release of adrenaline may cause the pain to diminish for a while. Perhaps, then, as Delacato thought, similar 'autistic' actions are actually a desperate attempt to 'remove the pain' caused by their hypersensitivity.

Donna Williams, who is hypersensitive to touch, provides two other possible explanations, neither of which are linked to hypersensitivity: hurting herself to 'test whether she was actually real' or banging her head at those times when her mind was 'screaming too loud' for her to use other methods to calm herself – an action which fought the tension by creating a hypnotic thudding rhythm (Williams 1992, pp.191–192).

Hyposensitivity

Carl Delacato identified hyposensitivity among those children with autism who eat indiscriminately, enjoy noise and strong smells and appear to feel no pain, as demonstrated by them hitting or slapping themselves. Is this really a separate condition to hypersensitivity? Perhaps the latter two reasons for self-abuse could apply equally here?

We should also ask whether these features bear any correlation to the child who suffers from MSD, whose attempts at spontaneous communication are almost nil, who dislikes being touched, spends most of his time in self-stimulating activities or ritualistic play, shows little curiosity, rarely relates in a positive way to visual, auditory or tactile stimulation and is often thought to be profoundly retarded? Many of these factors seem familiar, especially when we consider those who have residual vision/hearing and whose handicap is not that obvious.

Such children have a distorted perception of the world, have severe developmental lags and demonstrate apparently bizarre behaviour; problems which are compounded by frustration and often result in additional or increased inappropriate behaviours, eventually leading some of them to withdraw from the world. Although it is too early to draw conclusions, certainly so far the descriptions sound very similar.

In order to test Delacato's ideas, I carried out a survey. Unable to do this with children, I chose instead a group of thirty-three adults at an Autistic Community. While allowing for the fact that the picture was somewhat obscured by various 'learnt behaviours' and that as adults they had already undergone years of treatment, learning to cope with or compensate for their difficulties in various ways, I concluded that the two things did seem to be decidedly different; a finding backed up by my discussions with some of the parents and staff at the establishment.

It seemed that those adults who were hyposensitive fitted the description of the children with MSD except in the extent of their withdrawal, for although some had been very withdrawn in earlier times, none were now as withdrawn and many were making or beginning to make social contact – factors which one might also expect to find in adults with MSD.

White noise

This is the most difficult theory to either prove or disprove. Delacato defines it as a state in which sensory messages are garbled or overcome by 'internal' noises. He felt this type of child lives with a great deal of sensory interference where 'internal' sounds confuse incoming messages; for example, he hears his own heart beating and his digestion progressing and has a constant taste in his mouth. His body itches or he may shiver for no apparent reason and he attempts to deal with this by outbursts of tactile behaviours in which he will hit or slap himself. He also has many mannerisms associated with visual problems: touching, rubbing or poking his eyes frequently; looking inwards rather than out; and seeing things which are not there.

While some sufferers talk about hearing internal noises, and conditions such as tinnitus confirm that such disturbing noises certainly exist, there are many questions and some possible explanations for these phenomena.

How can we explain the fact that the 'internal sounds' could also happen if the person was hypersensitive to sound – as in Georgiana's case? And the auditory fuzz? Could it equally well apply to a person who was mildly hyposensitive or even one who is hypersensitive but whose hearing fluctuates? Might the itching be found in the person whose skin is hypersensitive? I have not yet found the answers to all of these questions, but certainly hitting and slapping oneself could be more a symptom of autism than a sensism.

Whilst dilated pupils could be indicative of hyposensitivity (or anxiety) I would ask whether trying to recreate colours by pushing or rubbing the eyes could be connected with visual sensitivity, that is, the eyes actually hurt. Alternatively we must also question whether they are linked to late onset problems, the child having seen colours but now finding them fading – about which more later.

In an earlier version of this book I suggested that the evidence was weighted against the idea of white noise, the reasons for my doubts being the questions I have already raised. The aim of updating this, though, is not merely to add new information but also to review each of my previous ideas to see if they are still valid. I do not doubt Delacato's observations so have to ask whether there is any way to explain them. One major candidate, which would fit in with the idea of digestive problems as well, is zinc – or rather a lack of it. This is because a deficiency can cause or contribute to a variety of sensory problems, including: tinnitus; unpleasant tastes in the mouth; a decreased ability to distinguish between different tastes and smells; and varied visual problems.

So now, with apologies to Delacato, I have to question my earlier judgement. Certainly there would seem to be at least one logical explanation for the problems which arise from 'white noise', although I had not come across it before. Maybe there are others as well? Perhaps further research into the subject will be able to clarify exactly why such problems arise and tell us how the third category of 'white noise' fits in with Tuormaa's third group in whom the problems fluctuate.

Conclusions

There are still many questions concerning the origins of these abnormal perceptions but I must agree wholeheartedly with Delacato when he said that careful observation of the sensisms would enable us to determine which senses were affected. It seems clear from the information about the visual and auditory problems that some of the bizarre mannerisms of autism fall within Delacato's category of sensisms and it is no coincidence that those which do mirror the mannerisms of children who are deaf or blind. So is there any explanation for the other stereotypes? To answer this we must look more closely at the varied effects which derive from sensory problems.

The effects of sensory problems

There have, over the years, been several investigations which have shown the vulnerability of the human personality to sensory deprivation. Donald Hebb, working in the 1950s, found that depriving a healthy university student of the sights, sounds and personal contacts that he would normally have, even for a few days, could disturb his personal identity. Such treatment could affect his capacity for critical judgement, give rise to hallucinations or alter his perception of 'his self' so that it was seen as 'separate from his body': experiments Hebb described as 'very unsettling' (Rimland 1964, p.103).

This and confirmatory results from other experiments clearly show that a few days of sensory deprivation can cause a person to become so totally disorientated that they begin to hallucinate. Could this account for the fact that a few people with autism do talk about hallucinatory experiences?

In 1975 Lipowski gathered together various scientific studies which had been carried out to determine the effects of sensory overload on the 'normal' population. He found that in every study the behaviour of the subjects resembled those behaviours which are termed 'autistic', ranging from withdrawal to obsessive or compulsive mannerisms. He concluded that such behaviours are triggered automatically by stress and could therefore be regarded as automatic 'defence mechanisms'.

This said, it is hardly surprising to find that sensory deprivation or overload (which may be caused by bombarding a person with noise at a certain pitch) has long been a technique associated with interrogation and torture. Although it may seem melodramatic, it requires little imagination (and, sadly, no exaggeration) to see that people with autism are indeed tortured by their senses, over which they have no control until they learn to withdraw.

Rimland suggested that the perceptual problems of those with autism could be severe enough to cause the type of psychosis (a mental disorder in which the person's contact with reality becomes distorted) found in those with sensory deprivation, enumerating apathy, detachment and irritability as characteristics of both conditions. Although I would question the use of the word psychosis in this context it is easy to see that people would also have severe problems if their reality is distorted, as we know it is.

Rimland also made one other very important comment which links this section to the comments made by Ornitz and by Newson in the previous section saying that: 'It is particularly noteworthy that a number of experiments have shown that it is not a lack of sensory stimulation *per se*, but lack of *meaningful* sensory stimulation, since subjects provided varying but non-meaningful stimuli also became psychologically disturbed' (Rimland 1964, p.104).

So just what would this be like if it happened to you? It is relatively easy to understand some of the problems caused by sensory deprivation but it may be more difficult to imagine those caused by abnormal perceptions – although anyone with severe tinnitus will understand the horrors of sound. Whilst I have already given an illustration of some of the visual problems, a simple experiment may help to re-create some of the difficulties which would be caused if your senses were extremely acute or did not receive the correct messages, (as in Darren White's case).

Look at the three well-known optical illusions shown in Figure 3.3. Concentrate on each of them in turn and you will gradually experience a switch in perspective as you move from one view to another. If at the same time you read this against the background noise of a radio tuned in-between stations to give an unclear signal and turned up until the sound has become unbearably loud, you will begin to understand some of the problems these people live with throughout each waking moment.

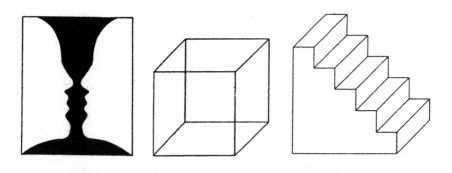

Figure 3.3 Optical illusions

Most of us are fortunate enough to have the ability to cope with illusions by recognizing them for what they are, but the writings of Darren and others lead me to assume that in their world, changes of perception or misleading perceptions, experienced both visually and through their other senses, are commonplace and 'normal'. Reality, as seen through all their early experiences, must (very frighteningly) be built upon shifting sands over which they have no control. It is hardly surprising if this provokes great anxiety.

We know that many people with autism do indeed lack meaningful sensory perceptions. How then do they cope with these overwhelming problems and the stresses they create? I would suggest that their only method of self-preservation is an automatic and defensive one in which the overwhelming stimuli and the anxiety they create are blocked out.

The following comments, all made by people who are hypersensitive, clearly indicate that this is so.

Georgiana Stehli said:

> I felt like I had to divert my attention a lot. I would try to get as far away as I could. Then I'd start daydreaming to distract myself. (Pascoe 1991)

Tony W comments:

> I daydreamed a lot ... I ... did my own thing such as make something and played ... not caring that anybody was in the room. (Volkmar and Cohen 1985)

Emilie F. told her mother that when she is daydreaming she cannot hear anything and cannot focus either, so that when people talk to her, all she sees is a blurred face with a mouth opening and closing and (like Miss Grandin) she hears absolutely nothing (Fisher 1987).

Are these really abnormal reactions? Surely not! Rather *very normal reactions to an abnormal situation!*

Combining these reactions with our knowledge of abnormal perceptions leads me to suggest that the stereotyped behaviours seen amongst people with autism should be divided into two categories:

1. **Sensisms** – those mannerisms which indicate the impaired sense; as with blindisms and deafisms.

2. **Autisms** – automatic defence mechanisms which are triggered by fear. These can be identified as *withdrawal* and/or *obsessions* or *compulsions* (the latter two of which may become increasingly complex or stylized in time).

Developing this idea further, it is easy to believe that the child can become trapped in an ever-decreasing circle, whereby the 'blocking' of stimuli leads them to starve their brains of the stimuli needed to learn; which further reinforces the confusion and the difficulties – as shown in Figure 3.4. To use a common analogy, they are 'not waving but drowning'!

It is small wonder that many people with autism appear to totally lack motivation. Apart from the immense effort needed to concentrate on and complete the simplest task, could this lack of motivation be yet another facet of fear? Are their other problems compounded because they are 'afraid' of trying new experiences, cannot predict the outcome or fear failure?

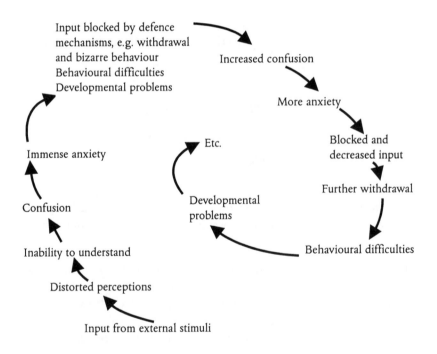

Figure 3.4 The ever-decreasing circle of stimuli-blocking

Why then, even now, do we insist that the cognitive process is at fault rather than looking more closely at the sufferers' perceptions and giving them the serious attention they warrant? Surely we have to conclude that, depending on severity, abnormal perceptions either cause serious delay or completely halt the 'normal' development of the comprehensive process, thereby leaving the child with continuing cognitive difficulties.

By the time I had reached this stage in the first edition I was firmly convinced that anxiety and fear play a large part in the development of autism. I still disagree with Bettleheim's assessment of the causes of anxiety, which I firmly believe are physical, but do agree that the withdrawal and obsessive or compulsive behaviours found in autism are reactions to a continuous overload of stress. Even whilst allowing for the new research incorporated in this edition this idea still appears valid. So, can I provide any further 'evidence' to strengthen this idea? I believe I can and hope that the inclusion of this section will at least give those who are sceptical some further food for thought.

We all know that the universal (and instinctive) reaction to physical pain such as a hot flame is withdrawal – moving one's hand from the object where possible. Similarly, as I hope we can agree, 'mental' anguish or severe stress can cause emotional withdrawal: a retreat into ourselves. So let us now look at some instances which detail the reactions to such stresses.

Moving away from autism, some inkling of this type of horror caused by stress can be found by looking at the reactions of ordinary 'normal' people forced, in recent years, to spend time in an isolated and terrifying situation over which they, quite literally, had no control.

Such terrors are eloquently described by Terry Waite, who spent the first years of his captivity in Lebanon in solitude, visited only by his guards who insisted that he was blindfolded whenever they were with him. Stopped from speaking out loud in case other hostages heard him, he lived one day at a time, spending much of that time writing a book in his head and revisiting his past.

Through his experiences we can gain an understanding of the devastating effects of solitude and fear; never knowing whether the advent of a guard heralded a beating or even death. Experiences and feelings recounted thus:

> I am again allowed one hour of freedom ... For some reason I am still interested in how far I walk so I count the number of paces. As I count, the familiar trance-like state comes over me. At the front of my mind I am still counting, elsewhere I am dreaming of all manner of things.
>
> It's become desperately important to arrange the day according to a pattern. If this is disturbed by the guards, it upsets me out of all proportion to the disturbance. I need a structure: ... and so the day passes. By creating a pattern in the vacuum in which I live, I exercise my choice, affirm my identity.

I recognise that I am in danger of swinging too violently in my emotions and must try to maintain a balance.

I invent the story all day and become absorbed in what is turning into a comic novel ... As night falls I find that I can't stop creating the narrative. My mind rushes on and on as the characters take shape in my imagination. I continue throughout the night and all the following day. After thirty six hours it is finished, and I am worn out. (Waite 1993, p.127, reproduced by permission of Hodder and Stoughton Ltd)

Terry Waite had a wealth of life experiences to draw upon in order to retain his sanity but even so he was aware of his desperate need for a routine and the fact that any interruption of this upset him unduly. The swings in emotion (against which he protected himself by retreating into his story); the obsessiveness of his novel; his counting and the solace which the latter brought are all things which should sound familiar to those who live or work with people with autism.

Are we to think that such experiences were unique? Of course not. There is indeed a common thread which runs through the accounts of all those treated in such an inhumane way as the writings of another hostage show. Thus, the writing of one of the American hostages, Brian Keenan says:

He had known more periods of isolation than the rest of us and had lost resolve, lost his capacity to be himself. Though we would have some hours of daylight during the day, I thought as I watched Frank that much of him remained in the dark ... But Frank had decided long ago to leave the reality of the situation. He was hurt deeply.

... His sense of reality was much distorted, and his conversation and behaviour evidenced the huge toll the deprivations and brutality had taken on him. For long periods he would sit with a blanket on his head, lost in his own world. For him we were not there. (Keenan 1992, p.285–286)

A description which explicitly demonstrates the horror of sensory deprivation arises when Keenan writes too of his reactions to a move (one of many) made to another prison during which he and John McCarthy were forced into a tiny compartment underneath a lorry for a lengthy agonizing journey made with them blindfolded, gagged and tightly bound:

All through those long, crushing, grinding hours this maniacal outburst continues. It is the only part of me alive during that hellish descent. I can't let go of it. I stare into the darkness within me and see its dark eye stare back. I feel that to give in to the darkness inside us is to live forever in the shadows, and I am not a shadow, I am a man ...

> This journey ends like all journeys. That the human mind can travel in those dark regions and return exhausted but intact is more a miracle than that word can ever convey. (Keenan 1992, p.285)

This quote may initially seem a little obscure in relation to the theme of autism but is included because I think the 'maniacal rage' felt by Brian Keenan parallels the 'blind panic' as those with autism are overwhelmed and engulfed by sensory experiences outside their control or by their own 'little understood' feelings: a panic which in some can seem like rage or, on occasions, result in 'flight'.

Brian Keenan also clearly describes his reaction to the continuing loneliness and deprivation and the apparent seductiveness of what he describes as 'madness':

> My days now seemed to pass in a slow, gentle delirium; like the comfort and reassurance that a child must feel as its mother rocks and sings it a lullaby. I found myself sitting on the floor and gently rocking myself back and forth, for how many minutes and how many hours I cannot tell. I looked wildly at the dead insect hanging in its cocoon. I felt a strange contentment. I derived reassurance from it. A new quality of strength pervaded me. I imagined I was moving inside that cocoon and I liked it. I was suspended in space. Minute and insignificant things in my cell intrigued me. I sat staring at them with fascination ... I felt no desire to leave this place. I found myself thinking with the shadows of panic rising in me that I was not ready to leave, that I did not want to leave...
>
> But then as if the coin of panic and fear had been flipped over I began to dread my growing attachment to this tiny cell. Something in me sensed danger and I told myself that I should not surrender to this temptation. I found an enemy within, powerful and insidious. I felt him caressing me and growing stronger, seeking to possess me. I had to find a way to take control, master my own mind, reasserting myself. I returned to an old strategy of thinking through the books that I had read as a child ... And began again to recall films and make them different or simply use them as a stepping stone to direct the mind away from this desire to remain captive. (Keenan 1992, p.73)

He returns to this theme later when sharing a cell with others, where we find that the seductiveness of refuge was common to all the hostages. As he says:

> Humanization is a reciprocal thing. We cannot know ourselves or declare ourselves human unless we share in the humanity of another ...
>
> The worlds we created and in which we found a refuge were more alluring than the vacant reality of the world outside ourselves ...

And this when there was no external stimulus, no window to look out
of, no door to walk through; when there was not the colour and the noise
of life. Then the idea of a return home was more than difficult. It was
frequently undesired ... (Keenan 1992, p.287)

So now you have shared a little of the fear and loneliness which engulfed the
hostages. Individual, albeit similar, experiences. Similar reactions to isolation,
deprivation and fear: panic, obsessiveness, compulsiveness, withdrawal,
distorted reality, a 'maniacal' rage, the need for structure, rocking ... Whilst the
recollection of things past was knowingly entered into, the compulsiveness
which overtook Terry Waite's story and the other features mentioned in the
hostages' moving accounts were not deliberately chosen 'avenues of escape'.
Just universal reactions to unrelenting fear and stress. No obscene experiments
are needed to replicate such things – man's inhumanity to man throughout the
years has produced all the 'evidence' the world should ever need.

Words are totally inadequate, but it is surely a great tribute to the strength
of the human spirit that people can not only survive such experiences but
manage, in spite of appalling treatment, to retain their sanity, compassion and a
sense of humour. A miracle indeed!

Such behaviours also echo those found amongst concentration camp
victims. Returning briefly to Bettleheim's theory I can only conclude that
although there was no social isolation in the concentration camps, the
prisoners faced such appalling and traumatic daily horrors, in addition to
starvation, that the reason only some became 'muslims' may be found in a
variety of factors including character, previous life experiences and (perhaps
most importantly?) inherent fragility. So are there any conclusions to be drawn
from this?

Remember Comings' idea that autism could be caused among people with
normal levels of serotonin because of other mutations or environmental
factors. The reactions of the hostages were caused by the stress-filled situations
and the environment in which they lived but other factors may have played a
part. We could also expect that the level of serotonin in the hostages would be
depleted because of a totally inadequate diet, the isolation, physical abuse,
their helplessness, sensory deprivation and the constant stress of the situation
– all of which would of course also alter the dopamine levels which are
involved in stereotyped behaviour.

My research has led me to believe that, because of metabolic problems,
abnormal perceptual experiences and processing difficulties, people with
autism live under constant stress, seeing 'the world' as a very frightening place
over which they have little control. This initiates various 'automatic' responses
which need no thought for they are common to everyone.

Thus they are forced to seek sanctuary within themselves; a sanctuary
which then becomes a prison, in which we can see constant reminders of the

shapes of fear. Unfortunately most people with autism have lived within their sanctuary/prison since early childhood and, unlike the hostages, have had few life experiences prior to their 'incarceration'. It is small wonder then that many of them appear to have no wish to build a lifeline to 'the world' or to escape their loneliness.

And yet to think so is to grossly oversimplify their situation, for while a number of people with autism see the world and 'us' as the enemy rather than identifying autism itself as the root problem, an increasing number are able to communicate their loneliness and question their 'handicap'. Many too, in their own way, seek to make contact with the 'world outside' or to escape. It is sad indeed that the escape route has so few clear signposts to help them. Those who fight and win the war (either on their own or with the help of others) are still a minority, although increasing knowledge may swell their numbers in time.

Moving on now, I have to ask whether there is any way to explain the similarities between autism and obsessive compulsive disorder. Returning to the hostages, we can conclude that although the abnormal situation in which they were forced to live made such reactions perfectly normal and understandable, to an untrained observer they might, during the periods of captivity they discussed, have seemed very similar to people suffering from OCD.

In obsessive compulsive disorder, the apparently bizarre behaviours are often seen (and treated) as the main problem. Fear generally appears to be absent even when the obsessions or compulsions are extreme. The experiences of the hostages, though, leads me to ask whether such people also suffer from overwhelming anxiety. This would certainly seem to be the case for as one adult sufferer of OCD, who is also a psychologist, says:

> Adult obsessives carry out their ritualized and aimless behaviours *to calm their piercing anxiety.* While there may be a slim justification for each obsession, OCs in their more rational moments know that what they're doing is totally senseless. What drives me and other obsessives to do this is the pain – the ceaseless anxiety that if we don't do it some unimaginably horrible event will occur. (Rapoport 1990, p.37, my emphasis)

The quote above and the fact that repetitive thoughts and stereotyped behaviours have a direct link to anxiety indicate that this could be the foundation of the obsessive compulsive behaviours. Thus anxiety would seem to be a common denominator between autism and OCD. What then is the dividing line? Could it be simply age and life experience?

Brain growth and development

Now, though, we need to make an apparent digression and return to the theories mentioned in the first chapter which divide into two groups – one which considers that the problems stem from psychological causes and the other which declares that they are of purely physical origin.

The argument regarding 'nature or nurture' has been applied to autism over the years and is obviously of vital importance for it determines the treatment method. Unfortunately each side has its own adherents, who often rigorously deny the validity or effectiveness of the 'alternative' approach. This has resulted in a continuing confusion which needs addressing if the sufferers are to gain the maximum benefit.

I will not deal with the issue of nurture in any great detail, for literature on the subject abounds. Certainly as most people would readily admit, it is of vital importance, particularly during our earliest formative years – an importance summed up in the Jesuit idea of 'give me a child until he is seven and he will be mine forever.'

While generally the word nurture relates only to the child's parenting and upbringing it must also be recognized that, for all of us, early development is subject to a number of other factors. When we are young, some, like moving house, are decided by our parents or circumstances such as job loss. Others like illness and hospitalization are beyond anyone's control. It must not be forgotten that these too can have an impact upon our lives which will be all the greater if happening within the first few years.

Now, though, to return to nature. Although he never explored it further, Freud once commented that the unconscious was based on the physiological processes, an idea supported by Pavlov's experiments, which explained functions previously considered to involve psychic activity on purely physiological grounds. In the most well known of these, he conditioned dogs to produce a normal reflex action, that of salivation, when they heard a bell ring rather than in response to the normal stimulus of food.

Moshe Feldenkrais, a physicist by profession, published a book in 1949 in which he looked at and analyzed the differences between nature and nurture in an attempt to reconcile the two apparently opposing views. While he concentrated on neuroses which may seem alien to autism, his ideas are worth considering, for they contain a useful study of anxiety which may have some bearing on our search.

His studies led him to suggest that functions which apparently stemmed from our emotional or mental state could actually be explained on purely physiological grounds. Feldenkrais believed that the most important primary reflex had, over the centuries, developed from an instinctive reaction to falling and suggested that any baby would, when startled by a loud noise, react by jerking her head – resulting in loss of balance and in fear. Even for an adult, an attack of vertigo is frightening because the person feels 'unbalanced' and the giddiness is accompanied by symptoms of fear, including rapid breathing, increased pulse rate, pallor, nausea and even vomiting. In the normal adult, this fear reflex should only be activated by the type of extreme fear found in a life-threatening situation, but in the neurotic person it is triggered by a comparatively minor stimulus, for it is a conditioned response which is 'misplaced'.

Feldenkrais concluded that emotional or mental disturbances and the negative feelings which stem from them were actually due to physical factors, that is, disturbed functioning of the central nervous system. This idea also led him to suggest that although psychological approaches might prove useful to people with neuroses they could never be wholly cured unless they also received some form of treatment to correct the physical problems.

Over the years his ideas have been upheld by research into the development of the central nervous system. However, before looking at the CNS and the role of the reflexes in greater detail I would first like to return to the work done by Doman and his staff in Philadelphia, which enabled them to help severely handicapped children suffering from a wide range of problems such as cerebral palsy or various 'mental' handicaps.

The staff at the Institutes for the Achievement of Human Potential regard brain growth and development as a dynamic process which can be stopped by severe brain injury or slowed by moderate brain injury but which, most significantly, can be speeded up by the correct treatment. They work on the theory that the brain cannot function at even the simplest level unless it receives incoming messages properly; hence a child who is damaged before learning to walk or speak will have far greater difficulty in learning such tasks than an adult who had lost his skills after a brain injury.

They developed an approach called *patterning*, which was designed to facilitate the transmission of messages to the brain, enabling the child to function in a particular area by re-creating the stages of development which he had missed. While the nature of the problem determines the precise methods used, the treatment gives the child stimulation in a particular area with increasing frequency, intensity and duration.

Although the technique is highly successful for many children who suffer from neurological problems or visual problems due to brain damage, there are some children for whom even intensive patterning proves ineffectual. Strangely, many of these children show little outward sign of brain damage for they are physically well-developed, but suffer rather from a wide variety of problems including hyperactivity, aphasia and dyslexia.

In order to try and remedy the situation for this group, Paul Dennison studied the relationship between the various parts of the brain and analyzed exactly how patterning worked. He determined that the clue to the problem lay in the relationship between the two parts of the brain.

The right hemisphere receives information via the senses, but although it can respond by making automatic (reflex) responses, it is unable to express itself or use the data creatively. This side also enables us to recognize a face in a crowd or name a song of which only a few notes have been heard. In contrast, the left hemisphere is logical, analytical and expressive and controls our ability to communicate. It is critical to our successful development that both hemispheres work together, for if they do not then various developmental problems occur.

Dennison identified the corpus callosum (midline) as extremely important in our development. Normally if development is unhindered, the two sides communicate spontaneously while the midline provides a 'bridge' over which messages pass. Thus the brain is able to listen, think, remember, make associations and internalize learning which is then expressed through actions or words. I would postulate that if, however, there are underlying problems which cause each side to work on its own or which hinder the development of this link the midline becomes a 'barrier' which blocks the process and great anxiety would ensue (Figure 3.5).

Left brain	Midline	Right brain
Critical, judgemental and analytical	Bridge to integrated learning *or* barrier leading to anxiety	Receives information from the senses but unable to use it creatively by itself
When working in isolation cannot remember what it learns and does things repetitively		

Figure 3.5 The midline as a bridge or barrier

Dennison came to the conclusion that whilst the process of cross-patterning would help to facilitate communication between the two hemispheres and improve myelination, a deeper type of repatterning was needed to bring about a more profound and permanent effect. In the 1970s he developed a more sophisticated 'treatment' called Educational Kinesiology (Brain Gym) (see Useful Addresses for contact details) which has proved of great success in helping people with developmental problems – as detailed in his book *Switching On* (1981).

Other studies into the CNS and the problems of neuro-developmental delay have been continued by researchers who recognize the importance of reflexes in our development and have carried out a detailed appraisal of their effect. It has long been acknowledged that the continued presence of some reflexes can contribute to, or be symptoms of, certain extreme conditions such as cerebral palsy, multiple sclerosis and Alzheimer's disease. It is now also believed that if these primitive reflexes remain after the first year they can cause or contribute to less serious problems which may disrupt normal development.

A closer look at these and the underlying problems suffered by children with dyslexia, aphasia and other developmental difficulties has resulted in some interesting ideas which deserve further and more detailed consideration because the research appears to add another dimension to the problems of abnormal sensory perceptions.

Peter Blythe of the Institute for Neuro-Physiological Psychology (INPP) (see Useful Addresses) mainly works with people with dyslexia although he also provides help for people with a variety of anxiety and panic disorders and some young children with more severe problems. He has spent many years studying the effects of such reflexes and he too has analyzed the reasons behind the inability of some children to respond to the patterning techniques carried out in Philadelphia. Blythe believes that the inability of some children to respond to patterning stems from a structural weakness in the central nervous system which creates problems as the child develops, for the body and mind are unable to work together in harmony.

This idea is supported by the work of Sally Goddard Blythe, from the same Institute, who says that the corpus callosum, cerebellum and vestibular system all undergo a spurt of myelination when the child is approximately seven or eight years old. She suggests that if the primitive reflexes are still active at this stage, they will interfere with the process and could possibly affect the instantaneous transmission between the hemispheres and the establishment of hemisphere specialization for specific tasks: both of which would obviously cause further difficulties. The results of their research therefore, whilst somewhat different, are not incompatible with Dennison's ideas.

A paper by Sally Goddard Blythe (1990) proposed that such problems could give rise to specific learning difficulties which then affect all the other systems in the body. Thus she suggests that although some children arrive in the world appearing 'normal' in all respects they are, from the very beginning, more vulnerable than they should be, an idea which seems to tie in with Kagan's study and the work of Brazelton.

Although such people appear to progress through life normally because they adapt, learning ways to cope or compensate for the weaknesses, their ability to function properly in specific areas which directly relate to presence of particular primitive reflexes may be impaired. This lack of development or malfunction might only become obvious at a later stage in the child's or adult's life. At this point he will begin to show demonstrable difficulties in several areas ranging from some panic disorders to those generally associated with dyslexia such as reading and writing or even the ability to understand language.

Goddard Blythe maintains that these aberrant reflexes may also be one of the underlying causes of elective mutism. Like others already mentioned in the course of this book she considers this to be a possible symptom of autism: characterized by the child who constantly and consistently refuses to speak either in one setting or in all, although he has both the physical ability to do so and a reasonable/good comprehension of language.

Such children will communicate with others through gestures of the hands and head and occasionally by single words or short sentences which may be spoken in a monotone. This problem may also be associated with other features such as excessive shyness, social isolation, withdrawal, clinging, temper tantrums, compulsive or controlling behaviour and sometimes bed-wetting. While elective mutism is often considered a psychological problem, for some children do indeed stop speaking following severe trauma, she believes that it can, in some cases, have an underlying physical basis.

The idea that some primitive reflexes are retained complements an earlier study by Minderaa and his colleagues (1985) in which certain primitive reflexes were found to be present in substantial numbers of children with autism. Although the reflexes tested were different to those mentioned in Sally Goddard Blythe's paper the authors postulated that in time the significance of their findings would provide a further insight to the problems of children with autism.

While all three papers are extremely interesting, I will only detail those reflexes which appear to have a direct bearing on our search. The first is the Moro reflex, which is the forerunner of the startle reflex and therefore the baby's instinctive reaction to danger. It is interesting to note that the emergence of this reflex approximately 9–12 weeks after conception coincides with the development of other vital systems, such as the vestibular system as well as the cerebellum and the hypothalamus.

Goddard Blythe felt that if the Moro reflex remained after birth some major problems would occur. These are detailed below, as are the child's probable reactions to such difficulties:

- The child will be hypersensitive in one or all sensory areas. He may 'feel' too much and therefore find close contact uncomfortable; a reaction which makes him seem rejecting. Paradoxically he is sensitive and may crave comfort, although he will have difficulty in expressing this or in demonstrating affection.

  His reaction to light is poor and bright lights can become a source of stress. Some children are so sensitive to alterations in light that they are constantly aware of things that most of us would 'block out', for example the flickering of fluorescent lights. When extreme, this 'overload' will cause one or more of the sensory channels to shut down, thereby blocking out the stimulus. When less extreme it will cause the child to tire rapidly and to lack concentration. This was certainly true of Donna Williams, who talks of the time when she worked in a shop whose ceiling was covered with fluorescent lights saying that: 'I was becoming terribly ill, finding it hard at times even to find the energy to lift an arm. I began to wear a sun visor and this prevented me from falling asleep under the effect of the lights' (Williams 1992, p.142).

- Adrenaline frequently 'floods' the system. As a result of this the child will try to anticipate or control future events so that he can avoid any 'unexpected' shock. Such children are frequently highly imaginative, possibly hyperactive and may suffer from night terrors (as some people with autism do).

- The child's level of internal excitation is high and, because he lives in a heightened state of stress, he can quickly reach 'overload'.

The tonic labyrinthine reflex (TLR) is concerned with balance. Equilibrium plays a vital role in the learning process as it provides us with a frame of reference from which to view the world. As the child develops and gains more control over his movements he becomes able to use both eyes and ears more effectively. If his balance is affected, the development of the eyes is also hampered. This may lead to the following problems:

- The child may constantly perceive the world as moving and readjusting. This will give him a distorted concept of his own size and may cause clumsiness. His view of distant objects and spatial relationships will also be confused – perhaps Darren who saw small shops as 'even smaller than they actually were' had this problem? He will have a poorly developed sense of direction which can affect his reading ability but in strange contrast he may also display an incredible memory for certain things, such as recognizing places he has only visited once before.

- The child may not necessarily see the object he is focusing on. A faulty vision of reality can cause tremendous learning difficulties and may also produce a lack of concentration as the child is unable to ignore the distractions which surround him and cannot distinguish a part from the whole. Thus he is unable to concentrate on one word as the whole paragraph keeps intruding.

- There may be automatic movements of the limbs when the body is lying down and a thrusting forward of the tongue when the head is in a certain position – factors which explain why some new-born babies arch away from the mother and have difficulty in feeding when held in the classic 'head in the crook of arm' position. As the tongue's movements during feeding not only contribute to our survival but also form the basis of the movements involved in speech, the tongue thrust of such children can later hinder the process of producing clear speech.

A combination of the Moro reflex and the tonic labyrinthine reflex (TLR) would lead to slightly different problems which culminate in certain identifiable difficulties:

- The child will have a low arousal threshold, suffering from *hypo*sensitivity, to which his system reacts by an increasing state of arousal and *hyper*activity. This in turn leads to an increase in tension and internal excitation which, when prolonged, results in fatigue and thus reduces the performance, so that his body can only maintain its equilibrium by struggling against the fatigue. This creates a vicious circle for his body can only maintain its balance by increasing the level of arousal, boosting adrenaline into the system through more excitement, constant activity, violent panic or angry outbursts.

- The child may react badly to some mild sedatives. As his body needs constant activity to keep it going, it reacts to the sedation by increasing the internal level of arousal and he may therefore become more hyperactive.

Finally we come to the asymmetrical tonic neck reflex (ATNR) which is concerned with how the tone of the muscles is affected by the position of the head. This helps in the complex process of hand/eye co-ordination and its continued presence can also affect balance, motor control and laterality so that:

- When the child moves her head to the right her body will stiffen on the right.

- Her head and eyes have difficulty in working independently and she will compensate for this by turning her head in the direction she is looking.

Thus the continued presence of the ATNR into later life will also impair the vision, giving rise to further problems as the movement of the head results in a temporary loss of image causing fragments of the picture to be missed.

A brief summary of the problems which could be caused by the Moro reflex and the tonic labyrinthine reflex is shown in Figure 3.6. A combination of both gives a picture of the hyposensitive child as shown in Figure 3.7.

Thus it seems as if the well researched and documented area of aberrant reflexes provides a major piece of the puzzle, for their effects would certainly explain some of the odd features connected to autism and Asperger's syndrome like those observed by Delacato and frequently commented on by the sufferers themselves. Perhaps, too, it enables us to make sense of Gunilla Gerland's problems in the gym:

> At a certain age we were supposed to be able to turn somersaults, and I was the only one who couldn't. When I got on all fours and put my head down, all sense of space, direction and body simply vanished. (Gerland 1997, p.113)

The work at the INNP seems to provide an explanation for the some of the physical effects already mentioned, for example hypersensitivity. If we add it to the information given by the sufferers we can begin to imagine just what some of the visual problems are actually like. Bear in mind too that some people may suffer from a combination of these.

First hypersensitivity (perhaps where too much light enters the eye?). This effect can be seen when you shine a very bright light onto a picture or look at other people's faces on a bright summer's day. The light will not only bleach some of the colour from the picture but also will obscure the finer features of other people so that only the most prominent parts are seen: something which would seem to explain the description of my husband mentioned in Chapter 2.

Try now to achieve the opposite effect by sitting in a darkened room or wearing sunglasses when inside the house. This again causes the colours and details of normal everyday objects to fade with results similar to those above. If this is how sufferers actually see then one would assume that the hypersensitive person would see more clearly in dim light and his problems would be worsened by strong sunlight whilst the opposite would be true of the hyposensitive person.

The next few abnormal perceptions can be imagined fairly easily, as in Darren White's description of things shrinking. This is reminiscent of Alice in Wonderland and could seem amusing but as a reality it would be horrendous. Then the double image mentioned by Richard Attfield (which would be caused if the eyes did not work together properly) – just looking at blurred print is difficult enough but if all your surroundings were seen in this way it would be extremely unpleasant and frightening. Then there is magnification, as in Georgie Stehli's description of a strand of hair.

Finally, try if you can to imagine lacking the ability to see movement – as when the ATNR reflex is retained. How would you see or avoid moving objects? Any one of these problems when as severe as in autism would cause enormous difficulties but when other people disregard them and expect you to act in a normal manner … how would you cope if it were you?

It will be interesting to know what effect these distortions actually have on the eye. Are there links here with the findings seen in studies on dyslexia in which the cells in the area of the magno system are more disorganized and approximately 25 per cent smaller, thereby giving slower reactions?

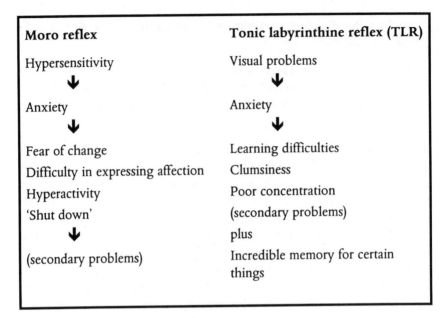

Figure 3.6 *Problems caused by Moro reflex and tonic labyrinthine reflex*

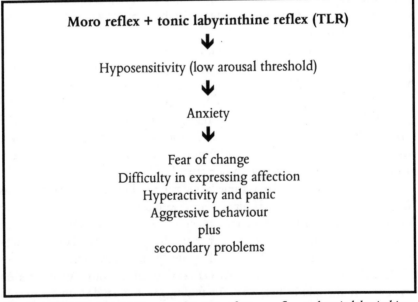

Figure 3.7 *Problems caused by a combination of Moro reflex and tonic labyrinthine reflex*

John Downing, an American neuroscientist, has developed a light treatment which is being used successfully with people with variety of disorders including hyperactivity, ADD, dyslexia and OCD. He suggests that some people have a reduced or narrowed perspective and that some visual problems are related to an enlarged blind spot.

One must also query whether the rods which are sensitive to dim light (scotopic) and the cones which are sensitive to bright light (photopic) in the eye work as they well as they should. Certainly if development is disrupted, as it obviously is in children with aberrant reflexes, then it would be no surprise to find that the normal development of vision is also impaired. It is interesting to find that Downing's technique also enhances such cells.

Could the work done at the INNP also explain the differences between individuals suffering from the 'same' condition, not only autism and Asperger's syndrome but also ADHD, dyslexia and TS? Certainly the TLR reflex seems to have a connection with Asperger's syndrome. Or does it? Perhaps it fits just too neatly?

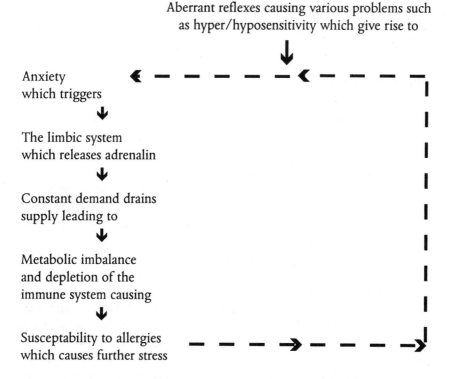

Figure 3.8 Possible causal sequence of problems related to aberrant reflexes (Based on the ideas of Sally Goddard Blythe, personal communication)

Moving on, we find that Sally Goddard Blythe (personal communication) suggests that one possible causal sequence could be similar to that shown in Figure 3.8, which includes metabolic disorders. It definitely makes sense, but whether it is so or not remains to be determined.

The reason why these reflexes remain is still unclear. Goddard Blythe and her colleagues feel that they can be triggered (generally temporarily) by vaccine or anaesthetic but also believe that approximately 50 per cent of the problem may be hereditary, sometimes stretching back as far as four generations. Thus a parent who has aberrant reflexes but who learns to adapt to the problems they cause could still pass an inbuilt 'weakness' down the line. It would be interesting to know how many families in which such reflexes occur also have a history of metabolic problems.

So now you have had the opportunity to read through the various factors which make up at least part of the puzzle of autism. Some of you may even have found aspects of yourself within this book. I certainly have, recognizing with interest why I am hypersensitive to some sounds, have mild visual problems, etc. It is still more fascinating to determine just how such factors affect daily life and behaviour.

Before coming to any conclusions, though, I would like to summarize some of the main facts and assess the various aspects to determine, if possible, which are specific to autism and just what part each plays in the development of this disorder.

Summary, discussion and ideas

Inheritance and causes

Here we must first consider the idea of a polygenic inheritance whereby various genes, inherited from both parents, combine to cause a specific disorder: an assumption which certainly seems logical, as too does the idea that many of the conditions investigated in this book are related.

It is believed that it is the inheritance of particular clusters of genes which predispose a person to developing autism, Asperger's syndrome and other related disorders. As previously mentioned, two chromosomes have now been identified by an international consortium of clinicians and scientists: the first on chromosome 7q and the second near one end of chromosome 16p.

Further research is ongoing and the researchers hope to identify the exact genes in time. Although there are very many potential genes, the researchers have already identified several possible candidates for closer examination. None of these tally with those mentioned by Comings (see Appendix J) although Edwin Cook and his colleagues (Cook and Leventhal 1996) believe that there is much to suggest that a dysfunction of the tryptophan/serotonin system is involved in many of the symptoms of this disorder. It will be very interesting to see if any of the gene research bears their ideas out and still more fascinating to find out just what the physical consequences of this inheritance are – that is, what the genes actually do.

Even without the answers we can surmise that such a genetic predisposition could in some way lead to disrupted development. So too, of course, could a variety of other factors including prenatal/birth problems, some of which could also cause a degree of neurodevelopmental delay.

Developmental difficulties would obviously result in problems at an early stage and could account for the aberrant reflexes; the fact that some babies are born with a 'hypersensitive' nervous system; perceptual problems; and/or the fact that some children have a slow/delayed physical development which is particularly noticeable in adolescence and adulthood. Perhaps it also explains why some people with autism have faulty myelination.

Comings found that some parents and relatives of people with Tourette's syndrome have low serotonin levels. Combine this then with the following findings:

- Many children in the AiA group have one parent who suffers from migraine whilst the other has allergies.

- Low sulphation levels are relatively common amongst the general population.

- Like those with TS, people with asthma also have abnormalities in their tryptophan metabolism.

As treatment for intestinal/digestive dysfunctions helps alleviate the symptoms of autism (as well as gluten allergies and juvenile asthma), we have to ask whether these factors indicate that some of the most significant symptoms amongst the parents and relatives will prove to be purely physical.

Shattock has long suggested that the abnormal urinary compounds found in over 80 per cent of sufferers might be opioid peptides. If research confirms this, the severe effect on brain function could account for many of the problems found in autism and Asperger's syndrome. Be that as it may, it is becoming clear that for many people the digestive system is implicated in the problems of autism. Research in several different areas and the benefits of secretin suggest that some of the problems originate in the liver, gut or pancreas and that these may then have devastating effects, as summarized in Figure 3.9.

Taking all these factors into account we can surmise that the reasons behind the success of secretin probably arise because correcting the problems in the digestive system improves the efficiency of the immune system. This, in turn, would reduce any food sensitivities and allow nutrients to be assimilated correctly; all of which would presumably result in a reduction of opioid peptides. One could also hypothesize that this should correct the serotonin levels, but whether this is so remains to be seen. Perhaps in time we will also be able to determine which of these factors were involved in the cessation of Parker's tics.

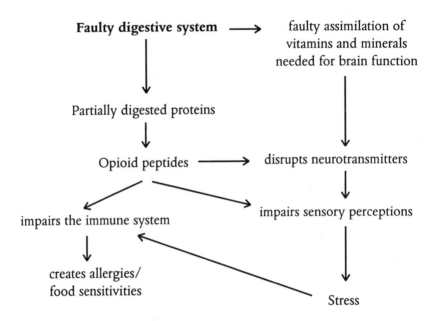

Figure 3.9 The digestive system and some problems of autism

Can we determine how or when the problems start? There are two obvious possibilities:

1. The genetic inheritance actually produces a faulty digestive system. Thus the problems could begin either before birth (where the foetus is affected by the mother's food) or at some point after birth – something which might be indicated by the type of allergy.

2. Physical problems like leaky gut, bowel disease, etc. and the consequent disruption of the digestive system begin at a later stage.

Either way it would seem that the production of opioid peptides could play a part in disrupting the normal developmental milestones, thus giving rise to neuro-developmental delay. It will be interesting to know whether such food intolerances or the underlying digestive problems alter or interfere with the blood flow to the frontal lobes as they do in ADHD.

At this point it would be helpful to take another look at allergy-induced autism, focusing specifically on the word 'induced'. It has been suggested that the onset may be the final stage in a slowly developing illness. There are several other points which might have some bearing on this:

- Many children developing problems at this stage have a gluten allergy.

- Children in this group often have one parent with migraine and the other with allergies.

- There are possible links between the MMR vaccine and intestinal problems.

- People with Tourette's syndrome often demonstrate symptoms of ADHD before the final onset of TS.

- The development of people with phenylketonuria remains normal if the problems are identified early and a diet is implemented.

If autism were to follow the pattern of these other disorders then two interesting ideas arise. The first, using Tourette's syndrome as a model, would suggest that it is possible that the children in the AiA group might demonstrate 'early symptoms' of neuro-developmental delay which could develop as ADD or ADHD. This would certainly account for any oddity of behaviour and could easily be mistaken for the beginnings of an 'illness'.

We could also postulate that this developmental delay would leave the child more vulnerable than others to additional problems arising from the onset of food or other intolerances, illness or infection. This could leave the child unusually vulnerable and thus any of these things could have a more devastating effect than normal, 'tipping the balance', so that the child's slight problems are aggravated and assume the severity of those associated with autism.

Does such a severe effect stem from an increase in the opioid peptides in the brain or because the mildly abnormal perceptions suddenly deteriorate and the child's whole world is thrown into chaos? An educated guess would suggest that both might play a part and that, as the peptides can produce perceptual problems, the former might, in some cases, cause or exacerbate the latter.

That then is a possible explanation for the AiA group, but could these developmental problems perhaps lead to an abnormal reaction to vaccine? At present it is hard to sort the fact from the fiction in relation to the damage which can be done by the MMR or other vaccines, for the arguments continue. Where does the truth lie? It is said that the children who had a severe reaction after vaccination and then developed symptoms of autism were all developing normally. Is that correct?

It has been postulated that some component of the MMR vaccine may cause damage to the blood brain barrier which thereafter allows opioid peptides to enter the brain more freely than they should – but perhaps we should also ask whether Sally Goddard Blythe's theory has any relevance here. Could it be that the vaccine (like anaesthetic) can instigate a return to previous 'submerged' reflexes? And that the bowel disease, opioid peptides, a damaged blood brain barrier, or even a combination of all these, prevents the sensory system correcting itself? If so we should expect to find that some children who have the new bowel disease also have perceptual problems, including an aversion to touch, auditory difficulties and bizarre visual experiences.

I have not been able to ascertain how many of the children in this group have such problems, for this question has not been asked before and I lacked the time to follow it up. It is, however, true in the tragic case of two young brothers who are now both affected by autism and in whom the onset appears to have a link with the vaccine. Both have bowel disease and their mother describes a degenerating situation in which the sensory problems have gradually gained in prominence.

Thus the eldest child now suffers from hypersensitivity to touch and sound. He originally demonstrated no visual problems but just a few months later showed clear signs of severe visual disturbances which he was able to explain through his drawing. This indicates that he is now actually registering two separate images so that his mother appears twice – once as a large figure near him and secondly as a small mummy at a distance, as the picture shows.

Not only do his eyes now trouble him greatly, being very dry, something he attempts to remedy by rubbing them with saliva, but, as the picture indicates, his eyes are now actually working quite independently from one another at times. A horrendous situation to find oneself in!

Meanwhile the younger has, according to school reports, gone from showing no signs of clumsiness to being identified as a clumsy child in a relatively short period of time. Sadly he now says that he can no longer see colours and, worst of all, his mother feels that he is gradually 'losing touch with his body'. Thus facial expressions and movements which were once freely done are becoming increasingly more difficult for him and (to his mother's distress) now attract attention and laughter for they have lost their spontaneity and are both laboured and exaggerated.

It is small wonder then that he has increasing behavioural problems, for he has suddenly found himself wrenched out of a normal childhood and thrust into a strange and incomprehensible world where his perceptual experiences no longer match previously known realities. How is he to understand a world turned into chaos? How indeed would we?

Of course doubts still remain as to whether, in such cases, the vaccine causes the autism. Many people think the link tenuous. The suggestion is that it is pure coincidence because the vaccine is given at approximately the age/time when one would normally expect the onset of such problems. Even though it is still officially believed that there is no link with the vaccine, questions remain to be asked – and answered – of which I include but a few.

Does the vaccine cause this new bowel disorder? If not, what does? What percentage of these children now have severe sensory problems? Are these being taken into account when looking at the possible links? How many of these children have another affected sibling who also developed autism or a related disorder after a vaccination? Were children in that group particularly vulnerable to the vaccine and if so why? For example, did any of them have an immature immune system, signs of NDD or a common genetic link which might predispose them to autism?

It is vital that the answers are found so that parents can either be totally reassured or, alternatively, so that we can determine just who will benefit from the vaccine and whether some children would be better with separate doses, homeopathic preventative measures, or even just take the risk of being left unvaccinated against one or more components of measles, mumps or rubella.

Indeed, if any component of the vaccine is eventually implicated in the bowel disease or in autism other questions will arise. In particular, were any cases of autism which developed prior to the introduction of the triple vaccine linked with a particular single vaccine and could any of the sufferers also be suffering from undetected intestinal disease?

It is time, though, to return to look at opioid peptides more closely. We have seen that high levels may be due to several different factors:

- disrupted development;
- incomplete digestive process;
- high serotonin levels;
- stress.

The first two have already been discussed in some detail, but what of the remaining points? Whilst the researchers link their findings to the digestive problems, particularly in relation to casein and gluten, they also need some attention. High serotonin levels have been found in approximately 33 per cent of people with autism. While obviously there is a big discrepancy between this percentage and the 80 per cent found to have abnormal urinary compounds as identified by Dr Shattock, perhaps these contribute to the levels of peptides in some people. It will be interesting to know why these high levels arise and when they begin.

Many of the problems of hyper- or hyposensitivity, which I believe cause stress, begin at an early age and do seem to affect a great majority of sufferers. Indeed an educated guess in line with the small study carried out by the Geneva centre would suggest a figure of approximately 80 per cent. This, though, leaves us with another conundrum for stress can lead to digestive problems including reduced enzyme activity in the gut and ulcerative colitis or irritable bowel disease. A vicious circle perhaps?

While the dietary factors obviously play a major part there is no real conflict between these ideas, for all these things could happen – albeit perhaps at different times. Thus delayed embryonic development could happen due to a faulty gene or a variety of other reasons, leaving the system immature and inherently fragile. This would obviously affect the child's future development. Alternatively, physical problems such as leaky gut or bowel disorder, abnormal levels of serotonin or peptides arising after birth, could also play a part – although here perhaps the problems would start at a later date.

It was initially confusing to find that some people with non-specific 'mental handicaps' and a group of people with Down's syndrome also had abnormal compounds in their urine. Can this perhaps be explained by the fact that many of these people also have 'autistic features' and that those with Down's syndrome do have an intolerance of milk?

Once again questions arise. We know that some children with ADHD show very definite food intolerances which seriously affect their behaviour. Considering the strength of the relationship between ADHD, Tourette's syndrome and the links with OCD it would be interesting to know whether people in these groups also have similar abnormal compounds. So too with people with candida, many of whom are intolerant of certain foods. One article refers to the 'fuzzy thinking' of people with candida: an idea which could surely be explained by opioid activity.

Having written this, I found that Paul Shattock and Dawn Savery already had some of the answers although they tended to classify them as 'false positives'. They found that many of the subjects who gave such results were completely devoid of clinical symptoms whilst others gave a clear indication of some other type of disorder – dyslexia, ADD, ADHD and OCD being mentioned specifically. It is interesting to note that in such cases the profile of compounds was similar to those found amongst people with Asperger's syndrome (i.e. 'high functioning'), rather than those with more severe forms of autism.

Do not misunderstand. The fact that some of these things are found amongst those with other disorders or even those with physical illness does not in any way decry the great importance of this research. The progress shown by those who have undergone appropriate treatment surely indicates that the intestinal and dietary factors and opioid peptides play a very major part either in the development or the exacerbation of autism.

While many of the people in these other groups do not demonstrate symptoms at a particularly early age, children with ADD or ADHD often begin to demonstrate problems between 18 months and 2 years. It would be interesting to know whether (like the AiA group) this is when the food intolerances are triggered and whether any such children develop problems post-vaccination.

Why though are the problems less severe than in autism? Is the food intolerance of the child with ADHD 'less harmful' to mental functioning because this is where the particular combination of genes finally shows its effect or are there other factors which could be significant? We know that some ADHD children have an abnormal blood flow to the part of the brain which controls the input of stimuli. Are any children with autism/Asperger's syndrome similarly affected?

At present there are no answers and the complexities of the digestive system and the brain will continue to make the identification of the 'fault(s)' difficult (although not impossible). Hopefully, though, further research into this area may begin to throw more light on such questions. Perhaps the fact that some of the research into pancreatic enzymes has already been done (albeit not in relation to autism) will shorten the time needed for research. I look forward to the outcome.

It is being said that treatment for the dietary problems effectively 'cures' the abnormal perceptions. This would seem perfectly feasible in young children but I would like to see more research in this area as I am not convinced that this is always so. While it certainly improves the person's ability to cope with many perceptual experiences which previously had a devastating effect, several people I know have sensory problems even after such treatment and continue to find other remedies helpful.

I am also told that those who undergo treatment at a later age still have cognitive deficits, which is only to be expected. We need to be very careful, though, not to confuse these with problems related to any remaining sensory difficulties or NDD. Each person will need individual assessment after treatment so that any further programmes can be specifically geared to their needs.

Abnormal perceptions

Although I have frequently discussed these, much of the 'evidence' I have presented has come from the sufferers themselves or from professionals like Delacato whose findings are based on lengthy observation. Judging from the way the sufferers are so often ignored and the reception that Delacato's ideas received, such things do not convince the sceptics.

Solid research has been done in the field of neurodevelopmental delay but, while the aberrant reflexes are clearly evident when tested for there is little general awareness about the methods used to test objectively for the other factors such as hyper- and hyposensitivities in vision and hearing. To date it has been all too easy for some professionals working in autism to dismiss such ideas and observations.

So is there any way of providing the proof necessary to convince the sceptics? Happily, in the two most important areas, the answer is now yes. I refer here of course to sight, which accounts for approximately 70–80 per cent of sensory input to the brain.

This confirmation comes from the work of Ian Jordan, an optician and inventor who has a keen interest in dyslexia. He has now clearly identified a variety of problems found in people with visual dyslexia which could cause the type of difficulties already mentioned in relation to both dyslexia and autism. Jordan lists those symptoms that may be noticed by the professional, to which I have added a few comments and questions (in italics):

- *Accommodation anomalies*
  In those children exhibiting visual dyslexia a significant reduction of focusing ability is very often experienced.

- *Convergence insufficiency*
  Normally both eyes rotate to a position to fixate on a close object. The ability to do this may be impaired in sufferers of visual dyslexia.

- *Saccadal eye movement problems*
  It has been shown that many children have problems with eye movements in reading. In the process of reading the eye has to focus, converge, move to another word, refocus, use small corrective movements and the brain must suppress any unwanted information. These small, jerky movements from word to word are called saccadal eye movements and problems associated with visual dyslexia may be due to a malfunction of these.

- *Pursuit deficiencies*
  People with visual dyslexia may have difficulties following moving objects. For example, they might be unable to follow the smooth movement of a squash ball.

- *Photophobia*
  Photophobia is the dislike of light. This can vary significantly from one person to another and gives rise to screwing up and watering of the eyes. In extreme cases it can be debilitating. *Having a mild form of this problem myself I worry that the word 'dislike' could give the wrong impression, that is, that it is a psychological problem rather than a physical one. I would instead concur with Helen Irlen's description of it as 'sensitivity to light' for it is certainly a physical inability to cope with light from a particular range of the spectrum. When extreme it could clearly account for the loss of definition similar to that found when looking at things under a very bright light.*

- *Unexplained visual acuity reduction*
  In a significant number of children with visual problems there is an unexplained reduction in visual acuity. It may be a binocular reduction or be observed in one eye only. *Could this relate to hyposensitivity and/or a lack of essential fatty acids?*

- *Fusional reserve reduction*
  In a significant proportion of those with reading problems there is a reduction in the ability to fuse the separate images from the eyes – *an idea which could perhaps explain the child's description of seeing two images of his mother.* (Jordan 1998, p.10)

Thus you can see that several of these problems have clear links with neuro-developmental delay and, hopefully, even the sceptics will now begin to fully appreciate the difficulties they cause. It is small wonder then that some experts comment that people with autism have a narrow focus but no grasp of the 'big' picture – for that is often literally true.

So now can I provide any proof to convince people of the auditory difficulties so frequently mentioned? Certainly auditory problems similar to some of those discussed by Bérard in relation to dyslexia are now actually being identified by the use of a SCAN test which is used to detect central auditory processing disorder (CAPD) (see Appendix D).

Such problems are found in children whose hearing is said to be essentially normal but who have problems in understanding speech when it is competing against background noise. These difficulties which, to me, sound similar to an inability to habituate can impair the child's ability to fulfil their potential in school or work.

Two points arise from the results of the SCAN tests which are particularly noteworthy, both of which point in a similar direction. First, it has been found that the ability to select a word from amongst background noise improves with age and maturation. Thus a low score on this aspect of the SCAN test is indicative of a delay in the development of the auditory system.

Second, it was found that when two different words were played into both ears simultaneously, young children typically showed better scores in the right ear than the left. This changes as the auditory pathways of the brain mature so that older children score more evenly. This indicates that the older child who demonstrates a better score on the right may have some developmental delay within the auditory system.

Hyperacusis, too, clearly exists as do its effects and can be measured objectively in several ways. Josephine Marriage has researched this subject and, interestingly, actually defines hyperacusis as a condition which has 'an impact on the quality of life by restricting what a patient chooses to do in day-to-day life' (Marriage and Barnes 1995).

Her research showed that the types of sounds which cause problems are very individual, varying in both intensity and frequency. They range from washing machines and vacuum cleaners to something as relatively quiet as a tissue being taken out of a box, a newspaper being folded or a distant dog barking. In my more informal research people have also mentioned a clock ticking in the flat next door, another person eating, a dog panting – even when in another room – and some low intensity sounds. All can be intolerable to people with hyperacusis and, in Marriage's words, cause 'physical pain' and 'nerve grating' as well as physical effects of sweating and an increase in the pulse rate.

Marriage notes that while many hyperacusics are reported to have normal audiograms their sound intolerance is often part of a larger 'global' sensitivity which includes bright lights and tactile stimulation. She concludes her study by suggesting that there may be a correlation between hyperacusis and a serotonin dysfunction which might relate to the fact that this hypersensitivity is known to co-occur with some other conditions including migraine, depression and B6 deficiency. I would also suggest that there is often a relationship between hyperacusis and an intolerance of loud noises – although exactly how this works is unclear.

There is also a study from Cornell University (Kiernan 1997) which seems to be relevant to this subject. The researchers found that children (aged seven to eight) who attended a school on the flight path of a nearby airport not only had poorer reading skills than other children but also, most importantly in this context, found it harder to understand and recognize spoken words. They concluded that this was because, in order to cope with all the noise, the children had learnt to 'filter out' certain sounds including speech as, I would contend, do many children with autism.

While much can be done by observation, combined with a knowledge of the problems which can arise from hyperacusis and the various visual problems, most of these difficulties can now be objectively and accurately tested. I hope that in the future all those diagnosed with autism will automatically be assessed and, where appropriate, treated for such problems.

So what then are we to make of the role of abnormal perceptions? We already know that varying degrees of this are found in a small percentage of the 'normal' population as well as in a larger proportion of those with dyslexia, ADHD, MSD and Down's syndrome and have been observed in other 'non-specific "mental" handicaps' too.

The parallel with deaf or blind children too is clear, for we can see that any child with such perceptual difficulties has much in common with them, but is far more handicapped by additional problems in the other senses. Only in autism and Asperger's syndrome (and perhaps some cases of MSD) do we find abnormal perceptions which generally cause severe distortions on *all* sensory channels thereby leaving the person living in a bizarre world where they neither see, nor hear, nor feel, nor taste, nor smell properly.

The story of Helen Keller, who became deaf and blind after an illness when she was nineteen months old, but whose other senses remained intact, vividly demonstrates the problems that such children face, as all communication with her was initially through touch. If that touch causes pain, or one cannot feel it properly, how does one receive help? To reiterate Rimland's point: '… it is not lack of sensory stimulation *per se*, but lack of meaningful sensory stimulation which is so disturbing' (Rimland 1964, p.104).

As I have already said, these difficulties will not be so obvious in the early months although the aberrant reflexes may cause problems with touch so that the child arches away from the mother when feeding or cries when held. While his response to sound will be unusual and cause increasing concern (and questions of deafness), the visual problems are less obvious although the hyper child may find bright lights difficult to cope with and the hypo child may seem to open their eyes very wide or blink less than normal.

The Developmental Profile of the Institutes for the Achievement of Human Potential suggests that convergence of vision takes place between 6 months and 24 months, 12 months being the average. It would hardly be surprising if the enormity of these sensory difficulties and their consequences were often not recognized until their overwhelming nature had begun to cause a lack of social interaction, communication problems and sensisms as well as all those defensive mechanisms which we term autism, that is, the development of compulsions or obsessions. Thus, unsurprisingly, I would add my voice to all those others who have suggested that for the majority of sufferers such sensory distortions play a major part in the creation of autism and Asperger's syndrome.

How these perceptual problems arise is still questionable. Certainly there is evidence to suggest that some are inherited. Then we have two stories which suggest that similar effects (which may or may not be reversible) can arise from some illnesses. One is an account of the onset of 'autistic' symptoms following severe illness when a child, after severe convulsions, suddenly began to show signs of hypersensitivity, blocking her ears and shielding her eyes. Second is the fact that a friend of mine, whilst recovering from meningitis, suffered for a time from severe auditory and visual problems. We know that aberrant reflexes can be 'triggered' by anaesthetic but whether this is irreversible and whether vaccine could have the same effect remains to be determined.

It is now clear that abnormal sensory experiences are common to both disorders but not yet clear which, if any, of the aberrant reflexes are most involved. It would therefore be helpful to discuss and clarify the differences between autism as defined by Kanner and Asperger's syndrome. So, we must now ask: which disorder?

Which disorder?

As you will recall, the most recent DMS IV criteria details both autism and Asperger's syndrome as having a qualitative impairment in social interaction and restricted, repetitive and stereotyped patterns of behaviour, interests and activities. Where it differentiates between the two is in regarding those with Asperger's syndrome as having: 'No clinically significant general delay in language nor in cognitive development or the development of age-appropriate self-help skills, adaptive behaviour and curiosity about the environment in childhood' in contrast to those with autism who have 'delayed or abnormal communication skills'. How, though, does this fit in with the people and problems already discussed?

I was completely puzzled by the differences between people like Georgiana Stehli, Donna Williams and Temple Grandin, especially as the latter two both refer to themselves as having autism. All are highly intelligent and lead independent lives but their writings led me to believe that their problems might differ. One aspect of this difference was evidenced by the fact that Donna Williams felt her tinted lenses lessened her auditory problems while Georgie Stehli found that she could cope with her other sensory difficulties once the auditory problems had been corrected.

Vision does in fact seem to be one of the major areas of difference between them; a discrepancy which initially led me to focus on the apparent clumsiness of those with Asperger's. This confused me more for I have met several children and adults who fit this particular aspect of the criteria of Asperger's syndrome but are extremely 'handicapped' and will never be able to lead independent lives. This led me to ask whether people with the 'same' condition could possibly have different symptoms?

I have already mentioned the problems of mono-processing which many people with autism share; the outcome of which is a delay in making connections that affects many aspects of life. What, though, of the other problem – hyperconnectedness – which, it was suggested, relates to Asperger's syndrome rather than autism? Such people also have mono-processing problems, but the difference is in how the incoming information is dealt with. As the description suggests, connections are made too rapidly thereby producing chaotic or haphazard responses; similar to those of the child or adult with 'attention problems'.

This description is reminiscent of the hyposensitive person described by Sally Goddard Blythe whereby the person lives, as you will remember, in a state of internal excitation, hyperactivity and tension, maintaining his balance only by continuously seeking to increase his level of arousal with excitement, constant activity, violent panic or angry outbursts.

Her ideas led me to question whether hyperconnectedness was simply a more 'adult' version of the attention 'deficit' problems some children have: a stage perhaps where formerly 'uncontrollable' motor activity has been 'tamed' and is then superseded by similarly uncontrollable thought processes which render the person unable to function as most of us do.

Before answering that there were other factors which I had to take into account. Initially I was tempted to think that the tonic labyrinthine reflex was most clearly linked to Asperger's syndrome but gradually my knowledge of people with autism, information on the various reflexes and the differences in information processing led me to review the idea again. Since then Comings' work has made me see the whole question in a totally different and very unexpected light; for the fact that the difficulties of those with Asperger's syndrome correlated closely to the description of the frontal lobe syndrome found amongst people with ADHD and other problems opened up new possibilities in terms of criteria.

So I now have to confess, controversially perhaps, that I no longer believe that Asperger's syndrome should be a term synonymous with those who are often clumsy and may be highly intelligent and of high ability; nor with those in whom the problems of communication, cognitive development, etc. are absent.

Carrying these ideas further I am led to conclude that, however strange it may seem, the problems of those with Asperger's syndrome probably fit into the hyposensitive category (with the combination of Moro and TLR reflexes) and that this condition may be associated with the frontal lobes.

Thus if such deductions are correct then some things formerly associated with Asperger's syndrome such as clumsiness, high ability and good memory would also to be found amongst those with autism: as indeed they are. In contrast, some people with an apparently lower ability could have Asperger's syndrome rather than autism. These are conclusions which, though now seeming inevitable, surprised me greatly.

This makes it tempting to extrapolate that hyposensitivity is related to frontal lobe dysfunction whilst hypersensitivity is more closely allied to the limbic system. This is an idea which would have implications in other areas as it could, for instance, help differentiate between children with attention deficit hyperactivity disorder and those with attention deficit disorder which, I would further suggest, have links to Asperger's syndrome and autism respectively.

To do so would, however, be premature for there is one conundrum in the construction of this argument which I have not yet solved. This is the question of how the low serotonin levels known to exist in some relate to the high levels of opioid peptides found amongst so many, for as you will remember, low serotonin levels are said to reduce the level of opioid peptides. Shattock provides one possible answer to this by suggesting that the opioid peptides may actually inhibit serotoninergic transmission and thereby reduce the levels of serotonin. However, only further research will provide clear answers.

I would now like to spend a few moments looking at the age of onset in relation to these two disorders. Just how do such ideas fit in with 'normal' child development? We can postulate that although children do not achieve the full flexibility of thought shown by most adults until approximately seven years old (see Appendix H), any problems which develop after the age of four, particularly in the areas of social relationships or communication, will be far less devastating. While each individual's development needs to be taken into account, one could surmise that generally problems developing after the age of four would fall into a different category.

Returning to Asperger's syndrome we must refer back to the DMS IV criteria. The emphasis on the age of onset (prior to age of three in autism) is absent in relation to Asperger's syndrome, although we are told that there is no significant delay in language with single words being used by the age of two and communicative phrases by three.

Neither are there problems with cognitive development, age-appropriate self-help skills, adaptive behaviour or curiosity – all factors which would indicate either that the problems are exceptionally mild or that development is 'normal' in the early years and that onset begins at a later stage.

Somewhat confusingly, all the people with autism/Asperger's syndrome whom I have met, whether they be children or adults who have married and have families, do have some cognitive problems and do demonstrate a rigidity of thought similar to that of the child of four years or under. Often, though, these problems are so mild, or the person is so adept at hiding them, that they may not be discerned during the course of a conversation. Indeed, sometimes one only realizes the extent of the person's problems when able to observe or work with them over a lengthy period of time.

So are we to believe that the problems of people with Asperger's syndrome are always much milder or begin later? Before answering we have to resolve two potential conflicts. One lies in the fact that the criteria for this syndrome actually seem to be describing children who relate most closely to those studied by Sula Wolff, that is, those who could be described as 'borderline'.

Another conflict arises from the link I postulated between hyperactivity and Asperger's syndrome. If my supposition is correct then the criteria and some diagnoses must be questioned, for many of the hyperactive children I have met do develop problems at an early age (often around 18 months) and either do not develop speech in the normal manner or gradually lose it after onset.

If this is the case it would be logical to assume that the age of onset and the development of Asperger's syndrome is in fact similar to that of autism and that the current criteria may unintentionally mislead; so that any child whose 'autisms' begin after the age of three is, at present, more likely to be diagnosed as having Asperger's syndrome or, like the child mentioned by Rapoport, with other disorders.

It would actually seem more likely that those whose problems begin after the age of four may have a variety of other problems such as obsessive-compulsive disorder. It will be interesting to know whether such assumptions are correct. Now, though, we need to look at that aspect of the problem which affects all sufferers: anxiety and obsessive-compulsive behaviours.

Anxiety and obsessive / compulsive behaviours

Comings' work was extremely interesting and helpful but I must beg to differ from him on two particular aspects for, although his view may now have changed, his earlier work implied that Tourette's syndrome was the worst of these related conditions and that OCD was part of that condition.

First, although appreciating the immense problems that TS causes for the sufferers, I believe that autism and Asperger's syndrome are in fact the most devastating of all these disorders, leading as they do in many cases to the inability of those affected to lead independent lives or to fully enjoy human relationships. Conversely some might argue that the fact that the majority are so severely 'handicapped' lessens the impact of their disability and that it is the awareness of the problems that magnifies the distress of those with Tourette's syndrome. I would counter that by saying that I do not believe that some of those deemed amongst the 'most handicapped' people with autism / Asperger's syndrome are necessarily as 'unaware' of their problems as we might think – an idea which would seem to be supported by the writings of a number of people who use facilitated communication.

Second, I would surmise that OCD is not merely part of Tourette's syndrome but, rather, a severe condition which can exist on its own – although it is also, in a number of people, part of other disorders. I would suggest that although obsessive-compulsive behaviours are a major feature in OCD they are also found in conditions such as autism and TS, as well as in people who undergo immense and/or continued stress for lengthy periods of time. Such behaviours have a direct link with:

- an imbalance in the neurotransmitters – especially serotonin and dopamine which can be unbalanced by stress or affected by genetic factors;
- fear/anxiety/stress.

While neither tested nor proven, it would seem possible that the latter also have a relationship with the aberrant reflexes and abnormal perceptions found amongst many people.

Most of these other disorders, however severe, are relatively mild when compared with autism. How then to differentiate, particularly in the case of OCD where the symptoms of stress are so similar? Perhaps the differences lie, not just in the fact that the digestive problems and abnormal perceptions, if any, are less severe, but also in the age at which they start?

To clarify exactly what I mean: the primary features of stress – withdrawal and obsessive/compulsive behaviours – are found in all these disorders. The secondary features are not. Could it be that cognitive problems and, most importantly, the stage at which the development of speech and thinking has been halted, are the clearest clues as to the age of onset? There are some exceptions to this found in those children who suddenly deteriorate but, in line with others, I would suggest that it is only where these problems start at an early age that we see the severe symptoms which are classed as autistic. This could also explain why some people with Down's syndrome and other 'non-specific mental handicaps' show autistic tendencies.

Here it would be helpful to leave the age of onset behind for a while and return to take a deeper look at the type of reactions that might be expected to appear in response to the stresses already mentioned.

First, two general points. The first is that compulsions and obsessions are common to all, albeit very individual. Many of these will change with time. Some will become obsolete only to be replaced by something different, whilst others may gradually become more and more intrusive. This can happen in two ways: by the range expanding, as when the person gradually increases the number of objects he has to touch or count; and as new 'features' are added to the original so that the action or thought becomes more intricate and, as is in the case of some compulsions, highly stylized.

The second general point is that the ability of the person to express or demonstrate their understanding of spoken language, although it is also related to the stage the person functions at, depends greatly on their auditory and processing problems. For some, things are only processed correctly after a delay, often when the moment for the response or reaction has passed.

Now let us look at the various levels of functioning, which, as you will see, carry the threads of withdrawal and agitation throughout:

1. People in this group are deeply withdrawn. This is the child who does not dare to 'expose' himself in any way. Thus he will not interact with, or acknowledge, others, demonstrates little or no curiosity and ignores challenges (although he may be hyperactive). He may demonstrate strange compulsions. Whilst often showing little awareness of or particular reaction to larger changes or stressful situations, when feeling secure he may very quickly notice and compulsively correct small changes. The people who Donna Williams identifies as 'having exposure anxiety' fit into this category, as did the description of Clara Parks' daughter.

2. People in this group are slightly less withdrawn but will generally only acknowledge other people when needing them to do something. Thus the child may attempt to move his mother's hand towards the drink or cake he wants or the door handle that he wants to turn, but will not attempt to take, eat or move things on his own for, fearing failure, he is unwilling to attempt any activity. Conversely he will, when feeling unobserved, occasionally demonstrate his skills – as with the child who is apparently too weak to hold a fork or cup and needs feeding, but who suddenly uses a spoon to eat his sister's pudding or quickly drinks her orange juice when no one is looking.

   Such children present a strange and puzzling picture as they continually refuse to attempt things which their parents know are well within their capabilities. This is the child of contrasts and contradictions, who in times past might have been the original changeling; a 'fairy' child left in exchange for a stolen human, who appears to inhabit a different world.

   Speech too may be present but will rarely be used. This child can cause more confusion by speaking when he feels unobserved – which would seem to incorporate some children/adults with 'elective' mutism. Whilst some children do literally elect not to speak after trauma, in this context the word 'elective' is misleading as the child is denied choice, either ceasing to talk because of overwhelming fear or being physically unable to speak.

3. This is the person who instigates limited interaction with others, perhaps by touching or speaking to them. This, though, is always on his terms and he will usually reject or ignore others, even turning and walking away from another's approach. Speech, when used, may be limited to a few very repetitive sentences or phrases which seem to bear little relation to the situation. He will show little curiosity although he may have a fascination (and even demonstrate skill) for things which demand

nothing in return (mechanical objects, things which spin, jigsaws, etc.). Alternatively he may lose himself in watching videos (or particular parts thereof) or listening to music, etc. He can get very agitated with changes in his surroundings or when demands are placed upon him.

4. This person actively seeks interaction with a few known 'safe' people. This will, initially at least, be on his terms although he does at times tolerate and even respond to their approach. Speech may be used to gain attention, although this is generally limited to safe sentences and phrases which are, at times, quite appropriate to the situation.

   Other interaction may not always be appropriate. For example, he may acknowledge the other person's presence by touching or hugging them over-enthusiastically or even hit out at them apparently for no obvious reason. He, too, may have similar skills or interests to those mentioned above or, being less withdrawn, may actually enjoy using a particular creative skill – once again generally those which do not require involvement from others (painting, music, etc.).

   At times an individual at this level will talk incessantly and, often, too loudly, repeating the same few phrases or anxiously asking repetitious questions to confirm what he already knows, whilst paying little heed to the answers. Such people often demonstrate physical signs of anxiety, too, walking constantly to and fro and/or making stereotyped arm or facial movements as they talk. It is worth noting that while repetitive speech seems to be a classic sign of anxiety it can, in some people, be a sensism originating partially from a desire to 'cancel out' a hypersensitivity to sound.

5. This group incorporates those who gradually learn to interact more easily with the world and with particular known people, although their difficulties generally continue to make this hard to do in relation to their peer group. Many of them will be able to live in establishments with minimal support or live independently.

   They will find a variety of mechanisms which will enable them to cope with the difficulties arising from their anxiety and perceptual problems. For some this will be through the acquisition of various 'characters' which will ostensibly enable them to deal with most situations, allowing them to seem (superficially at least) quite sociable and often hiding their cognitive difficulties.

   Even though they are often very independent, their lives (or parts of them) may be ruled by obsessions and compulsions and they retain some rigidity of thought. Some may have had few problems with the acquisition of speech but for others speech will gradually progress from echolalia to a more 'normal' pattern although when under stress they may revert to earlier patterns of speech. I suspect that there are also a number who reach this stage but never speak, relying instead on FC or other types of communication – although such people are likely to continue being 'cared for' by others rather than achieving full independence.

A number of people at this level will go throughout their lives without ever being diagnosed. While they may be regarded as obsessive or compulsive some will develop relationships, have families and frequently successful careers but, regardless of these, they will often feel like 'outsiders'.

This list is not comprehensive but does, I hope, offer some insight into these very complex behaviours. To make things even more difficult these, of course, are further complicated by the fact that, like the rest of us, the person's responses vary according to a number of factors. Physical well-being, mood, the situation and people around can all have an effect on the ability to function, which may therefore fluctuate. Thus different situations will produce a range of effects which, again, are very individual. In some this may lead to one person literally 'freezing' in a particular situation whilst another might demonstrate his distress and confusion either verbally or physically: becoming increasingly repetitive and loud and/or losing control of himself and becoming physically agitated (often towards himself as much as towards objects or other people).

It was only as I collated this list that I gradually realized that what I had initially considered to be different levels of fear were not that at all. This will sound as if I am merely playing with semantics, but there is an important point to be made. After much reflection I had to conclude that the categories mentioned were not simply reflections of fear but rather different expressions of defence mechanisms, that is, individual responses.

Once this was clarified I was able to look at this area from a different perspective and this led me to make what I consider an important discovery. This is the fact that the different responses relate directly to the levels of functioning generally used to diagnose the various degrees of 'mental handicap'/learning difficulty: so that those who are most withdrawn are often considered to be most handicapped whilst those at the other end are given a much better prognosis and considered capable of development. It is even more confusing to find that those with the most severe problems are similar to a number of people with multi-sensory deprivation who do respond to treatment, whilst those with whom facilitated communication has been used successfully – and through which some demonstrate a wide understanding of language – are often people whose handicap is considered to be in the moderate/severe range. Confusing! Or is it? Certainly, if I am correct, the implications would be serious but they will have to wait while I share some of the questions and the answers which led me to such startling conclusions.

So, what exactly turns children into withdrawn, obsessive-compulsive and dependent people? What are the factors which dictate their ability to function? First we must take into account the possibility of increasing physical difficulties, perhaps because of a build-up of phenols and other toxic substances, opioid peptides, a restricted blood flow in the brain or faulty myelination. We will also have to determine whether children who have developed the new bowel disease identified by Wakefield and his team have more problems with pain than others.

Then we have the severity of the perceptual problems, which would make a temptingly easy answer. Balance this with the fact that a number of people with autism who are very independent have managed to overcome many of the obstacles placed in their path by tremendous perceptual distortions. How? Is it simply that over time they learnt to cope with/adapt to the problems? This scenario would seem likely for although their childhood problems were severe both Temple Grandin and Donna Williams initially made a great deal of progress without treatment. So, although the perceptual problems obviously create tremendous anxiety this seems unrelated to the way people function: which confusingly but effectively disassociated anxiety from functioning – not at all the answer I expected.

Alternatively some may ask whether people are able to cope well with such problems because of their intelligence. This could be a possibility but one then has to account for the fact that, as already mentioned, many of those who demonstrate previously unacknowledged skills via FC fall into the apparently 'less intelligent' and more handicapped group.

My work with several children (under the age of six) with, apparently, very varied abilities and problems also leads me to doubt this, for although some appeared more handicapped than others, all, in my estimation, were of average or above average intelligence: a judgement proved in part by the way these children coped with and adapted to their sensory difficulties, albeit in a variety of ways. You have to be reasonably bright to do that!

Whilst the differences between the male and female brain (see p.118) may play a part, one other physical factor which might be involved in this is, of course, the reticular activating system mentioned by Rimland. H.J. Eysenck linked the RAS to our character, suggesting it would be strong in extroverts and weak in introverts. So could this too have an effect on the level at which people function? This would certainly seem to be a possibility for, despite their difficulties, I know a few people with autism who are indeed somewhat extroverted.

Figure 3.10 uses the information we already have on perceptual problems and neurotransmitters to demonstrate the way in which this might work and this suggests one possible reason for the differences in the severity of the problem.

Whilst this subject may initially seem a little confusing, one could further postulate that if reversed, so that an extrovert with a strong RAS received weak/delayed messages, the degree of problem might again be lessened. This is a possible candidate, then, although obviously further research will be needed before its validity can be assessed. Intriguing too to speculate on the causes of the delayed connections and hyperconnectedness.

One further puzzle remains. How do we account for the fact that the majority of adults I have met in residential homes gradually respond to the security of routine, consistency, other people's expectations and a particular type of environment, with a consequent alteration in their level of functioning?

Some people then retain this progress so that in time they are able to move on and lead a more independent life than may originally have been thought possible. In contrast, although others may effectively 'move up a level' in certain circumstances or when in the presence of particular people, they 'slip back' to a former level when/if things change. So let us consider some psychological factors.

First the Pygmalion effect, demonstrated in experiments in which children of equal aptitude were divided randomly into two groups: one being labelled potentially 'high achievers' and the other 'academically poor'. Both groups fulfilled the teacher's 'expectations': an effect now borne out by numerous studies. This is further confirmed by my observations in a residential and day care establishment. One woman in particular responds well and will carry out a variety of tasks when with staff who demonstrate confidence in her ability to do them but, when placed in another situation with staff who clearly think she is incapable of even the most menial task, she withdraws completely and will do nothing at all ... and who can blame her?

While the words 'mentally handicapped' are no longer generally used about those with autism, some of the parents of children I know have, even in the 1990s, been told that their child is 'a hopeless case' and will never achieve anything. What does this do to those parents? While many are strong enough to believe in their own assessment of their child such words can easily undermine them.

This process often continues when the child goes to school and is treated as intellectually 'deficient': as in the case of Neil, an intelligent young man who has very good comprehension and demonstrates much fluency in his writings. Hampered by a lack of similar fluency in his speech he spent many years returning to the 'basics' each time he moved classes or changed schools and even intervention by his parents has not always been able to convince his teachers of his abilities. Imagine then their frustration and anger at not being able to influence his treatment in school whilst knowing that his abilities far exceeded the tasks he was given.

Introvert

Information enters via sense organs eyes, ears, skin, etc.	Information passed via neuro-transmitters	Weak reticular activating system	Brain	Responses
Information entered correctly	Information passed correctly	Information is amplified	Over-stimulated	Avoids too much stimuli
Information distorted or incomplete	Bombardment of fast information (hyper)	**Normal** Information is amplified	Bombarded by an overload of information	Delayed connections in mental and physical activity and speech
		Weak Increases the effect		Severe problems
		Moderate No effect		Moderate problems
		Strong Decreases the effect?		Mild problems

Extrovert

Information enters via sense organs eyes, ears, skin, etc.	Information passed via neuro-transmitters	Strong reticular activating system	Brain	Responses
Information entered correctly	Information passed correctly	Inhibits all messages	Under-stimulated	Seeks more stimuli
Information distorted or incomplete	Information delayed (hypo)	**Normal** Inhibits all messages	Waiting! Waiting! Waiting!	Hyper-**activity** Hyper-**connectedness** Hyper-**speech** These may at times produce **Total inaction**
		Strong Increases the effect		Severe problems
		Moderate No effect		Moderate problems
		Weak Decreases the effect		Mild problems

Figure 3.10 The reticular activating system, its link with introversion and extroversion and its possible involvement in autism

Even more importantly we must ask, 'What does such consistent "discrimination" do to the child?' We have already heard Jim Sinclair's views on this, of which I shall reiterate the most important points. As he said:

> I am not taken seriously. My credibility is suspect. My understanding of myself is not considered to be valid, and my perceptions of events are not considered to be based in reality. My rationality is questioned … My ability to make reasonable decisions … is doubted … My greatest difficulties are minimised, and my greatest strengths are invalidated. (Sinclair 1992)

I can understand how he feels for I have come across care staff, teachers and others with whom the child has contact who make comments which can be disparaging and which (even when said 'out of earshot') may be heard by the hypersensitive child. Sometimes it is simply a lack of knowledge which may lead the adult to wrongly assess the child's abilities or 'talk down' to him but the effect is still the same and the attitudes conveyed may be adopted by other children. Sadly, all too often these perceptions follow the child into adulthood where they are then perpetuated by the other people they come into contact with.

Then again, as Jim Sinclair says, there are those who minimize or disparage the very real fears and physical difficulties which people with autism have, such as the 'special needs' teacher who made it clear to all that she saw no reason for her pupil to wear tinted lenses. Such children and adults may also face problems in the community, as in one instance where a family friend demonstrated a total lack of empathy by referring to the child as a 'silly cow' because she persistently banged her head against walls.

A 'chat show' on racial discrimination in the United States discussed the effect such treatment has on the person discriminated against: gradually wearing away their self-esteem and spirit. If it is difficult for 'ordinary' people to live with discrimination because of their colour or race how much harder must it be to cope when one also has the myriad problems of autism. When discrimination begins in the early years any seeds of self-esteem will be trampled and crushed before they have the opportunity to grow. This can also have a physical effect, for feelings of lack of worth (which surely must arise if you know other people regard you as handicapped) can actually have a physical effect, lowering serotonin levels in the brain; thereby adding yet more difficulties.

It is sobering to reflect that we, as parents, teachers or carers can also influence the level of withdrawal: either by helping and supporting the person to take the tentative steps needed to go from one stage to another until withdrawal is minimized or sometimes, through ignorance or mismanagement, driving them even further behind their castle walls.

It would seem that those children who are considered primarily to be physically handicapped (as in MSD) rather than socially or cognitively impaired might well have a greater chance of achievement. However, this aspect of things can be changed. The challenge is to change our perceptions too. We must recognize that children who suffer from abnormal perceptual experiences, whether hyper- or hyposensitive, are not only far more greatly handicapped than those whose problems lie in one or two areas, but also continue to have their difficulties compounded by society's lack of understanding.

After all this discussion I can now summarize the answers to the question I posed about the origins of this 'handicap'. Certainly several factors are probably involved in determining the level at which the person functions. The foundations of anxiety are laid by the physical problems which may make the child feel extremely unwell and render him unable to cope with many apparently ordinary tasks. It would also seem that the RAS may be integral not only to the child's character but in determining the level at which he is then able to function.

I would also suggest that, whatever the apparent level of functioning, each child continues to learn, despite lacking some of the basic foundations. Unfortunately, though, his ability to demonstrate what he has learnt will be limited by three things: first, his physical ability, which may make some tasks virtually impossible at times; second, his particular level of functioning; and third, the opportunities – or lack of them – that others offer, something which is all too often determined by his presumed ability to function.

Then there are the psychological factors already mentioned which can allow the person to overcome the invisible barrier and move to a different level. Thus, I would postulate that although one can effect an improvement in the level of functioning by our expectations, without treatment the underlying anxiety will remain in the majority of people with these disorders, although it will be less apparent and impinge slightly less upon the person's daily life.

Perhaps this accounts for the success of facilitated communication, which would seem to work by bypassing the 'normal' level of functioning and minimizing the processing problems. These two things decrease some of the anxiety and thereby allow the person easier access to their thoughts. While it may not apply to all, the use of information technology (IT) and FC are beginning to show that, even if a person is generally unable to demonstrate the correct response at the appropriate time, his understanding may be well in advance of his apparent abilities.

Intelligence

This is a subject that has not yet been explored in any depth although it has been mentioned obliquely in the course of this investigation. I hope I have shown (and convinced?) you of the reasons why a great number of people with autism are mistakenly regarded as 'mentally handicapped'. Certainly my initial view that the majority of people with autism are of normal intelligence has been reinforced, both by those I know and by some of the ideas that have been considered. I would therefore still contend that the vast majority start life as potentially intelligent people: people who are so handicapped by their perceptual processing and other difficulties that only some ever fulfil their true potential.

How do such ideas fit into current thinking? If we consider the criteria proposed by Creak – her list being one of the most comprehensive – could they now be rearranged in order to prioritize the problems? Are the previous comments given to illustrate the points still appropriate? I will answer these questions by both readjusting the list on page 16 and writing alternative comments. This would give:

1. *Abnormal perceptual experiences.* Definitely present, although of different types.

2. *An unawareness of the child's own personal identity to a degree inappropriate to age.* Certainly proprioception (body sense) is lacking in some people – which could inhibit self-awareness.

3. *Acute, excessive anxiety* which is, most definitely, not illogical.

4. *Sustained resistance to change in the environment and a striving to maintain or restore that sameness.* Naturally!

5. *Pathological preoccupation with particular objects or certain characteristics of them without regard to their accepted functions.* More accurately described as defence mechanisms.

6. *Gross and sustained impairment of emotional relationships with people.* Hardly surprising given their problems. Whilst this will affect all children in whom the bonding process has been disrupted, many do want relationships but are frustrated by their inability to express (or even understand and cope with) their own feelings and therefore may only be able to relate in an 'unusual' manner.

7. *Speech may have been lost, or never acquired, or may have failed to develop beyond a level appropriate to an earlier stage.* While the latter two points are probably an indication of the age when development slowed or halted, I would suggest that 'lost speech' may be associated with the sudden onset of serious problems, that is, when the child starts deteriorating and his

previous skills and acquisitions begin to be overwhelmed by the onset of the sensory problems.

8. I will leave this point to last as it warrants much further discussion.

9. *Distortion in mobility patterns.* This does not occur in all children and is therefore perhaps one of the least important, although it is certainly an indicator of delayed development and is often related to aberrant reflexes or visual perceptual problems.

So let me now discuss point 8 (point 9 on the original list) which, you will remember, reads: *A background of serious retardation in which islets of normal, near normal or exceptional intellectual function or skill may appear.*

It must be remembered that most people can, with practice, become either extremely competent or exceptionally skilled at a particular task. One simple example of this is found in the use of speed reading techniques which, by teaching the reader to make use of peripheral vision and other ideas, is said to increase the reading speed from an average of 200 to an incredible 2000 words per minute: something I would not have thought possible (Russell 1979). We have to acknowledge that the person with autism may practise a task repeatedly, often from an early age and, with few other interests, will spend much more time on it than the majority of people ever would. It is no surprise, then, that their skills in particular areas, which are generally based on practical matters such as mathematics, art or music, rather than 'people-based', should be so finely honed or that some are regarded as exceptional.

The logical conclusion to be drawn from this is that the 'islets' of normal, and near-normal, intellectual function or skill are simply those abilities which are not 'masked' by the level of functioning – abilities which sometimes 'escape' when the person feels unobserved or safe – while the exceptional intellectual function or skill is similar but is that which has been honed to a fine degree as mentioned. Thus we can occasionally catch a glimpse of their innate abilities and potential which, for the main part, may lie hidden or fallow. It would therefore be more accurate if the eighth point were to read:

A background of normal, near-normal or exceptional intelligence which is submerged beneath, or obscured by, the problems of autism.

This complements a theory put forward by David Waterhouse, who says that although it is assumed that only a small percentage of sufferers display an area of outstanding ability, it is in fact expressed by a far greater percentage, although in those who are considered more 'handicapped' this is often in such an inappropriate manner that it is not recognized – an idea illustrated by the following examples:

- Mike constantly plays practical jokes which require a great deal of thought and planning. One of his most successful was carried out late one night after the majority of staff had gone home, when he unscrewed the hinges on the doors and then carefully propped them up so that the first person in the next morning was, quite literally, staggered as he touched the knob and the doors toppled over.

- That exploit took some beating but was, for me, overshadowed by another, in which Mike was seen at a distance by a member of staff who thought that he was walking in a peculiar way. When she came on duty a little later he seemed perfectly all right, so she thought no more of it. However, when Mike arrived home the following day, his mother found that he was wearing two sets of clothing: two vests, shirts, jumpers, etc. The previous day had been a 'dummy run' to see if anyone would notice!

- Nick is apparently severely handicapped. His speech is limited to only a few words and he generally appears to have a very short concentration span. Nick likes to play with small 'twiddles' such as dust caps or the tiny plastic 'plugs' which hold up shelves. Surprisingly (?) he managed to remove these from under several shelves in a glass-fronted wall cupboard, closing the doors extremely carefully so that the shelves stayed in place – until the doors were opened and the contents of the cupboard came tumbling out.

Jasmine Lee O'Neill supports David Waterhouse's theory, saying that although some savant gifts appear useless in the eyes of 'the world' they may, in fact, be evidence that others lie dormant. She also points out that: 'Frequently they [people with autism] will hide their skills, surprising others later on' – for she regards the fact that they are self taught as 'a sign of high intelligence' (O'Neill 1999, p.58).

Other questions relating to intelligence arise from the use of facilitated communication (FC), which I have already touched upon. People have suggested that the physical skills demonstrated by those being facilitated were so far beyond 'normal' capabilities as to be impossible. This is partly because many seem to have acquired a high understanding and use of language when they were thought to be so handicapped that they could neither read nor write – which will receive more attention in Chapter 5 – and also because they rarely look at the keyboard when typing.

To counteract the latter criticism, proponents of FC have fallen into the trap of placing great emphasis on the fact that the client should be encouraged to look at the keyboard as much as possible. While sceptics may deride the comparison, it should be noted that this is actually unnecessary as many typists touch-type, looking at the copy rather than the keyboard. In the case of autism it may also be counterproductive for, as severe visual problems do affect many of them, looking at a keyboard may not actually give the person concerned much coherent information.

That such remarkable skills fail to be generalized across other areas of learning is one of the frequent paradoxes to be found in autism. This may perhaps be a result of their withdrawal from the world and their inability to understand the reason behind many of the things they are expected to do. If FC is seen as positive and washing has often been a unpleasant negative experience, why on earth would you want to waste your time washing?

It is strange, then, that some professionals cannot accept such skills when they are happy to accept many of the skills of the 'savants', which are quite extraordinary. Do they ever question the fact that Stephen Wiltshire has the ability to draw buildings accurately from memory or that others are able to do fantastic mathematical calculations? Of course not.

Paul Shattock and Dawn Savery attempt to explain the origin of such skills. They suggest that an inability to filter out irrelevant stimuli could, in part, explain some of these unusual feats of memory. They postulate that, rather than a deliberate retention of material, such skills actually result from an 'inability to forget'. As they say:

> At the end of the day one runs through the events of that day and decides which are worthy of retention and which should be discarded. (Is this a function of dreaming?) If the filtration processes are faulty then detail in inappropriate material will be retained. Maps, dates and numerical data will be remembered with uncanny accuracy. The uncanny musical and artistic skills which are shown by some people with autism are explicable in the same way. (Shattock and Savery 1997, p.15)

Another controversial theory which could shed some light on this comes from Ian Wilson in his book *Superself* (1989). In it he reflects on the abilities which he links to a sixth or 'super' sense (which some people would term the unconscious). He feels that this enables us to achieve things which would otherwise seem beyond our normal physical capabilities, as in the extraordinary skills found amongst people who produce art or perform sport at a level way above most of us. He views the abilities of savants such as Stephen Wiltshire and Nadia (who drew the most amazing pictures of horses as a young child only to gradually lose this skill on learning to speak) as possible examples of this. He also proposes that when a person concentrates too hard on learning something it comes less naturally; as with the story of the millipede who was walking along perfectly happily until asked which foot he moved first.

Indeed, Wilson feels that:

> ... there can be no doubting that, deprived of one or more of its five monitors of the external world, the inner entity we are calling the superself has no shortage of compensating heightened sensory resources to call upon. It is equally clear that ... it often does so in ways the normal consciousness finds difficult if not impossible to comprehend. (Wilson 1989, p.58)

He also quotes two examples which may be of interest here. One is of Nijinsky, who in addition to his superb ballet skills was able to play any piece of music by ear after hearing it once, even though he was unable to read music – a skill also demonstrated by one savant. The second, stranger one, which may be interesting in the context of the reading skills that some people demonstrate through FC, was of a woman who, under hypnosis, correctly sang the words and tune of a song that she had seen in a book which she had simply flicked through (not read!) many years before.

A similar theme is expounded in *Autism and Sensing* (Williams 1998), the gist of which is the proposal that in the early stages of development we all have a system of 'sensing' which is gradually lost by most people as they go on to develop another system: that of interpretation. The author suggests that whilst this enables them to make sense of the world its development usually cuts them off from their earlier abilities – which people with autism retain.

That suggestion seems to indicate a link with neurodevelopmental delay. We already know that those with a retained TLR reflex have an incredible memory for some things; something which would seem to give added weight to this theory. The idea of developmental problems also gains support from Rita Carter. In her book *Mapping the Mind* (1998) she points out that an eidetic (photographic) memory is commonly found amongst young children although as the brain grows and the neurons are pruned such skills are generally lost. She suggests that if this pruning process were incomplete these abilities would remain: a fact which she feels could account for the savant skills as well as playing a part in the development of various problems.

While such ideas certainly provide explanations for the incredible skills of the savant and for the other abilities which some find so questionable I shall leave you to make up your own mind as to their credibility.

Social skills

While difficulties in social relationships and both verbal and non-verbal communication skills are often severe, especially when the child is young, it is interesting to find that (many?) people with autism or Asperger's syndrome do have/develop a degree of some of these skills. Here it might be helpful to look at the various aspects in turn, commenting where necessary.

People with a damaged or incomplete sense of proprioception:

- *Lack 'body sense', that is, lack 'body connectedness'.* This would account for the problems with motor control which affect many people particularly in early life although they often learn to compensate for this as they get older. It could also, in some cases, lead to/cause a lack of self-awareness.

Those with alexithymia:

- *Lack self-awareness.*
- *Find emotional experiences confusing and overwhelming: to be avoided.* This would seem to echo the idea of one's body being an 'enemy' which 'floods' one with uncontrollable feelings.
- *Have little ability to distinguish between the different emotions.*

- *May demonstrate confusion between emotions and bodily sensations.* Thus she may, on rare occasions, weep copiously for no apparent reason: a basic confusion which may lead to complaints of vague medical symptoms when they are really emotionally distressed. I have come across the uncontrollable and seemingly inexplicable weeping but not the latter (which would presumably only affect the more verbal sufferers), although some of you may have experience of this.

- *Seem to have no 'inner life'; being devoid of emotions, fantasies or vivid dreams.* While this certainly does not reflect the experiences of many of the people mentioned in this book, the word *seem* is crucial for this apparent deficit may, as previously suggested, be more a reflection of an inability to express their feelings or our lack of awareness than actuality.

- *Lack the words to describe their emotions.* Yes.

- *Lack intuitive signals (gut feeling).* While their gut feelings may not stem from experience many of them are able to judge people accurately and even those who are least verbal seem to have a sixth sense (Ian Wilson's 'supersense'?) about some matters. Thus, as already said, they are frequently attuned to other people's emotions and, although these may not be interpreted or expressed verbally, they may copy or mirror the other person's feelings or even 'act out' their concerns.

- *Are unable to correctly recognize and interpret either their own or other people's feelings – giving rise to a lack of both insight and empathy:* the latter being clearly linked to Baron-Cohen's idea of *mind-blindness*. While many people with autism do demonstrate an intuitive understanding of and considerable empathy towards other people with autism. Could this 'attunement' or 'sensing' also provide an explanation for this?.

Whatever the truth behind this, my observations and experience lead me to suggest that people with autism certainly do have all the emotions which we feel but unfortunately many of them lack the ability to correctly recognize, interpret or express those emotions. This gives them the impression of being different and in some way 'alien' – something which is felt keenly by many sufferers.

People with dyssemia:

- *Misinterpret facial expressions or body language –* as also happens with distorted vision. This can result in them 'misusing' expressions, asking intrusive questions, talking about themselves or one subject all the time and ignoring attempts to change the topic – all of which are common amongst those with autism (although whether the latter two have a connection to obsessiveness is a moot point).

- *Have a poor sense of personal space. That is, they stand too close to others or encroach on their space.* This is certainly true of a number of people.

- *Show little awareness of the emotional content of speech (prosody) so that they talk too shrilly or flatly.* This type of speech is definitely heard in some people with autism. Why this should be a moot point, for after the description of Christina and Rimland's comments one has to ask whether it has a connection with either a lack of proprioception or the processing problems.

So, while many of these factors are indeed found in autism and Asperger's syndrome, each of these conditions exists on its own and symptoms of each are also found, albeit to a lesser extent, in some of those with disorders such as ADD, ADHD or OCD. It would seem as if such problems could also account for an inability to interpret other people's expressions and the difficulties in internalizing social rules which form part of the 'theory of mind'. I would be interested to know whether any of those people with alexithymia and dyssemia whose development is otherwise 'normal' have difficulties with proprioception or suffer from any of the visual or other perceptual problems, for it would certainly seem possible.

Discussion and conclusions

We have now explored a variety of factors many of which are common, although never as severe, in other groups of people, as can be seen from Figure 3.11.

So are we merely going around in circles or can any conclusions be drawn? It seems clear that while many other disorders share the 'symptoms' mentioned they are generally milder than those found in autism and Asperger's syndrome and thus many of their effects can therefore be compensated for, coped with or even hidden (as is often the case in OCD). Only in autism and Asperger's syndrome do we find the combination of these problems arising with such a degree of severity.

Leaving the genetic inheritance aside, four points are common to both these disorders and would seem to be found in the majority of people; although there may be a few to whom the first two points are not applicable. While the order of the first two may be arguable, these are:

- A faulty digestive system which affects the functioning of the brain causing, in the majority, normal development to be disrupted.

- Neurodevelopmental delay which causes severe disruption to the perceptual system. This effectively hampers the child's interaction with other people and bars him from exploring his environment, thereby reducing his ability to learn from or to understand the world around him.

	Tryptophan	Low sulpat.	Food intolerances	Leaky gut	Opioid peptides	Low serotonin	Ab reflexes	Auditory problems	Visual problems	Processing problems	Stress	Immune system
General Population	X	X	X	X	X	X	X	X	X	X	–	–
Asthma	–	X	?	?	?	?	?	?	?	?	–	–
Candida	–	–	X	X	X	–	–	–	–	–	–	L
Dyslexia	–	?	L	X	X	?	X	X	X	X	X	L
ADHD	?	?	X	X	X	X	L	L	L	L	L	X
OCD	?	?	X	–	X	X	L	L	L	L	X	L
TS	X	?	?	?	?	X	L	L	X	X	L	L
Autism	?	X	X	X	X	X	X	X	X	X	X	X
Asperger's syndrome	?	X	X	X	X	X	X	X	X	X	X	X

Key:
 X Affects some people   – Unknown
 L Likely to affect some   ? May affect some

Figure 3.11 Incidence of symptoms of autism and Asperger's syndrome which are also found in other populations

- Severe and ongoing stress.
- Chronic and acute anxiety.

In autism these things combine to trigger the fifth aspect of the problem:

- Withdrawal and/or obsessive-compulsive behaviours. These are the symptoms we know as autism, which further detach the child from 'normal' childhood experiences.

Apart from the severity of such problems the only other difference between those with autism or Asperger's syndrome and the people in these other groups has to lie in the combination of mutant genes they have inherited – which for simplicity I shall simply refer to as mutant gene(s) (Gm/s) from now on. Thus I would suggest that in the majority of cases the development of autism/ Asperger's syndrome is dependent on the age of onset and those five specific factors, all of which are interdependent (Figure 3.12) – an idea I will expand in the next chapter.

These ideas give support to Bender (1959), whose ideas I have already touched upon. Remembering that in the 1960s autism was often confused with childhood schizophrenia it is interesting that see that the full quote says:

I have long argued that autism is a defence mechanism frequently occurring in young schizophrenic, or brain damaged, or severely traumatized or emotionally deprived children who thereby withdraw to protect themselves from the disorganization and anxiety arising from the basic pathology in their genes, brains, perceptual organs or social relationships. (Bender 1959, pp.81–86)

How unfortunate that her hypotheses did not receive more attention and were not thoroughly researched at that time.

Let us move now to the next point. As I hope this chapter and those preceding it have made clear, the apparent conflict between the concepts of nature and nurture has no basis in reality, for the two things are actually complementary: a fact which can be used to illuminate some facets of behaviour, as I hope to show in the next chapter.

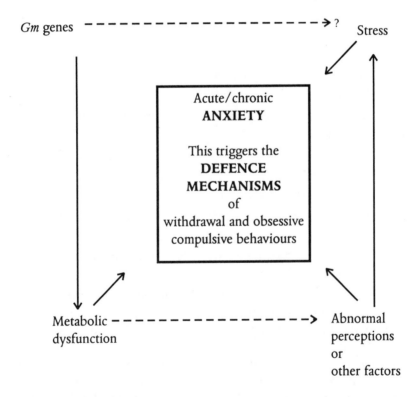

Figure 3.12 Factors involved in the development of autism/Asperger's syndrome

Before finding the answers we must, however, return to the various lists of diagnostic features and the majority of theories I have detailed. These suggest that their authors still accept one vital point which, if questioned, might enable them to take a second look at the condition and usefully alter their perspective. Although they recognize that people with autism display a variety of symptoms, there is a tendency to think of autism as a single condition, with perhaps more than one cause.

This idea must be analyzed, while taking into consideration the fact that over the past twenty or thirty years there have been stories of people or children with autism who progressed greatly or have even recovered. Thus while some learn to cope with their handicap, as in Grandin's case, others recover to the stage where they no longer exhibit any of the 'autism' they once displayed and are able to lead a full life, which includes 'ordinary' relationships with other people. One of the latter is Raun Kaufman, whose parents developed the Option Institute (see Useful Addresses) which receives more detailed discussion later. Raun, who was considered to be severely handicapped at an early age, graduated from university and is doing extremely well – a far cry from the child to whom the doctors gave an extremely poor prognosis.

Claims like this have usually been received with some scepticism and greeted by comments such as 'perhaps the original diagnosis was wrong' or 'the "cure" is exaggerated'. There is, however, growing evidence that some of these claims are true, which suggests that while some people's symptoms can at best be alleviated, a cure may be possible for others. Could this be so if all people with autism suffer from the same problem?

And then we have the child with OCD. Where does he fit in? Can we clarify the link between abnormal perceptions, anxiety, OCD and autism? Are there any explanations which answer such questions and give a coherent picture? How then to conclude?

It would seem that there could be several different causes of the problems:

1. Those few children who demonstrate severe developmental delay from birth onwards and later develop severe problems. Do they either inherit a faulty digestive system and/or some degree of neuro-developmental delay or encounter problems during the foetal stage which culminate in NDD? Could this combine with the food intolerances at a later stage, thereby increasing the severity of the problems?

2. We could postulate that the majority (?) may initially have only moderate perceptual abnormalities (which could be seen as symptoms of ADD or ADHD). These could then be exacerbated by the digestive problems, illness (or vaccine?) whence they would increase in severity. Unless the underlying problems are treated this situation could become permanent, the problems being intensified by opioid peptides in the brain.

3. What, though, of those who show no sign of sensory problems and others whose difficulties could be classified as mild: difficulties which

could, in the right circumstances, be coped with or adapted to? What happens then to take away or destroy their ability to cope and turns them into children with the obsessive-compulsive and other behaviours of autism or Asperger's syndrome? While these features may be exacerbated by digestive problems, illness or vaccine, the perceptual problems (where they exist) remain mild. This would indicate that perhaps here 'external' factors play a part: an idea I will expand in the next chapter.

Whilst obviously there may be several causes for inherent fragility and for the 'oddities' of behaviour noted amongst the children in the AiAs group prior to the development of autism, it would seem that some degree of neuro-developmental delay could account for both.

Using phenylketonuria and andrenoleukodystrophy (which gained attention in the film 'Lorenzo's Oil') as models offers another perspective. Their development leads me to question whether, if the problems could be diagnosed at a very early stage and relevant treatment such as a diet implemented, the handicap of autism would still arise.

More research is obviously needed to determine whether that is a valid assumption. If it is, though, we have to consider the possibility, based again on these other disorders, that while some children might respond to (and be cured by?) a dietary approach there are others who might need to maintain a particular diet for a lengthy period (life?) in order to maintain optimum mental and physical health – a small price to pay when weighed against the potential desolation and frustrations of a life with autism.

Certainly I know of some children who have 'recovered' and have heard and read of others which suggest that it is the case, although whether this is so remains to be seen. Perhaps this is where the difference in genetic inheritance shows itself. Could the 1 gene/2 gene theory, which in view of the polygenic inheritance would be better written as 1/few genes or several genes, also provide an explanation as to why Jeremy's problems were so quickly reversed or are there other answers?

It begins to seem that even though these conditions are genetic, the effect of the genes can be modified or altered and, in some cases, autism can truly be 'beaten'. Of course many questions still remain but we *are* getting nearer to some of the answers and these should improve the quality of life for many.

It will no doubt be said that I should not assume that the pattern of one disorder can be transposed onto another and perhaps that I am jumping to dangerous or misleading conclusions which may prove hurtful to the parents and families. Although you will have to judge for yourself, I do not believe that this is so. While, as a researcher, I am qualified by experience rather than training I have now spent nearly ten years researching the ideas for this book in addition to working with both children and adults with autism. During that time I have observed their perceptual and other problems and listened to and/or read their own accounts. At times it seemed that I was the stranger: learning a new language and translating it, often with difficulty, into mine.

Many hours have also been spent identifying the shapes of anxiety and differences in perception; discussing these problems, those of neurodevelopmental delay and the digestive problems, with people working in these areas who are remarkably open-minded.

In the first chapter I requested you to shelve any preconceived ideas you might hold about autism and view this exploration with an open mind. I tried to do so too. I had no idea when I began my research of the many fascinating ideas that I would find to challenge *my* preconceived ideas. Thus when theories seemed to clash I tried to reconcile the differences by looking at things from another angle. This has changed my ideas radically, particularly in relation to the importance of the metabolic/digestive problems which I dismissed much too lightly before. I now accept the idea that some people either begin life with a severe genetic problem or have a genetic predisposition to metabolic problems, although whether this is the cause of inherent fragility remains to be determined. Whatever the truth, though, these factors do contribute to a wide variety of problems which have a domino effect.

It would seem that several of the problems mentioned, while genetic in origin, relate to enzymes which disrupt the normal functioning of the body. It is fascinating, then, to find that in the 1870s Thudichum believed that:

> ... the great diseases of the brain and spine will all be shown to be connected to the specific chemical changes in the neuroplasms. It is probable that by the aid of chemistry many derangements of the brain and mind which are presently obscure will become accurately definable and amenable to precise treatment. (Comings 1981, p.313)

We must hope they do.

So how are we to make any sense of all these different pieces? Is there an underlying pattern to it all? Where does this knowledge lead us? Do we have enough pieces to make the puzzle? Enough evidence to make a judgement? I think we do, but whether you'll agree ...!?

CHAPTER 4

Hypotheses

It is the nature of a hypothesis when once a man has conceived it that it assimilates every thing to itself as proper nourishment; and from the first moment of your begetting it, it generally grows the stronger by every thing you see, hear, read or understand. Laurence Sterne

Introduction

So, you now share all the information that I have. While some pieces of the puzzle still remain to be found, I will attempt to unravel the knots and draw the various threads together to make a coherent 'whole' by putting forward some hypotheses which can then be examined in detail. [Note, though, that the complexity of these disorders will mean that some questions will remain unanswered until further research is done.]

Hypotheses

- Autism and Asperger's syndrome can result from a combination of different factors.

- In the majority of people these originally stem from the inheritance of mutant (*Gm*) genes which are not directly linked to the specific disorders of Tourette's syndrome, autism, ADHD or OCD but instead cause a dysfunction in the liver, pancreas or gut.

- This can include low sulphation levels, a deficiency of tryptophan oxygenase or phenolsulphotransferase-P and a variety of other factors.

- This predisposes them to develop various anxiety related disorders, *if given a particular set of circumstances.*

- The vast majority of people with autism/Asperger's syndrome have a faulty digestive system and/or problems with the blood brain barrier.

- These dysfunctions can eventually impair both neurological function and physical development and weaken the central nervous system. They can also cause high levels of opioid peptides, an imbalance of neurotransmitters and may possibly damage the reticular formation.

- Such problems can lead to some degree of neurodevelopmental delay and/or inherent fragility. NND is involved in the aberrant reflexes and abnormal perceptions.

- Whether there could be different genes or groups of genes which result in the same effect remains to be seen but, while the jury is still out in the case of vaccine damage, this idea could account for the fact that some children are more susceptible to such external factors than others.

- The abnormal sensory perceptions either create a form of sensory deprivation or alternatively (and most frequently) leave the child without meaningful sensory stimulation. Either can render the child unable to understand 'the world' and the people around them properly.

- Such problems affect the way in which the person deals with information processing resulting in mono processing. The thought processes are unusual too (delayed or hyper) and can affect the implementation of actions and speech.

- The culmination of these factors:
  - creates enormous and constant stress. This arouses the automatic 'defence mechanisms'. These are a fundamental sign of autism inhibiting curiosity and disrupting the child's ability to learn;
  - hinders a number of people from developing a link with their 'self' (although in some cases this is gained before being gradually lost). Thus their own desires and feelings can seem alien and overwhelming;
  - makes relationships and communication extremely difficult to comprehend.

- The majority of people with autism and Asperger's syndrome are, like the general population, born with average or above average intelligence, which gradually becomes submerged (and may remain hidden) by their immense difficulties.

- It would seem possible that autism is linked to the limbic system. I would suggest that it is a childhood form of obsessive-compulsive disorder and may also have some relationship with panic attacks. In contrast Asperger's syndrome could be more directly associated with the frontal lobes, low serotonin levels, ADHD and various phobias.

- The example of Tourette's syndrome, current research and the fact, noted by Rimland, that several parents are 'high flyers' leads me to suggest that:

  - some – but not all – parents or relatives would have some symptoms *not* of autism/Asperger's syndrome but either of a physical nature (autoimmune diseases, allergies, migraine, etc.) or an inherent fragility which might give rise to metabolic or mild perceptual/processing problems or other related disorders. This idea would seem to link with a study which found that a subgroup of parents (with elevated blood serotonin levels) are more likely than other parents to suffer from depression or OCD (Cook, Charak and Arida 1994).

  - those in the latter group might demonstrate features of hyper- or hyposensitivity adapting to and coping with such difficulties so that they do not impinge on their daily lives.

  - some family members may be high achievers who have learnt to control and channel the traits which arise from this type of gene into positive attributes.

- It would seem that autism is likely to be polygenic (having more than one cause). Whilst autism is likely to fall into the pattern of autosomal inheritance those with low serotonin levels (with Asperger's syndrome?) may fit the pattern of semidominant, semirecessive inheritance.

- A significant proportion of the population may carry the type of mutant gene(s) that can weaken the CNS.

- There may also be others with autism who have received their inherent fragility or perceptual problems from the sex-linked fragile X chromosome or from other sources during conception and pregnancy.

- Those born prematurely or of very low birthweight are obviously more susceptible to fragility as are those born with lower levels of vitamin B6 than 'normal'.

I would further suggest that there are several different categories of autism/Asperger's syndrome, all but the last beginning before the age of four. Thus we have:

1. PERCEPTUAL autism (hyper) linked to a damaged limbic system – and possibly other cerebral problems?

PERCEPTUAL Asperger's syndrome linked to frontal lobe problems (including a decreased blood flow) and – probably – a hyposensitive system.

2. REACTIVE autism (limbic system).

REACTIVE Asperger's syndrome (frontal lobe).

Later onset causes:

    i)   Obsessive-compulsive disorder II

    ii) Delayed Asperger's syndrome.

3. INDUCED autism (limbic system).

INDUCED Asperger's syndrome.

Late onset can cause:

    i)   Obsessive-compulsive disorder or anxiety/panic attacks

    ii) Frontal lobe syndrome or phobias

    iii) Physical anxiety-related illnesses

4. SECONDARY autism caused by accident or illness.

Before looking at these in greater detail I would like to add a few general points.

1. *Onset:*

    i)   Onset relates to the level of self-awareness rather than age. 'Autisms' are experienced (and seen by others) as an integral part of the character. Those with OCD experience obsessions and compulsions as being external to themselves.

    ii) If onset occurs before bonding is complete, the development of social relationships and emotional intelligence will be hindered.

    iii) If onset occurs after bonding the child will already relate to others and have language and other skills appropriate to her stage of development. Onset can halt or hinder progress, (or cause deterioration) in all aspects of development.

    iv) When onset is late (as in a minority of cases), problems with cognition and language will be non-existent or slight. The level of self awareness at onset could lead to confusions/misdiagnosis and might leave them prone to later mental illness and depression.

2. *Whichever group the child fits in to he will also:*

    i)   display a variety of sensisms;

ii)   demonstrate a range of autisms which will alter with age;

iii) function at a particular level which can fluctuate depending on the situation, mood, etc.

Regardless of the severity of perceptual problems some people will eventually lead independent lives whilst others will have more severe difficulties and will remain dependent on other people throughout their lives.

3. *Possible additional problems:*

Some people with autism and Asperger's syndrome might be prone to any (or several) of the following difficulties. The first three can occur in childhood. The latter three would be most obvious in adolescence or adulthood and are generally most easily recognized in 'high functioning' people, although they are not exclusive to them:

i)   self-abusive behaviours;

ii)   mutism;

iii) tics or grimaces;

iv)   anxiety/panic attacks/phobias;

v)   depression (which is most likely to be found in those with low serotonin levels);

vi)   addictive behaviours.

It is time now to look at the different aspects in more detail, starting with the aberrant reflexes and perceptual problems which are shared by those with both reactive and induced problems.

Sensory or perceptual autism/Asperger's syndrome

Perceptual difficulties can affect children whose initial problems fall into two broad groups:

1. A relatively small proportion of children will be born with specific brain damage, foetal problems/distress or birth trauma. These can arise from a variety of causes as already mentioned.

2. The child will have several autism-related *Gm* genes (which may include an inability to tolerate certain foods, particularly milk and wheat). He may be intolerant of foods eaten by his mother if breast fed.

Children in both these groups will initially show signs of severe neuro-developmental delay, being either overly placid or restless and easily agitated. Depending on the reflexes involved this may include any of the wide range of features already mentioned, for example feeding difficulties and a number of sensisms. His unusual response to approaches and touch are early indicators of the problems.

Those with a food intolerance will gradually accrue a build-up of toxins and opioid peptides in the brain whilst the nutrients will be depleted and this may worsen their sensory problems.

Those in group 1 will develop 'autisms' at an early age whilst those in group 2 are predisposed to autism. In the case of those with unrecognized food intolerances onset will vary according to their diet. Those with a milk allergy will often show signs of autism during the first 6 to 12 months whilst those with an intolerance of wheat will begin to demonstrate problems between 12 and 18 months.

Symptoms of perceptual autism

1. *Abnormal sensory perceptions*

   These perceptions seem to be directly linked to particular aberrant reflexes. Although it is possible that other reflexes may also be involved, the one of most importance here is the Moro reflex.

2. *Anxiety*

   Present knowledge would suggest that these symptoms are interrelated, the anxiety being caused by the abnormal sensory perceptions. The anxiety leads, as I have already shown, to the onset of various instinctive defence mechanisms, which in their turn cause a variety of secondary problems (Figure 4.1).

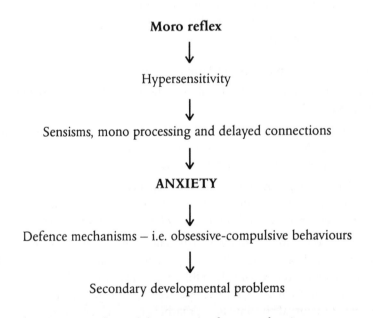

Moro reflex

↓

Hypersensitivity

↓

Sensisms, mono processing and delayed connections

↓

ANXIETY

↓

Defence mechanisms – i.e. obsessive-compulsive behaviours

↓

Secondary developmental problems

Figure 4.1 The Moro reflex and the symptoms of perceptual autism

Although each person has their own individual difficulties perhaps we should also anticipate that some people in this group could have high or fluctuating serotonin levels and would also have any or several of the problems which Goddard Blythe and Comings linked to the limbic system:

- metabolic imbalance and allergies;
- difficulties in co-ordinating the two hemispheres of the brain;
- anxiety/panic attacks.;
- polydipsia;
- sleep disorders.

(I omit parts of Comings' list since some things are already in my description whilst others obviously relate more to Tourette's syndrome than autism.)

Perhaps Delacato's third category of 'white noise' belongs here too? I have already mentioned the possible role of a zinc deficiency to which I would also now add a fluctuation in serotonin levels. It is also possible for some aberrant reflexes to contribute to a similar effect for, according to Goddard Blythe, the Moro reflex combined with a cluster of other retained reflexes can make the child feel extremely uncomfortable within his body. So, even though other factors may also play a part, I include it in here until research clarifies the matter.

To complicate matters still further I would suggest that the tonic labyrinthine reflex might have a place here as well. As you will remember, this leads to automatic movements of the limbs when the body is lying down and causes the tongue to thrust forward when the head is in a certain position. This can make early feeding difficult, hinders the development of clear speech and could account for the fact that some children do seem unusual from birth. The TLR reflex can also give rise to a number of other problems as shown in Figure 4.2.

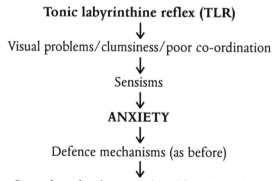

Tonic labyrinthine reflex (TLR)
↓
Visual problems/clumsiness/poor co-ordination
↓
Sensisms
↓
ANXIETY
↓
Defence mechanisms (as before)
↓
Secondary developmental problems including
poor concentration plus an incredible memory for certain things

Figure 4.2 The tonic labyrinthine reflex and the symptoms of perceptual autism

In contrast to the global problems caused by the Moro reflex, those caused by the TLR are mainly concerned with vision. The child would have great difficulty in repressing visual background information and the constant impingement of this could cause a delay in dealing with information efficiently. If only the one sense were to be affected (albeit severely) then one could assume that any processing problems or delay in making connections would be slight. As experience suggests that most people with autism seem to have problems in all their senses, I would suggest that if this reflex is found it is highly likely that a cluster of other retained reflexes will be present too and that these will give rise to mono processing and delayed connections.

I firmly believe that, regardless of the reflexes involved, many people with autism are able to hone a particular skill to a fine degree. However, it would be interesting to know whether the incredible memory associated with the TLR is actually related to those with savant abilities.

Features associated with onset

These are shared by those with autism and Asperger's syndrome as well as those with reactive and induced problems:

- Either the development of perceptual problems or a serious and dramatic deterioration in perception with all the attendant problems that brings. Delayed or hyper connections.

- Constant anxiety.

- Withdrawal and/or the development of obsessive or compulsive behaviours.

- A lack or a decrease of interest in others and in play etc.

- Halted development or a loss of previously acquired skills.

- A slowing or halting of language development or a loss of previously acquired language.

- A possible lack of, or a gradual loss of proprioception and self-awareness.

- Symptoms of alexithymia, that is, an inability to talk about/understand one's feelings or to empathize with others.

- Symptoms of dyssemia, that is, an inability to understand non-verbal cues.

Symptoms of perceptual Asperger's syndrome

1. *Abnormal sensory perceptions*

   Here the reflexes are combined giving rise to slightly different problems. Once again, individual assessment would be needed to determine this accurately.

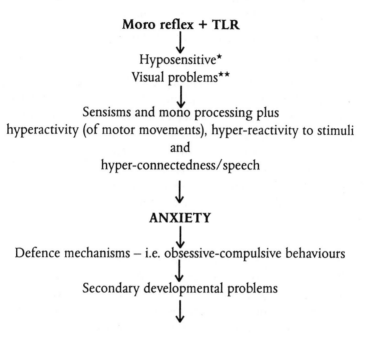

Moro reflex + TLR
↓
Hyposensitive*
Visual problems**

↓
Sensisms and mono processing plus
hyperactivity (of motor movements), hyper-reactivity to stimuli
and
hyper-connectedness/speech

↓

ANXIETY
↓
Defence mechanisms – i.e. obsessive-compulsive behaviours
↓
Secondary developmental problems
↓

Figure 4.3 The Moro reflex and TLR and the symptoms of perceptual Asperger's syndrome. (*Hypersensitivity to sound is sometimes found in such children – perhaps as a compensatory feature? **The visual problems can be associated with either reflex and could include hyposensitivity to light and distorted vision as with the TLR, or hypersensitivity as associated with the Moro reflex. Once again individual assessment will be needed to detail the problem areas accurately)

2. *Anxiety*

   While again the anxiety is caused by the metabolic problems and abnormal perceptions, it may be less visible because it is submerged by the other more obvious difficulties – problems similar to those found in frontal lobe syndrome. These and the secondary problems could include any of the following:

   • Impairment in perception and the formation of concepts.

   • Speech and communication problems.

- Problems with attention, concentration and thinking processes.

- Impaired motor functions.

- High achievement in some areas/low in others.

- Difficulties with reading, writing, etc. similar to, but generally more severe, than those of dyslexia with a variability of performance (day-to-day or even hour-to-hour).

- Disturbed sleeping patterns including night terrors or nightmares.

- Problems with relationships and social behaviour.

Perhaps acknowledging the sensory problems and recognizing the far-reaching effects of altered serotonin levels could explain why a few sufferers do have hallucinations – a factor which has caused confusion and, in a number of cases, a diagnosis of 'childhood schizophrenia'.

One final point. Obviously individual assessment will be needed to determine whether other reflexes like the asymmetrical tonic neck reflex (ATNR), which gives rise to fragmented vision and affects balance, motor control and laterality, may also have an involvement in either of these conditions.

Reactive autism and reactive Asperger's syndrome

Generally, although not exclusively, the child in this group has several autism-related *Gm* genes. This inheritance probably includes digestive problems and an inability to tolerate certain foods which leaves him more 'at risk' from stress or trauma during early childhood than his peers.

Prior to the onset of autism he will probably show signs of moderate neurodevelopmental delay which could make him appear very placid or restless in the early months. This will eventually lead to problems consistent with attention deficit disorder or attention deficit hyperactivity disorder.

Some of these signs may initially be mistaken for indications of precocity rather than delay, as the child may learn to walk without crawling or creeping much first; may have precocious (but unusual) speech patterns; may be able to give a quick and accurate repetition of tunes at a very early age, etc. This combination of factors will leave him susceptible to anxiety-related problems which, given a particular set of circumstances, will develop at some point during his life.

Without research it is difficult to make an assessment, but one has to allow for the possibility that there may also be a few children in this category who only have an inherent fragility or mild NDD, as described more fully in the next section.

The onset of these reactive problems would again be during the first four years – often between 18 months and 3 years. It is generally associated with stress or trauma but *not maternal deprivation*. It is possible though that there may be a few instances in which it is linked with abuse and unrelated to the genetic inheritance – an idea discussed more fully on page 218.

Onset is precipitated by a period of stress or a 'traumatic' event, either of which will probably contribute to a further build-up of opioid peptides and alterations in the neurotransmitters, particularly adrenaline. The child will react by beginning to display autisms. In the case of stress the onset may be gradual whereas it is likely to be more sudden if he is subjected to a trauma.

Potential stresses and traumas

The following list gives examples of some of the major events which are generally acknowledged to cause stress although obviously there are others: one child I know finally developing autism after her stomach was pumped in order to save her life. Even an 'ordinary' healthy young child would need a great deal of support to deal with some of them but while he might regress for a time, he would certainly not develop the obsessions or compulsions common to the child who is predisposed to such conditions:

- Early separation from the family – particularly the mother.
- Birth of a sibling.
- Death of a parent/close relative.
- Divorce.
- Moving house or school.
- Going away on holiday – for while this may be seen as pleasant and is obviously necessary, it can prove stressful for the vulnerable child.

These then culminate in the types of problems detailed on page 206. Once again I will reiterate that although maternal deprivation as a general cause is definitely a myth, a variety of circumstances beyond parental control can be potentially traumatic for the growing child and, if occurring in the first weeks of life, could also affect the bonding process – for example, separation from the mother through illness or postnatal depression.

Trauma at a later stage of life may precipitate either obsessive compulsive disorder II or delayed Asperger's syndrome. These, too, generally fall into the column relating to the inheritance of several *Gm* genes, onset being after the age of four. The reason for this idea is threefold.

First, people with OCD have many of the features of autism except for the very concrete thinking of the young child. Second, while many people with OCD respond well to behavioural therapies which actually slow the activity in the brain, others respond better (only?) when their treatment includes medication and thus it would seem that there may be an inherent difference between them. It would be interesting to know whether this relates to the serotonin levels for whilst one report (Zohar, Murphy and Zohar-Kadouch 1990) says that people with OCD have low levels of serotonin another (Coccaro and Murphy 1990) suggests that they actually have higher levels than normal. Third, Tourette's syndrome, whilst devastating, does not appear at birth although there are various symptoms (such as ADHD characteristics) before any tics appear.

If so, one could expect that whilst both groups might have moderate perceptual problems those with OCD II will demonstrate symptoms of ADD and have some mono-processing problems. If this condition is closely related to autism, as I believe it is, it is also possible that many of the people in this group would have high or fluctuating serotonin levels and problems associated with the limbic system previously mentioned.

In contrast, those in the Asperger's group may initially display symptoms of ADHD and have hyper-processing problems, an underactive nervous system, low serotonin levels and features of frontal lobe syndrome (with a reduced flow of blood in this region?). In time perhaps research will show whether, if the initial symptoms remain mild and onset was late, there would be a possibility that panic disorders or similar might be the result even with this predisposition.

Induced autism/Asperger's syndrome

The child generally has one/few *Gm* genes although again there may be some exceptions. These can cause an inherent fragility which, in many cases, may be associated with physical problems such as food intolerances, allergies or migraine. Whilst some will have mild signs of NDD including mildly abnormal sensory perceptions it will be interesting to see whether those who do not have NDD carry the 'seeds of shyness' identified by Kagan.

Onset is generally associated with a number of physical factors, including illness, which lead to a variety of severe physical and other reactions. To complicate matters still further, one could postulate that in some cases the central nervous system of the young fragile children could simply be 'unbalanced' by any of the precipitating factors and, rather than causing the development of severe symptoms, merely leaves them even more vulnerable than usual; a traumatic event of the type previously mentioned in the reactive category could prove to be the final straw, leading to the development of autisms.

The onset generally occurs between 15 months and 2 years when the child's development is disrupted by any one of a number of physical problems, including:

- Repeated courses of antibiotics.
- Adverse reaction to vaccine.

- Onset of bowel disease, e.g. Crohn's disease, coeliac or ileal-lymphoid-nodular hyperplasia.

- Measles, meningitis or encephalitis.

- Undergoing a general anaesthetic.

- A build-up of problems associated with leaky gut, candida, food intolerances, etc. (Although generally I would expect at least one other factor to be involved in sudden onset of physical symptoms described below, this will remain a moot point until more research is done.)

Any of the above can precipitate the following physical symptoms which culminate in withdrawal and the development of defence mechanisms:

- An increase in the severity of the aforementioned perceptual difficulties. (These thrust the child into an unknown environment and, in addition to halting development, can often cause the loss of previously achieved milestones.)

- Dramatic change in diet. An intolerance to certain foods whilst craving others. Indiscriminate eating (things other than food).

- Excessive thirst (polydipsia).

- Pale complexion with red face/ears – which may be especially evident after eating. Dark rings under the eyes.

- Dry skin.

- A high temperature for no apparent reason.

- Excessive sweating (particularly at night).

- Bad catarrh.

- Intestinal problems, diarrhoea, bloating, stomach pains.

- Disruption of the digestive system and/or damage to the blood brain barrier.

- Asthma, eczema or urticaria (nettle rash)

- Hypoglycaemia with symptoms of weakness, tremors, nervousness, breathlessness or excitement and, occasionally, a loss of consciousness.

- Possible petit mal epilepsy.

- Tendency to become ambidextrous or even to change handedness.

These will lead to a general regression in all areas and a deterioration in behaviour as well as many of the other points detailed in the sections on perceptual problems of both autism and Asperger's syndrome. It is also possible that the social relationships of those with induced problems could show a greater deterioration than those of children in other groups as the physical problems become increasingly worse – for example the perceptual problems or untreated bowel disease.

One factor not yet mentioned is onset arising from repeated (severe) seizures or ear infections, for this is slightly different to the others and may possibly involve children who have several *Gm* genes as well. One would assume that these factors will not generally cause a deterioration of the sensory problems although they will halt development and, as long as they continue, may make it increasingly hard for the child to retain the skills and knowledge he had previously acquired.

This inherent vulnerability may mean that any similar problems after the age of four might precipitate obsessive compulsive disorder or frontal lobe syndrome which share the characteristics of the induced conditions already identified. I would also postulate that the differences between the two groups are similar to those I suggested between autism and Asperger's syndrome with its links to the frontal lobes. And once again I would suggest that OCD is more specifically related to problems which have a primary effect on the limbic system.

Generally, though, those whose inherent fragility is not compromised by any of these physical problems in childhood may well make their way carefully and successfully through life by learning to compensate for their problems. Many will become fully functioning adults who are generally able to cope with the normal pressures of life adequately although some of them may be prone to anxiety-related physical illnesses or even possibly panic attacks or a variety of phobic behaviours.

So now we have explored the three different types of autism in which metabolic and perceptual problems play a major part. Before moving on to the next section, though, I would like to answer some of the questions which may arise.

- *Can the metabolic problems and sensory perceptions be altered by 'treatment'?* The short answer is of course 'yes'. However it must be acknowledged that while the various treatments currently available do not inevitably lead to a 'cure' for the problems of autism they should certainly contribute to giving the sufferers a greater quality of life than they might otherwise have.

- *Is the degree of handicap and withdrawal determined by the severity of the abnormal perceptions?* Definitely not, as you have seen from the discussion in the previous chapter.

- *Does the passing of time lessen the disturbing effect of the perceptual problems?* While it would be true to say that many older people with autism do not appear as disturbed as they did in childhood or adolescence it is difficult to determine whether the problems have decreased through treatment, increased maturity, reduced anxiety, or whether the person has merely adjusted to living with them. Darren White's account suggests that some of his problems had ceased while the idea of adjustment would seem to be supported by Gunilla Gerland who says that she is finding that a great many aspects of life are now much easier, although some remain unchanged. Hopefully the increasing number of books and articles written by the sufferers themselves will gradually throw more light on this.

Now, however, let us look at some of the other problems in more detail.

Secondary autism/Asperger's syndrome

This type of problem can be acquired at any age after an accident. It would be interesting to know whether those people who develop obsessive-compulsive behaviours in such a way have also received some degree of perceptual 'damage'.

The patient is most likely to receive treatment in a centre specifically geared to coping with people with brain injuries. While obviously these problems vary in severity, great strides have been made in the treatment of severe brain damage over the past few decades and improvement might be possible in the long term.

Moving on now I would also like to discuss two other groups of children who demonstrate autisms but in whom, as you will see, the causes and the major problems will remain unclear without extremely careful assessment. The two groups consist of those who have undergone severe deprivation and those who have suffered child abuse.

Severe deprivation

One research project identified some 6 per cent of very severely deprived and undernourished young children in Romanian orphanages as having 'autistic-like' features even though the children were said to show more signs of social interest and had a far better prognosis, with most improving considerably between the ages of 4 and 6.

Six per cent initially seems very high, but we have to remember that whilst many of the children who comprise this group come from impoverished families others have been placed into an orphanage because they already had some type of problem. A true figure could only be arrived at by looking at the total population and so we must treat this percentage as atypical.

While such conditions are rare in most affluent countries it is a fact that severe deprivation and undernourishment can, in some circumstances, be a cause of 'autisms' although, as not all children in similar situations develop the same problems, we could conclude that inherent fragility also plays a part. Is this the whole answer?

An article in the *Sunday Times Magazine* (Scott 1998) offered additional and interesting information which helps elucidate the question. This discussed the varied problems found amongst nearly 1000 children who had been adopted from the orphanages in Romania. While many have adapted well others, although coping well at school in the early years (ages 4 to 5), have, by the age of 8 or 9, begun to drop behind.

Several of these children, although not suffering from autism, have a variety of other problems ranging from passivity to hyperactivity and an inability to pay attention. Whilst one child was said to be unable to respond to visual clues she and some of the other children in this group also have a condition known as central auditory processing disorder (CAPD) which leaves them unable to filter, process or sort information correctly; problems which are reminiscent of the processing problems already discussed and which seem to parallel the processing problems of some people with ADHD and ADD.

In contrast, other children seem to be more resilient. They have few problems; something which is put down to numerous factors including heredity, prenatal nutrition, less illness, a shorter time in institutional care (custody?!) and/or stimulus.

Harry Ghugani, a paediatric neurologist, is currently looking at the problems of such children in greater depth by using PET scans to observe the activity levels in the area of the brain concerned with social behaviour. Although the results are not conclusive he claims that the emotional deprivation these children suffered has resulted, not only in the type of emotional damage mentioned in the early studies, but also in actual brain damage. Ghugani postulates that because emotional exchanges were absent in their early years the normal connections in the brain have not developed as they should.

Ronald Federici, a developmental neuropsychologist, has collected data on similar adoptees over a period of twelve years and has researched the environmental and medical factors that may have interrupted brain development. Generally these range from environmental factors (many orphanages being situated in polluted industrial areas), the length of time for which the children were institutionalized (which seems to relate directly to the prognosis) and pre- and postnatal factors. This includes prenatal malnutrition, parental health problems and last, but not least, childhood illnesses. Indeed, many of the children had suffered illnesses and even chronic ear infections which, being left untreated, would have caused them constant stress.

During the period of 'care' such children often suffered from general neglect: some were also malnourished, having to fight for handfuls of food. A number of them also suffered from abuse of a physical and (in at least one case) sexual nature. This being so it is easy to see why the area of the brain dealing with social behaviour would be less active than in other 'normal' children. It is hardly surprising then to find that some have severe emotional problems.

Although the figures may vary, Federici says that while approximately 25 per cent of children in this group escape both emotional and neurological damage, others are less fortunate. He estimates that approximately 40–50 per cent have moderate but manageable problems including learning and behavioural difficulties and that the remaining 25 per cent have severe problems involving some form of brain damage and mental retardation.

It is not just learning difficulties which affect such children for other problems exist too. One mother described her eight-year-old adopted son as having a damaged soul, for, like many another severely deprived child he had learnt very early on that he could not rely upon other people for comfort. As she points out, he had to care for himself until he was a year old and thus is now unable to let anyone else care for him, pushing them away when they try.

This description seems indicative of Docker Drysdale's 'caretaker self'. It is incredibly difficult for a child to learn to hug, kiss or otherwise show emotion when their deprivation has been so great. Such children will need much specialized help before they begin to be able to develop normal relationships with other people. While, sadly, that may be impossible for some, the work of Docker Drysdale and others offers hope that it will not be the case for all; a point to which I shall return in a moment.

What, though, is the foundation of the learning difficulties, hyperactivity, central auditory processing deficit, etc.? I would suggest that these are not simply an offshoot of the emotional problems but may rather indicate some degree of neurodevelopmental delay.

It is clear that children who are malnourished are at risk of disrupted development, but we also have to take into account the lack of opportunities such children had to develop the various skills we all take so for granted. We know that many of these children spent hour upon endless hour confined to a limited space, whether a shared cot or playpen, which severely limited their scope for exploration. And we know that development is dependent upon the series of building blocks and initially needs constant practice. The child must learn to crawl before he can creep and then walk correctly – all things which many of these children had little opportunity to do. Similarly the child who has no toys to reach for will have great difficulty in developing hand/eye co-ordination.

This being the case I would surmise that at least some (and perhaps the majority) of those with learning difficulties will have some aberrant reflexes. One rather hopes that this will turn out to be the case because then some aspects of their physical/mental 'impairments' might respond to treatment.

Thus I would hypothesise that here again we have a spectrum of problems with a variety of causes. We can anticipate that:

1. All those institutionalized at a very early age who are denied an attachment, or whose attachment is broken by being taken away from their mother, will have emotional problems stemming from the lack of or disruption of bonding.

2. Those who were confined to a cot, playpen etc. and had no freedom to explore and develop their crawling, hand/eye coordination etc. skills may well have aberrant reflexes and other developmental problems, for depending on the conditions such children will have suffered a degree of sensory deprivation.

3. Those with the most severe problems (i.e. autistic features) were either inherently fragile and/or had severe developmental delay (perhaps because of the lack of opportunity/conditions in which they were kept) and/or suffered severe trauma during their first three or four years – possibly including abuse.

4. Those who have less severe learning problems (akin to ADD or ADHD) are likely to have some form of developmental delay which may respond to treatment.

5. Children who were able to develop a relationship with a carer will have fewer emotional problems than many of the others, as would those who were institutionalized at a later stage.

Some children will of course suffer from both neurodevelopmental and emotional difficulties. Breaking down each child's problems into their constituent parts should allow us to devise individual treatment plans before their lives are further blighted by their ongoing difficulties.

We already know that treatment for aberrant reflexes and for other physical problems caused by slowed development is available from a variety of sources. Indeed, while little help is currently available in Britain early intervention programmes in the United States very sensibly do focus on post-traumatic stress, sensory integration, CAPD and the treatment thereof.

What though of the emotional damage? We must not mistake this for post-traumatic stress, for the effects are different. Bowlby's report in 1951 offered little hope for those who were so institutionalized, indicating that in almost all cases the damage caused by the lack of attachment would last for life. This though is not the end of the story for, as previously mentioned, Barbara Docker Drysdale, who based her work on that of Donald Winnicot, developed programmes to help alleviate the results of such damage.

She divided these children into the different categories already discussed. She founded the Mulberry Bush School in Oxford and, through her work there, clearly showed that even children who have been severely emotionally damaged could and do respond to the correct treatment programme. Whilst realistically a 'cure' may not be possible for all, there is certainly some hope that some of these damaged children can be helped to overcome their early traumas and move forward into rewarding relationships.

Child abuse

In the section on reactive problems I noted that the child would generally have inherited several *Gm* genes. There is, however, a possibility that the child subjected to abuse could also develop severe problems, even without that type of inheritance.

This subject is made even more difficult by the emotive words which used to be used to blame autism on the parents. To ignore this topic would be cowardice but I hope that by now it is abundantly clear that the anxiety which denotes autism/Asperger's syndrome *normally* arises from internal problems and that autism linked to abuse is relatively rare.

I was recently asked whether a child who had suffered very severe child abuse (having various limbs broken, being locked for long periods of time in a small cupboard, etc.) could be suffering from autism solely due to the abuse: for, unsurprisingly, he displayed many of the stress/anxiety features I have mentioned. This, of course, is extremely difficult to ascertain for while he certainly suffered from sensory deprivation, one would need not only a full history but also observation to determine whether 'internal', that is metabolic, perceptual and processing, problems existed.

We have to acknowledge that, in a few families, the original internal problems of some children can lead to a situation where what may have begun as discipline slides gradually into abuse as detailed by Svea Gold in her book *When Children Invite Child Abuse* (1986).

That said, we cannot hide our heads in the sand and refuse to admit that is also a possibility that the converse may happen. Everyone is aware that a small minority of families have an abusive relationship with a particular child or even, occasionally, all their children. It cannot be denied that such abuse, if happening in the very earliest years, could cause withdrawal and other 'symptoms' indistinguishable from many of the difficulties found amongst those with autism even though the perceptual and other problems would be absent.

Certainly (and unhappily) the sensory deprivations and abuses suffered by the child mentioned above are similar (but more severe) than those of the hostages and, as such, could quite conceivably have triggered a variety of defence mechanisms, which depending on the child's age at the time of the abuse could lead him to be classified as 'autistic': problems which would perhaps be better classed as 'acquired'.

The causes of abuse are beyond the remit of this book but because of the particular problems of autism there are some relevant factors I would like to discuss as they might be helpful in identifying whether abuse is actually taking place.

My limited experience of this subject (of sexual abuse of a person with OCD rather than autism) suggests that when abuse is perpetrated within the family the abuser often takes one of two courses of action. One is to refuse to attempt any type of treatment which they feel might have beneficial results for the person they are abusing. Alternatively, if they cannot find some logical argument to dissuade others from that course of action, they will then in some way 'sabotage' that treatment in order to protect themselves. This can even extend to causing a breakdown between the home and those responsible for the child – social worker, school or residential home – a breakdown which can lead to the appointment of a new social worker or to the abused person moving to a new establishment. Sadly at present the confusion regarding the relevance of certain treatments makes it relatively easy for any such people to question/undermine treatments.

Such abusers do not actually want to see the child/adult make progress for fear that they might then begin to talk about the abuse they have suffered. This is something which, on reflection, I feel is also the case in other types of abuse – physical or emotional – and whether carried out by a member of the family or by a 'carer'; the latter also being in a position to disrupt a treatment programme.

The other type of abuser I have come across (although unfortunately I only recognized this with hindsight) was an intelligent person who despite much knowledge of the child/adult with autism and their problems *repeatedly* mishandled situations thereby precipitating incidents of difficult behaviour and (in the case I know of) severe self-abuse; something I will touch upon again in relation to FC. This can, of course, happen inadvertently too but when it occurs frequently or consistently one must question the person's motives.

Unfortunately the sensory and other problems leave the person with autism only too open to abuse caused in a variety of ways. As the significance of these problems is still dismissed by some, professionals, parents and carers are still in a position to 'choose' to ignore the evidence. Thus at times a person with autism may be subject to perceptual bombardment which is done inadvertently or thoughtlessly. At other times, though, one must question the motives behind some actions as with the man who, with a good knowledge of autism and, whilst acknowledging his child's dislike of noise, insisted on playing a particular tape (which was flawed and screeched in places) whenever the family went on long trip in the car – and who commented quite coolly that the child then got extremely upset!

Each case needs to be examined extremely carefully, though, for the points mentioned above are not the sole preserve of the abuser. Indeed there seem to be a small (and thankfully rare) number of parents who have some complex and confusing ulterior motive for the way in which they deal with their children. These are people who behave in a bizarre fashion (perhaps because of unresolved problems of their own) undermining or refusing to try any treatment even though it is clearly obvious that it might have beneficial results.

I have come across a couple of people whose children would definitely fall into the perceptual category but who were determined to prove that a particular treatment was not of benefit: organizing things in such a way that the treatment failed. One such was a well educated person who had read all the latest research information. Instead of implementing a diet gradually, it was done overnight; so suddenly that the child was bound to stop eating. This obviously resulted in the diet having to be stopped soon after onset because 'it' caused the child so much distress. Thus *the diet failed*. Not so! This was clearly a case in which the parent actually caused the distress even though they were, no doubt, able to deny any responsibility – even to themselves – for surely otherwise it would not have been openly talked about?

Another example was the intelligent person who, having read much information on food intolerances and, despite the fact that one child in the family had a serious food intolerance which had caused great ill health until identified and treated, still refused even to have the child with autism tested for similar intolerances – 'justifying' this on the grounds that eliminating that food would mean the child would not be getting the correct vitamins etc. which, intellectually at least, the person knew was quite contrary to the facts.

Why would any parent act in such a manner? Not being a psychiatrist I can only wonder if in some way this type of person 'needs' to have a 'handicapped' child because they themselves then attract both sympathy and attention. It is sad to think that the reverse is in fact true for, if treatment were effective, not only would the child's future be happier but the parent could actually gain more attention through the child's progress, as with those parents who have recorded their children's improvements.

You may have a different viewpoint on the motivation behind this but whatever the cause the child ends up paying a very high price for their parent's problem. Whether those people with such problems have the insight needed to analyze and alter their actions is a moot point. I can only hope that their spouses, partners or other people involved with the family may be able to recognize such problems and give the person the support they need to resolve their underlying problems.

Discussion

So now you have read through my ideas and have had the opportunity to decide their validity for yourselves. Whether such hypotheses are accurate or not will remain open to question until more research has been done but certainly it would seem that they could help explain some of the conundrums.

Assuming that they are correct we must ask whether such hypotheses help in any way. Do they have any real relevance? I think so, for even though some answers are still missing clarification of the type of difficulties should enable us to predict (and perhaps avoid) potential future problems whilst enabling us to devise and give the most appropriate treatment. It should also help to determine the efficacy of current treatments and identify those for whom they are best suited.

If these suppositions are correct, it becomes vital that accurate diagnosis is made, for it is only by determining the answers correctly that the most appropriate treatment(s) can be developed and progress monitored. While current assessments give a clear picture of the person's abilities I hope that in time some other aspects can be added. These are:

- tests to determine the underlying metabolic problems;
- assessment of the reflexes and perceptual problems involved;
- assessment of the person's emotional stage;
- assessment of their level of functioning.

Logically such assumptions would imply that treatment which would be helpful to one group would not necessarily be of value to another and might even prove detrimental. This would certainly appear to be the case with holding therapy, which while sounding as if it belongs to the 'physical' range of treatments is, in fact, based on psychotherapeutic lines. While it might possibly prove of some benefit to children suffering from reactive problems, its confrontational approach must, at the very least, be an extremely traumatic and terrifying experience for any child who is hypersensitive to sound or touch.

My concern at present is that too many treatments are offered without careful consideration of the individual's problems. It is clear that those who are hyposensitive will generally need different treatment from those who have hypersensitivity, and that their emotional level also needs to be taken into account. Similarly people whose problems are mainly dietary and perceptual will need a different type of treatment from those Romanian children, for instance, whose difficulties derive from undernourishment and deprivation – for the latter would need physical care, stimulation and, possibly, help for emotional disturbance. This also applies to any child whose problems stem solely from abuse, for, in contrast to the others, he would need a primarily psychotherapeutic approach.

However there is hope for, although there is no definite way of effecting a cure at present, greater knowledge and understanding of the causes is gradually leading to a change in the prognosis as present treatments are enhanced and new ones developed. Encouragement is twofold, for while various treatments are already having some success both in autism and in other differing fields, success is not exclusive to those with the mildest problems. With co-operation and co-ordination, it should be possible to increase the chances of success.

Initially I thought that the criteria would give a guide to any 'cure', suggesting that if defence mechanisms were still used for lengthy periods of time after treatment to the detriment of social relationships and communication. The person cannot be said to have been totally cured. This was naive. Great care will be needed in judging this, as those who have been socially isolated for lengthy periods of time (i.e. those who reach adolescence or adulthood before undergoing treatment) will have effectively 'lost' many years of their lives and the corresponding experiences.

It is to be hoped that once the underlying anxiety has gone, the strategies they have built up over the years to enable them to survive will gradually be replaced by a genuine ability to cope and that with help they will be able to begin to build upon the language and comprehension skills that they already have. We must recognize, though, that even those who are most apparently independent will initially have problems in socializing and/or may converse only about a limited range of subjects, for much will have passed them by during their years in 'solitary'.

I was fascinated to find, when reading *The Empty Fortress* (Bettleheim 1969), that three of the children who made progress at the Orthogenic School were used as examples by Bettleheim, in part because he felt that those who were mute or extremely limited in their use of language skills were 'more damaged' than those who had speech. While this supposition seemed logical at that time, hindsight would now suggest that it was unfounded. Rereading his accounts would suggest that his criteria may have resulted in a study of children who had reactive problems. Could it be that this made them more responsive to psychotherapeutic methods than others, thereby artificially reinforcing the idea that the underlying problem was psychological?

One thing on which the 'experts' have no difficulty in agreeing is that there is a spectrum of autistic behaviour which ranges from extremely severe to very mild. An article in the *Daily Telegraph* (Highfield and Berry 28.8.91) said that Francesca Happé, of the Medical Research Council's Cognitive Development Unit, had suggested that at one end of the scale were the very withdrawn and unsociable people who treated people as objects. As an example of this she quoted the tragic case of a man who threw a baby out of a window in order to silence it, which, in the light of our knowledge of hypersensitivity, is still terrible but sadly all too understandable. At the other end of the range were the eccentrics and what she termed 'mad professors', some of whom would seem either to fit into the fifth category of functioning (see page 178) or who might even have late onset problems of one type or another.

Certainly, I would agree that there is a spectrum of behaviours but would suggest, in line with the discussion in the previous chapter, that this correlates to the way in which people with autism and Asperger's syndrome function – and is often confused with their intelligence and sociability. I would emphasize, though, that to react so terribly to sound is not necessarily the prerogative of a person who is unsociable and thinks of people as objects, even if that was so in the case mentioned.

I do not intend to confuse but would suggest that there are actually two different sorts of spectrum. On one side is the type of scale mentioned by Happe. On the other side we have a spectrum, not just of autism, but rather of a wide range of disorders, all of which are part of the same coin and vary in intensity and, presumably, in the genetic inheritance. This idea is now being supported by researchers in other fields, such as that of Tourette's syndrome: a development which offers positive hope for the future for if researchers from different areas join forces answers may be found earlier than expected.

Thus the diagram by Comings which relates to Tourette's syndrome could be modified to include the various disorders mentioned overleaf (Figure 4.4). It is, of course, possible that further research into the genetic problems will also implicate other factors such as other amino acids and neurotransmitters. Could this invalidate the chart? I would suggest not, for two reasons. First, regardless of the genes involved, it is highly likely that the opioid peptides and/or other factors have some effect on the serotoninergic and dopaminergic pathways thereby also affecting the level of norepinephrine. Second, even if this postulated relationship between these neurotransmitters and autism etc. is dismissed, the connections between the limbic system, the frontal lobes and the problems mentioned would, I believe, still be valid. I would point out, however, that the diagram probably makes it look more simplistic than it actually is for the complexities of the brain leave many questions unanswered.

Whilst Comings' work indicates that Tourette's syndrome is connected with low serotonin levels I would surmise from the work on opioid peptides that those with the most severe problems, whether of autism or Asperger's syndrome, probably have high serotonin levels whilst those with milder problems have lower levels.

A query now. Should the section on problems caused by several mutant genes be broadened to include some 'apparently' physical problems? If so I would suggest that the final box in Figure 4.4 might read as shown in Figure 4.5.

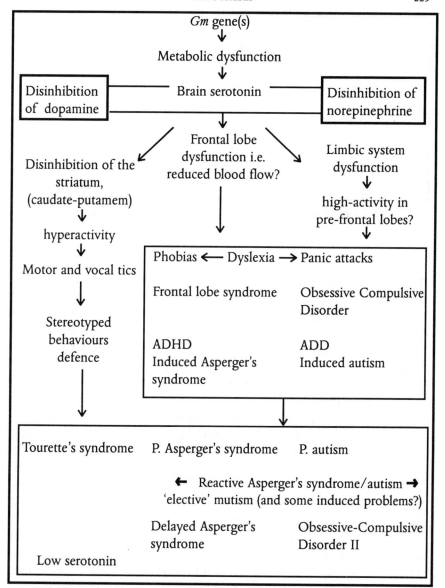

Figure 4.4 Disorders resulting from genetic problems   (P = perceptual)

The reason for the inclusion of MSD and PKU should by now be clear. Should Rett's syndrome also have a place in this list? And some types of cerebral palsy? Certainly some 'palsy'-type movements seem similar to the various kinds of tics found in TS whilst some people with CP have aberrant reflexes and dyslexia and others demonstrate 'autistic' tendencies as well. I am starting to believe that in time perhaps we will find that other 'mental' disorders like schizophrenia may also fit into the wider puzzle. Do such theories hold water? I shall be interested to hear what other people think.

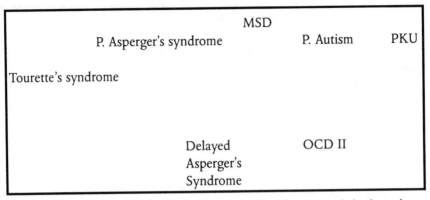

Figure 4.5 A version of the final box of Figure 4.4, broadened to include physical problems

Research

It would certainly seem that many of the research findings to date plus the outcome of research in other areas lead one to another, as shown in Figure 4.6.

While the different types of aberrant reflex could certainly account for the differences that occur between individuals, it would also be helpful to know more about the relationship between aberrant reflexes, neurotransmitters such as serotonin and the various parts of the brain i.e. the limbic system, prefrontal and frontal lobes, as this might give a clearer indication of the way problems could (and do) develop.

Bérard's treatment of people with depression clearly demonstrates the strong links between many of the physical problems and the psychological factors. There is one report to suggest that this 'physical' treatment actually has an effect on the neurotransmitters.

Glenn Doman believes that the type of programming he uses can affect acetycholine. If a similar effect happens with other treatments and neurotransmitters too, this could have great implications for the future.

Research into the effect of tinted lenses for people with autism has already been started by the Irlen Institute who are involved in a project at Modena University in Italy looking into the relationship between these and various neurotransmitters. It will be interesting to see how this progresses. If the lenses correct vision, as we know they do, then one can postulate that, by reducing stress, they should reduce the levels of opioid peptides and alter the level of adrenaline.

Unfortunately some of the other treatments are not currently being assessed in an objective manner, which makes it exceptionally hard to choose which is best for a particular individual. I hope that in time this will be addressed for this would enable us to gain an accurate picture of which person is likely to be responsive to which treatment; a vital factor in helping minimize each individual's difficulties.

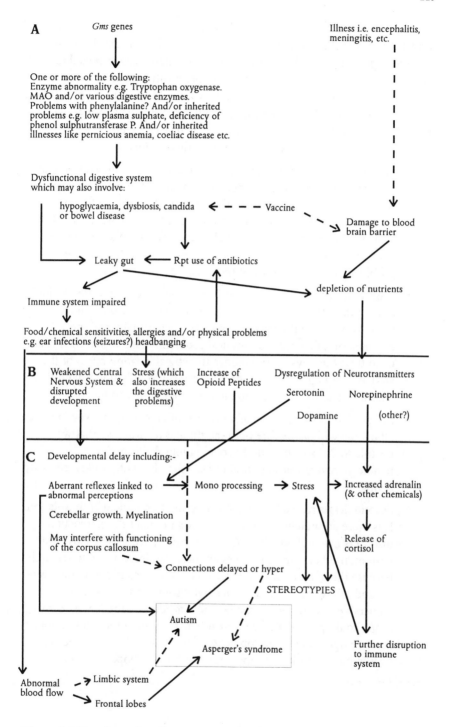

Figure 4.6 How the various factors associated with autism might correlate

Another important area for research might be in determining the sex differences. Overall it seems that males are at a biological disadvantage from the very beginning. Whether this is because of genetic factors linked to the X chromosome (such as MAO), testosterone, brain differences or other factors remains a moot point. Either of the first two would seem to be particularly good candidates. I will be interested to know the answer(s) although whether this will enable us to redress the balance remains to be seen.

In conclusion I would like to make a few final points:

- First, even the word autism has tended to mislead, concentrating as it does on the symptom of 'aloneness', which, as I hope I have shown, is only the product of several other factors. While I would not suggest that a change be made (for the public are more aware of the problems than ever before) I would certainly like to see far more emphasis placed on the role that both anxiety and the perceptual problems play in the onset of these disorders.

- If only this can be done we will be in a much better position to look at the problems of autism and Asperger's syndrome objectively seeing them for what, in the majority of cases, they actually are: the culmination of a cluster of physical problems. This would then enable us to treat the physical symptoms, thereby alleviating much of the anxiety; helping sufferers (where necessary) to fully understand their emotions and to find ways to increase their ability to function.

- I hope that this will eventually make a difference to the way in which all people with *autisms* are both taught and regarded so that we will be able to discard the sad old connotations of 'mental' handicap/severe learning disabilities which currently follow so many people.

- Second, let us remember that autism cannot be looked at in isolation. It is more accurately assessed as one of a range of developmental disorders many of which, as Comings rightly feels, have close links with each other. This idea gives an increased importance to research, because the number of people affected rises dramatically to between 15 and 20 per cent. Knowing just why some people are more vulnerable than others, and being able to identify them at an early stage, could potentially be of great benefit. If only the information concerning all these developmental disorders could be pooled we should be able to look to the future with much hope.

Heresy? Or is it?

Summary

This chapter has made several distinct proposals.

Different types of autism

There are different types of autism, each needing specific types of treatment. The different types comprise the following.

PERCEPTUAL AUTISM/ASPERGER'S SYNDROME

- Genetic in origin or linked to a variety of factors, for example foetal/birth problems.

- Some problems are present from birth although they may not be obvious for some time. These are initially demonstrated by sensisms.

- Onset is generally noticeable during the first 6 to 18 months.

- This then causes the onset of instinctive defence mechanisms.

- In some children this will lead to disrupted bonding whilst all will have later developmental problems.

- There are differing types of abnormal sensory perceptions.

- People with autism may have processing problems, delayed connections, problems connected to the limbic system and, initially, signs of attention deficit disorder.

- Those with Asperger's syndrome have processing problems and hyperconnectedness. They share many characteristics associated with ADHD and frontal lobe syndrome.

- Treatments vary, but those which aim at diminishing the effects of dietary problems, abnormal sensory perceptions and the anxiety are most likely to have a lasting effect.

- Some family members are high flyers whilst others may suffer from stress-related illnesses, autoimmune diseases, anxiety or other related problems.

REACTIVE AUTISM/REACTIVE ASPERGER'S SYNDROME

- Origin genetic. Probably linked to neurodevelopmental delay.

- Early signs of moderate NDD and problems consistent with ADD or ADHD. May be seen as precocious.

- Triggered after birth by some event of a stressful/traumatic nature.

- Onset of problems demonstrated by a variety of 'defence mechanisms' and behavioural symptoms which lead to secondary developmental problems.

- Onset generally occurs between 18 months and three years.
- Family history as for perceptual autism/Asperger's syndrome.

Late onset may cause:

DELAYED ASPERGER'S SYNDROME AND OCD II

- Onset after the age of four.
- Might have mild perceptual problems and processing problems.
- Onset will cause obsessive or compulsive mannerisms.
- Symptoms of dyssemia.
- Will be verbal but has limited interests and speech may therefore be used to discuss these repetitively.

Autisms can also be 'acquired' through abuse:

- This would occur at an early age.
- No genetic predisposition to problems is necessary although it may be present.
- Would not necessarily have any perceptual or processing problems.
- If abuse is the sole cause, treatment would probably need to be based on psychotherapeutic methods.

INDUCED AUTISM/ASPERGER'S SYNDROME

- Origin may be genetic causing an inherent weakness or linked to mild neurodevelopmental delay, etc.
- Possible family history of various allergic disorders including asthma, eczema, hay fever and migraine.
- Onset often occurs between approximately 15 months and 2 years.
- Likely causes of onset include intestinal disease, digestive or metabolic problems or (possibly) vaccination.
- Onset causes many symptoms including:
  - changes in diet, complexion and behaviour;
  - physical problems, i.e. digestion, allergies, hypoglycaemia and possible petit mal epilepsy;
  - increasing sensory problems;
  - loss of previously acquired skills;
  - withdrawal and obsessive-compulsive mannerisms.

Late onset may cause:

FRONTAL LOBE SYNDROME AND OBSESSIVE-COMPULSIVE DISORDER

- Origin and causes of onset as for induced problems.
- Triggered after the age of four by stress or trauma of some kind.

SECONDARY AUTISM

Caused by severe illness or accident resulting in brain damage:

- Could occur at any age.
- Treatments need to be geared towards the particular type of brain damage and recovery will obviously be of varying success, for it will depend on the severity of damage.

Need to clarify criteria used for diagnosis

The criteria used for diagnosis should be clarified. This would enable the problems to be clearly defined. Once this has been done, it should be possible to develop individual treatment programmes specifically geared to each child's need. If the fundamental problems are dealt with satisfactorily, the secondary problems should gradually decrease, although the prognosis may be better for those who begin treatment when young. Certainly older children, adolescents and adults will have both more to learn and to 'unlearn', thus making progress slower.

Autism not an isolated disorder

Autism should no longer be seen in isolation – it is part of a continuum of developmental disorders, albeit one of the most serious. If these disorders are all gradations of the same basic difficulties which cause a dysregulation of serotonin and dopamine levels, the problem is much greater than anyone has previously acknowledged. Although the statistics do not seem excessive when each disorder is considered in isolation, when taken together it appears that a large percentage of the population is affected to some degree.

CHAPTER 5

Diagnosis

Diagnosis – 1.a. the identification of diseases from the examination of symptoms. b. an opinion or conclusion so gained. 2.a. thorough analysis of facts or problems in order to gain understanding and aid future planning. Collins English Dictionary

After the initial joys of pregnancy and the birth of a good-looking child may come a creeping realization that all is not entirely well. Even worse, the child may have developed normally until the second year but suddenly seem to be regressing.

In the past, a diagnosis of autism and the all too common prognostications of gloom have often led parents to despair for, quite naturally, we all want the best for our children and set our sights according to our own experience and expectations. Now, however, the picture is gradually improving and there is more hope – a very valuable commodity!

Although, sadly, previous expectations may need some adjustment if your child proves to have autism, an accurate picture of his problems will enable you to define his needs clearly and seek the best treatment available. There is now enough knowledge for families to begin to make a difference themselves and the earlier the symptoms can be diagnosed the greater the possibility of helping the child. Recognizing the problems has the added benefit of helping you to understand why the child is regressing or seeming distant and/or reacting in an odd manner. This will enable you to make allowances for the 'peculiarities', adapting your responses to meet his needs.

Unfortunately I am aware that many parents with young children are currently receiving little practical advice or help and still have to actively push to get the services (and sometimes even the diagnosis) that they are entitled to; although some areas are better than others.

Some 'experts' still appear reluctant to give a clear diagnosis of autism or autistic tendencies. Is this because of the disturbing trend which shies away from 'labelling' people: the implication being that diagnosis is a hindrance rather than a help? I can understand this concern, for over the years I have come across several children and adults who were incorrectly placed as a result of their 'classification', but I would argue strongly that such things happen only when the original diagnosis was incorrect. More worrying is the other issue which I have heard from some quarters as to whether financial considerations play a part. One would hope not.

Unfortunately, political correctness has resulted in the introduction of the vague term 'learning difficulties', which covers a multitude of problems while defining none. Some advocates of this term argue that the generalization has helped to remove the stigma which is often attached to more specific terms, but this is a short-sighted view, for the lack of a clear diagnosis can only further handicap those who most need help by denying them access to the correct services. How can families ever get the correct type of help if the need remains undefined? Or know of the potential benefits of dietary and sensory programmes if they do not know exactly what the problems are?

In confirmation of this one mother says:

> Although the diagnosis of autism connotes many negative images, it relieved us greatly. Having a NAME that accurately described all of Jason's developmental delays, we were able to quit searching. We could shuck all the conflicting pieces of data those well-meaning but poorly-informed professionals had laid as our feet, and we could align ourselves with a COMMUNITY, the community that would help us understand Jason and offer us ideas about how to help him. Realising that the diagnostic label of autism encompasses a whole spectrum of ability and that some treatments/therapies work for some people some of the time, we had at least some knowledge of where to look for help. We had a starting point, a frame of reference. (Stehli 1995, p.6)

The way in which the term 'handicap' is generally used is little better because when combined with the words 'mental' or even 'developmental' it again becomes a blanket with which to cover a multitude of problems. I prefer the use of the term 'special needs', which encourages us to consider the ways in which each child can best be helped by assessing his ability to cope and his level of development. This then allows us to deal with his specific needs by building on his strengths and alleviating his difficulties.

One example which highlights the need for this came when I heard that, in one county, children diagnosed as autistic attend a 'Special Unit' for those with autism whilst those diagnosed as having Asperger's syndrome are sent instead to a 'Language Unit'. Such simplistic decisions bring discredit on those involved in them and do little to help those affected. So, accurate diagnosis is not enough: whilst there are many who help and support such children and do secure the place best suited to the child's needs, re-education of others in the position to make such decisions may also be needed.

Still; enough of that. First and foremost an accurate diagnosis is essential. Initially I proposed a guide which attempted to correlate the behavioural and developmental symptoms with a table describing normal child development until the age of six and to describe some of the obsessive-compulsive 'defence mechanisms' in detail. Now, however, Simon Baron-Cohen and his colleagues (1992) have developed the Checklist for Autism in Toddlers (CHAT) which is being used to diagnosis autism and Asperger's syndrome at an early age. I am delighted that such a guide now exists (and being far simpler and more concise than the guidelines I initially proposed will be used with greater ease by both parents and professionals).

If you feel in any doubt about your child's development do ask your health visitor or doctor about the CHAT, for when used in conjunction with the explanatory notes it will clearly indicate whether you need to seek a second opinion. It will normally be used during the 18-month developmental check-up and asks a series of questions designed to identify whether the child is making normal progress in several areas. For the parent these include questions designed to assess the level of social interaction with family and peer group; his ability/will to explore; his imagination and his ability to point to objects. Those for the health visitor or doctor include questions designed to assess eye contact; the ability to respond to interest in a toy and to look at a particular object; his imagination and his ability to respond to instruction.

If necessary your child can then be referred for specialist assessment. This may involve the Diagnostic Interview for Social and Communications Disorder (DISCO) developed by Wing and Gould. This is much more detailed than the CHAT and more time-consuming for it involves interviews with parents and carers from which precise information can be obtained about the child's difficulties. It is very helpful in clarifying the problems, especially in those cases where diagnosis is difficult (as in some older children).

I would like to include some signs of neurodevelopmental delay here as this covers some areas not included in the CHAT which I feel might be of relevance. Please note that Sally Goddard Blythe (see Useful Addresses) stresses that only a cluster of developmental factors (seven or more) would indicate that NDD may underlie some of the presenting symptoms.

Some Indicators of NDD
History of learning difficulties on either side of the family.

Pregnancy

Accident or infection	Severe sickness
Threatened miscarriage	Placental insufficiency (small for dates)
Smoking during pregnancy	Excessive alcohol and/or drug use

Radiation   Toxoplasmosis
Uncontrolled diabetes
Viral infection (in first 12 weeks or between 26/30 weeks)
Severe emotional stress between 25/27 weeks

Birth
Prolonged labour or precipitated labour
Placenta praevia   High forceps extraction
Breech   Caesarean
Cord around the neck   Foetal distress
Premature (more than 2 weeks early) or postmature (more than 2 weeks late)

New-born disorders
Low birthweight (under 5 pounds)   Incubation
Distorted skull   Prolonged jaundice
Required resuscitation   Blue baby
Heavy bruising   Feeding problems (in first 13 weeks)
A very still baby (in first 6 months)

Infancy
Made violent rocking, moving the pram/cot
Banged his head deliberately into solid objects
Illnesses involving high fever, delirium, or convulsions in first 18 months
Tremendous difficulties in learning to dress himself after any of the above
Adverse reaction to the triple inoculation
Repeated ear, nose or throat infections
Infant eczema or asthma; allergies
Very active and demanding: requiring minimum sleep with continual
screaming (between 6 mths and 18 mths)
Late learning to walk (after 18 months)
Did not crawl and creep but rather 'bottom-hopped' or 'rolled' before
standing
Late learning to talk (after 18 months)
Severe allergic reactions
Difficulty learning to dress – buttons, shoelaces, etc.
Thumbsucking (until 5 years plus)
Bedwetting (after 5 years)

Childhood and school history
Poor hand/eye co-ordination
General clumsiness/lack of co-ordination

Difficulty:

> in physical education classes, for example forward rolls; handstands; cartwheels; climbing ropes
> learning to swim
> learning to ride a two-wheeled bicycle
> learning to read or write, or in making the transition from printing to cursive script

Occasionally puts letters back to front or misses letters or words out when writing

Speech and articulation problems

Travel sickness – headache/nausea (especially when reading in car, boat or plane)

Overreacts to sudden, unexpected noises or movement

Mixed handedness (after 8 years)

Inability to sit still or remain silent (up to the age of 11/12)

Finally I also include two other lists, amalgamated from a variety of sources, which will give an indication of any auditory or visual problems.

Auditory difficulties

Ignores sounds/speech. May initially be considered deaf. Speech difficulties.

Puts hands over/in ears or moves away from noisy situations

A very light sleeper – wakes easily

Frightened of some animals, especially household pets

Hears noises which others might not be aware of – fluorescent lights, people breathing, etc.

Can often correctly identify distant noises or overhear distant conversations

May dislike bathing, haircuts or shaving because of the noise of the water, scissors, razor, etc.

Dislikes crowded situations, shopping, rainstorms, wind, seaside, etc.

Enjoys sounds that he makes himself

Learns/concentrates better in quiet surroundings

Enjoys/seeks loud rhythmic noises, for example washing machines, vacuum cleaners, lawn mowers, fire engines, ambulances, or makes loud noises himself

Likes crowded situations, shopping, storms, wind, etc.

Enjoys being in the kitchen and/or the bathroom as both are noisy; likes playing with running water, flushing the toilet

Likes the seaside, crashing waves, etc.

Likes/does things that make a noise – squeaking toys, tearing paper, banging doors, etc.

Visual difficulties

Eyes are watery under bright light

Suffers from headaches/migraine

Looks at things with short quick glances

Looks 'through' people

Squints periodically

Has bouts of blinking

Uses peripheral vision

Avoids eye contact, that is, cries or looks away

Likes to look at faces close to (after 18 months)

Seems startled when approached

Is slow to recognize people at a distance

Misinterprets facial expressions

Has dilated pupils

Opens eyes wide/stares when asked to look

Attracted to light sources; stares at the sun

Rubs, pokes or hits eyes

Shields one eye with hand

Wiggles or turns fingers in front of eyes

Switches lights on and off

Does jigsaws accurately: enjoys doing intricate work, for example tapestry

Looks at feet when walking

Afraid of/has difficulty with heights, for example goes downstairs one step at a time, has problems using escalators

Takes large steps when entering a room, stepping off a kerb, etc.

Steps back and forth (often for long periods) from one surface to another or stumbles/falls when stepping from one surface to another

Doesn't appear to look where going   Bumps into things

Rocks frequently   Likes to spin objects

Enjoys/avoids/distressed by:

being in the dark   bright sunshine/lights

going through tunnels   going through an avenue of trees

night driving

Is fascinated with *or* dislikes:

shadows, reflections   certain colours, stripes/patterns

mirrors, shiny objects   things blowing in the wind

small objects, for example a strand of hair, bits of fluff/dust, saliva, water

Is very adept at *or* has difficulty in:
picking things up   catching a ball
putting a peg/object in a slot/hole (especially if the hole is black)

Has difficulty colouring within lines
Creates extremely intricate designs

When writing:
has problems when copying (better with large print)
uses large letters;   runs words together
stops frequently/becomes tired quickly shuts or rubs eyes

When reading:
misreads or combines words   repeats words/lines
skips words/lines

Has difficulty in distinguishing letters/words on a blackboard/whiteboard
or on a page

I would also like to include a word here about hyperlexia. This developmental disorder is characterized by an intense fascination with letters and numbers; precocity, with self-taught reading before the age of five and an inability to learn language through normal spoken channels. This results in introversion and severe social problems and can be found amongst some children with autism/Asperger's syndrome.

One mother whose son has what she describes as high-functioning autism and hyperlexia felt that the fact that he is hyperlexic excluded any visual problems. However some of the accounts in *Dancing in the Rain* (Stehli 1997) make me query whether this applies to all, for some of the children described there as having hyperlexia clearly also suffer from visual discomfort.

Thus a mother comments that Danny (who has both autism and hyperlexia) had a slack and expressionless face when a baby and, as a toddler, peered sideways at parallel objects such as rails and power lines, twirled his fingers in the air, liked making intricate patterns, etc. He also focused on shapes, letters and images. Although she felt she did not wish to tamper with his vision, seeing it as a 'great strength', she also says: 'We knew there was something peculiar about Danny's vision...'

Similarly the description of James talks about his ability to point out things which caught his attention from a great distance. Fascinated by shapes, he could identify jigsaw pieces simply by the shape (even if they were upside down) and by the age of three knew most countries of the world on a map in the same way. His mother also comments on his amazing memory for places.

Thus both descriptions are indicative of visual problems. Whilst one would need further information before ascertaining the actual problems in Danny's case these, in relation to James', would seem to indicate magnified vision. One is also tempted to suggest that a combination of the TLR reflex could tally with his 'phenomenal memory'.

Bear in mind the fact that many people with severe visual problems nevertheless learn to read (although not necessarily with meaning), write and even drive cars. Thus, even though there may be some children and adults with hyperlexia who do not have visual problems, I would certainly not exclude this possibility until testing had been carried out.

CHAPTER 6

Treatment

Speak not so loudly
For I am in pain
Your voice's sharpened edges
Are cutting my brain.

Larry Winters (Boyle 1984, p.37)

Introduction

The future for children with autism is frequently portrayed as bleak, but there are various treatments which can help.

Treatment should be implemented as early as possible in order to maximize the chances of success for, as Annabel Stehli points out, research in Brooklyn, New York, shows a high cure rate amongst children who have been treated with AIT at the age of two – as is also the case with some children who have received dietary intervention at an early age. It must be recognized though that in many cases several different types of help may be needed if we are to maximize the chances of success.

This *does not* mean that you should give up if your child has reached adolescence or adulthood for, following the correct treatment, I have seen great changes take place in adults whose behaviour was previously described as ingrained. Certainly the experiences of adults who have undergone dietary and/or sensory treatments suggest that some adults can make huge strides in dealing with their anxiety and other problems.

Others will be more difficult to treat effectively, for they have missed out on many vital learning experiences and some of their obsessive or bizarre behaviour could be ingrained. While many will have learnt regardless, we should be able to rectify any actual loss of learning by careful analysis of their needs and by devising appropriate methods of help.

The alleviation of anxiety should diminish the need for some of the defensive behaviours but, depending on diagnosis, some obsessions and compulsions may prove more difficult to deal with. However, as the study by

Baxter *et al.* (1992) into OCD indicates, even this may not be insoluble once the underlying problems have been dealt with. Their study involved exploring the conflict between nature and nurture which has always affected the way in which practitioners look at and decide on treatment: that is, medicinal (drug therapy) versus the psychotherapeutic approach. In this experiment half the patients received the standard drug treatment (Prozac – i.e. fluoxetine). The other group were given behaviour therapy in which they were repeatedly exposed to the object of their obsession or compulsion without being allowed to perform it: for example, patients with a hand-washing compulsion were put by a sink but not allowed to wash. During this, they learnt to question the fears that underlay their behaviour.

The result of the behaviour therapy was that gradually, over a period of months, the compulsions faded just as they did with the medication: a result confirmed by PET scans which showed that both the behaviour therapy and the medication had caused a significant decrease in the activity of the caudate nucleus which controls instinctive stereotyped behaviours. Treatment which might help specific individuals.

It will be interesting to see if other treatments used for dealing with stress-based problems such as post-traumatic stress disorder will have any relevance in dealing with any residual obsessive-compulsive behaviours. Obviously though if, whatever the original cause, brain damage is now present treatment may not be as successful as one would like. However, even in such cases, it is possible to provide the security and help needed to enable even the most severely handicapped person to live happily. Despite their difficulties in interacting and communicating, such people have a great deal of warmth to offer those who are able to understand and accept them.

Fortunately, more help is now available than ever before and films like 'The Rainman' are slowly increasing public awareness. This should benefit both the families and their children, although conversations with the parents of several young children sadly show that once their children were diagnosed they had still found themselves very much alone and felt that they were left to find information for themselves.

However, at present, information on the most helpful treatments can be confusing for even the experts disagree. One, who had the temerity to mention to a 'professional' that she had heard various vitamins might be helpful, was even told that was 'nonsense'! It is surprising then that the Autism Research Institute has consistently advocated and advised parents on the importance of vitamins for many years.

Unfortunately the issue is further confused by some therapists who tend to feel that their treatment is a 'cure-all': some of whom even state that once completed other types of treatment will be unnecessary. Although this may occasionally prove to be the case, especially when treatment is initiated early, such practitioners generally have little overall experience of the problems of autism and may therefore miss those difficulties outside their own specialization. This can make their advice misleading. I would therefore suggest that you assess the depth of their knowledge and either make your own judgement or seek independent advice on this.

Britain has produced some very interesting ideas concerning treatment but, while people in the United States are generally open-minded and do not hesitate to try out the non-invasive techniques that are available, we are often slow to follow. Although it is in some ways understandable that the professional organizations are reluctant to advocate any ideas which have not been fully tried and tested, they do sometimes hesitate to the point of inertia – to the detriment of the sufferers. Surely it is time that more emphasis was given to instigating a programme of research into the various treatments for those with autism and Asperger's syndrome; research which is currently idiosyncratic and does not attract the necessary funding or commitment from those organizations concerned with autism.

There is also another point which relates to the implementation of treatments. We know that some 80 per cent of children are affected by diet but cannot as yet determine whether this will be needed merely in the short term or for life. Indeed, if autism is something which occurs only in early life we could anticipate that if a diet were implemented early enough it should be possible to relax this once the child has passed the critical age – although if my hypotheses about the links between autism and OCD are correct this might leave some of them vulnerable to later onset disorders. Even so, I know that some parents are reluctant to follow a diet, feeling perhaps that it is unkind to remove 'treats' like chocolate cake and sweets from a child who is handicapped and has few other pleasures.

Whilst I can sympathize with this view and do appreciate the difficulties of implementation (which can generally be overcome), no parent would pursue such a course if their child had diabetes or phenylketonuria. Indeed, if a diet is needed to maintain mental and physical health I believe it is a small price to pay.

This is similar to the case with tinted lenses for, as yet, the problems are not fully understood and have received little publicity. Thus some families and people with autism themselves feel, with justification, that tinted lenses (especially when they are a bright colour) make the person 'stand out' further. It must be recognized that these are not cosmetic tints and are therefore effectively no different to the thick lenses worn by a short-sighted person. Whilst the look of the lenses may be unusual, denying the person the opportunity to correct their visual problems is counter-productive – condemning them, unnecessarily, to remain in their frightening world.

This is a difficult area, though, for whilst it is obviously right to correct the visual problems we are losing a great deal of the benefit if it makes the person look unusual and their families uncomfortable. While this effect may be lessened by greater knowledge, recognition and acceptance of the visual problems, it is now becoming possible to find ways around this with the lenses and also through the growing use of contact lenses in which the brighter colours become less obvious once on the eyes.

Treatments vary in price, with some being quite expensive. However, expense has no correlation to effectiveness and, as you will see, some of the lowest cost options may in fact be most effective. If you do feel there is something which would help, it may be possible to obtain finance from the various statutory bodies, who may need to spend less in the long term if some of the problems can be alleviated now. The Charities Digest, available in libraries, indicates various charities which may give grants, while many places and even some firms also have their own funds specifically for people who live or work within a particular area.

It will be interesting to see if those organizations which currently offer help with the problems of autism will eventually take it upon themselves to routinely provide at least some of the treatments mentioned or, alternatively, offer help with funding. Before embarking on the detail, though, I include some words of advice given to me by parents:

- Although your child needs help it is important not to rush by trying too many different types of treatment at once as this will obscure the results and will make it difficult to decide which treatment is effective.

- It is also important to remember that, even if implementing an intensive programme of some type, your child will need some 'time off', as indeed we all do. One mother, having first tried an intensive programme seven days a week, said later that the benefit of giving her daughter a regular break from the programme had actually enhanced her progress.

I would also like to point out to those who do not know me that, although I did take over the Alternative Approaches to Autism Consultancy from Donna Williams, I have no financial interest in, nor am I in a position to endorse, any of the other treatments. That said, certain treatments are helpful, although obviously they may not benefit everyone. So, where should you start? Figure 6.1 shows the major problems and attempts to correlate the possible outcome of some current treatments – although others have been omitted due to time constraints. I should point out that although a particular treatment may have several question marks by it, this does not invalidate that approach, but merely indicates that to date I have found no hard evidence to support my ideas – even though someone somewhere may have done a study on it.

	Food intolerance	Leaky gut	Opioid peptides	Neuro transmitters	Ab. reflexes	Auditory system	Visual system	Processing problems	Stress	Immune system
Dietary	*	*	*	?	*/x	*/x	*/x	*/x	*/x	*/x
Reflex treatment	?		?	?	*	*/x	*	*/x	*/x	*/x
Tinted lenses			?	?	?	x/a	*	*/x	x	x?
AIT			?		?	*	?	x	x	x?
Medication			?	*	a?	a?	a?	a?	*/x	x?
Lovaas			?	?	a?	a?	a?	a?	*/x	*
Higashi			?	?	a?	a?	a?	a?	*/x	x
Option			?	?	a?	a?	a?	a?	*/x	x
Giant steps			?	?	*	*	*	*/x	*/x	*/x
Behaviour modification			?	?	c?	c?	c?	c?	x	?

KEY

* Treats and rectifies the problem in the majority of cases.

X Reduces the problems.

? Where treatment may have an effect but is as yet unconfirmed. For example, it is possible that tinted lenses and AIT reduce the effects of the other sensory problems whilst any treatment which reduces stress may possibly alter the levels of neurotransmitters/opioid peptides in the brain and boost the immune system.

a? May alleviate the problems.

c? May teach (enable) the person to compensate for difficulties

Figure 6.1 Possible outcomes of some treatments for symptoms of autism

It is time now, though, for a more detailed look at some of the treatments which are currently available. Further information on some of these is available from the addresses in the section on Useful Addresses at the end of the book.

Although this is not a definitive list it will give you a brief 'pen picture', not only of the most well known treatments, but also a few other interesting ideas, plus my comments and opinions along the way in an attempt to estimate their chances of success. Many of these will already be only too familiar to those of you who have kept pace with the continuous stream of books and ideas upon the subject, but I include them for those who have little previous knowledge.

Treatments

Alternative approaches to autism

This was started by Donna Williams who has undergone a dramatic, albeit gradual, change over the past few years. She used her own experiences and those of her friends to develop a holistic approach which looked at the underlying problems of people with autism and Asperger's syndrome and those with autistic tendencies. (I particularly mention the latter because I know that some parents were quite hesitant about approaching her if their child did not have a 'proper' diagnosis of autism.)

The consultancy offered advice and help with metabolic, perceptual and processing problems, referring people on to other specialists as necessary. Because this book had led me to conclusions which were similar to hers I was extremely interested in her approach and gave my support and involvement for two main reasons. First, it provided the most effective 'programme' I have come across and second, it appealed to me because it was relatively inexpensive – a vital factor for many.

Whilst I now run this consultancy, offering advice and support, I do not claim to run it in exactly the same way – although I hope it will prove just as effective. I also offer AIT (something which Donna and I disagree on).

This book should, however, give you the advice necessary for you to begin to identify the problems and instigate treatment. Effective treatment may consist of several parts but even before you begin you can help the person by providing structure and consistency, for this is a vital part of any treatment programme and will help alleviate some anxiety.

TREATMENT PLAN

1. Identify the problems, looking carefully for any sensisms and metabolic problems.

2. Minimize the anxiety. (Delacato eloquently terms this the Survival Stage.)

   This should be done as soon as possible in order to minimize the development of the defence mechanisms. It can be done in a variety of ways through:

   • tinted lenses, the Downing technique;

   • AIT;

   • Delacato's methods;

   • dietary intervention;

   • reflex inhibition/sensory integration programmes.

It is important to note that the first three ways have the advantage of giving benefits in a short space of time, thereby reducing stress levels. They can also have a positive effect on the other sensory difficulties.

3. Reassess the problems periodically.

4. Construct a treatment plan to deal with the remaining problems.

5. Reassess progress on a regular basis; either continuing as before or updating the plan as required.

Once this has been done you need to clarify which type of treatment will initially be most suitable. Obviously in the majority of cases the dietary and sensory problems are of major importance. Diets, though, are not always easy to implement so for some a more practical approach will be to reduce stress through an alternative method before moving on to this.

How, though, to choose which one to start with? I would suggest that those who are hyperactive would benefit from AIT or the Downing technique first as these often have a calming effect and this will then allow other treatments to be implemented. This would also apply to those who are very withdrawn and unable to cooperate with other treatments.

In contrast, the person who is able to make an informed choice, whether verbally or through FC, could benefit from lenses and this may then give them an incentive to try other things.

Once these aspects of the problems have been dealt with you will have a far clearer idea of the depth of the person's withdrawal and be able to assess just what their residual problems are – that is, any emotional, social or educational deficits. It is at this point that an individual plan may be of benefit.

Complementary and alternative approaches

THE DIGESTIVE SYSTEM, DIET AND FOOD INTOLERANCES

There are some who, despite growing evidence, are still wary of connecting digestive problems with autism but my research has certainly convinced me that these – and various dietary factors – do indeed play a major part in the development of autism. While this may not apply to everyone, it is vital to explore these areas and I would strongly recommend that every child and adult with autism be assessed professionally either so that any digestive problems, intestinal/bowel disease and/or food intolerances can either be eliminated or so that the necessary treatment can be implemented.

In this context it would be helpful to take a brief look at various treatments which may improve the digestive system. Secretin obviously has a high priority amongst them, for there is currently a great deal of excitement in the media concerning its use, with some seeing it as a miracle cure. More realistically, despite the fact that the results to date are limited in number, it should perhaps be described as a very promising treatment. Rather than attempting to keep up with the rapidly changing research which is available from several sources, however, I would prefer to make a few comments most of which I have not seen expressed elsewhere.

The acidity of the contents of the gut during the digestive process triggers the release of two digestive hormones, one of which is secretin; these, in turn, stimulate the pancreas to produce various digestive enzymes. While the effects are probably dependent on any underlying problems, it would seem likely that secretion may work by increasing the efficiency of the digestive system, assisting the functioning of the immune system (thereby eliminating or reducing food intolerances) and rectifying the biochemistry of the brain. It may also correct, or at least improve, abnormal perceptions. The combination of these effects in someone with autism would, of course, be to reduce stress and thereby lessen the obsessive/compulsive behaviours.

Results to date (May 1999) suggest that while many people respond positively to treatment with secretion and show improvements in sociability, speech, eye contact and awareness, some react differently. Thus there are those who improve only slightly and a minority who have become hyperactive or even aggressive for a few days or weeks after a secretin infusion, although these behaviours are said to be relatively short-lived. It has been suggested that such difficult behaviour may in fact be 'normal', although there is also speculation that other factors may be responsible.

Certainly, some people with autism do display such behaviours periodically anyway, but two other possible explanations spring to mind. The first is an allergy to pork (from which secretin is produced) which could give rise to physical discomfort and/or difficult behaviour. The second is linked to my major concern, which is that for some people, rectifying the underlying problems *too quickly* could also cause stress and might lead to additional problems.

Many people with autism have, over the years, learnt to live within the limitations imposed by their sensory problems and some remain unaware that their senses are playing tricks. Imagine then how it must feel if your vision or hearing is suddenly altered dramatically, which is what could happen during such treatment. This was certainly the case with one child who, on being given glutamine (mentioned later), had an exceptionally strong reaction. The glutamine was so effective that it corrected his severe visual problems and, in so doing, transported him suddenly into a totally different world, which left him extremely confused, distraught and 'lost'. Add to this withdrawal, the problems of functioning and the cognitive difficulties, and you can see the reasons for my caution.

Returning to the analogy of the hostages, it is known that, after being freed from captivity and returning to their own countries, they needed a period of readjustment before their lives could return to 'normal'. Some people with autism actually think of themselves as 'aliens'. We cannot and should not expect them to suddenly feel 'at home' in 'our world' unless they are given the support, time and space which they need to readjust gradually. It is too early to state this conclusively, but I do wonder if some people might be better served by a slow but gradual increase in the dose of secretin so that they can more easily deal with any changes which occur. It would be helpful if those organizations dealing with the problems of autism could be more involved this treatment, so that parents and others could be made aware of possible problems and all concerned could be given the support to work with any changes in a positive manner.

That said, I would also like to see some research into the physical effects – whether the levels of opioid peptides, serotonin and stress-related chemicals alter during treatment with secretin. I would suggest too that everyone undergoing this type of treatment should, where possible, be assessed prior to starting treatment in order to determine whether any food intolerances, candida, aberrant reflexes, sensory problems or such like exist. If so, regular testing thereafter should determine whether the patient improves or whether in some cases secondary treatment such as a controlled diet will be needed.

Should we also ask whether there are any other treatments which could improve the digestive system and might therefore prove beneficial? Certainly glutamine is one of these. It has a variety of uses of which four are of particular interest in relation to the digestive problems involved with autism. These are:

- detoxification
- maintenance of the intestinal wall
- maintenance of blood sugar balance
- protection of the immune system.

The results with people with autism include an enhanced ability to deal with incoming information.

Shattock and Savery mention glutamine in their booklet *Autism as a Metabolic Disorder* (1997) but, as with many of the items in this area, there is as yet no research to support its use; although many parents have found it helpful for their children and it is now being prescribed by some doctors of complementary medicine. Note, though, that high doses can cause headaches, particularly in those who are intolerant of monosodium glutamate.

Some speculation now. While it would seem that there are several facets of the digestive system which could be awry in people with autism, problems with the pancreas have cropped up several times. Bearing this in mind I would like to return to the work of Bland (1983), who discusses many facets of research connected to the digestive system, one of which was the fact that people with a gluten intolerance often respond well to pancreatin, a pancreatic enzyme in general use as a medication for various problems. As many people with autism have a gluten intolerance, I have to ask whether pancreatin (or its vegan equivalent) would also be helpful to some of them? Perhaps this is something which should be researched? Similarly, it might be helpful to assess the range of formulae called Ultra Clear which contain various amino acids and other nutrients that boost the body's ability to detoxify itself. These were developed by Dr Bland and his colleagues for use by people with digestive problems and might, therefore, benefit some people with autism.

I hope that in time we shall regularly assess each person with autism/ Asperger's syndrome for digestive and dietary problems (and those with other non-specific 'labels' too). I am intrigued by the possibility that similar approaches, in both assessment and treatment, might prove relevant to people with Tourette's syndrome, ADHD and other related disorders. I wonder if they will?

Finally, although treatment is available for ileal-lymphoid-nodular hyperplasia some families are not in a position to follow this up. If this is the case for you, the homeopathic approach might also be worthy of exploration in relation to people thought to be suffering from Post Vaccination Syndrome.

Dr Bland (1983) also gives advice on dietary matters, two points of which are certainly relevant here:

- Any alteration to the diet should take place gradually, not overnight:
  the reason being that Bland believes the pancreas may produce
  enzymes which are consistent with the food one is used to eating. He
  suggests that changing things too quickly could result in the very
  malabsorption which one is trying to correct and in physical
  discomfort.

- It is essential that fluids be taken with each meal in order to make the
  digestive process as efficient as possible. Bland suggests one or two
  glasses of liquid served at room temperature.

While milk products and gluten are most strongly implicated in dietary problems it is known that other food intolerances may exist. The idea that phenolics may play a part in the development of autism and many other conditions could also be very important, particularly in relation to foods containing gallic acid or malvin. However, do be aware that the general application of a diet may simply result in one allergen being replaced by another (as with replacing cow's milk with soya milk, to which some people are also allergic) so professional advice will be needed.

In the meantime, if you have a young child you feel could be at risk it is also worth taking note of Dr Brazelton's advice on the feeding of infants (Brazelton 1993). He found that allergies could be avoided by introducing individual foods one at a time with an interval between each new food enabling it to be stopped if it caused any allergic reaction, such as eczema rashes or a stomach upset. Beware of mixed foods too unless you can be sure that only one new ingredient is being introduced at a time.

Note, though, that a baby under six months of age may not react very quickly even if he has an allergy. However, any allergy should show within a week although an intolerance would be slower to appear. Dr Brazelton also states that wheat and eggs were most likely to cause food sensitivity and suggests that they should not be given until the child is nine months old.

Many of the reactions in autism will be of a behavioural rather than a physical nature. Thus although some children will respond to a particular food within a few hours with a sudden bout of hyperactivity or by headbanging, the reaction is often a more gradual one, as the child develops an intolerance which may be more difficult to assess. Careful observation should be helpful in picking up any early signs.

Professional assessment may not, of course, be immediately practical in your situation in which case you might be wise to try the suggestions in the following section.

VITAMINS, MINERALS AND HOMEOPATHY

The Autism Research Institute has, over a period of years, collated a great deal of information on the use of vitamins and minerals in helping people with autism. This organization is happy to give advice when requested. Many studies have now shown vitamin B6 and magnesium supplements to have a good rate of success, results ranging from a significant improvement in the ability to relate and communicate to a decrease in frustration and 'self-stimulatory' behaviours. B6 may also be helpful in boosting the immune system, which is often damaged or 'under par' in autism.

Two other products receive their recommendation too. One is dimethyl-glycine (DMG), which closely resembles water-soluble vitamins such as those in the B group but which is technically classed as a food. Research shows that it also enhances the effectiveness of the immune system and has a beneficial effect on the physical and athletic performance of both man and other animals. I was interested to see that it is also being tried with some people with obsessive-compulsive disorder and that its beneficial results compare well with the various medications currently used in alleviating this condition.

Reports from parents of people with autism who have tried it over the years tend to confirm such findings, for they have noticed improvements similar to those given by vitamin B6. Beneficial effects in autism include a reduction of hyperactivity, hypersensitivities and various other problems. While some researchers in Britain continue to be cautious, Rimland has advocated its use for many years and can offer further information and advice.

The second is the GTC formula (Rimland 1989), which contains a variety of high dosage vitamins and minerals (at safe levels). It was developed by Williams and his team to improve the functioning of the brain and other organs in people who require a higher than normal intake of such things.

In their booklet (1997), Shattock and Savery review some of the 'alternative' treatments which have been used over the years. The authors make a variety of suggestions and detail other interesting facts such as the suggestion that the lack of activity in the sulphur transferase system can be remedied in part by the use of Epsom salts (magnesium sulphate crystals). As these have a laxative effect many parents have, instead of giving them orally, been mixing a cupful in the bathwater so that the child soaks in the solution. While this has not been investigated by researchers, anecdotal evidence suggests that it is of help. I understand that Glauber's salts (sodium sulphate crystals) also have a similar effect on the sulphur transferase system. Once again these can be taken orally but are said to have a purgative effect.

While it is generally safe to give most vitamins in large doses, some have phenolics in them and minerals given in excess can create problems of toxicity. Advice should, therefore, always be obtained first.

While much information is available from ARI (see Useful Addresses), some parents have found, when mentioning megavitamins or allergies to their doctors, that they have been referred to a dietician. In such cases I would suggest that you check whether the person has any knowledge of autism and the role of leaky gut, food intolerances, etc., for if they have not, you will be wasting both your time and theirs.

Remember, too, that if vitamins and mineral supplements do prove helpful it is highly likely that there is an underlying metabolic problem, as previously discussed.

This whole area offers great potential for research, particularly in conjunction with those researching these other related conditions. While parents should not try it without expert advice and guidance, it would be interesting to see some controlled research into the possible benefits of St John's Wort (said to be nature's Prozac) and 5HTP, a precursor to serotonin, which has now replaced tryptophan. Whilst Comings did not find the latter particularly helpful to his patients it is said to have proved beneficial to people with OCD, anxiety and depression and other conditions; although it has not, to my knowledge, been used with people with autism/Asperger's syndrome.

Two final points. Many children have problems in sleeping, which can obviously increase the stresses of family life. Valerian has long been used as a 'relaxant' and it may be helpful in this context. It is certainly worth seeking advice on this as other herbal remedies could be beneficial too.

One other interesting remedy used in the United States is Calmplex 2000. It is recommended by Heidi Wagner (see Useful Addresses) who used it successfully with her child. She has since become involved in selling it to other parents, of whom she says 90 per cent have perceived some benefit to their child (and often also to themselves and/or siblings). Calmplex 2000 is not available in Britain at present – the nearest remedy available here is Avena Sativa Comp which contains five of the seven ingredients of Calmplex. It is made by Weleda and sold by most chemists. Some children may be allergic to coating on the tablets so it is worth asking advice from a homeopathic chemist, who may be able to supply it in liquid form.

Desensitization

The significance of abnormal sensory perceptions is now acknowledged by many people who are working positively to alleviate the effects. I have already touched on various methods of desensitization which I shall detail more fully but meanwhile Delacato's book and advice will be helpful to all those dealing with sensory problems in the home, school or residential situations.

If the sensory problems are indeed linked to the type of aberrant reflexes identified by Sally Goddard Blythe, as I believe they are, then young children or anyone with the motivation may benefit from a reflex inhibition or sensory integration programme, although these take some time to show results.

REFLEX INHIBITION PROGRAMMES

Before each individual reflex inhibition programme is designed, the child undergoes a series of simple tests to determine the stage at which the problem lies. These tests can give a fairly accurate picture of which reflexes are involved although, in some cases where the problem is more minor and the person has learnt to compensate for some of his difficulties, the full picture may only develop once treatment has begun. Once it has been ascertained that treatment is applicable an individual programme will be designed which can then be implemented at home.

Although the INNP do not generally work with children under eight years old some of their associated therapists do. The Centre for Brain Injury Rehabilitation and Development (BIRD) also works in a similar way. While they work predominantly with children (from an early age) they do see older people as well: the only criterion being that the person can, at least passively, co-operate.

These treatment techniques aim to mimic the various reflex movements through a series of exercises (involving repetitive movements) designed to recreate the movements which would normally have been done either in the womb or early in life, when each reflex fulfils its function before it makes way for the next.

Research at the INNP has been further extended by Stephen Clarke, who works with people with developmental difficulties. He has identified some of the very earliest reflexes that occur in the womb and has modified the INNP's approach to take account of this. Thus instead of using movement as the basis of treatment, he uses touch to mimic these early reflexes, a technique which involves stroking specific parts of the body with a soft brush. Once the person has been assessed the parents are taught the technique, which can then be implemented at home.

Although it sounds unusual, this type of therapy is now used for children and adults with a range of problems from dyslexia to hyperactivity, learning difficulties (including autism) and stress disorders. This controversial idea has been taken up enthusiastically in Sweden where the success rate is claimed to be approximately 80 per cent. In contrast there have been varying reports about its success in Britain and many professionals and some parents in Britain remain extremely sceptical about this approach. Research into the efficacy of this treatment is due to begin in 1999 which should help to determine just which children benefit most. Meanwhile I should point out that one hesitation comes from the fact that a number of children respond better to deep pressure than gentle touch, which they could find intolerable – as would certainly be true of those who are hypersensitive.

SENSORY INTEGRATION

This technique was originally developed by the late Jean Ayres after many years of intensive study of the neurophysiology of development and learning. The therapist looks at the child's history, behaviour and physical abilities in order to determine which aspects of the sensory motor process system need remediation.

This is then done by involving the child in various pleasurable therapeutic activities, involving such things as pressure touch (similar to that described by Temple Grandin). The purpose of sensory integration is to facilitate the development of the nervous system. There are three specific goals. The first is to help the person to reach a state of calm awareness so that they begin to pay attention to the things around them. The second involves motor planning, that is, helping the child to organize the sensations they feel into information. The third goal, of intervention, allows the person to acquire the concepts that underlie learning – which can occur simultaneously with the achievement of the first two goals.

Although a relatively new approach in relation to autism, sensory integration can produce significant improvements both in behaviour and in the level of functioning.

This section includes some of my ideas plus others from the various sources mentioned in the text.

Hypersensitivity

Once hypersensitivity has been recognized, it is important to monitor the environment in which the sufferer lives and plays in order to ensure that he is not subjected to stimuli which might prove overwhelming for him – for example, is there too much background noise in the house? Much of his discomfort in feeding, being touched, cuddled, dressed or played with can then be minimized by a sensitive approach.

Remember, though, that this hypersensitivity affects all the senses so that even smell can be painful. One simple example which springs to mind is the use of the baby slings in which the baby sits facing the parent. This must be anathema to him for his face is turned towards the parent and he cannot escape from the overwhelming variety of odours. Once recognized, it is relatively easy for you to limit the number of different odours, making sure that, where unavoidable, those used are mild.

Brazelton's book gives very helpful advice on many aspects of parenting although, as you will by now have come to expect, I did not fully agree with everything he said, especially when shortly after mentioning hypersensitivity and 'autistic' movements he went on to discuss ambivalent parents! This does not, however, negate his many positive ideas.

He suggests some ways in which the hypersensitive child can be helped to learn to screen out unimportant stimuli. One is to reduce the external stimuli to which the child is exposed by creating a calm atmosphere with soft lights and using low-pitched quiet voices. Another is that parents should slow down their actions so that they do things one at a time. Thus the child should first be picked up and held but not looked at or talked to. Only once he is relaxed should you begin quietly talking to him, gradually building up the interaction. This will be a slow process as each separate action may initially cause him to tense – a reaction which should gradually subside.

One of the most important 'contact' times for the baby is of course during feeding. This can be a major problem because holding him in the 'normal' feeding position (i.e. resting his head in the crook of your arm) may invoke a reflex response which causes him to arch away from you. Sally Goddard Blythe suggests that you should instead hold his head in the palm of your hand whilst tucking his body under your arm – so that his head faces your breast in a slightly raised position. Raising his head slightly may prevent the arching away and the tongue thrusting which causes him to seem rejecting in the other position: an idea which may also be helpful when holding him at other times.

Once the baby is weaned it will be wise to stick to fairly bland foods initially but if this is not always possible, a spicier food could perhaps be mixed with mashed potato, for instance, in order to 'dilute' the flavour – although, in the light of the research from the Autism Research Unit, diet will need careful consideration.

Gail Gillingham (1991) has spent much time reading the accounts of sufferers as she felt they did not receive enough attention. While her conclusions are not the same as mine, I was interested to find that she had devised a programme specifically designed to help those suffering from hypersensitivity. This includes making all the people who work with the person aware of the problems of 'supersensitivity' as she calls it, so that they become aware of the effect their voice has, for instance. This is similar to earlier work by Delacato, whose treatment varied according to the symptoms which had been diagnosed, but involved the hypersensitive child in a programme of desensitization in which, for example, noise was reduced by means of ear plugs.

Desensitization enables the hypersensitive person to begin making progress in other areas, learning to give and receive affection and communicating with others more freely. Perhaps we should ask who leads the most satisfying life and who will in the long term make the most progress: the person who copes with the demands of daily life but remains isolated, or the apparently 'less able' person who needs and approaches others?

Hyposensitivity

Much work has been done in dealing with the problems presented by children who suffer from multi-sensory deprivation, whether hyposensitive or hypersensitive, although more success is achieved with the former group. While I have no first-hand knowledge of the following treatment, I understand that the programme has proved successful with a number of children, although the results are dependent on several factors, such as the type of damage as well as the age at which treatment was started.

The main aim is to help the child develop an adequate basis for communication and an understanding of the environment, by gradually increasing his exposure to sensory input. This is done through a programme of intensive intervention, the primary objective of which is to make contact and establish an emotional bond, thereby giving a firm basis for further learning. The stages of interaction which might be expected from each child generally follow the pattern shown in Figure 6.2, which gradually enables them to move into and interact with the 'outside world' – and which could easily be a blueprint for a treatment plan designed for children with autism – especially those who are hyposensitive or have Asperger's syndrome.

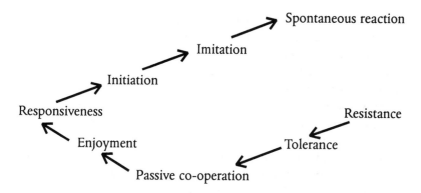

Figure 6.2 Stages of interaction which enable a child to move into and interact with the outside world.

This treatment is used to 'draw the child into the world', teaching all the skills he will need in daily life so that his limitations are minimized. It will continue until he has progressed as far as possible, thus fulfilling his potential, although I suspect that many of these children, like those with autism, will continue to progress and develop throughout their lives.

Further ideas and details will be found in books which deal with the management and care of such children. However, some common-sense ideas are included here:

- The child needs to be approached sensitively so that he is aware that you are in the room near him before you pick him up or dress him. This can be done simply, forewarning him by talking clearly and slowly, standing where he can see you and then touching him. Remember though that some of these children are actually *hyper*sensitive to sound so you will have to assess this and alter your voice accordingly.

- He is vulnerable to everyday hazards and therefore toys must be chosen with care, so that sharp edges or those small enough to be swallowed are avoided. They should also be easily cleanable, as he will probably continue to explore with his mouth for longer than other children. Various toys can be used to stimulate his interests, so choose those that are both brightly coloured and give vibrations when shaken.

Now, however, let us look at the main problem areas in turn.

SIGHT

The recognition of these visual perceptual problems amongst some people with autism is an exciting development and the preliminary results offer the hope that some of the most devastating consequences can be overcome.

I have already touched upon some of the improvements that can be gained from the use of tints but am sure that you would like to know exactly what the lenses do and how they work.

Technically, each different colour stops a particular range of light from entering the eyes, thereby allowing other colours to become clearer. The use of tinted lenses to correct this type of problem goes back at least as far as the 1920s. It came to my attention in an article in The *Sunday Telegraph* (Le Fanu 1999) on the artist Claude Monet who had already achieved great acclaim for his paintings from the critics of his time. By 1918 his paintings had changed and colours lost their intensity so that reds appeared muddy and pinks insipid – something which caused him great distress.

The cause of this deterioration was the onset of cataracts which diminished his visual acuity and, because they had a yellowish discoloration, made everything appear dirty. This blocked out light from the blue end of the spectrum and increased his sensitivity to blues and greens.

After undergoing a successful operation to correct this he found that he was left with another problem for, although he could see clearly now, his retina had become even more sensitive to the blue/green end of the spectrum and blue dominated his vision so that although he could see blue, he lost the ability to see red, yellow or a certain violet. This was solved quite simply by a Parisian ophthalmologist who suggested he should wear yellow tinted lenses; these rectified the difficulty and completely restored his vision.

Cutting out light from a particular part of the spectrum obviously alleviates the strain of photophobia but it also, in some (all?) cases, corrects any lack of convergence. This is borne out by the experience of a friend who wears tinted lenses for migraine. Although she considered that she had extremely good sight, particularly when looking long-distance, she found, in middle age, that her migraines were caused by the fact that her eyes did not work in conjunction with each other. Since wearing lenses she has found that she suffers far less eye-strain and migraine because her eyes are now working together properly. She can even look through binoculars, an impossible task before, although, intriguingly, her long-distance vision is not as good with the glasses on.

Just why the tints should correct a lack of convergence is, as yet, unclear but ongoing research should eventually provide the answers. Meanwhile I would hazard a guess that it has something to do with the reduction of strain. The other question to arise is whether the lenses will also work for those with hyposensitivity. This condition seems in some ways similar to Monet's when the cataracts first developed and the answer is, of course, yes, although other treatments might be appropriate for some.

While it is advisable for each person to have an eye examination the problems identified by Ian Jordan are not, at present, detected by the most frequently used tests. Obviously, though, diagnosis and treatment play an important part in reducing stress and, in turn, alleviating many of the other problems. Currently only a few organizations are able to carry out relevant tests and offer tinted lenses.

One of these is the Irlen Institute (see Useful Addresses). While those able to respond accurately are easy to assess for tints the Irlen Institute, like myself, are also working on testing people who are unable to co-operate; something which is obviously more difficult and time-consuming.

Treatment for the visual perceptual problems is now also available from various optometrists (using the colorimeter) throughout the country. Whilst suitable for people who can communicate this may not help those who cannot unless they have some way of accurately indicating their likes and dislikes, for example through FC. Some optometrists are willing to try, though, as at the Institute of Optometry in London who have successfully worked with some people with severe communication difficulties.

If using either of these methods it should be noted that:

- If the tint is correct a piece of white paper will generally remain white when looked at through tinted lenses, although this does *not* accurately indicate the depth of colour needed to correct the particular visual difficulty as a lighter shade of the same colour can give the same effect.

- The colorimeter makes a slight humming noise.

Whilst currently some of the problems may not be obvious when tested in a conventional manner this is an area in which much exciting research and work is being done. Thus, as Jordan's book *Visual Dyslexia* (1998) tells us, the DP system, which is currently under development (and named after his two sons, David and Paul):

...consists of a multi-stimulus machine which allows the input of:

- different light sources and intensities
- varying degrees of pattern glare
- variable reading texts (if required)
- computer screens

It allows a comparison of the effectiveness of the following treatments:

- tinted lenses
- prismatic treatments
- reading additions
- occlusion

The principle on which the machine is based is that of quantifying both the input of stimuli and the individual's response to them by using different treatment regimes, thus allowing effective comparison of treatments. (Jordan 1998, p.17)

In the meantime anyone who tries tinted lenses with a person with autism should be aware that some people may initially be reluctant to wear them. This may simply be because, being unaware of the problems they have, the person may be confused when the lenses (in correcting the problems) initially make everything seem distorted – an effect which should wear off after a while.

You also need to remember that anyone who has seen in a distorted manner for years could initially suffer from eye-strain or even headaches if they immediately take to wearing glasses all day and every day. Although many people seem to adapt without problem a gradual introduction to the glasses may work better for others. Then, too, there can be a problem unconnected with the lenses, the cause being solely the feel of the frames around the head and ears.

Until accurate assessment of such visual problems is achievable, the environment can be adapted in order to take potential problems into account. Here are a few general points:

- Fluorescent light should be avoided for it can cause sleepiness and can create an inability to concentrate, especially in those people who have metabolic problems. Unfortunately the majority of shops use this sort of lighting, which can make shopping difficult – although sunglasses may help minimize the effect.

- White or very light walls will tend to reflect the lights. It will be easier for the child or adult if the furniture is dark, for when lightly coloured it has a tendency to merge into the background, making the object indistinguishable from its surroundings.

- Particular care, too, should be taken in the choosing of light fittings. Table or standard lamps or even wall lights of the up or downlighter type create a far better environment than ceiling lights (especially those with wide bases which pour the light onto those below). Lights which can be dimmed are clearly desirable.

- Stripes can cause visual distortions and discomfort. These are to be found in many places including books, clothes, avenues of trees, road surfaces, etc.

- Finally, remember that the person may have particular difficulty in seeing things which are clear, for example a glass or even water. If you feel that this is a problem you could try serving drinks in a coloured glass or a mug. Water (especially in a white bath and under electric light) may also be confusing so a coloured bath is preferable; alternatively salts could be added to enable the person to distinguish the water more clearly – though beware of the smell!

While I'm sure many more ideas abound, further information on visual problems for the partially sighted, whose problems are similar, can be obtained from the RNIB (see Useful Addresses).

The Downing technique

This neuro-sensory development programme was developed by Downing during 20 years of research and observation although its use in Britain is restricted to a small number of practitioners.

The treatment, using a machine called a Lumatron, involves sitting comfortably in a darkened room and looking at various colours of light for 20 minutes over a period 20 days (which do not need to be consecutive). It uses narrow bands of coloured light to enhance the light receptor cells (i.e. the rods and cones).

It is thought that increasing the amount of light energy flowing through the brain:

- allows it to function more efficiently;
- enhances stimulation of brain activity;
- affects neural pathways;
- balances biological rhythms;
- results in an expansion of the visual field.

The treatment has shown benefits for people with dyslexia, hyperactivity, cerebral palsy, OCD, visual discomfort and has also been used successfully with some people with autism.

SOUND

The importance of sound is clearly stressed by Annabel Stehli, for correct diagnosis and treatment provided the key to Georgiana's recovery. It is worth noting, though, that her new ability to hear properly was just the beginning of the process which was reinforced and enhanced by a great deal of family input; helping her to learn those things which she had previously missed out on – for example how to approach people.

Controversy still surrounds Auditory Integration Training as the method by which it actually works is unclear. It is said to help by 'levelling out' the frequencies at which the person hears so that they are no longer 'overwhelmed' by particular sounds. In conjunction with this, personal experience would also suggest that it enables the person to habituate to noises they previously disliked and increases the loudness tolerance level, allowing the person to cope with louder noise levels without having to block them out; both of which make life much more comfortable.

Certainly there now are several studies mentioned on the Internet which support its use. It is interesting that whilst initially it was thought that 'high functioning' individuals like Georgiana might benefit most it would now seem that those who are apparently more severely handicapped have shown the greatest behavioural benefits. Perhaps in time it will be possible to accurately identify those people who will benefit most from this treatment.

Meanwhile AIT appears to be helpful for some children who are hyper- and those who are hyposensitive to sound. It has been said that people with frontal lobe syndrome respond well to AIT but whether it is more effective for those with Asperger's syndrome and those who are hyperactive than for people with autism remains to be seen.

We can also surmise that anyone whose speech patterns are unusual, as in those who consistently mispronounce words and those who mishear words and sentences, should at the very least be tested for potential problems. Bonnie Glow points out that:

> The message of AIT is spreading but I could so easily have missed it ...
> Dan and I had no indication of any sound sensitivities in Steven. He hadn't appeared to block out noises. We would never have guessed that his irritability, hyperactivity, inappropriate speech and odd behaviours were in any way sound-related.

Whilst there are no guarantees, it is certainly helpful to many people with autism and, as Pauline Stone of the Sound Learning Centre (see Useful Addresses) says, it has the benefit of initiating change in a very short time.

So what exactly are the benefits? Here I would like to quote from four people (Stehli 1995, pp.86, 100). The first is a six-year-old who describes the benefits succinctly when he said, 'The motorcycles are gone from my head, and I can still hear people blink but I can tune it out.'

Second is Charlie who, a month after AIT, said, 'When I laugh it doesn't bother me anymore.' To repeat his mother's question: 'Can you imagine your ears hurting when you laughed?'

Sharisa Kochmeister has undergone Auditory Training twice and is therefore well qualified to comment upon the results:

> ...AIT has enabled me to sleep better, be calmer while I'm awake, and understand what I hear more quickly and clearly. I can handle noises which had previously caused me to withdraw or panic. These included applause, sirens, dogs barking, vacuum-cleaners, dishwashers, certain voices, the sound of fluorescent lights, or piano music, computers, and sound of the ocean. I believe it also reduced sensitivities in sight, smell,

taste, and tactile sensations. I'm much, much happier and less inclined to anger. I am, in many ways a much nicer person to be around. It has also increased my ability to type independently, without hands-on facilitation, and my desire to be independent in many areas. With typing and AIT, I am able to attend regular school for the first time my life and to make friends.

Finally I would also like to mention Joey, who a few weeks after AIT, noted the difference in his hearing by commenting that his teacher (whose diction was very clear) 'must be taking speech therapy'!

I have already noted that it should reduce anxiety and this idea receives some backing from the fact that AIT did in fact have a physical effect on one child (Stehli 1995), reducing the levels of homovanillate (HVA) and vanillymandelate (VMA), which are associated with stress. It would be interesting to see more research in this area.

Apart from the physical effects of treatment there is another benefit which may accrue. I am told that the 'distorted' sounds heard with AIT are how some people with autism actually hear speech and it has been suggested that this could also have a positive psychological effect on the person being treated who may feel that, possibly for the first time, their difficulties are actually being recognized by others.

Prior to auditory integration training the person is generally given a detailed audiogram to pinpoint the frequencies at which the problems occur, although this is not always possible, especially with non-communicative children and adults who may additionally be feeling extremely anxious due to the strange situation. In the latter case successful treatment is still possible, although without a hearing test one is at a disadvantage as it is then not possible to verify results except through close observation afterwards.

Treatment involves 20 half-hour sessions during which the person listens through headphones to a variety of music with a wide range of frequencies. If an audiogram is obtained the music will be programmed specifically to meet the person's need but if this has not been possible the various frequencies are modulated at random. While Bérard has written a book detailing his work (Bérard 1993), further details of AIT are available from a variety of sources.

It has been noted that the person with autism may well become more hyperactive or withdrawn, or even more obsessive, during the first few days of AIT. Having tried the equipment on myself initially for two sessions, I found that I was left with a buzzing sensation in my ears which lasted about two days and that on the first day I developed a mild headache (which was quickly cured by a painkiller) and felt slightly nauseous. Such reactions may well account for the apparently 'deteriorating' behaviour of the person with autism during treatment, who may be unable to indicate precisely what he is feeling. Indeed, if your child does demonstrate behavioural changes he may actually be feeling slightly unwell.

Those using AIT should give you guidelines on how to deal with such situations and on 'after-care'; but generally both during AIT and afterwards the person will need support and encouragement to help him to build upon any changes which have taken place. Do not expect overnight changes, for he has lived with the problems for many years, although if treatment is successful his anxiety should decrease and his behaviour may gradually change as his confidence increases and his ability to cope improves.

Be aware, though, that some children may initially demonstrate a deterioration in behaviour after treatment has finished. It has been suggested that this happens as they gradually adjust to a 'totally different world' in which sounds are no longer as frightening as they used to be. While I would agree with Stephen Edelson (who has much experience of AIT) when he suggests that this deterioration of behaviour is generally short-lived, lasting anywhere from two days to two months, I would also suggest two other possible causes for deterioration apart from the physical reaction already mentioned. One is the fact that, as Christine Goss says:

> Sound-sensitive children have learned to block out the uncomfortable sounds that bother them. After AIT, they are not able to do that because their hearing starts to normalize; thus for a short time afterwards, they hear certain sounds louder until their hearing adjusts. (Stehli 1995, p.100)

Second is the idea that a 'sudden' improvement in hearing will not only make familiar sounds seem strange, but may, in correcting this aspect of the problem, make the person more aware of their other sensory problems – particularly the visual; this was certainly experienced by some of my clients. The connection between the senses can also mean that the visual and other sensory problems gradually undergo some beneficial change (as with those who begin to make more eye contact after AIT) although this has not been fully researched.

Although some audiologists are very open-minded about the use of AIT, the potentially devastating effects of hypersensitivity in autism are not always recognized by others whose work is geared mainly to alleviating the problems of deafness, even though Bérard's work and the research done in the USA (which can be obtained from ARRI) already clearly show that it is beneficial to many people who suffer from autism.

There are also some people with autism who are wary of using AIT. To address the doubts that I have heard expressed I would like to respond to a point made by Jasmine Lee O'Neill:

> Therapies can help to desensitize the over acute sense, as well as increase the one considered to be deficient. This may not be a wise idea always. When you tamper with something someone has been given, it's not always for the good. Unless the autistic individual is showing distress very often

concerning too sensitive senses, it's best to leave nature alone. I myself, love all of my senses, and cherish the profound experiences they bring to my life. They fuel creativity as well as provide a lovely feeling to me. Even in non-creative autistic individuals, the same feelings are useful because they give pleasure. (O'Neill 1999, pp.27–28)

Thus it would seem that some people may be under the misapprehension that AIT will actually diminish their hearing. I do not have autism but have spent the greater part of my life suffering from hyperacusis in my right ear. Whilst nowhere near as severe as for some people the former increasingly caused problems, especially in any noisy situation when I found it difficult to hear the person I was talking to. I also had a low tolerance to sound in that ear so that at concerts and shows I could only cope with what I perceived as 'noise' by sitting with a finger in my ear.

Whilst it is said that one's hearing 'levels out' I know that my hearing has not diminished since the AIT, for I can still hear exceptionally well in the right ear. There has been a major change, though, for sounds which were previously uncomfortable or painful no longer worry me at all even when loud. This has made life a great deal more comfortable and has also enabled me to obtain great enjoyment from attending concerts.

Thus, even though we obviously need far more information about this area I firmly believe that it is helpful to anyone who has an inability to habituate or whose tolerance of noise is poor. It has been said that for some the improvement has been small but this could perhaps be because the person suffered from problems akin to tinnitus, which is more difficult to treat, or he was hyposensitive – for while Bérard successfully treated his own deafness this condition does not always respond as well as hypersensitivity. Alternatively the person may have had no real auditory problems in the first place – something which can occasionally happen, especially where testing has proved difficult.

How, though, does this tally with the findings from the study done by Oliver Mudford and his team at Keele University into the efficacy of auditory training. While, at the time of writing, analysis of the results was ongoing I understand that the preliminary report suggests the findings were not positive enough to recommend that AIT should be carried out as a general rule.

This must be balanced by the fact that current information (February 1999) on the Internet gives a slightly different picture, for so far there have been fifteen different studies into Auditory Integration Training of which the majority have been positive – only three being negative. While I am sure that all such studies have assessed the results scrupulously there would certainly seem to be specific pitfalls in this area.

I came across one of these recently when I did a follow-up study of one man in his late twenties who had undergone AIT. He lives in residential care, attending a day centre and visiting his mother for weekends and holidays which gave me the opportunity to get three views. I had expected some differences but was surprised to find just how great these were.

The form filled in by a member of staff from one establishment said that the man was making slightly more eye contact; was slightly more affectionate and slightly more active but added that no one else had noticed any changes. His mother found him slightly more sociable and less obsessive. She also said that his communication skills and understanding had improved but again added that no one else had commented on these changes.

Then I read the final form which had been completed by team of people. This was totally different to the first and commented that his listening skills, attention span, eye contact and appropriate communications had all increased dramatically. It also noted that social interaction, independence, appropriate laughter, self-control, etc. had all improved slightly and that other people had commented on the changes. No wonder it is often difficult to tell subjectively whether or not AIT has been successful!

I would like to see a study which includes objective tests for hyperacusic as well as tests to ascertain whether or not the stress levels have been reduced via blood pressure, heart rate and urine tests to check the levels of HVA, VMA, etc.

TOUCH

This section was written prior to my involvement in Alternative Approaches to Autism. Now I would recommend that people generally try a more indirect approach as discussed in *Autism – An Inside-Out Approach* (Williams 1996) which if done sensitively will give the person the encouragement in time to seek contact with you.

Certainly I know that parents who consulted Donna Williams were amazed at the way in which their child, who usually avoided all contact, would begin (each in his own way) to make contact with her, not because of her autism but because she simply gave them the space to do so. This made me totally reassess my approach, although in doing so I think that much of my 'work' with touch only began once the person knew me well enough to feel reasonably safe with me (at least I hope so). That being said I have left the rest of the section in, for in some teaching or caring situations touch may, of necessity, be used and in such cases this discussion may have something to offer.

Temple Grandin (Grandin and Scariano 1986) sought and found her own answers to this problem by desensitizing herself to the pain of physical touch after observing the effect of a 'cattle crush' (used to gently restrain the cattle) on her aunt's farm. She decided that she would experiment and tried climbing inside it while her aunt shut her in. Having found that its effects were comforting, for it held her firmly and safely without causing pain, she used it to provide herself with a feeling of security and now believes that this has enabled her to both give and receive affection.

Grandin later designed a similar piece of equipment which has proved beneficial by encouraging relaxation and gradually reducing hyperactivity. This 'squeeze machine', which she says gives the 'feeling of being held, cuddled and *gently* cradled in Mother's arms', enables the user to remain in control of the amount of pressure used, so that he can progress at his own pace. Perhaps in time it will be redeveloped as a chair?

There are other interesting observations in her book. She discusses the fact that she found a soft, gentle touch was more painful than a firm grip and she talks about feeling uncomfortable when the wind touched her legs while she was wearing a skirt. Could this also account for the fact that many sufferers seem to react more to changes in the weather than is normal, so that they often get very excited or agitated by the wind or a storm?

In another article (Grandin 1989) she talks of a parent who gently encouraged her child to tolerate more and more holding and who was rewarded by increased affection and improved eye contact. I know of many similar efforts by both parents and professionals, particularly in the United States, where a similar decrease in stereotyped and self-injurious behaviour has been achieved.

In my experience, it is possible for carers and teachers to achieve a similar effect by using a sensitive approach by touching the person several times a day. In doing so, it is important that the child or adult knows you well and is aware of your presence and your intention so that the touch is expected or anticipated and does not happen suddenly 'out of the blue'. The touch should initially be brief but firm and in a place which is not too sensitive (and does not therefore feel too uncomfortable or threatening) – perhaps on the shoulder or the forearm. It must stop before the person becomes too uncomfortable but the duration can gradually be increased as the person becomes more able to tolerate it.

It has been said that staff working in a caring situation with adolescents or adults should not touch their clients in case their actions are misinterpreted. Certainly in this day and age there is, quite correctly, far more awareness of what is appropriate, especially when the person is 'vulnerable' because of his disability. Staff in any establishment must be aware of the potential problems and ensure, by discussion with senior staff, that 'touching' is done in an appropriate manner and is in accordance with any policy the organization may have. While I sympathize with the difficulties of such situations, if any member of staff should have any concern about the way in which their clients are being dealt with, they should ensure that this is reported and discussed immediately, for failure to do this, as has sometimes been reported in the press, is not only a lack of care but a total breach of their position, which implies collusion.

However, to suggest that the sufferers should be denied this most basic of human needs, for it is indeed a need, is to totally misinterpret the situation. Admittedly, the adolescent or adult may not be aware of his need but even though he is, through circumstance, cut off from the 'normal' range of human emotion we have no right to knowingly exacerbate his condition by withholding our help.

Experiments with monkeys have confirmed what most people know intuitively, which is that the monkey who had only a wire figure for a substitute mother became far more disturbed than one who had a furry figure to cuddle up to. So too with people. The person with autism is no exception here, for those who are denied touch may remain far more aloof and unresponsive than those we touch. With the majority of sufferers it would be futile to wait until they make the first approach; we must take the initiative.

When used correctly in a sensitive manner, touch makes few demands but is more immediate and less easy to ignore than the spoken word and, in my view, provides a good way of making contact with those who suffer from autism.

This approach contradicts Donna Williams' idea (1992) that any touch ought either to have been initiated by her or only used if she had been given the choice, but perhaps this stems from the fact that she has problems in this area, as no-one in her early life ever used touch in a therapeutic way. Indeed, she does suggest that for some children another approach is needed, saying, 'I must, against my own feelings, suggest a strongly persistent, sensitive, though impersonal, approach to teach the child that "the world" will not give up on it and that it will relentlessly make demands of the child. Otherwise "the world" will remain closed out' (Williams 1992, p.194).

The idea of 'making contact' of course leads me neatly on to the ideas discussed in the next section.

'Holding' therapy and bonding

I have already stated my views on holding therapy but would like to expand them here. The bonding process is recognized as crucial to the child's development and thus 'holding' has many advocates amongst both parents and professionals, who see it as a way of re-creating that bond. Its proponents offer parents more hope than they usually receive elsewhere but it is hope which may prove unrealistic and may, in the case of failure, have a devastating effect upon the parents who will have made a tremendous effort to achieve results.

While I agree that the bonding process is vital, I cannot accept the method used. The therapists, like others with differing views, treat all children the same and seem to assume, as did Bettleheim, that the child is choosing to withhold his affection, speech, etc. and that deep down he is actually extremely angry.

Treatment is meant to enable (force?) him to express his feelings towards his parents who are also encouraged to tell him just how they feel about his behaviour and the effect it is having on them. During treatment the child is held forcibly until he no longer has the energy to protest. At this point, when he finally gives up the struggle, he receives a 'reward' as the holding stops. This is reminiscent of the experiments done several years ago whereby children were placed upon an electrified floor. The resultant shock they were given forced them to seek the safety of their mother's arms – the intention being to 'encourage' social contact. A shocking idea in more ways than one! However, while the shock was short-lived, 'holding' may unfortunately go on for lengthy periods of 30 to 90 minutes.

Many people with autism who are able to communicate have expressed their horror at holding therapy, one person even being physically sick during a programme advocating its use. While in contrast I do know one man who felt he had been helped by it, the majority support Temple Grandin's view that its possible effectiveness might lie in the area of desensitization, perhaps because the physical effort used by the struggling child induces the release of endorphins which calm people. Even if its effectiveness could be fully proved and validated, I believe that other gentler forms of treatment, *if implemented with the same amount of persistence and determination*, could prove equally successful and far less stressful for all concerned.

Martha Welch (1988) places a great deal of emphasis on the position in which the younger child is held, suggesting that this should be with his face towards his mother so that he cannot escape from making eye contact. I know there are people working in other areas who also feel that it is vital to encourage the child to make visual contact, but once again I must strongly disagree. While aberrant reflexes may actually dictate against holding in this position we must also remember that any child who is hypersensitive may well find this physically painful.

Eye contact should *never* be forced. Indeed, while the possibility of visual problems should be assessed and treated or eliminated first, I believe that in some cases it will develop gradually and naturally as the child's anxiety diminishes.

A gentler method of bonding is frequently used in therapeutic communities dealing with emotionally disturbed children or adolescents, who for a variety of reasons have 'missed' the normal bonding process. Although the stage and age of the child will determine exactly how the process is implemented, the basic principles remain the same. Thus while the child who has suffered disruption to the bonding process must regress – move backwards emotionally to the point at which the problems arose – before he is able to progress, the 'frozen' child must start at the beginning. In fact regression often occurs quite naturally amongst small children who have just acquired a new brother or sister, whose parents suddenly find that they have two babies to deal with, as the older child returns to the bottle or becomes incontinent even though he has already progressed far beyond that stage.

The most effective treatment usually takes place within a structured setting, where the demands made on the child are limited by his ability to cope. The first vital step in the bonding process, which may take some time, is to make the child dependent on the adult, whether parent or carer. This is done simply by 'creating' a situation in which the child becomes the focal point of the adult's attention – just as the infant would: something which happens in several programmes designed for people with autism, such as Option and Lovaas.

In a therapeutic community this would entail enabling the child to spend a great deal of time with his 'special' person, who would take care of his needs, albeit in an age-appropriate manner. When this process first begins, the older child or adolescent may well be resistant but will gradually come to rely upon 'his' special person and start to show similar emotions to those of the young child, for example demonstrating jealousy when attention is given to others. Disturbed children are often subject to 'tantrums' or panic attacks, as is the child with autism; and it is here that one particular aspect of this therapy (a different type of 'holding' technique) becomes relevant, for any child in such a state feels totally insecure and this creates a vicious circle leading her to panic further. At this point the child should, in the early stages of treatment, be held gently but firmly until she has calmed. The effect is to provide security – she knows she will not be allowed to hurt either herself or others.

When successful the eventual outcome of this process is the child's ability to 'restrain himself': he refrains from panicking or hitting out and learns to talk about his feelings and find more acceptable ways of dealing with them. This treatment may take a long time to take effect, but will enable the person to begin to 'grow' emotionally with resulting changes in personality. Although treatment obviously takes a longer period of time to complete when started in adolescence, the outcome is an emotional stage appropriate to the age. Having seen this in action I have first-hand knowledge of several highly disturbed and delinquent adolescents who had undergone such treatment. While some still have difficulties, many are coping successfully, bringing up families of their own and leading productive lives.

Some people may feel that such ideas are far-fetched and will ask how such treatment could possibly instigate what is apparently a change of personality. Although I know it works, it was something I found very difficult to understand until the information on proprioception and alexithymia cast new light on it. If this developmental process is linked, with one skill being built upon another, proprioception (self-awareness) would seem to be the basis of the whole process. Thus I would suggest that this treatment puts the child in touch with his 'self' initiating the development of self-awareness which, in some way, then allows him to move on to the next stage, that is, 'tuning in to' and understanding his emotions.

Are these ideas actually of relevance in the treatment of autism? Yes! Having seen the 'holding' process in action with adults with autism I know that it is often successful when dealing with extremely difficult behaviour and does gradually have a far-reaching effect which leads towards self-control.

In one instance, it was noticeable that the person immediately began to take long deep relaxing breaths (almost as if he were about to sleep) and calmed in a matter of minutes whereas had he been left on his own his 'tantrum' would on past experience have gone on for half an hour or more and involved some self-abuse. Another instance involved a young woman who had for many years displayed extremely disturbed behaviour, on a regular and frequent basis. This involved kicking or hitting out at others, breaking windows and furniture. 'Holding' was therefore used every time such an incident occurred and after some time she gradually began to take control of herself. Initially she was held by others but then progressed to lying down by herself when asked (at the beginning of an outburst) and, later, would instead sit (and stay) in a chair albeit while shrieking loudly. As she has good verbal skills she will hopefully progress to the next stage, which entails coping with her problems by talking about them, before they overwhelm her.

I must though make it clear that speech and the ability to discuss problems is *not* a criterion for using this type of holding for it works equally well with people who are unable to communicate verbally. Thus although I originally thought that this whole treatment was only of importance in terms of bonding and would not be relevant to any children who had successfully bonded prior to the onset of autism I would now suggest that any person (child or adult) who has a lack of proprioception or symptoms of alexithymia could obtain benefit particularly from the holding techniques designed to calm and reassure the child when he is in a panic/rage.

It is relatively easy to use when the child is small but once the child is larger, restraint will be more difficult, although it is generally possible to do with two people. *It should never in any circumstances be used in anger or in panic.* It is applied by 'holding', *not* in the manner of 'holding therapy' facing the person but simply in one of two ways. A small child can be sat on one's lap – facing away from the adult – and simply held firmly until he has calmed. Beware, though, for if the child is tall an agitated jerk of the head can leave you with an aching jaw or sore nose.

Alternatively, lie the person on his front, with a cushion/pillow under his head to ensure that he does not hurt himself. While the child or adult may continue to talk or shout, particularly at the beginning of this process, conversation on the part of the person holding him should be limited to the repetition of a few simple words such as 'get up when you feel better', whilst restraining him gently but firmly until he has calmed. This method should only be used when the child is totally out of control or when he or others are in danger of injury. It provides the agitated person with the security he so badly needs and reassures him that he will not be allowed to get out of control and thus enables him to calm down. It is very important, though, to stop as soon as he is calm, even if the procedure needs to be repeated again moments later.

One parent queried this idea. He believed that his child *chose* to have a tantrum and tear the place apart and felt strongly that, because it was her choice, she should simply be left until she had calmed down and that she would gradually learn that it was counter-productive when she later found all her toys broken.

This view concerns me for, although the loss of toys is irrelevant and such behaviour can be tolerated in a child, it is unacceptable in an adult. Having known several adults (including some rather large ones) who continue to have panic/rages I know that this type of behaviour handicaps them severely and can also lead to further difficulties. If she is left to continue in this way how will she ever learn that breaking toys is different from breaking windows or hitting out at other people?

Obviously I am looking at it from a very different angle but to reiterate I am convinced that such 'tantrums' do, in fact, stem from a deep sense of panic. None of us are born with self-control. Anyone involved with small children has seen how a game can go from creating high excitement to something which is 'over the top' and out of the child's control. It is this 'out of controlness' which is similar to that of the child or adult with autism when they are in a panic state. While eventually the panicked child will cease to have a tantrum as she runs out of steam, 'holding' will short-circuit this process and, most importantly, give her the means to begin developing self-control and awareness.

Earlier I suggested that it was better to try one treatment at a time so that you could see exactly what was happening. This does not, however, apply to 'holding', which should be implemented every time the child has a panic attack regardless of other treatments.

Although it would need careful consideration, perhaps in an adapted form, this type of treatment could also help those people who have over the years developed various 'characters'. These give them a sociable veneer which enables them to deal with most situations but would seem to leave a large gap. At present this 'skill' is often used as a foundation to enable them to cope in social situations. Is this right? Surely it would be better to find a way in which to allow them to learn to get in touch with and *be* themselves. While it may be impossible to help the older independent people who are already in the community and coping in this way, surely it should not beyond our scope to devise imaginative programmes which would have a similar effect.

Many people shy away from the idea of restraint and some have expressed the feeling that staff should not be taught how to use it, on the basis that once they know they are less likely to try other methods first. Such an assumption does a great disservice to the majority of caring people in this line of work and can contribute to a lack of confidence which may, in times of stress, have disastrous effects. Clear guidelines should always be given as to how and when restraint is carried out and great care must be taken so that the risk of injury is minimized. Generally, the registering authorities will be only too pleased to give advice and guidance on such matters.

Donna Williams saw self-injurious behaviours (and behaviour which was intended to shock or embarrass others) as a 'test' to see if she was actually real. I would suggest that being held firmly and sensitively, in a non-threatening manner, could awaken a sense of self-awareness which she would seem to indicate was then lacking.

Note too that she also talks about relieving her tension by hitting her head in order to create a rhythm which would block out all external noises. She suggests that it is for this reason that people with autism may bang their heads against a window, bite their hands or hit themselves. In contrast to my ideas she maintains that such behaviours can be stopped by another person clapping, tapping or banging rhythmically, for the person with autism will then be unable to hear anything but this noise and the external 'horrors' will diminish (something which can also work in a different context as when the child is 'stuck' in the middle of a particular action). This would certainly allow the person, in time, to learn and develop their own skills in dealing with tension but whether it would eventually put them in touch with their feelings is something I cannot answer.

Behaviour modification

Behaviour modification is not so much a treatment but more a type of 'training'. Some readers may already have strong views on this. The outcome of this approach can range from extremely positive to detrimental, although the latter is not usually the fault of the 'training' itself but rather of the way in which it has been interpreted.

In its purest form, behaviour modification simply refers to the behaviour used by a parent with each child. For instance, any ordinary child enjoys life with his family, sharing meals, playing games and watching television. At times the family will all go out together to the park, cinema or for a meal simply because it is enjoyable. If he has just pulled his sister's hair or broken a window his parents may stop him from having a bar of chocolate or refuse to let him go out to play with his friends; similarly a temper tantrum may result in him being sent to his room until he has calmed down. If, on the other hand, he has been especially good or has passed his exams, he may be given a treat. Thus he is encouraged to do a variety of nice things, but may be stopped from doing them if he behaves badly.

Behaviour modification should always be used positively, so that good behaviour is continuously reinforced while negative behaviour is ignored if possible. Everyone should be entitled to everything from meals to trips out. Appropriate behaviour should be 'rewarded' and encouraged. While tangible rewards, such as a sweet or even the opportunity to indulge in some type of obsessive behaviour for a limited period, may be appropriate for some, the best reward for good behaviour is very often attention from a parent, carer or teacher, although this may not always be the case in autism. Conversely, 'difficult' or 'challenging' behaviour should result in the withdrawal of attention, although this is not always possible as some situations need speedy intervention.

This approach, when implemented properly, is of great importance in dealing with an 'eruption' of anxiety, especially when the severe agitation which results gives rise to apparent aggression, or self-injurious or destructive behaviour. I use the term 'apparent' advisedly, for it does not accurately represent the actions of the majority of people with autism who 'hit out' because they are confused, hypersensitive, upset or even ill. In the majority of cases, the person concerned has no intent to hurt and no understanding of the pain caused when he has done so; although admittedly that is no consolation to the person who has received the blow.

Detective work may be needed to establish the cause of sudden difficult or unusual behaviour which has not happened before, for it can be caused by a variety of factors, either physical or emotional. Medical and dental checks may need to be carried out. We must also take into account any changes in the home or school as these may also have an effect. One example of this was a little girl who, after the birth of a sister, began to bite and scratch others, although she had previously been the most easy-going and placid of children.

All these behaviours are easier to deal with if tackled in the early stages before they get out of hand. Detailed knowledge of the person concerned will enable such behaviour to be anticipated and lead to early intervention.

While each individual and situation is different, it should not be difficult to adapt the basic ideas to suit if the following guidelines are used:

- Define the problem behaviour and an alternative appropriate behaviour which could be increased.
- Determine how often each behaviour happens.
- Identify the probable causes of each type of behaviour.

- Identify changes that can be made to increase or decrease these.
- Plan a programme to do this.
- Ensure that everyone concerned is aware of and understands the programme.
- Check that it is implemented consistently.
- Evaluate the programme at regular intervals but do not expect too much too soon.
- Modify or discontinue the programme when you have succeeded.

Remember that if a particular type of behaviour has been 'used' for many years it will not be changed easily. It is therefore important to note that each particular approach may need to be tried consistently and for a lengthy period (at least three months) before it either proves a success or is deemed a failure. If one tries to rush the changes they will be doomed.

Unfortunately, behaviour modification has often been misused. This can be seen in situations where bad behaviour is 'punished' by a great deal of attention (which then becomes a reward), while the child whose behaviour is acceptable is ignored. This type of approach is misguided and can perpetuate and even cause inappropriate or challenging behaviours, as the 'good' child may begin to act badly in order to gain attention and the 'bad' child seeks further attention by increased misbehaviour.

Another common problem is a 'confusing' delay between the inappropriate behaviour and the 'result', as can happen in some families where the child, having done something wrong, is told, 'Just wait till your father gets back!' Many people with autism (and small children) are totally confused by such a delay, especially if, having behaved perfectly for the hour before Dad came home, he then told them off for their earlier 'misdeeds'.

Other questionable 'treatments' which endorse the 'punitive' approach have also been used in some places throughout the years although (I hope) no longer with people with autism. These include aversion therapy(!?), which attempts to 'stop' a particular behaviour which is considered unacceptable by a thoroughly unacceptable punishment, for example an electric shock, or ammonia sprayed into the face. Similarly, there are places where 'rewards' have to be earned by good behaviour, so that the person has to earn tokens in order to purchase a bar of chocolate or a packet of cigarettes. In the past, some places have even used tokens for the purchase of meals and the person who does not earn enough has ended up living on Complan or its equivalent.

While despair and impotence seem to underlie many of the more punitive approaches, there is no way in which they can or should be justified. If such 'treatments' were inflicted on physically handicapped children in order to make them leave the wheelchair, or on animals in a circus, it would result in

uproar. To think that children with autism, whether displaying challenging behaviour or not, should be treated in such a fashion, shows a lack of both imagination and humanity. Such 'treatments' are immoral, unacceptable and should never be inflicted on anyone, especially not people who are 'handicapped'.

That said, are any behaviour modification programmes helpful?

The Lovaas behaviour modification programme mentioned by Catherine Maurice in her book *Let Me Hear Your Voice* (1993) certainly seems to be better than many, although one gets the impression that, as with many things, much depends on the interpretation of the method by the person implementing the programme. While I would (obviously) like to see the dietary and sensory approaches explored first it must be recognized that this programme has been successful in treating some children with autism. Why is this? Certainly it facilitates the development of imagination and so one would think that it must be having some effect on the brain. This in fact makes sense when we find that studies have now verified Donald O. Hebb's hypothesis (Rimland 1964) that memory and learning are actually associated with structural changes in the brain's synapses thus enabling them to function more efficiently.

Without more information I can only postulate that perhaps the Lovaas programme is most effective either for children who have received other treatment first or for some who develop autism at a later stage, as Maurice's children did. Why this should be so is yet unclear and will be difficult to clarify unless we can identify the reason why her children developed problems. Once again more research is needed before we have the answers.

Finally I would like to mention an interesting book on successful intervention techniques by Marcia Datlow Smith (1990), which describes work done in America with adults who suffer, to varying degrees, from autism and its related problems. In addition to the intervention techniques, the book also describes the community services which are available in Rockville, Maryland. While the levels of staffing mentioned were different from those generally found in British establishments, it is interesting that many of the people with autism, even those with quite severe difficulties such as challenging or antisocial behaviour, were able, with intensive support, to cope with and maintain productive jobs.

The support was given by a job coach who learnt the job thoroughly himself before the person with autism began work. There were usually two people with autism working in each situation who were coached in the various skills they needed and were then supported for as long as necessary. Such programmes proved highly successful for both the employee and the employer, to the extent that one employer actually offered further employment to other people with autism.

Like many others of my generation, I was brought up to believe in the 'work ethic', so that in order to feel fulfilled one had to be actively and productively employed. In contrast, the younger generation has, over the last few years, seen a rise in unemployment and, in tandem with it, an increasing awareness of the positive aspects of leisure activities. Indeed, studies have shown that those who retire early have a greater life expectancy than those who continue working into their later years. Bearing these facts in mind, it must be asked whether it is right, or indeed relevant, to expect that people who are severely handicapped should achieve any great feeling of satisfaction in completing a day's work or holding down a job which many of us would consider to be repetitive, dull or unpleasant. Are we right to impose our own expectations upon them?

Although I do not have an answer, such questions need to be asked for, while work may provide increased opportunities for growth through meeting people or having to cope with unexpected situations, it may also, because of increased stress, 'slow' or halt progress for a time.

There are obviously two sides to the argument, for things which are repetitive may well be good for the person with autism and may create a sense of security which will let them bloom. Dullness, though, is a different matter, for all too often their intelligence is underestimated and, like Neil Mitchelhill, they are expected to do things which are far below their level of ability. This links in with the other aspect – that of unpleasantness. I baulk, for instance, at the idea of anyone with hypersensitivity doing the job of cleaning toilets. Am I wrong to do so?

Obviously each person has specific needs which need taking into account when making a decision about such matters. Other factors need consideration, too, for we must assess whether it would be more relevant and important for the person to take part in a variety of other activities in sport or leisure, or perhaps continue to work in a more sheltered environment where his flexibility can gradually be increased, than to step out into a work situation.

Oliver Sacks (1986) had some experience of the difficulties posed when making such decisions whilst working with Rebecca, a young woman who, due to a congenital condition, had both cerebral and mental defects. She brought his attention to the type of dilemma that I find myself in here; one which was happily resolved to her benefit and satisfaction. As he says:

> ... Rebecca, like all our 'clients' (an odious word then becoming fashionable, supposedly less degrading than 'patients'), was pressed into a variety of workshops and classes, as part of our Developmental and Cognitive Drive (these too were 'in' terms at the time).
>
> It didn't work with Rebecca, it didn't work with most of them. It was not, I came to think, the right thing to do, because what we did was to drive them full-tilt upon their limitations, as had already been done, futilely, and often to the point of cruelty, throughout their lives.

However things were to change for the better for, as he explains:

> Rather suddenly, after her grandmother's death, she became clear and decisive. 'I want no more classes, no more workshops,' she said. 'They do nothing for me. They do nothing to bring me together.' ... 'I must have meaning,' she went on. 'The classes, the odd jobs have no meaning ... What I really love,' she added wistfully, 'is the theatre.'
>
> We removed Rebecca from the workshop she hated, and managed to enroll her in a special theatre group. She loved this – it composed her; she did amazingly well: she became a complete person, poised, fluent, with style, in each role. And now if one sees Rebecca on stage, for theatre and theatre groups soon became her life, one would never even guess that she was mentally defective.

Thus, unlike many people with autism, Rebecca was able to affect her own future by discussing her needs and, most importantly, by being listened to! Let us make sure we listen too.

One parent said that it was the quality of life rather than the length which was of paramount importance, but really the two things go together, for anxiety diminishes when things are going well and the resulting relaxation and happiness of the person concerned may possibly contribute to a longer life.

Structure and consistency

These are not specific types of treatment but their importance must be acknowledged, for helping the person (child or adult) with autism to feel secure within the world will not only lead to less anxiety, rendering some of the defence mechanisms unnecessary, but may also contribute to a gradual reduction of some of the secondary symptoms.

Routine plays an important role in helping the person cope with his anxiety by providing a feeling of security, so that he knows where he is today and where he will be tomorrow – just as it does with 'normal' children. This goes together with consistency, for he needs to know and understand the adult's expectations of him and the limits to which he can go. The person who was allowed to play in the garden yesterday will, understandably, become upset if the garden is suddenly 'out of bounds' today.

Unfortunately, these are often the most difficult things for the family to provide, for life is constantly subject to change and does not adhere to rigid patterns. Indeed, it must be noted that while routine is initially helpful in overcoming some problems, over-adherence to it may encourage extreme rigidity, which can create further problems. In the film 'The Rainman', Raymond (the central character who suffers from autism) has additional difficulties imposed on his life by the hospital routine so that he will not go out in the rain and will only eat certain foods on certain days.

How can these two apparently diverse views be reconciled? In my work over the years, I have seen several different ideas proposed and tried with varying success. One approach which proved successful was that suggested by an experienced psychiatrist with a particular interest in autism. He was consulted by the mother of a small child who had begun to create tremendous difficulties when travelling to school because of a diversion caused by road works, which had forced them to take a different route. The result was several miles of loudly screaming child and a huge sigh of relief, followed by aspirins, as the mother gratefully left her now silent daughter with the teacher. The advice given was that, as her daughter was going to have a tantrum anyway, the situation would be resolved more quickly if Mum forced the issue by varying the route every day, so that the constant factors became Mum, the car trip and the arrival at school, rather than the route. Without this type of approach the child is in danger of becoming so rigid that she may then 'tyrannize' the parents, by throwing a tantrum every time the slightest change takes place.

The child or adult entering residential care will need a routine, whereby days are organized with meals and activities at regular times in particular places. It is of the utmost importance that a consistent approach is taken by all staff. However, great care should be taken to ensure that over-rigidity does not rule the day, so that meals are varied throughout each week and are not repeated on the same days in following weeks, while activities, although taking place in the same room, also vary at times. The intention is obviously to make the person feel secure while, at the same time, instilling in them the idea that things do change. Once the person has settled, he may become attached to particular members of staff and it is at this point that further changes can be slowly introduced, for the security will be provided to some extent by the presence of the person he trusts rather than solely by external factors.

Even so there are certainly some people with autism who, even after many years with the same people, panic when faced with a new situation and need great reassurance. One man used to get very agitated whenever he went on holiday and over a period of three years always had to return before the others. Once the problem had been identified it could be remedied by a sensitive approach: arrangements were made for him to visit one particular holiday cottage on a regular basis, starting with an overnight stay and gradually increasing. Success is no longer elusive, for eventually he happily stayed with the others throughout the whole period and was reluctant to return home.

Regardless of the apparent degree of handicap it must be recognized that people with autism and Asperger's syndrome are not similar to other groups of people who have 'learning difficulties'. They do *not* thrive on excitement and change and may not be able to make valid choices (as described further in the section on facilitated communication). Indeed just the opposite, for what we consider exciting can lead to added stress and even a deterioration in behaviour.

There is a tendency nowadays for some care homes and day care centres to offer freedom of choice which, while a nice idea, can in practice create great uncertainty (and increased anxiety) for the person with autism. Thus their specific needs should always be taken into account even if they lead to one individual being treated differently from the others in the group.

Psychotherapy and play therapy

There are many different types of therapy in use today (depending on which philosophy the therapist adheres to, whether it be Freud, Jung or others), but generally all have one thing in common: acceptance of the person as they are.

Most therapists aim, through observation and by their interpretation of actions or words, to help the patient recognize why he behaves as he does in certain situations; for once the underlying causes are recognized, change can be effected if necessary. In the context of this book, it needs to be asked whether such therapies are useful for people with autism.

Initially I felt that play therapy would be not be particularly beneficial to children with sensory/perceptual autism although it would certainly not be in any way detrimental once the child had assimilated it into his routine. The writing of some sufferers casts a different light on this, however, suggesting that communication can be through symbols of various kinds, which in the hands of a skilled therapist might provide an opening through which to lead the child.

However unless the therapist is *fully aware* of the problems created by autism, certain pitfalls await. One lies in the misinterpretation of play, drawings or information which could easily cause further confusion for the 'patient' (examples of which are to be found in both *Nobody Nowhere* and *A Real Person – Life on the Outside*); while another is that it could merely encourage some more verbal people with autism to indulge and reinforce their obsessive need to talk continually about perceived problems. Another drawback with this type of therapy is that it could prove frustrating for the parents who expect to see some change in the behaviour of their child. I believe that this type of treatment is generally unlikely to effect much change unless combined with other treatments which tackle the underlying problems. This view must, though, be tempered by the fact that some people find that the therapist becomes increasingly important, so much so that he or she is eventually considered a 'friend'; which for people who are usually isolated because of their problems is a gift of great magnitude.

Conversely, both psychotherapy and play therapy (depending on age) should have some effect in treating acquired autism associated with abuse. They might also have a role to play in helping the person deal with the various 'traumas' associated with reactive conditions. We must be aware though that neither method is likely to affect the underlying anxiety for as many older sufferers of OCD acknowledge, this is only alleviated by the rituals and their insight of the problems does not help them overcome the obsessive or compulsive feelings.

I must therefore conclude that, while helpful to those who have suffered abuse, such therapies are only of use in the treatment of the latter group when used in conjunction with other methods specifically designed to alleviate anxiety. Unless these additional measures are taken, parents should be aware that the 'therapeutic session', even when carried out several times a week, will take a long time to effect any change.

In contrast, though, behaviour therapy has been shown to reduce obsessive-compulsive behaviours and to cause a physical change in the brain as previously mentioned. This indicates that it might be a useful adjunct in helping people to deal with their obsessive-compulsive behaviours once the underlying problems have been treated – although any cognitive problems would also have to be taken into account in planning a treatment programme.

We can also learn from the fact that all the children with autism who recovered or progressed during their stay at Philadelphia's Orthogenic School had one major advantage. Not only did they receive individual therapeutic sessions but they also lived in an environment which was geared to meet their needs – possibly the most important factor in their recovery. This leads me to suggest that therapeutic sessions will be most successful when combined with an environment in which the child's needs are understood and catered for – whether at home or in a therapeutic community.

Option method

The Option Institute (see Useful Addresses) teaches a philosophy of life to adults and also runs a programme for families with 'special children'. This was developed by Barry and Suzi Kaufman, whose son had been deemed 'severely mentally handicapped' and for whom doctors prophesied no hope: a child who has fully recovered. Its main aim is to ensure that interaction with others becomes a pleasurable 'fun' activity so that people gradually become more important to the child than obsessions.

The attitude of the parents is seen as crucial to the success of any programme and thus they are helped to accept and be happy with their child as he is, thereby removing any pressure on him to 'succeed'. The Option Institute puts great emphasis on the fact that 'we do the best we can and there is no sense in which we should or even could do better' – an idea which must be very beneficial for parents, many of whom have frequently met with the opposite opinion.

Treatment is intensive for it lasts throughout the waking hours and is provided by joining the child in his 'world', doing the things he enjoys so that he feels he is 'in control' of the situation, although the therapist/parent is constantly looking for opportunities to encourage and develop his interests. This is done in the belief that once he has seen that interaction is fun, the former chain of cause and effect will be reversed and the brain will gradually develop in those areas where it is lacking. The method appears to owe much to the therapeutic approach, where the emphasis is upon total acceptance of the child, who is then allowed to develop at his own pace without pressure. I would suggest too that by bringing the adult and child together in this way it may also support/enhance the bonding process.

Another advantage with this method, apart from the amount of time and effort expended in the 'treatment sessions', is the fact that the child is living in an accepting situation where the adults (presumably) try to act consistently at all times.

Treatment takes place within an area designed to provide everything needed, thereby reducing external stimulus. While I would suggest that such an approach is well suited to the child suffering from reactive problems, this method should benefit the child with perceptual difficulties, too. This is because studies into autism and the effects of a stimulus-free environment with reduced auditory input showed that social interaction and concentration spans improved, whilst conversely the amount of self-stimulating behaviour decreased (i.e. anxiety lessened). Similarly the hyperactivity of the hypo-sensitive child would probably be reduced by the limited stimuli and the adults' acceptance of him.

My overall impression of this programme, both through children I have met and through my research, is favourable. It also has the additional advantage of encouraging and obtaining help from enthusiastic volunteers who might otherwise not wish to work with a 'difficult' child.

Giant Steps Centre

Although I only have a few details of this from the Toronto branch (see Useful Addresses) it sounds an interesting programme which provides co-ordinated therapy, educational and social services. The Centre was founded in 1981 and now operates in several places in Canada, USA and Australia. The programme provides an approach which could benefit some children and should certainly be given serious attention.

Giant Steps combines a variety of treatments aimed at providing a holistic approach for children with, what they term, neuro-integrative dysfunctions, that is, those who are impaired in their ability to use/organize sensory information. Refreshingly it regards parents as a vital part of the team and provides in-house observation, support and training plus educational and therapeutic 'home' programmes.

The programme aims to facilitate change by initially dealing with the primary dysfunction. Thus during the first year the child will receive intensive individual therapy on a full-time basis at the Centre. In the second year, if ready, the child is gradually integrated into a community school while Giant Steps provides support (on a one-to-one basis where needed). This is done by a member of staff who co-ordinates between the school and Giant Steps, supporting the child for as long as necessary.

While I would obviously like to see the addition of dietary treatment etc., this seems to be a very practical and sensible approach and, again, I particularly like the way the parental involvement is encouraged.

Higashi School

The aims of the Higashi School (see Useful Addresses) are for children to develop as closely as possible to normal children physically, emotionally and intellectually and to achieve social independence and dignity. Great emphasis is placed on physical exercise, the effectiveness of which was commented on by a team who visited from the National Autistic Society (Gould, Rigg and Bignall 1991).

Having watched a television programme on it, one image which remains in my mind is that of a line of children, each holding on to the shoulders of the child in front while running from place to place. The first benefit of this type of treatment is obvious for the physical exercise helps calm anxiety. I would suggest that it could also have more specific effects: helping the hyposensitive child by enabling him to know exactly where he is in relation to others and the hypersensitive child by accustoming him to being touched on the shoulders in a non-threatening manner, which may be the first step in the process of desensitization.

I do not know if Kiyo Kitahara, the founder, had analysed her ideas in this way, but if she did not, her intuitive way of working produced some extremely good ideas, more of which appear in an interesting article by Graham Upton (1992). He discusses the work done in Japan at the Musashino Higashi Gakuen, the forerunner of the school in Boston.

Upton found that ritualistic/obsessional behaviour was definitely discouraged, but went on to talk about a synchronized cycling display given by twenty-two children, ten of whom were autistic (and were on unicycles) plus various other physical and synchronized activities. It would seem that such activities provide not only security, but also an acceptable substitute for obsessive behaviour. It would be interesting to know whether this approach gradually weans the children away from the need for their own obsessional behaviours or whether these are still in evidence when they reach adolescence and adulthood.

This treatment does give positive benefits and seems particularly successful in dealing with the basics such as toilet training, sociability, etc. It has gained great favour in Britain with several families making great sacrifices to send their children to the Higashi School in the USA. Plans are now under way to introduce such a school to Britain (see Useful Addresses).

As you would expect, I would like to see the dietary and sensory problems taken into account and dealt with as part of the treatment programme – something which, in my opinion, would enhance the work already done.

Communication

There are three particular methods of communication therapy which I would like to mention here, for even though I feel that speech is a secondary problem in terms of diagnosis, it plays an extremely important part in all our lives. Indeed, if the child's communication skills can be enhanced in any way, much of his frustration will be diminished.

SPEECH AND LANGUAGE THERAPY

This may play an extremely important part in helping some children towards communicating with greater fluency, but I shall say only a little about it for it serves a wide range of very individual needs and specialist advice is needed before deciding how best to help a particular child.

For many children the major role of the therapist begins when he provides a relaxing and secure atmosphere involving a variety of methods including play and music. In such a situation each child can gradually begin to work on his individual needs, whether it be the learning of useful words or expressing himself more clearly.

Unfortunately, though, I have heard of situations where a child with acute 'exposure' anxiety, has been expected to sit opposite a speech therapist who then insists, not only on eye contact, but also on the repetition of particular words or sounds: a situation which I thought was almost guaranteed to make the child retreat even further into himself or to develop a coping mechanism. However, not all children react in this way even when confusion remains. Donna Williams (1995) describes an encounter with one child. As she says:

> Michael began to teach me. He took my hand ...
>
> He put my hand in front of his face, spat on it, and broke into cheeky, secretive laughter. Michael seemed to think this was hilarious. At first I didn't.
>
> Michael expanded on his game, making strings of sounds as he held my hands in front of his face: 'K,k,k,b,b,b,t,t,t.' Suddenly it occurred to me that he must have had speech therapy. He wasn't spitting on my hand after all, he had been demonstrating the letter 'p'. I chuckled quietly to myself thinking how irrational speech therapy must have seemed to him, some perverse game where he was taught to blow and spit upon the hands of a stranger. He had, at least, found entertainment value in what might otherwise have been a meaningless session where he was expected to make sounds without ever being told why. Even if he had wanted to, who would explain all this to him? Who would know to explain why on earth he would want to use words according to his own value system? Who would even think he was listening or understanding when he found it too difficult to express his awareness, even to himself? (Williams 1995, p.22)

I include this quote, not to question nor diminish the role of the speech therapist but merely to emphasize that it is vital to ensure that those being given speech therapy can and do actually benefit from it. Great sensitivity and careful assessment will be needed to plan a therapeutic programme (taking auditory problems, literalness and processing difficulties and the level of functioning into account) and it will then need to be evaluated periodically to ensure that it is helpful. If this is not done we may merely, as with Michael, be subjecting the person to a confusing situation in which he is asked to do things which he cannot fully comprehend.

SIGN LANGUAGE

Sometimes of course the therapist and others may deem it more appropriate for the child to learn sign language as part of the therapy. Opposing schools of thought seem to surround sign language, much as in the 'deaf world'. Some decry its use for they feel that it will discourage the child from using speech, while others advocate its use in conjunction with speech believing that its continued use will enable the child to communicate in a way which may eventually lead to speech.

I do not have enough experience of the subject to state whether either opinion is right or wrong, but some time ago I read a book in which several deaf people discussed their lives. It was interesting to find that the majority, even some of those who had been taught only speech, appeared to feel that sign language should have been made more readily available to them. Although virtually all people who are born deaf have some residual hearing which can be enhanced by aids and may increase with use, many of those writing said that they had had great difficulties in making their speech understood. They felt that sign language gave them a wide vocabulary which enabled them to 'talk' fluently and that this give them increased social contact and greater confidence. The situation may have changed now as the people writing were all adults whose upbringing and schooling took place some time ago when hearing aids were far less sophisticated and ideas about sign language more rigid.

One suspects that the success of sign language with children with autism is very individual, for their problems are greater and more misunderstandings may arise. For example, one adult I know always kisses people on the cheek when she wants them to go, while another will run through all the signs he knows regardless of their meaning if he wishes to do something and does not achieve the required result immediately.

My major hesitation is that the use of signing in conjunction with speech may cause confusion to those with processing problems and could contribute to an overload of information. However, if we are aiming to ensure that the child feels happy and confident within his world and accept that some children may indeed be 'afraid to speak', then we would be doing them a disservice to decry its use. I must stress, though, that any child for whom signs are deemed to be of use should be assessed frequently, to ensure he is not merely being subjected to endless hours of boredom as relatively useless information is wafted in front of him.

FACILITATED COMMUNICATION

This method of communication was developed independently in several countries over a period of time and is now used in many parts of the world with different groups of people, including those classed as physically or 'mentally' handicapped and others with multiple difficulties.

The earliest detailed account (Crossley and McDonald 1980) of its use comes from Australia where Rosemary Crossley, a teacher in a special hospital, began using it with Anne McDonald, a young woman who, disabled by cerebral palsy and classified as mentally retarded, had been institutionalized since the age of three. Until she was sixteen it was thought that Annie would never communicate but only two years after Rosemary began working with her, Annie decided, despite much opposition, that she wanted to leave the hospital. Eventually, after a Supreme Court decided that Annie was indeed able to communicate and manage her own affairs, she went to live with Rosemary Crossley.

Facilitated communication is a support strategy which enables some people with severe communication difficulties to communicate with the assistance of a facilitator. It is helpful to people with a wide range of abilities, some of whom will use objects, symbols or pictures to indicate their likes and dislikes while others are able to communicate through writing or typing. A number of people have even shown previously hidden and unexpected literacy skills by demonstrating their ability to read and spell in this way.

Unfortunately there has been – and continues to be – considerable controversy regarding the authenticity of FC since pointing or touching the typewriter is initially achieved with physical contact between the user and the facilitator.

Its advocates make it clear that FC is not a cure for autism but merely an aid to help the person communicate, in which the aim is gradually to decrease the amount of support given until the person can function fully on his or her own. It is suggested that the support of the facilitator helps counteract various difficulties like tenseness, poor eyesight, visual disturbance, or lack of co-ordination which can interfere with pointing, typing or writing.

FC was introduced in the United States by Douglas Biklen, director of a facility for special education and rehabilitation at Syracuse University (Biklen and Cardinal 1997). Initially sceptical of the Australian results, he now believes that this method is an important step in helping the sufferers communicate. While he still faces stiff opposition from some quarters he is continuing to develop his work in this area.

So let us look at its use with people with autism. There are several strands here which need unravelling. They will, no doubt, receive an adverse reaction from both 'sides' but nevertheless it is important to consider them all.

While the results have proved astounding in some cases, Bernard Rimland urges caution for, while he believes that more people may be able to communicate through this method than was previously recognized, he feels that the percentage may not be as high as we would hope. Others who live or work with such people take heart from the fact that for many of them, both children and adults, the first sentence is often 'I can read' or 'I am intelligent'.

However, some critics have said that 'the helper is putting words into their mouths', a position they support by pointing to the fact that the person will often only work with certain helpers. This is in fact quite natural, for people with autism often work well with one person and not another, just as they can react differently once a situation changes, although whether this stems from their anxiety levels with different people or the rigidity of autism is a moot point.

Hello Alex. I do speak to you indirectly through the written words because I cannot explain by speaking to you in person.

I think you asked me what I wanted to learn at school and you was always trying to discuss things with me to decide what I was to decide to do.

I have told you that I want to learn physics, chemistry, mathematics, artists.

Why will you not respect my wishes and listen to my opinion.

I want to know these subjects. How would you feel if you did choose to learn and people frustrated you.

I think Alex you are really special person who cares what does happen to other people and trys to help reach autistic children. Tries to help them find within themselves their person that is. Mother found myself. Taught words to communicate.

The silly behaviour attention seeking is your interpretation of why was the reason I did silly things.

My friend you were but you did the reasons decide were incorrect. We do still stupid things because try real reasons to explain to you. Fuss we decide to make.

I autistic am I did know this when I was a child by listening to doctors talk about me.

Peaditicians said that I was retarded not intelligent but you thought that I was clever and I decided that you were my extra special friend.

I am intelligent you should have asked appropriate questions for college students as we are just equally as capable of learning.

I was happy with you because you tried decisions to help me make. A friend dear which I knew.

You Alex treated me with respect as a friend.

Richard.

Figure 6.3 Letter to a teacher from Richard, who suffers from cerebral palsy and 'classic' autism (reproduced with the permission of Richard Attfield)

A comment by a fifteen-year-old named Jeff Powell on the usefulness of this technique tries to counteract the criticisms, for he types, 'People who doubt that facilitated communication is real have no idea what it feels like to be locked in your body. Please tell people that autism does not mean retarded.'

Some would query the results by suggesting that 'the very fact that they can talk about themselves must mean that they are not autistic because people with autism have no self-awareness.' I have even seen it suggested that 'we may be discovering a new population', by which I assume they think that these users of FC, formerly diagnosed as autistic, may in fact be the sufferers of some new syndrome: an idea which makes no allowance for the fact of the overwhelming physical problems and acute anxiety which can effectively mask any innate abilities. Instead I would agree with Jeff when he clearly states, 'I am not autistic at the typewriter.'

Richard, who suffers from cerebral palsy and 'classic' autism, learnt to communicate at the age of fourteen, via a typewriter. He gives us some insight into the problems in a letter to his teacher, as shown in Figure 6.3.

It is a fact that a number of these children and adults do indeed use FC to write about a variety of ideas, feelings and happenings of which the facilitator is unaware. I am convinced that in many cases the writings that have been sent to me by families who have been using this technique for varying lengths of time *definitely* record happenings of which the families themselves and/or the facilitator could not possibly be aware.

One example of this is found in a description of the problems faced by one young man who identified visual difficulties of which his parents were totally unaware. He wrote:

> It's not that I am lazy it is just that I find it difficult to process information given directly to me, I panic and my mind goes blank … I would like to take the register to the office but I can't because I feel as if the walls of the corridors are going to crush me, they seem to be moving inwards as I walk. (Reproduced with permission of Neil Mitchelhill and family)

Similarly, in some cases, thoughts and ideas which would clearly not have emanated from the facilitator raise their heads. One example of this comes from Helen, who frequently writes about 'living underground', a concept her mother had never considered.

It has been suggested by its advocates that motor deficits are a major factor in the inability of people with autism to communicate independently. Further evidence of this is found in an FC video from Syracuse university in which one man comments with great feeling, as he shakes his fingers after typing, that it was 'hard work' while a young lady types that 'even moving a marker' on a games board 'is very difficult' for her. Certainly it is very clear that some of these people find all physical movements hard: something already discussed in relation to proprioception.

In addition I would offer some other potential explanations for the difficulties. These relate not only the acute anxiety which accompanies autism but also to the type of problems associated with aberrant reflexes such as those of vision and balance, for all could play a major, though often unrecognized, part in this (see Figure 6.3).

That the use of this technique with many other groups of people has rarely brought about such acrimonious debate perhaps merely underlines the complexities of dealing with the problems of autism. As mentioned, there are currently two sides to the argument. The first is of great importance for it is not only people like Rosemary Crossley and Bicklen who advocate FC. We must not ignore the fact that many people with autism speak or write very positively about its use. Indeed, while FC is often used in an educational setting to involve the children in studies at a level similar to their peers, it has also given some the opportunity to express their feelings for the first time in their lives whilst others use it positively to discuss their difficulties.

The negative approach of those who resist the idea (possibility?!) that such people are far more capable than they appear has indirectly been strengthened over the last few years. This has happened as some families (in both Australia and the USA) have been torn apart when their children have accused them of abuse, through writings facilitated by a third party: a nightmare situation which has, quite obviously, caused tremendous distress to all the members of the families concerned.

Whilst, in some cases, the allegations were proved to have been totally unfounded, we cannot bury our heads in the sand and deny that, sadly, abuse (physical, emotional and sexual) does occur both in the general population and in residential situations. Regardless of our feelings we have to acknowledge that some children *are* actually abused.

This was certainly the case for Sharisa Kochmeister, who has both cerebral palsy and autism. Her parents are divorced and her father has custody of her. She now types independently but originally began typing with a facilitator. As Annabel Stehli tells us, Sharisa, typing with support, levelled accusations of abuse which ultimately resulted in grave consequences for her mother.

Sharisa's accusations initially raised questions about the validity of her ability to communicate. It was placed in doubt, as was that of Sharisa's facilitator, who it was felt was making the damaging allegations for her own sick, misguided reasons. As Stehli says:

> Sharisa was outraged. Even though it appeared to be neurologically impossible, she taught herself to type independently. Her evidence of abuse was accepted, and resulted in the denial of her mother's visitation rights. (Stehli 1995, p.81)

This is a very thorny subject, for studies also show that some children may 'invite child abuse' (Gold 1986) because their behaviour is perceived as unacceptable and, quite literally, becomes intolerable at times. Then too there are a minority of people who do actually make false accusations of abuse. Unfortunately the problems of autism can further confuse an already complicated issue and so each case will need to be looked at in great detail bearing in mind several factors.

How are we to deal with the growing concerns about abuse and the frequent criticism that 'the facilitator is putting words into the client's mouth'? Whilst obviously proven to be untrue in Sharisa's case, the latter is an idea which was, in contrast, compounded by another facilitator (also involved in a child abuse case) who said publicly that she had not realized it was possible to influence the person being facilitated! Such factors arouse serious questions about the validity of this method and have naturally made quite a few parents reluctant to give their children the opportunity to try FC at all. However, having read many reports both for and against FC, it seems to me that at least some of the negative points arise because of a lack of understanding, on the part of people like the facilitator mentioned above, of the nature of autism.

First, I would like to make some points which relate not only to cases of abuse but also to daily life. People with autism generally take things too literally to lie but as anyone who has lived or worked with people with autism should know, it is possible to influence some of them into giving a particular answer. Certainly, as already discussed, many people with autism are acutely aware of other people's feelings at times and can often offer answers which they feel will please the other person. This, of course, is really unsurprising, for as Anne Donnellan and Martha Leary (1995) point out: 'human beings are supposed to influence each other's conversation!' – although generally not to the extent seen here.

Such attempts to please can sometimes have unintended (and unwanted) results. One father told me of his son's comment after a test to prove or disprove the efficiency of FC which was instigated by people who were actually opposed to the idea. When asked if it had gone well the child replied: 'they got the answers they wanted'. This type of response may be more common than we would like to think, for others use it too. Gunilla Gerland describes an episode when an ambulance came to take her mother to hospital:

> ...before they left, they [the ambulance men] asked whether any adult would be coming home soon, *and I heard in their voices that they wanted me to say yes, so I did. 'Yes.'* (Gerland 1997, p.156, my emphasis)

Trying to please can inadvertently cause problems too. For some families the joy of finding that their child is far more capable than they had previously thought can lead them, like many parents in other situations, to push their child too far too fast, forgetting that they should not confuse the ability to communicate with the will to want to. This can lead parents or carers to expect a flow of communication from the person which he may not be ready for. In such situations FC may be used unwittingly to pressure some children who then feel obliged to give the responses which they deem are required, even though the feelings expressed are not necessarily their own.

Alternatively, if two answers are offered when a question is asked some will always choose the first answer while others repeatedly go for the latter. None of these points invalidate FC; they merely mean that great care must be taken so that the questions are put in different ways and, if the matter at hand is a serious one, these may need to be repeated a few days later.

In some cases of alleged abuse which have come to court a test of the facilitator's ability to influence the person has been carried out. As with tests carried out for research purposes the 'examiner' must not ignore the facts above. Thus the questioner may unintentionally get the answer she expects even at the very beginning when the person is asked if he is willing to take part in a test. She must also be aware that, whatever the answer, any unfamiliar place and people will make the situation extremely anxiety-provoking and this could affect the rest of his 'test performance'.

So, if this area is not to remain fraught with problems we must also take several other factors into account, some of which are also relevant to the general use of FC.

Recall the different levels of anxiety which relate directly to particular types of behaviour. Some people with autism are 'unable' to allow themselves to function on their own in front of other people (although when they feel unobserved they may do things). If they are at this stage they will gladly abdicate all responsibility to another and thus would be unwilling (or unable) to attempt to write or type on their own.

Although it may seem very strange, a person at this stage actually needs to believe that the other is doing the work and may even demonstrate his own 'inaction' by looking elsewhere. Remember too that even if he generally copes above this level, any new or stressful situation may make him take one step (or several steps) backwards. It should be no surprise then that the query about who is actually responsible for the words arises.

The anxiety evoked by any strange situation may also mean that it is extremely difficult to get a valid response, even when such anxiety is not apparent. Do not forget that many of these people have spent long years learning to withdraw from the world and hiding their fears. In some cases this anxiety is not apparent – except perhaps to the seasoned observer – for the person may 'hide behind his eyes' while outwardly looking just as he did when he was concentrating on you moments before. Perhaps at such times words and answers come by rote?

We must also not forget that many of them have spent long hours undergoing tests, the purpose of which they may not fully understand. While the processing problems can exacerbate this confusion can lead them to be deliberately unco-operative or to do things well below their actual ability. Two quotes from different children give a clear picture of their reactions to tests – reactions which need little comment.

First, Helen, who went to the Maudsley Hospital in London for an assessment. On arrival her parents left her with Dr X. A few months later she had a conversation with her mother via facilitated communication in which she said that when at the hospital she had played with some nice blocks. She continued:

Helen: He wanted me to match the colours.

Mum: And did you?

Helen: Yes but I did them wrong.

Mum: It was too hard for you to do?

Helen: No I could often do them but I liked to do them wrong.

(Reproduced with the permission of Helen Fox and family)

The second comes from Neil, who feels that he was not always autistic:

Things became so difficult that we went to X Child Development Unit for help but that was the last thing they gave us. I was given play therapy but I did not co-operate and the staff thought I could not play, they were wrong. One thing really infuriated me and that was the two-way window in the play room. I did not want to be spied on, I hated the thought of it and I started having screaming fits to avoid going to the hospital. I behaved as if I understood nothing and the doctors believed me, a three year old and not my mother. She said I was much cleverer than I let on but they said I couldn't keep it up so long, but I could. (Reproduced with the permission of Neil Mitchelhill and family)

Unfortunately this type of response can cause great problems or have negative consequences which are unforeseen by the person concerned. Neil paid dearly for his ability to mislead the people assessing him for, as he says:

Looking back I can now see that pretending I could do nothing was not a good idea. I was angry and frightened and I enjoyed teasing the staff. It backfired on me and the doctors said I could only go to a school for children with severe learning difficulties. (Reproduced with the permission of Neil Mitchelhill and family)

It is easy to put all the blame for such misjudgements on the professionals who, you may feel, should know better. But really it is only now, as the use of FC has become more widespread, that we are finding out more about the way in which such children think.

Jasmine Lee O'Neill sums up some of the difficulties of testing when, in relation to IQ tests, she gives several reasons why the person could score at a misleadingly low level. As she says:

1. ... that person may actually be mentally retarded.

2. The person didn't completely grasp how to respond to the testing questions.

3. The person may be annoyed by the questions and simply refuse to answer them, or purposely answer questions incorrectly. This happens frequently with a highly intelligent child who is bored and frustrated.

4. The individual's personal Autism may largely prevent the correct answers from being given. A short circuit may be occurring within the brain. The correct answer awaits within the brain but it gets lodged – and can't be transferred outwards to lips or to paper. It is a freezing up that is very often caused by stress. (1999, p.56)

It is apparent that any of the above could cause problems in communication. Now, though, let us look at abuse itself.

One of the most important factors is that children with autism are often extremely hypersensitive and can therefore perceive apparently everyday occurrences as a form of 'torture'. This is especially noticeable in relation to their hearing and in their inability to tolerate touch. Perhaps some of the ways in which other people relate to them or the way in which they are treated may at times feel, quite literally, like abuse. Such was certainly the case for one poor child whose auditory hypersensitivity was mistaken for a phobia and who was then subjected to a foolish and misguided attempt to rectify the perceived problem by being actively exposed to the very things which he found painful!

Another such episode is to be found in *Somebody Somewhere*, with this description of events seen in a classroom:

> In the infant room ... I saw a girl of about four years old curled up in the dark interior of a crate ... The staff had been advised that in the safety of her self-controlled isolation she might begin to explore her surroundings. Hung inside the crate were various mobiles and objects.
>
> The two supervising staff were excited by the novelty of their ideas and the equipment ... Like over enthusiastic relatives on the first meeting with a new-born child they were half in the tiny crate with her ... They bombarded her personal space with their bodies, their breath, their smells,

their laughter, their movement and their noise ... I got the feeling that if they could have used a crowbar to pry open her soul and pour 'the world' in they would have done so and would never have noticed that their patient had died on the operating table. (Williams 1995, p.22)

Even though done with the best intentions, such things are abuse indeed!

Unfortunately it must also be recognized that there are some unpleasant people who learn to use these sensory perceptions and the other difficulties inherent in autism as an abusive weapon. Thus, as previously mentioned, you may find a person who, despite experience of autism, mishandles situations in such a way as to cause the person with autism to become agitated or even to lose control and perhaps hurt themselves. Many of those working or living with people with autism will have done this accidentally at times but *where it happens frequently or consistently* one must seriously question whether this (perhaps unconsciously) is being used as a form of abuse.

We must also remember that the emotions and feelings of some people with autism may, at times, be similar to those of a small child where things are seen as black or white. Helen was a fragile child who has a degree of hyperacusis and possibly some visual disturbance but her autism only developed after her brother's birth when she was 3 years old. Now in her forties she has been writing with her mother since 1969. Although her speech is limited and repetitive her writing is not and it has consistently shown an understanding of many concepts and words far above anything her parents originally thought possible. She continually challenges the idea that people with autism are 'mentally handicapped' for her writings give a clear insight into the way in which she has learnt things, by secretly reading dictionaries and newspapers as well as listening to conversations.

Unfortunately this has at times caused her great distress as she interprets things literally. One particular incident happened when she became extremely agitated and anxious after a letter arrived saying that she had been given a place on a waiting list at a particular hospital. Finally her mother, via FC, discovered that Helen had read (months before, when her parents were unaware that she could actually read) an article about a resident from that hospital who had died there during what the local press had termed a 'mischief killing': an incident which was in fact quite accidental. Helen's feelings about her place on the waiting list were summed up only too clearly when she wrote to her mother: 'Yes we thought you were wanting to have Helen killed' (reproduced with permission of Helen Fox and family).

She has also frequently used her writings to express her feelings towards her brother who she 'wanted to kill' and towards her mother who she saw as being wholly responsible for disrupting her (Helen's) life. Her mother has courageously catalogued these feelings over the years and with great good sense understands that 'wishes to kill', although looking far more horrific on paper than when said by a toddler, are in fact just that: the expression of feelings which her daughter had as a toddler and which, because of her other problems, she has only partially resolved.

Many young children express their angry thoughts through words which imply 'I hate you'. Such words are easily ignored or the feelings talked through but, unfortunately, once they are written, especially by an older child, adolescent or adult, they gain dramatically in their power to shock.

Finally we must also question whether their writings may sometimes reflect the type of confusion or rigidity found in the person's speech where, for instance, the word 'hit' or 'push' is used for both intentional and unintentional physical contact.

Clearly all the points above need to be taken into consideration for they can cause great confusion and underline just how difficult it is to make judgements in alleged abuse cases.

Now, though, to pass on to more general matters. A person without communication difficulties can easily make it very clear to others when they wish to be left alone – as the parents of most teenagers can testify. Those using FC as a 'lifeline' to the non-communicative person must not lose sight of this need for space, which is all the more important when FC only begins to be used later in life.

The fact that many of the people with autism who use this method of communication are able to make observations and 'converse' via a typewriter at a sophisticated intellectual level which can contrast with their vocalizations leads to further scepticism. Maybe it is here that a link with Tourette's syndrome can be found, for those with TS certainly seem to be unable to control their own speech at times. However, it may also be that there are other explanations behind the seeming 'nonsense', as with the following, related by a young man who wrote about an episode with a member of staff in the residential school he attended. The sequence of events is shown overleaf.

Sceptical? As this was reported via FC I fully expect that some of you will either disbelieve the whole tale and/or my interpretation of it or may think that such things are so rare as to be mere chance. And yet this is not so, for looking back to Kanner we find an even better example. This was a description of an incident which took place with his first 'case', Donald, who when asked to subtract four from ten replied that he would 'draw a hexagon' (Kanner 1943). Kanner initially described Donald's replies to his and other questions as peculiar or metaphorical although he was later to acknowledge that:

> The autistic child has his own, private, original, individualized references, the semantics of which are transferable to the extent to which any listener can, through his own efforts, trace the source of the analogy. (Kanner 1946)

Picture 2

Picture 3

Picture 4
Illustrations by Paula Cloonan

We also find that when he reviewed the case later (Kanner and Lesser 1958) he then stressed that Donald had obviously known the answer. This sheds quite a different light on the answer which, as Bettleheim pointed out, constituted:

> an ingenious solution to the problems confronting the boy: how to show that he understood the question, could readily have answered it, and that his intelligence even exceeded what the question required. By his response he showed that he not only knew the answer, but could even give it in Greek. He further asserted his independence by replying on his own terms instead of those of the questioner. So he offered to draw a six-sided form instead of answering 'six'. (Bettleheim 1967, p.388)

Ingenious indeed!

Before concluding this section I should like to quote from Richard Attfield again. He has been using FC for several years now and is able to clearly identify the many benefits it has given, amongst which have been the acquisition of two 'A' levels (with a top grade in English Literature).

This passage was dictated to me over the telephone, using computer aided speech and underlines the importance of FC to those who are unable to communicate verbally. As he says:

> I was a child that had no way to communicate. All my life I felt disowned by society, left to rot in a prison of my own body. I felt that I had no means of escaping; that I was shut away, hidden from view. I found myself through the written word. I was unable to hold on to my own identity until I could express my thoughts and my feelings.
>
> I wrote that letter [Figure 6.3] seven years ago and I felt I had a chance to free myself from all the pain of being autistic but, what I never knew then was that the pain of not being able to communicate as a child goes with you throughout life. And that one can try to outrun it but it follows you like a cloud of dark misery. Even though I have gone on to achieve all my dreams, gaining an education and doing well I can never recapture a lost childhood.

Richard is adamant that children without speech should be given the opportunity to use Facilitated Communication as early as possible so that their childhood years are not 'lost' as his were.

While trying to look at the questions and doubts objectively I have touched only relatively briefly upon some of the arguments both for and against the use of FC, for greater details of the debate can be found in more depth elsewhere. How though to sum up? Perhaps before answering that I should first ask whether we actually have the right to withhold what could, for some, be an extremely helpful tool in dealing with everyday life. To deny those people a voice. Would we deny those with multiple handicaps the opportunity to use every modern technological aid which might help, simply because it might at some point cause misunderstandings? Of course not. Progress brings many advances, some of which could always, in the wrong hands, be misused – but only a tyrant or a fool would wish to stop it.

Therefore although it would take a Solomon to judge situations in which abuse has been alleged I feel that, on balance, facilitated communication is a valid and useful technique *when combined with knowledge and understanding* of the many pitfalls which can occur.

One person asked what use it was if it could not 'cure' autism. This is an extremely short-sighted view for, at its best, facilitated communication allows sufferers to take an active part in the world by making decisions and communicating their ideas, hopes and problems. In the long term, too, it may contribute greatly to the fight against autism by enhancing our understanding of the abilities and problems of the people themselves – which is what we should be working for.

Let us ensure that FC gives maximum benefit by using it carefully and treating the writings of those who use it with respect.

Other ideas

To the best of my knowledge, neither of the ideas in this section are used to treat people with autism, although they could possibly, with adaptation, be of use in treating specific areas once the metabolic/dietary and sensory problems (if any) have been treated. The descriptions below offer a brief description of their use at present.

The Dennison Laterality Programme (Brain Gym; see Useful Addresses) consists of a number of simple exercises designed mainly to help children suffering from dyslexia and which have proved extremely successful in helping them overcome some of the difficulties they face. Once the problem has been diagnosed by some simple tests, the programme aims to correct the disparity between the two hemispheres and help the two sides of the brain co-ordinate and work together: a method which might be helpful later in treatment – after any abnormal sensory perceptions have been corrected.

The Feldenkrais method (see Useful Addresses) has been used for many years by people who wish to alleviate their feelings of anxiety. It can be divided into two: Awareness through Movement, whereby a group of people learn together and Functional Integration, which involves individual teaching and would obviously be the most appropriate for those who are severely handicapped. The aim of both is to reduce and eventually eliminate anxiety through a series of physical exercises which can be specifically geared to an individual's needs and abilities and might again be beneficial at some point.

Medication

This is an area which causes controversy for a variety of reasons, perhaps the greatest being a misunderstanding of how drugs work. Some time ago I came across a report of a carer who had, quite recklessly (and stupidly), tried some of the medication which had been prescribed for one of his clients. He found that it had a detrimental effect on him and therefore decided to reduce his client's medication without any reference to the doctor; although how such a sudden reduction affected the client was not recorded.

It is vital to stress that reductions or alterations in medication should only take place under a doctor's supervision and need careful observation, for, even if the treatment seems to be having little effect, any dramatic changes could cause serious side-effects, possibly comparable to those felt by any drug addict who stops suddenly.

While the carer may have thought that he was acting logically it was, in fact, a dangerous experiment based on ignorance. Each medication is given to deal with a specific problem and it will not produce similar results in a person who does not have that particular problem. Our metabolic makeup too means that a particular medication may cause a different reaction even when taken by two people with a similar complaint, such as when one person's headache responds to one painkiller while another needs two to clear the same condition. The explanation for this is that the liver functions more efficiently in some people than in others. It is also possible, once the body has become accustomed to a particular drug, for the liver to begin to eliminate it more efficiently, thereby leaving less in the bloodstream, which is the reason why dosages may need to be increased at times.

I do not in any way advocate medication for all, for whether or not it is given is a matter which should be discussed thoroughly by all concerned before any decisions are taken. However, it would be foolish to ignore the fact that it can be helpful to some people and is far better than treatments given in times past. A British television programme 'The Liquid Cosh' focused on some of the detrimental effects seen with long-term use of 'neuroleptic' medicines such as largactil (used less frequently nowadays) and haloperidol. These can certainly have side-effects, but correctly monitored they may, for some, give great benefits which, sadly, are all too easily ignored or forgotten.

I know some parents whose children suffer from autism who, after watching the programme, mistakenly jumped to the conclusion that medicines given for epilepsy should also not be used. This would presumably not have been the case if the person concerned was diabetic or had a heart condition which necessitated taking a particular medicine for life. Many people with epilepsy, whether suffering from autism or not, may need to take medication throughout their lives in order to have the quality of life that they deserve and are entitled to.

Remember that stress not only causes physical reactions such as raised blood pressure, accelerated heartbeat and sweating but can also cause difficult or apparently 'aggressive' behaviour. Thus medication may sometimes need to be considered to help the person cope with the pressures of daily life.

If you are advised that medication might help your child, do not dismiss it out of hand. Ask for information. Question the alternatives. And remember that a number of people with autism, like Temple Grandin and David Miedzianik (1986), have received great benefits from various types of medication, through a reduction of their anxiety levels and/or a lessening of their agitation.

It is always difficult to remain objective when this type of decision has to be taken for a relative who is unable to decide for themselves, but once again, quality of life has to be a crucial deciding factor. The child or adult who is constantly agitated because he cannot cope with anxiety is not happy and if the problem cannot be alleviated by other means, medication may well have a vital part to play.

It is, however, *very important* to note that some people with autism do not always react to medication as others might. While it is an area that needs more research there are several possible reasons for this: from the underactive 'hypo' nervous system, possible allergies, digestive problems etc. – all of which could affect the uptake of a particular drug. If the serotonin levels do vary and/or tryptophan oxygenase in the liver is eventually implicated in the problems these factors will also have to be taken into account.

Close observation will be needed to ensure that the desired effect is given, as the person may not be able to make others aware of how he feels when taking a specific drug. This is particularly true in relation to those with a hypoactive system where tranquillizers often have the opposite effect to that intended.

We also need to be aware that a weakened immune system, so often found amongst those with autism, may impair the effect of vaccinations and it is therefore important that immunity is double-checked. This of course will be of particular significance in large establishments where clients are immunized against life-threatening conditions such as Hepatitis B. Some medications can also affect the visual and auditory systems and the doctor involved should be made aware of the person's sensitivities and specific difficulties in these areas in order that the most appropriate medication can be prescribed. It may also be helpful to note that the contraceptive pill interferes with the tryptophan/serotonin cycle and that those taking it may need vitamin B6 supplementation.

As already mentioned, some drugs used for panic disorders may be more effective than tranquillizers for certain people. Beta blockers, used to slow the heart rate (and taken by many people in public life, for example sportsmen prior to a match or musicians before a concert), have successfully alleviated the agitated behaviour of some people with autism, although they are not appropriate or suitable for all. I am aware of more than one case where an adult with autism suffered from extremely high blood pressure and it may be that some are prone to this or associated heart complaints owing to the continuous anxiety they live with. If this should prove true, then beta blockers could be helpful in diminishing the possible severe implications of such problems.

Another medication which appears to be having positive results for some people with autism is Naltrexone (Nalorex). This is an anti-opioid drug which was originally developed to help people who have stopped taking narcotics to remain drug-free, by preventing the 'high' feeling which they induce. Naltrexone was initially tested on two children aged ten and twelve who had displayed self-injurious behaviour since the age of seven. They appeared insensitive to pain and displayed other autistic features, but had not responded to other medications. During the trial period, their social behaviour increased while the self-injurious behaviours decreased, results which were similar to other later tests. Although not helpful to all, current information suggests that it can give beneficial results for both children and adults who display agitated behaviour, whilst some studies show that it can be effective even when given in a very low dosage.

Shattock and Savery (1997) give their considered opinions on the medications which might prove most helpful. They state that drugs which enhance dopaminergic transmission such as haloperidol (marketed as Seranace, Fortunan and Haldol) or sulpiride (Dolmatil) can be effective even in low doses. Similarly they feel that Respiridone, which enhances the transmission of serotonin and dopamine, may show some promise. Shattock has also suggested that Eltoprazine could perhaps have potential benefits when used specifically in autism, but this idea has not yet received much attention and the research remains to be done.

The presence of opioids can diminish transmission in the CNS and so, in contrast to the above, the authors consider that any drugs (like the neuroleptics which affect dopamine) which reduce transmission further would be of little use in this context.

There are, however, two other groups of drugs, the tricyclic antidepressants and SSRIs (selective serotonin reuptake inhibitors), which might yield potential benefits. While the reasons above may dictate against the use of some of these, it is worth noting that those mentioned below have been found helpful to people with ADHD and/or OCD (James 1997). This could indicate a potential benefit to some people with Asperger's syndrome or autism.

The tricyclic antidepressants are broad spectrum drugs which affect a great many brain chemicals, especially noradrenalin, although they also raise serotonin levels. This group includes:

- *Clomipramine (Anafranil)*. Used with some success for people with obsessive-compulsive disorder to diminish the bizarre behaviour which inhibits their ability to lead an ordinary life, although recent studies suggest that it is not suitable for children (Sanchez *et al.* 1996)

- *Clonidine (Catapres)*. Generally used for people with hypertension but has also proved effective in reducing tics and some of the symptoms of ADHD. It also helps those with anxiety-related problems such as phobias and OCD as well as a number of people with depression.

- *Impramine (Tofranil)*. Interestingly, while this takes a few weeks to have effect for those suffering from depression, it works well with some people with ADHD where it provides an almost immediate effect.

- *Desipramine (Pertofran)*. This is again used for depression and was found helpful by Comings in his work with people with TS but whether it would also prove useful in the treatment of autism or Asperger's syndrome remains to be seen.

The SSRIs were specifically developed to raise serotonin levels in the nervous system and are said to work with 75 per cent of patients. While used to treat depression, all are also said to be effective in the treatment of OCD. They are generally considered to have fewer side-effects than the antidepressants and are not fatal in overdose. This group includes:

- Fluvoxamine (Faverin). This has been used successfully to treat some cases of OCD and other disorders. Of particular interest and relevance here was an article in *The Times* on 3 July 1992 (Struttaford 1992). It discussed the work being done by Christopher McDougle of Yale University who was using Faverin to treat children and adults suffering from Asperger's syndrome, with results which were described as 'encouraging and in some cases dramatic'.

- He had found that 50 per cent of his patients improved when treated with the drug, becoming more relaxed and sociable. Unfortunately, while part of the article discussed improvements such as greater social contact (which was demonstrated by the buying of presents for relatives and writing to them), it also included a very odd story which leaves the level of 'improvement' open to question. This was in the description of two people who got married, for one of them actually dated over the telephone in order to avoid eye contact! While this may merely be confusion on the part of the media, the criteria for improvement need to be clearly defined if the general public is to understand them.

- Fluoxetine (Prozac). One of the most commonly known drugs used for the treatment of depression. While, like the other medications in this group, it was originally developed to raise serotonin levels it is also said to be effective in those with obsessive-compulsive disorder, regulating the originally high serotonin levels found in a number of people with this condition. That being the case one would think that it might be helpful to some people with autism/Asperger's syndrome? More research would certainly be needed first, though, as there are reports that indicate a link to deteriorating behaviour and, confusingly, it is believed that it can increase anxiety in a significant percentage of people.

One final point. We know that the prolonged use of neuroleptic drugs can sometimes cause an adverse effect known as tardive dyskinesia which initially consists of involuntary facial movements (i.e. tics) and that, as the condition progresses, the body and limbs can also be affected. Growing evidence suggests that vitamin E is effective both in preventing symptoms of tardive dyskinesia and in alleviating the symptoms if the disorder has already developed – even when it has been present for years.

Complementary ideas

There are several techniques and activities which may prove useful when used as part of a wider treatment plan. These can be divided into three groups.

First, there are a variety of tried and tested 'relaxation' techniques:

- **Music**. Most people find music relaxing and enjoyable and it will generally elicit a positive response from even the most handicapped person, although care must be taken in the choice of music and sound levels when the listener is hypersensitive.

- **Massage**. This can be beneficial but must be introduced with sensitivity and care. It would certainly be helpful to the hyposensitive child as it would stimulate and may gradually develop his sensitivity to touch. Hand or foot massage may initially be all that a hypersensitive person can tolerate, but with perseverance this will help desensitize him to the painful feelings he experiences when touched.

- **Relaxation tapes**. It is advisable to test these first as many have a 'voice over' which could be inappropriate or even irritating. Equally some have patterns which may not necessarily be soothing (one had an awful spiralling effect that changed colour constantly) and might not be good for anyone suffering from epilepsy.

- **Snoezelen**. This idea from Holland offers a room with soft-cushioned walls and areas on which to lie under soft, constantly changing lights while tranquil music is played and can be used for both adults and children. Although the effect of the lights and the sound should to be monitored, reports suggest that it has a beneficial result for many people.

Second, there are activities which encourage some interaction from the participants and which are already proving beneficial in a variety of situations:

- **Music therapy**. This is an extremely useful therapy, especially when used from an early age. In contrast with the idea of music played simply for enjoyment and relaxation, music therapy is used on an individual basis or within a small group and entails more positive involvement from the person/people concerned. The child or adult is gradually encouraged to respond to the music played by the therapist and to initiate her own music, thereby communicating with the therapist.

Music can also be used, to great effect, to interpret how the person is feeling. This can help him to understand his feelings, and may gradually encourage him to express and show them in an appropriate manner.

- **Art therapy**. This encourages each person to give expression to his ideas and feelings through the use of various coloured mediums. It would be a mistake to feel that all people with autism will be able or even want to express their feelings in this way or that their art work should be analyzed to help our understanding of them. Some will paint merely for pleasure, as do many 'normal' people.

Third, leisure. There are many different 'leisure' pursuits being used successfully with people with autism, some of which have a definite 'therapeutic' value. These involve various types of physical exercise, including swimming, sailing, horse riding, jogging, skiing and even abseiling, all of which encourage and demand a certain degree of active involvement.

Whichever activity is chosen it must always be remembered that the person involved may not fully understand what is being said and that he could feel extremely anxious about trying anything he has not experienced before. New activities need to be introduced gradually and with care, even if you consider them pleasurable yourself.

One example of the difficulties involved occurred with a young man who suddenly refused to go to the pub, an activity he had previously always thoroughly enjoyed, as evidenced by his eagerness to get ready and go. Suddenly his pleasure vanished; he was reluctant to put his coat on and became extremely agitated when asked to get in the minibus. No amount of reassurance helped; he simply refused. It was some time before the staff understood the problem but when they did the answer was simple. His last trip in that particular vehicle had taken him on an unwelcome and traumatic trip to the dentist, not the pub. Solution: take him to the pub in the car before gradually reintroducing him to the minibus.

Conclusions

There are many and various types of treatment, most of which have some merit. Unfortunately at present things are too haphazard for, although one can make an educated guess in some cases, we still do not know why a particular treatment is effective with one child and not another. It is clear that the aim has to be to help as many people as possible. The only way that this can be achieved is by serious, open-minded research. Perhaps our starting point should be investigation of the stress levels?

Meanwhile I would like to see the advocates of the various approaches take account of the other ideas, incorporating some of them within their own methods. Alternatively it should be possible to take the best features of each approach and meld them into something even more effective. Indeed, if the dietary and sensory approaches continue to prove effective we will also have to instigate and develop new ideas to help people who are increasingly less confined by fear but whose background will have left them with certain deficits of experience, particularly in the social and emotional areas of their lives.

CHAPTER 7

Implications

The major impact for all concerned must stem from the discovery that the majority of people with autism are actually suffering from some form of physical impairment or damage which was definitely not caused by the parents. Hopefully this should help eradicate the feelings of guilt still felt by many parents and dispel any remnants of the myth surrounding their contribution to the problems for, even if there is a genetic link, such things are as far beyond their control as cerebral palsy or blindness.

Most importantly, this should have a beneficial effect on the confidence of the sufferer, who may have been told, or more correctly, in whose hearing it may have been said, that he 'is severely (mentally) handicapped/mad/ psychotic and does not understand/will never be able to learn.' This, combined with treatment which is often inappropriate, has in the past 'trapped' the sufferer, because many of his actions, which are perfectly normal considering the difficulties he has, have been judged odd or peculiar.

The problems he faces leave him in a similar condition to a stroke victim who has lost the ability to speak. He hears what we say, he understands it (and is often extremely hurt by it), but does not have the ability to contradict us or to converse freely enough to convince us of our mistakes.

I hope that these ideas will alleviate some of the distresses felt and also enable people to understand that effective treatments are available which can help.

My next point has received strong criticism from Gunilla Gerland, who feels that my opinion is one-sided. She believes it could be hurtful to those people who have come to terms with their autism. Please accept that this is certainly not my intention.

The controversy arose when, in an early draft of this book, I wrote that:

...those of us who are actively involved in the 'treatment' of autism must always remember that whilst we may see it as a fortress which locks us out, those who are imprisoned may have become so accustomed to the walls that they ignore them, seeing only the sanctuary. Storming castles may be appealing but it has to be done with *great sensitivity* so that the person inside does not become a casualty of war.

People like Donna Williams have fought against their problems and, as she says in *Like Color to the Blind*, now clearly recognize that obsessions and compulsions are not their character. Others, though, identify only with their 'autism' and, quite naturally, find 'letting go' a very painful process. They may feel that 'treatment' will cause them to lose their 'identity' and will be unsure where this will leave them or what they will 'become'. Thus 'the world's' gain could initially be perceived as a major loss – a fact which needs clear recognition.

Whilst 'counselling' may not be relevant we must recognize that such feelings are very real. They could be devastating unless we find ways of providing the support necessary to enable them to understand that the loss of fear and anxiety will finally 'allow them to be themselves', enabling them to walk into the future valuing themselves for what they are.

Gunilla Gerland wrote to me making several interesting comments about the above three paragraphs, the gist of which should be included here. She points out that there is a third group consisting of people who, despite having perceptual and other problems, have, in a healthy way, come to terms with their autism. She says people in this group are happy to be as they are and feel comfortable about their autism which is part of their identity – as evidenced by a growing disability and self-advocacy movement. She compares this to people in the deaf community who fall into three broad groups: those who fight their disability, others who over-identify with it and still others who are quite happy being who they are – which includes their deafness.

She further notes that: 'Acknowledging it is a difficult handicap which requires interventions and support is not the same as the people being "imprisoned" and that if they feel okay this would be because they (we) are "accustomed to the walls".'

Whilst the words 'great sensitivity' are of the utmost importance (a point to which I shall return shortly) my comments were not directed at the latter group identified by Gerland but were rather made with two different groups in mind.

First, I had in mind those who are considered to have 'severe learning disabilities' or mental handicap whose daily lives are, of necessity, in the care of others. It is not that such people over-identify with their autism – they know nothing else. Unfortunately they are so firmly gripped by anxiety and other people's (often minimal) expectations that they are frequently denied those opportunities such as FC which would help them make any sort of choice.

One cannot ignore this and should, in some small way, attempt to alleviate some of their problems so that their potential becomes more recognizable to others and they can then obtain the help and encouragement needed to begin to make valid choices of their own.

Second, there are the more independent people I know (or know of), who do decide to ask for support in coping with the demands of daily life. For a number of them one of the main topics of conversation is their lack of 'real friends': something which can, in some cases, lead to depression. Whilst support groups, penpals, etc. may help many they do not always adequately address the issue of friendship.

Informing such people of the treatments available is not to invite them into my world, or to attempt to 'normalize' or patronize them in any way, but merely to state that life without anxiety is far easier. So, whilst some people will no doubt continue to disagree, I must reiterate that I believe that alleviating the underlying anxiety will allow each person the freedom to begin to relate to other people in the way they would wish. It must be recognized, though, that this is no magic wand, for friendships will take time to develop, just as they do for the rest of us.

Gerland's points reminded me of my first meeting with Donna Williams when she asked two particularly disconcerting questions: firstly just 'what "my world" has to offer people with autism'; and secondly, 'Why do I assume that they (people with autism) would want to relate to me?'

As I said in the first version of this book, I thought about these questions very carefully for they needed an answer, as did Gunilla Gerland's comments. Those people who are independent or who are able to communicate accurately through FC or other means are the lucky ones. They have the skills to cope with life on their own terms and may no longer be dependent on others for many of their daily needs. Most importantly, they all have the ability to make their feelings and needs known, which enables them to join us or reject us as they wish.

It is only natural that some people with autism should feel very strongly about such issues for many of them have, over the years, felt (and been) discriminated against. There would seem to be two aspects to this. First, unfortunately, mankind has always had a tendency to be frightened and wary of those who are in any way 'different' and this fear, combined with a person's own inadequacies, can lead him to mock or bully those who seem 'unusual'.

Such things, though, are often compounded by another factor. This arises from the arrogance of some professionals who have persisted in interpreting the 'autistic' behaviours in the light of their own experiences; as when 'abnormal perceptual experiences' are translated into '*abnormal reactions* to perceptual stimulation'.

Admittedly one can make some excuse for this because some of the perceptual problems are only just gaining recognition and there are often difficulties in testing. And yet ... should either of these points really be a problem? Professionals like Delacato and Helen Irlen have been identifying and alleviating certain aspects of such problems for long periods of time, and people with autism have been talking of their perceptual problems now for many years.

Why then have they and those professionals been ignored? One has to question whether the apparent 'mental' handicap has distracted people's attention from the real issues, for this is certainly not the same for other groups. Thus, for instance, while testing is now available to determine whether a baby has been born deaf, it was not always so, much initially having been done by observation.

Since beginning to write this book I too have had some small taste of how it must feel to be ignored or laughed at, as I have tried, often unsuccessfully, to convince other professionals of the role of anxiety and the fact that serious (but correctable) visual problems exist amongst people with autism. How much worse then it must be to be on the receiving end of comments (often from a very young age) which indicate that one is 'abnormal'. No wonder it can result in extreme frustration and anger. It is understandable that this, all too often, leaves the people concerned feeling alienated from 'the world'. It is sad, though, that a number of them feel that all of 'us' are tarnished with the same brush.

Such feelings come across strongly in Jasmine Lee O'Neill's book when she says:

> Autism is not a terrifying crippling disease. It is, of course, not an illness at all. Nothing is *wrong* with a person who was simply born autistic. There is only something *unique*. A different function of the brain doesn't mean that brain is damaged or incomplete. I fail to comprehend or accept how a great number of medical professionals, researchers, and even parents wish to eliminate a particular personality type, to stamp out something that makes some rare individuals stand out wonderfully from the crowds. How could I accept it? If their plan succeeded, I wouldn't be who I am. (O'Neill 1999, p.119)

While I understand the feelings behind the passage above I clearly do not agree that the treatments I am proposing would in any way diminish Jasmine's personality. That said, however, I would certainly not presume to tell either her or others who have come to terms with their autism that they 'should' join 'my world' for that choice is theirs alone and they and the choices they make should be treated with the same respect that we are all entitled to.

However, whilst I may be wrong, I cannot see that 'autisms' or the abnormal sensory perceptions which give rise to them are actually part of a person's character; their personality. To do so would be to imply that those people whose autism has been minimized or those who have 'recovered' lose something essential to their being – which is *definitely* not true of the people I know. Perhaps in time the people in this position will explain the differences and tell us how it feels. In the meantime I would argue that all they have lost is their anxiety and the restrictions it placed upon their lives. (I exclude here those people who have merely 'conformed' to the expectations of 'the world' rather than lost their anxieties.)

I must, though, emphasize again that the words 'great sensitivity' are central to any type of treatment; for sadly there have indeed been situations in which 'treatment' has been forced upon people insensitively – especially children and those who are least independent. This can cause further damage and leave the person in danger of losing touch with himself or of being forced into deeper withdrawal.

Moving on now, I hope that such ideas also empower parents who, armed with knowledge and understanding, will be in a better position to demand correct diagnosis and treatment. Increased knowledge should give them additional confidence when talking to 'professionals', although whether they will get what they ask for is a moot point.

Unfortunately in the past, when information about the condition was sparse, many general practitioners had never come across the problem. The mother's views were often disregarded when she approached the doctor to say, 'I know something is wrong', as the child appeared fit, healthy and had, perhaps, not reached the stage of displaying glaring problems. In some cases, after several unproductive visits, the case notes read 'neurotic mother' – a view which then followed them down the years, thereby adding to their difficulties.

Fortunately this has changed, as the problems of the condition have gained more recognition and diagnosis has become easier, although one still occasionally meets a professional(!?) – happily rare – who says that the parents would 'prefer not to know what the problem is' as they 'don't know how to deal with the information'. Perhaps this is caused more by their own fear of having to 'break' such news and cope with the aftermath?

It has even been said that emotional attachment may blur the parents' judgement or make them over-anxious, but this is generally not true. Obviously some people are more naturally anxious than others and the strain, which all these parents share, of constantly coping with bizarre and inappropriate behaviours can only increase such feelings.

However, as the true professionals readily admit, the parents are the people with first-hand experience who are most knowledgeable about their children's abilities and needs. They know their child intimately through sharing each day with him and will see facets which would be hidden to the visitor or outsider. Generally they are only too glad to share this with someone whom they feel understands the problems and empathizes with them, for most are desperately seeking knowledge so that they will know where to go for the help and support in dealing with the situation; as would anyone in a similar position.

Acknowledging any type of handicap is extremely difficult, especially when the baby appeared normal for the first few weeks or months. While many parents already feel that something is wrong, confirmation of such fears should be communicated clearly, concisely and in a way that allows for hope. Sadly, the varying and often depressing prognoses which have frequently been connected with autism have caused additional (and often unnecessary) distress to people in an already traumatic situation. While the line between pessimism and realism is often thin, increasing knowledge should offer some optimism.

Parents not only have to assimilate the news of the handicap, which brings with it natural (but unrealistic) feelings of guilt, but also the realization that their expectations of the future have been drastically altered. Some feel they should support their partner by keeping a stiff upper lip and consequently they refrain from expressing their real feelings about the situation, which can then lead them to feel isolated. In reality more support will be generated by an open discussion and exploration of their feelings than by silence.

They also have to face breaking the news to siblings, whose difficulties in coping with a handicapped brother or sister are often underestimated. The older they are the easier it will be for them to understand, but their need for support in coping with the problems which arise must be recognized too. They may have genuinely ambivalent feelings when their handicapped sibling consumes their parents' time and attention or behaves in a bizarre manner in front of their friends. Fortunately, some support groups do now provide a forum for these youngsters too.

Further difficulties arise when telling relations and friends, some of whom may have been cooing over the pram and making complimentary noises. Many parents have found it best to tell other people as soon as possible, for delay creates even more anxiety. Unfortunately, family and friends may make well-intentioned remarks which appear awkward or unsympathetic simply because they do not know how to react. On the positive side, however, involving others gives them the opportunity to offer practical help which may be welcomed (and much needed). At this point I must stress the importance of some form of respite care, whether it be a babysitter for a night or a place to which the child can go for a weekend or holiday. It is all to easy to become overtired when caring for a child with the varied problems of autism/ Asperger's syndrome and this can have a detrimental effect on relationships. Many parents are understandably reluctant to leave their children in someone else's care but it is extremely important for all involved to take a regular break to 'recharge the batteries' – and one's sense of humour.

Sadly, but hardly surprisingly, some families fall apart under such pressures, which are often added to as the child grows older – as when members of the public misinterpret the child's actions as 'bad behaviour' for which they blame the parents. Perhaps it is more astonishing that many families cope so successfully even while functioning under such strains.

Parents obviously want what is best for their children but many, for whom I have great sympathy, are at present hampered from pursuing and achieving this for a variety of reasons.

First, the way in which many relevant treatments work cannot always be fully explained. Add to this, uncertainty as to which person will respond to which treatment. This plays into the hands of the critics, who are more easily able to deride the treatments. This again creates confusion amongst parents who, at a time when they may be coming to terms with and learning to cope with the problems caused by living with a person with autism, have to be particularly single-minded to ignore such 'experts'.

This is especially true when the person with autism has reached adulthood, for parents, too, will find it especially hard to accept new ideas and go against what may have become a self-fulfilling prophecy: their 'child' having spent many years being thought of and treated as mentally handicapped and perhaps even thinking of himself in such terms.

This ties up with the second problem, which is of course the cost. Some of these treatments are costly but – given the potential benefits in terms of education and care and the money that a reduction of the difficulties will save – the parents should not be responsible for paying. However, this is a 'catch-22' situation for until their efficacy has been fully proven, which is problematic given the complexities of autism, it continues to be difficult for families to get funding (although this is not always the case); something which must be particularly difficult for those families who would like to try but cannot afford the costs. I hope that as the metabolic and other difficulties become better understood we shall see such treatments offered under or funded by the National Health Service or other relevant authority as a matter of course, not only for those with autism but for those with related disorders too. Perhaps this book will go some way to help.

Finally, parents have to contend with other people's/professionals' expectations of autism which, regardless of the lip service paid to political correctness, still often see the 'less functioning' person (a horrible term!) as 'mentally handicapped': one who will be unable to achieve very much at all. And about whom occasionally hangs the, albeit generally unspoken, question: 'Why bother?'

Quite understandably, many parents are reluctant to go against such 'perceived wisdom'. Thus they do not even try treatments which might be of benefit. Meanwhile those who wish to try must fight (or pay) to get things which should be readily available to anyone, which greatly adds to the stress of coping with a family member with autism.

Such attitudes may be compounded by the fact that a few other professionals, who have little in-depth knowledge of autism, are very reluctant to take new ideas aboard. Thus one family I know have had great difficulty in arranging a NHS hearing test for their child and were, at the time of writing, finding it almost impossible to arrange for a test for bowel disease because their doctor is unwilling to refer them to a specialist in their area. (I have always thought that the American trend of suing people for the slightest thing was 'over the top' but perhaps it is not always such a bad idea after all!)

One final point. Those families or individuals who do, successfully, try some of these treatments need to be aware that an improvement can sometimes induce feelings of anger and/or loss regarding time wasted in the past: a reaction which needs clear recognition.

Education

Once a diagnosis has been made, the onus falls on the educational system to make the correct provision for each child. He will be assessed, or in official jargon 'Statemented', so that his needs can be accurately determined by everyone concerned.

Currently it would seem that the child's level of functioning will usually determine where he receives his education. It may be in a school for children with developmental handicaps, one for children with autism, or, for some, an ordinary school. Each individual's needs are different and while some may gain a great deal from attending on a daily basis, others may benefit more from attending a residential school as a weekly or termly boarder, especially if it is geared to their specific needs. Before any choice is made the parents should visit and compare various places and see exactly what facilities are provided. Once a school has been determined, the parents should discuss the child's strengths and needs in detail with those who will be responsible for him.

The exact method by which the child will be introduced to the school should also be well thought out, for some children will cope better if there is a transitional period, when they can visit with a parent for instance, to introduce them to the staff and the new routines gradually: an idea which can also be helpful when changing or leaving school.

In some countries there has been a move away from 'special provision' to a more integrated educational system, whereby children with special needs are catered for amongst the mainstream classes and this is also being looked at in Britain. The intention, of course, is to remove the stigma attached to special schools and bring about a greater acceptance of those with difficulties and a more positive attitude within society in the future. However, although this type of placement can be entirely appropriate for some, it may be totally wrong for others. In some cases the very support designed to help the child can in fact make matters worse, as Ann Coward, the Headmistress of Clarendon School for children with special needs, pointed out. In an article in the *Daily Telegraph* (1998) she wrote that the difficulties faced by children with special needs attending mainstream schools can be increased by the support they receive, which draws attention to them, embarrasses them, and cuts them off from other children. It is therefore very important that each case is looked at individually and that the drawbacks of mainstreaming are neither forgotten nor ignored.

The major problem which I foresee is for children who are hypersensitive, who will be constantly bombarded by the normal hurly-burly of school life, for even in the best-run schools they would be subjected to a great deal of visual stimulation/confusion and noise which could cause increased anxiety. If they are to maximize their chances of success, they will need some 'protection', as indeed would those with a physical problem such as brittle bones.

The effects of such problems are highlighted by Gunilla Gerland who in discussing her school days makes several telling comments:

> It was often no use asking (the way to a room) because they might reply 'This or that corridor on the left, number this or that on the door'. This was no use. I didn't really know left from right, and all the corridors were so alike that they merged together, sliding into each other. Nor was there enough difference between the little numbers on the right of the doors.
>
> All this was also made more difficult by the constant murmur created by hundreds of pupils in an old stone building with high ceilings. This murmur was torment to me, as if eating into my mind, as if penetrating between my thoughts and making them dusty and hairy. My thoughts grew ragged at the edges, and I couldn't dismiss the sound if it lasted too long. Trying to block it out was usually too much of an effort. All that was left to me was to let go and switch off the whole system. To retreat inside myself. (Gerland and Tate 1997, pp.148–149)

Then too we have the added isolation that some of the symptoms of autism may bring as the child is unable to pick up on the normal verbal and non-verbal cues which would enable him to make friends and he gradually becomes regarded as an oddity. As Gunilla Gerland says:

> I was very lonely, and increasingly suffering from it – not from my actual solitude, but more from comparing myself with others and wanting to be as normal, right and ordinary as they were. My actual solitude – being on my own – was easy … Yet that emptiness was my eternal companion, like a vague loss of something; though at the same time I was so used to it, I couldn't imagine things could be any other way. (Gerland and Tate 1997, p.139)

Finally we need to be concerned with teasing and, worse still, bullying. It is all too easy to pick upon the 'odd' child, who may in fact fuel the situation by his naivety and quite often will not hit back. Whilst the books of Gunilla Gerland and Jasmine Lee O'Neill provide heartrending descriptions of the treatment they received, a simple comment brought this home vividly when twenty-five year old Michael visited me. In the course of the conversation he painfully recalled his years at junior school, asking in a bewildered voice, 'Why did the other boys always hit me?' Why indeed?

Continuing to play Devil's advocate, though, I must point out that, while there are several arguments to be made against mainstreaming, you will need to look at each potential placement carefully. Clearly not all schools for children with learning disabilities have a clear understanding of autism/Asperger's syndrome and the problems thereof. This, as you have already seen, can create additional stress for the child's sensory and information processing problems may be ignored and their level of functioning can be misinterpreted or misunderstood. This can result in a range of additional problems as they are subjected to 'exciting' opportunities which may leave them confused or distraught or, like Neil, are made to repeat basic school work year after year.

Whichever type of school you finally decide upon you will need to ensure that the staff do indeed understand (or are willing to learn about) the specific problems relating to these disorders. Close ongoing contact will also be helpful to ensure that the individual teachers are aware of the issues that can arise around bullying. Indeed, in mainstream schools it may sometimes be helpful to explain the child's difficulties to his peers so that they too can be aware of the potential problems and his vulnerability.

Choices in adulthood

For the parent

The choice of provision for school leavers is an individual one for each family and no guilt should be felt by parents who feel that they wish to look for an 'alternative' home for their son or daughter. The decision is obviously more difficult for those whose child is handicapped in some way, as the natural tendency of most parents to continue thinking of their son or daughter as a child is exaggerated by awareness of his or her difficulties in coping with particular aspects of life. Nevertheless, a choice will have to be made at some point, taking all factors into account.

While many parents wish to continue providing for their child at home, those who feel otherwise should be reassured by the fact that leaving home is a natural process for people in their late teens or early twenties; the difference being that most children instigate this move themselves rather than waiting for their parents to do so. The process is natural for the parents, too!

Many parents actually find it helpful to prepare the adolescent or young adult for an independent way of life and see him settled long before they themselves reach the stage of not being able to cope. And, like most of those in their teens or early twenties, even people who are apparently severely handicapped may, after a careful transition, enjoy the feeling of independence and gain from living with their own peer group.

Unfortunately, residential care has sometimes received bad publicity, but at best it can provide a safe and secure future for the many sufferers whose families feel they wish to conform to the 'normal' pattern and provide their child with more independence, or for those whose situation or behaviour makes a move away from 'home' the only viable alternative.

So: what are the choices? Residential homes fall into three broad categories:

1. **Group homes**. These provide care in a small house in a local town or city. Clients in these homes may attend a local Adult Opportunity or Community Resource Centre during the day although some homes may provide their own form of work or day-care.

2. **Communities**. These provide care in a larger establishment where several houses may be grouped together. Clients may live in a house with a few others: such communities are often set within large grounds and may provide day-care on site. Some of these may have links with group homes to which clients can move as they progress.

3. **Villages** such as those run by Care, Camphill, Home Farm Trust, etc. In these there are many separate houses with day-care/work provided on site.

I omit hospitals from this list as the service is in a state of flux at present with many hospitals closing and moving their patients to live in the 'wider community' in a group home.

Each type of home will have different services to offer, which may or may not be appropriate for the person concerned. While the trend nowadays is towards group homes which are situated in 'the community', this is not suitable for everyone. Each situation needs to be assessed according to the needs of the individual, as indeed it would be for ourselves. Many people with autism enjoy the space and, perhaps, the slower pace of life often found in a more rural setting (which can be especially beneficial for those who present difficult behaviour at times), but others will welcome the opportunity of living in a town and both should be catered for.

Any residential home which is able to offer a place will be only too willing for parents to visit in order that they may meet the staff, ask questions and assess the facilities. While the state of the buildings and furnishings will indicate whether it is well run, the most important guide will be the atmosphere. A home where the clients are happy, well cared for and treated with respect is obviously better than one which looks like a candidate for an Ideal Home award, where the furniture receives more care than the people.

Once the person is 'installed' in his new home, parents should never feel inhibited about asking questions or querying decisions. Unfortunately, I have come across situations in which parents refrained from asking about important matters because they felt their child would be adversely affected if they, as the parents, 'displeased' the person in charge.

In a well run school or home the relationship with the parents of the client is very important and any questions or concerns will be answered or dealt with without hesitation. Open and forthright communication is of paramount importance if both parents and staff have the welfare of the person concerned at heart. All reputable organizations welcome the opportunity to sort problems out promptly: if not, there is something wrong. In this case further steps may eventually need to be taken, by approaching the Registration Officer or even the Ombudsman if necessary.

Communication is a two-way process and it needs to be recognized that some parents experience difficulties, not only in leaving their child in someone else's care but also in accepting that anyone else can care as well as they do. The feeling may be exacerbated if the child or adult settles happily in the new situation, becomes attached to particular staff, or even appears to have fewer problems when away from home. The latter can in fact happen, for staff in a residential setting have the major advantage of not having to cope on their own twenty-four hours a day as the parents may have done for many years. They can enter the situation with a fresh viewpoint, setting limits which might be quite impossible to adhere to in the home situation, where allowances may have been made over the years in order to ensure the family's survival.

Such feelings are quite natural to every parent whose child leaves home. They need discussion, for if left unspoken or unrecognized they can create great ill feeling and have, in some extreme cases, led to 'competition' for the child or adult, which has only increased his already severe problems.

It is vital that parents and staff understand the potential difficulties and work together for the benefit of the person concerned, for in any tug of war he will inevitably be the major loser. Similarly, staff need to work together towards common agreed goals, rather than each going their own way (as is sometimes done) in order to try to impress others by the way they cope.

From my experience of working in care, I have found that there are times when the staff may feel that limited risks need to be taken in order to move their client towards further independence. This is often difficult for parents to accept as they still feel protective and they, rather than the client, may not be ready for such a step. Such fears are common to all parents, especially, I am sure, those with teenage daughters. They should never be ignored or left unexpressed, but should rather be discussed openly by all concerned, including the client himself, for very often it is he who is pushing to have more independence. As long as an appropriate programme is worked out, whereby the risks are recognized, limited and carefully monitored, success will prove extremely beneficial as it will result in increased confidence and pave the way for further learning.

For the client

Any discussion of choice must also consider life from the client's point of view, leading us to examine the concept of self-advocacy which is so often discussed nowadays. This, at first glance, would appear to be alien to the person with autism whose impaired communication, social skills and lack of motivation may initially make it appear irrelevant. In spite of this, self-advocacy can be initiated and developed to varying degrees by a sensitive, supportive and careful approach.

Those with the ability to live more independently should, with help, gradually learn to make many decisions concerning matters that affect them. Much will depend on the support and encouragement they receive and the ability of other people to respect their opinions. If any degree of self-advocacy is to be attained, parents, carers and teachers may find themselves having to reappraise and perhaps change their attitudes and behaviour. The degree of protectiveness aroused by the handicap may make this an extremely painful time, as it could involve the more capable person in taking risks and possibly making decisions with which the parent or carer does not fully agree.

Not all the person's ideas have to be accepted or acted upon, but any rebuttal must be done sensitively and the reasons carefully explained. The parent or member of staff will need to find positive ways of channelling the person into something more suitable. This may entail them intervening at times, as for instance if an independent client decided to go without meals while spending all his money on alcohol. Initially, it may be very difficult for the client to understand why staff do not act upon an opinion they encouraged him to give and, in extreme cases, he might then begin to feel that it is pointless to express an opinion and withdraw or become depressed. The client should also not, as happens in some places, be given the idea that he has the absolute freedom to do what he likes regardless of others, for this will only hinder his progress towards becoming a responsible member of society.

Unfortunately, problems can occur for many people with autism simply because they take others at face value, lacking the ability to understand other people's motives. They are therefore vulnerable to exploitation in a variety of ways and this is particularly true of those people who have more independence, living within the community.

One extreme example of this occurred with an independent woman with Asperger's syndrome. As with many people who suffer from this problem, she liked people and was aware of and often depressed by her lack of friends. She did, however, get a job in a jeweller's shop where she worked happily for several years. Imagine her pleasure when a junior member of staff offered to take her out to lunch and spent time talking to her. Their 'friendship' grew until the day when the unscrupulous assistant asked her to open the showcase and give her a tray of jewellery so that she could 'take them home to show to her husband'. Poor Janette still does not understand why she lost her job or why she was taken to court and eventually ended up with a year on probation; in her eyes she was merely lending the tray to her friend.

One other relevant point: as new experiences are often seen as frightening, even the most capable person may take the easy route by rejecting all suggestions out of hand. If this is the case, he should be encouraged to join in or at the very least be expected to give a valid reason for opting out, for otherwise he might miss out on experiences which would be of great value. Indeed, it is possible that his more handicapped and less verbal counterpart might gradually become more flexible in attitude, because being less able to make her wishes known she may therefore be more easily encouraged into experiencing a wide range of situations.

The scenario which arises with a severely handicapped person is different, for he may never be able to exercise his right to full self-advocacy, although he can (and should) be encouraged to exercise choice in as many areas as possible. Where practical, this might include a choice of meals, clothes and the colour of his room. He will, however, continue to need an informed advocate, a parent, sibling or professional, to be involved in the decisions concerning his future and welfare.

Spouses and families

One other aspect of this problem has been brought to my attention recently which affects both those people who are most independent and their spouses and families. While this group probably includes people similar to those studied by Sula Wolff in Edinburgh (1993), it was only comparatively recently that I became aware of just how many people with such problems were living and coping in the community, going to school and/or university and building solid careers.

While a high level of intelligence has meant that these people have avoided being diagnosed or categorized as handicapped it has also allowed them to make their way in life, often very successfully in career terms. Their home lives, though, are not necessarily easy and it is often here that things first begin to go wrong. Many such relationships obviously last for years, in some cases, but the lack of empathy and other social problems can make life very difficult, particularly for their spouses and especially if the children inherit similar problems. This can put immense strains on the marriage which, in some cases, eventually ends in divorce.

One lady whose husband has now been diagnosed with Asperger's syndrome discussed her problems on TV and in the newspapers only to find that she was flooded with letters from people in a similar position. Since that time I understand that the NAS have also been overwhelmed by people asking about a support group for people in similar situations, support which is certainly much needed.

An understanding of the problems will enable those involved to appreciate the problems and thereby help ease the burden placed on them by oddities of behaviour etc. Regardless of diagnosis (or lack of it) it may be worth investigating whether the person has any of the metabolic and sensory problems previously mentioned, for treatment of these might alleviate their underlying problems and open the way for those affected to obtain help, where necessary, for other problems.

The future

It appears that there must now be a greater possibility of achieving success through co-operation with other researchers who are working in the fields of neurodevelopmental delay, multi-sensory deprivation and obsessive-compulsive disorders than has previously existed. Additionally, new areas for research are opening up, which must give more hope to parents and sufferers alike.

Early knowledge will have two benefits, enabling appropriate treatment to be started as soon as possible and also making the parents aware of the problems, which would help them create an environment in which to alleviate the child's discomfort. While it would be premature at this point to suggest that tests could eventually lead to the elimination of the problems of autism the future is becoming brighter. How then can we achieve this early recognition?

While the Checklist for Autism in Toddlers (CHAT) and Disco will be vital in determining which children are suffering from autism/Asperger's syndrome, once more accurate information concerning the causes is available, perhaps it will be possible to find ways of testing each baby, either at birth or slightly later, to see if he suffers from a metabolic disorder or an inherent fragility which may cause later difficulties. In time, perhaps, the genetic aspects will give a clear indication of which are the most vulnerable children and may possibly open the way for new treatments although that point has not quite been reached yet. Meanwhile there are several ideas which could be of importance.

First is the Neonatal Behavioural Assessment Scale (NBAS) developed by Brazelton which, as you will remember, is used to evaluate the new-born baby within the first few days by assessing the way in which she responds to both human and non-human stimuli. In Britain there are currently several systems in use (depending on the area in which one lives) and I have not been able to assess each one. The use of the NBAS does seem to have the advantage of alerting the parents to any weaknesses from the beginning. It could indicate if the child would benefit from close monitoring, especially in relation to the introduction of new foods. If vaccines do prove to be a factor for some, perhaps a follow-up done prior to vaccinations would give an indication of how the child might react to the MMR and clarify whether it would be safer given in three separate doses. Similarly the assessment of any neuro-developmental delay/aberrant reflexes might be helpful here.

Then, too, we have the work of Paul Shattock and his colleagues. If opioid peptides are a clear indication of problems it would be helpful to know when they first appear (although one assumes that this is after the problems begin?). Although the age for testing would have to be carefully gauged – being done more than once in some instances (to ensure that those with late onset problems do not slip through the net) – perhaps initially it could be used to screen all those most at risk, including: families with a history of autism or OCD; children with some degree of neurodevelopment delay; those identified by CHAT or Disco; and those who fit Waring's criteria (e.g. one parent with migraine and the other with allergies).

Some of the problems may prove to be extremely hard to reverse, particularly in relation to learnt responses to fear but work with brain-damaged people suggests that there is some hope. While the brain is at the height of its plasticity during the early years, some adults with brain damage can and do make great progress as the undamaged parts of the brain take over the functions of the damaged part.

In the case of autism and Asperger's syndrome many of the problems seem to stem, not directly from brain damage, but rather from the fact that the brain is subjected to high levels of opioids and also because some of the sensory systems are wrongly wired and continuously pass incorrect messages to the brain. If the metabolic function could be corrected so that the 'poisons' are eventually eliminated and the sensory systems 'rewired' correctly through the appropriate treatment then the future should hold great hope for many.

Staffing in residential establishments

Here I would like to digress briefly from the topic of autism to discuss two points which concern me. I was tempted to omit them from the book altogether until told by one reader of the original that she found it of interest. I hope others find it so.

The first point, often ignored, is that in the majority of residential establishments there has historically been a divide between teaching staff or instructors and those who care for the child or adult during the morning, evening and weekends.

This division has been reinforced by the training, higher salaries and more sociable hours worked by the 'day' staff, although parity of pay with ordinary social workers has been introduced in some residential homes who tend to term their staff as residential social workers. Others, however, are still classed as 'care assistants' and, as such, receive very low wages commensurate with their perceived status, justified by the phrase previously applied to nursing: 'but it's a vocation'.

Many residential staff used to come into the work to gain experience prior to following some sort of formal training, which frequently seduced the younger people away from residential care, with the higher salaries and more sociable hours of the other types of work. Many others I know are women returning to work after having had a 'family' break, who are often entering a job which is completely new to them. It is sad that they remain, in some cases, so undervalued for the majority, particularly in the latter group, are highly committed people who give a great deal to the people in their care.

It surely time to acknowledge that, for people living in residential care, the carers assume almost the importance of the parent. They play a vital part in ensuring that the person in their care leads a happy and satisfying life regardless of the limitations imposed by his handicap. It is generally recognized that the child who is unhappy at home will gain little from school, for home life underpins everything: this applies equally to people with any type of handicap who live in a residential school or home, for if they are not happy, little will be achieved by their teachers or instructors in the daytime.

All too often these caring people leave what could have been a productive and satisfying career because there are few prospects and little status: the latter being highlighted for me, by the lone parent (out of many) who never managed to remember or use my name until I was promoted!

This apparently low status often creates a divide between the carers and staff working in day-care establishments who are paid at much better rates and, in my experience, often leads to one group 'looking down' on the other. This can be, unnecessarily, hurtful to the carers.

Sometimes, though, the consequences can be quite amusing, as when I offered to stand in at short notice and lecture on autism at a particular college. Whilst speaking to the lecturer who was organizing the course I told her that my background was in care. A chilly pause was followed by a considerable change of attitude and a quickly curtailed conversation, to be followed by a letter saying they had decided another lecture would be more appropriate! Would her attitude have been the same if I had begun by saying that I used to be Deputy Principal of an establishment with residents, day attenders and over 50 staff? I doubt it!

It is vital that the necessary training and commensurate salary/status is provided for all 'care staff' so that their skills and dedication can not only be acknowledged but enhanced for this would, in the long term, provide greater security for those in their care.

My second point is to stress the need for careful vetting of all staff working with these most vulnerable people, for it has to be acknowledged that the 'caring' professions can attract the wrong type of people at times. I am not talking here about paedophilia but rather about two particular types of people, some of whom I have met during my career.

One is the person who goes into this type of work because they have particular needs of their own and seem to feel, mistakenly, that these will be fulfilled within a 'caring' situation. Fortunately such people often have a relatively short career once the realities of the job actually hit them.

The other type, though, concern me far more. These are people who, unfortunately, seem to have particular personality traits which lead them to seek out this type of career. Although this type of person is often adept at presenting a very caring front to parents and professionals from other fields they do, on closer or longer acquaintance, lack the empathy necessary for such work and often seem to enjoy power (which may be one of their motivating forces in entering this profession).

Thus those people in this category who work directly with the clients can be quite insensitive to their needs and, when feeling unobserved, may be overbearing and bullying towards them. Likewise others, who reach managerial positions, can also come, in time, to abuse their power: not necessarily directly by abusing the people in their care (although there are instances where that has happened), but rather by the way they treat their staff and manipulate or even bully the management committees of the establishments they are supposed to work for. Many committees are made up of parents whose children are in the care of the person concerned and sadly this can leave them feeling vulnerable and reluctant to 'rock the boat' by opposing or complaining about such a manager.

Whilst I may have been unlucky, I have observed the latter situation on a couple of occasions. Thus I was quite disconcerted to hear that one national organization proposed having some of their clients on one such committee: a move which could easily, in a similar situation, leave a manipulative and powerful manager in an invincible position.

How can one avoid such situations? Obviously the vetting of staff should be as thorough as possible, but this will not preclude the appointment of such people for they are only too adept at presenting a 'public face'. To counter this I would suggest four things. First, an ongoing assessment of staff throughout their careers (regardless of the heights to which they rise). Many places already have an appraisal system to do just this but the manager may be excluded from it. I would suggest too that appraisal of the manager should be done only by committee members who do not have children placed at the establishment in question.

Second, I would suggest that the profession also needs tough external regulation. Critics of this idea will say that the registering authorities fulfil this role, but this is not entirely true. Their powers only extend to looking after the welfare of the clients and they are unable to intervene if a situation arises in which the parents of those clients feel intimidated and vulnerable because of their children's placement: something which definitely needs rectifying.

Third, each establishment needs to ensure that the staff feel able to report any problems to the appropriate people so that they can be investigated and, if necessary, dealt with as soon as possible.

Finally, I would also urge each organization to give detailed consideration to the extent of each manager's powers and to the methods by which they can be removed should it ever become necessary, and to ensure that such things are clearly spelled out in any contract.

CHAPTER 8

Conclusion

... all men are created equal ...

Thomas Jefferson (1743–1826)

Sadly, these children are not born equal. I hope to have shown by my arguments that the majority, while severely damaged, are not mentally handicapped, but are normal children whose problems leave them isolated and unable to express, or sometimes even understand, the feelings they undoubtedly have. Their problems may be similar to those of children with dyslexia and aphasia, whom society would not for one moment suggest were mentally handicapped. Unfortunately, though, their problems are far more severe and therefore the outcome is crippling: causing them to suffer from one of the most awful handicaps presently known to man.

The phrase, 'Does he take sugar' has frequently been used to highlight society's attitude to those with severe physical disabilities, handicaps which have often ensured that the sufferers have been treated as feeble-minded. These people have objected quite vocally to such treatment over the past few years and have gradually made some impression on the general public. In contrast, sufferers of autism are still frequently misunderstood by society and are often thought to have severe 'learning difficulties'. Their sad plight is paralleled in the film 'One Flew Over A Cuckoo's Nest', where a 'normal' man had himself admitted to a hospital for the insane in order to escape a prison sentence. Once there, all his actions, however normal, were seen from a different (abnormal?) perspective and he was treated as insane. The film concentrates on his struggle to convince the staff of his sanity; a struggle which is savagely, and predictably, lost.

How can we expect these children to convince us of their normality, when from their earliest days they are besieged and tortured by problems which activate a conditioned response 'forcing' them, in an unconscious act of desperation, to isolate themselves from the world? This isolation becomes a self-perpetuating problem which ensures their silence while their problems are further compounded by society's demoralizing attitude. One might fairly assume that each child then unwittingly becomes a 'willing' accomplice in the 'crime upon its soul'.

I would like to quote a very moving passage written by Joan Martin Hundley (now sadly deceased) in her book *The Small Outsider* (1971). Her son had, she felt, appeared odd from birth, neither seeing nor hearing in the same way as her other children and, because of this, he was an extremely anxious child. His mother described her experience thus:

> I once had a strange dream about him. I dreamt I saw the fear step away from his body and stand alone, like a shadow of himself. His own body stood stiff and silent like a wooden doll, and I stepped into the shape of the fear. I became one with the fear, his sensitive self: I felt as he does and saw with his eyes. I saw human beings through one eye in the forehead of the fear; I saw a narrow vision of the world. And through one ear I heard disjointed sounds coming and going. I saw a world peopled with strange moving shapes, human beings, shapes that didn't stay in one place but kept moving out of my range of vision. And just when I got adjusted to them standing in one place for a little while and assessed them against one background, they moved and flickered back and forth like reflections in a stream when the surface of the water is disturbed. I heard the voices of human beings – strange chattering noises coming out of holes in their heads, distorted heads. They never said the same thing twice in the same way. Every time the words came out they sounded different, of a different pitch. Sometimes there was a blackness, a nothing all around me, and I felt afraid and I reached out and clung to something solid, a piece of furniture that stayed in one place. Then I heard music and was comforted. I liked the music because it followed recognizable patterns and I knew what to expect from it ... (Hundley 1971, reproduced with permission of Curtis Brown (Australia) Pty Ltd)

Using the 'insight' she obtained from this dream, she then continued:

> These are the children who walk in the shadows, and the road they walk is lonely and empty. They don't know how to take advantage of the warmth of human company. If a child can't find safety in his mother's arms, where else can he find it? How can a child develop into a human being if he doesn't know how to make contact with human beings? (Hundley 1971, reproduced with permission of Curtis Brown (Australia) Pty Ltd)

Whatever the reality behind her dream, it must be recognized that trauma is the constant companion of people with autism, remaining so throughout their lives unless treated. And while some successfully help themselves, the majority, especially of those most handicapped, will only achieve that most precious of gifts, a human relationship, through our unremitting efforts.

In the beginning, I simply intended to challenge some of the fallacies about autism and detail my thoughts about anxiety, which I considered to be a major factor. A secondary aim was to speak for those unable to speak for themselves. I had no idea that this would eventually lead me as far as it did, or to the conclusions I have reached.

Once started, however, it became a puzzle which I had to solve. I encountered a snowball effect, as the more I read of other people's ideas, the more avenues for exploration opened. While following the 'clues', I was at times puzzled and confused as I tried blind alleys or 'went round in circles'. Although many theories and ideas had previously been explored and discarded by others, I became a 'doubting Thomas', investigating many of them myself just in case a vital point had been missed. I was often close to despair but four things stood me in good stead: I have worked with both emotionally disturbed and 'mentally handicapped' people; I bear no allegiance to any particular theory or type of treatment; I graduated early from Enid Blyton to detective stories, which continue to fascinate me; and finally I can, as former colleagues would no doubt testify, be extremely stubborn (some might even say obsessive!) and there was no way I would admit defeat.

It was never my intention to challenge so many different aspects of the criteria and current theories but looking at them objectively gave me no option. I have been accused of being selective and fitting the facts to my theories but while the sceptics may continue to mock, those who have followed my search will understand that such a thing was never necessary. I began exactly where I said – with anxiety – and merely followed the path that opened in front of me.

Although the various clues initially seemed contradictory and confusing, all contained at least a grain of truth, which fitted together to form a pattern, affording insight into the underlying problems of autism and Asperger's syndrome. One of the major problems seemed to be that all too often researchers have emphasized or concentrated on one facet of the problem rather than taking the necessary overview. And as a result they have headed in the wrong direction. Perhaps one of the most notable 'red herrings' has been the recent emphasis on cognition, which distracts attention from the fundamental causes.

I found the genetic factors particularly exciting, offering, as they must, more positive hope for the future than we have previously seen. It is ironic then to note that, as those who read the first version of this book may recall, at one point I wrote: 'I am not convinced that autism ever arises solely from metabolic disorders or allergies ...' How foolish that now seems! Now I am totally convinced that such problems underlie the many other factors which cause anxiety and which, in my view, contribute to those behaviours we identify as 'autism'. Indeed, I now find that after all my criticism of red herrings and misleading information I have, in truth, probably contributed to the confusion – for which I must and do apologize.

Perhaps people will be more convinced by Donna Williams' theories, for she has lived with and within such problems. Or will they? Unfortunately, I know that a number of people feel that she is 'the exception', thereby making it easy to dismiss her experiences as irrelevant to those who are apparently different from or more handicapped than her.

I find it strange that my approach, built upon the foundation of my original book and looking at the subject from a totally different perspective, has led to answers which in many respects closely parallel hers. Is this merely another coincidence? Obviously I firmly believe that it is not, but you must judge for yourselves.

And what of the sensory disorders? Looking back at Rimland's book *Infantile Autism* (1964) I was fascinated to find the following:

> The prevailing theory that autism is a form of psychosis rather than mental retardation has been explained as an expected consequence of effective sensory deprivation (or more exactly of perceptual disability). (Rimland 1964, p.103)

Thus the idea that autistic behaviours could stem from perceptual problems was considered seriously by several people in the 1960s. Even the use of the term psychosis (a form of mental disorder in which the person's contact with reality becomes distorted), although not quite right, was close to the mark for, if reality is distorted, as it is, it is small wonder that the sufferers have problems in dealing with it: as would we all. Perhaps such ideas were simply ahead of their time?

What amazes (and depresses) me is that such ideas were mooted in the 1960s and 1970s and have been supported by the writings of sufferers for years, yet the cry of 'anecdote' still resounds. One account could be anecdote. Two might (possibly) be coincidence. But three, four, five, six ...? My credulity doesn't stretch that far. Does yours?

I am told that a new idea has to pass through three stages:

1. When it is regarded as ridiculous.

2. When people say, 'well ... it's possible, but where's the proof?'

3. When everybody dismisses it as obvious.

My hypotheses about the different types of autism may still be at stage one. If so, don't ignore them, find instead the evidence to disprove or prove them. Results will only be achieved if we keep looking!

The major part played by anxiety (which is now gradually gaining more attention) is probably nearing stage two, although its role in the development of obsessive-compulsive behaviours may still lag behind. While the origins of this anxiety are multiple, sadly to find proof needs no research for it already exists. You only have to read the factual accounts from people who have suffered from isolation and fear and judge for yourselves.

What, then, of the metabolic and dietary problems? A number of professionals remain sceptical even in the face of growing evidence. How long can they remain so? I too was a sceptic. I too made foolish comments concerning this. Even so I cannot ignore the evidence from the Autism Research Unit and elsewhere, or dismiss the very real improvements that I have seen when diets have been implemented.

While not everyone will have such problems, it would be foolish to dismiss such ideas without a thorough investigation of each individual. No: not foolish but, rather, irresponsible, for we can only design appropriate treatments once the problems have been evaluated correctly. Stage two going on stage three perhaps?

But what of the distorted sensory perceptions? Surely people must now start to believe the sufferers! No anecdote there – just horrifying, terrifying experience. Abnormal perceptions devastate lives – are devastating *their* lives. They must not be allowed to cry in the wilderness any longer. Surely now this must be an idea whose time has come.

Appendix A: Glossary

Amino acids. Make the enzymes (proteins) necessary to our functioning. Some 'essential' amino acids cannot be produced by the body but must be obtained from food or supplements. There are eight of these including **tryptophan, leucine** and **phenylalanine**.

Tryptophan is the precursor of **serotonin** and also promotes **melatonin**. Phenylalanine is needed to make **tyrosine** which can raise brain levels of **dopamine** and **noradrenalin**. Vitamin B6 is used in all of these reactions.

Glutamine is a non-essential amino acid which has many uses. Besides being an important energy source for the immune system it keeps the lining of the digestive tract in balance and is involved in liver function and detoxification. It is said to help with a variety of digestive problems, for example leaky gut and Crohn's disease. It is used by the brain for clarity of thinking and mental alertness. It also helps to control the blood sugar balance, thereby helping those who suffer from hypoglycaemia.

Any compound of two or more amino acids is known as a **peptide**. These facilitate the passing of messages in the brain.

Aphasia. A partial or total loss of the ability to communicate, especially in speech and writing. This is thought to be due to a disorder of or damage to the central nervous system.

Central nervous system (CNS). Made up of the spinal cord, brain stem and brain.

Dysbiosis. A condition in which abnormal bacteria are present in the intestines. The bacteria render the lining of the gut more permeable than it should be and this can disrupt the normal digestive process with subsequent food sensitivity and vitamin deficiency.

Endorphins. Have a calming effect and also give pain relief.

Enzymes. Control the types of chemical reactions that take place in the body and the brain. There are thousands of enzymes within the body.

A mutant or damaged gene can sometimes cause a particular enzyme to be ineffective. This impairs the function of the specific chemical reaction normally controlled by that enzyme and, in turn, disrupts many of the other processes carried out by the brain.

Essential fatty acids (EFAs). Have two important functions. First, they form part of the structure of nearly every cell membrane and are therefore present in large quantities in the nervous system. It has been suggested that the development of the nervous system is to some extent dependent on the availability of EFAs: a theory which, if proved true, might have implications for the dietary requirements of pregnant women.

Second, EFAs provide the raw material from which **prostaglandins** are made. These are produced in every organ of the body and either regulate that organ or its immediate surroundings. Prostaglandins are involved in many vital functions, including the development of vision and the synapses, the transmission of messages through the nerves, the memory, the regulation of respiration, blood pressure and immune responses.

Lack of EFAs can cause behavioural impairments, impair the ability to learn and impair the memory. Essential fatty acids are also, for some as yet unexplained reason, needed far more by males than by females.

Hypoglycaemia. Stems from a pancreatic dysfunction. It results in low blood sugar which may cause symptoms of weakness, tremors, nervousness, breathlessness or excitement and can, when extreme, lead to a loss of consciousness.

Leaky gut. There are several potential causes of leaky gut, including illness, intestinal infection, candida, poor digestion, ingestion of allergenic foods and dysbiosis. This condition can result in deficiencies in the supply of nutrients to the brain, the development of allergies, toxicity in the body (which can affect the blood supply to the brain), hypoglycaemia and hormonal disturbances.

Malnutrition. Has severe effects, particularly during the first two years of life and, although the body usually suffers first, eventually the brain's development will be severely impaired. Where this happens it results in a brain which is smaller than normal, with a reduced number of glia cells, fewer connections between neurons, less myelination and a reduced level of enzymes. The cerebellum suffers most from malnourishment in relation to size and, as it is responsible for the integration of limb movements, malnutrition can result in poor co-ordination.

Melatonin. Has several functions, influencing body rhythms such as digestion, mood and sleep patterns. It is a hormone which is secreted by the **pineal gland** in response to light coming in through the eyes, with less light giving increased melatonin. Thus at night the melatonin levels rise, our blood pressure falls, the heart beat slows and we feel sleepy.

Myelin. A fatty protective sheath around the neurons which insulates them and allows the impulses to move along the nerves faster and more efficiently. The process of myelination begins prior to birth and is mainly completed by the age of two although in some areas it continues much later, even into adolescence.

Nerve cells (neurons). React to a variety of stimuli, that is, external factors, emotional stimulation or motor commands from the brain. The neurons which receive information from the senses are called **receptors** whilst those which trigger a response are known as **effectors**.

Nervous system. Divided into two parts which work opposite each other. Thus the **sympathetic nervous system** accelerates the heartbeat, dilates the bronchi of the lungs and inhibits the smooth muscles of the digestive system whilst the **parasympathetic nervous system** does the opposite, slowing the heartbeat, constricting the bronchi, etc.

Neurotransmitters. Chemicals which transmit messages throughout the various areas of the brain. The main ones mentioned in this book are:

   i)   **Acetylcholine**, which is linked to the functioning of memory, the ability to learn and the attention span.

ii) **Dopamine**, which plays an important role in controlling complex muscle movements. Dopamine abnormalities are implicated in conditions associated with uncontrollable muscle movements such as Tourette's syndrome, Parkinson's disease and even some cases of attention deficit hyperactivity disorder. It is known that stress can cause a decrease of dopamine in the frontal lobes leading to hyperactivity, short attention span and irritability.

iii) **Norepinephrine (noradrenalin)**, which is a precursor of **adrenaline** which plays an important role in response to stress. One of the key changes which occur under great stress are in the **locus ceruleus** which regulates adrenaline and noradrenalin. Associated with the sympathetic nervous system, it increases blood pressure and the heart rate. It helps to modulate dopamine and allows us to filter out irrelevant stimuli or to block out a stimulus once it has been repeated several times (as when sleeping in a noisy environment).

The amino acids **tyrosine** and **phenylalanine** are needed to produce norepinephrine. Low glucose levels (as found in hypoglycaemia) increase the level of norepinephrine which has the effect of making us more active. This in turn makes the limbic system more reactive to external events. Thus the person may more easily become irritable or act more impulsively than usual if they miss a meal.

Homovanillate (HVA) and **vanillymandelate (VMA)** are two organic by-products of norepinephrine and adrenaline which stimulate the nervous system. High levels of these have been found in some people with autism.

iv) **Serotonin**, which acts as an inhibitor. It is involved in the control of a wide range of areas such as sensitivity to pain, appetite, blood pressure and sleep. It also plays a role in anxiety and depression. Evidence (Cook and Leventhal 1996) now indicates that serotonin levels differ between races and ethnic groups.

Low levels of serotonin can disturb day and night activity rhythms. They can produce feelings of depression and unease and are thought to have a link with low blood sugar levels. Low serotonin levels are found in a number of people with particular disorders such as ADHD, OCD, Tourette's syndrome, autism, depression and bulimia.

Increased levels of serotonin can also produce numerous effects. Thus it can cause depressed appetite; sustained rapid eye movement; an overreaction of the reflexes; clumsiness; restlessness; high body temperatures and sweating; muscle contraction/relaxation in particular parts of the body. In addition, it can cause changes in the person's mental state.

High levels of serotonin are found in a number of people with obsessive-compulsive disorder, anorexia (although they decrease when the person is fasting) and autism as well as those who are 'mentally handicapped': the levels in the latter being even higher than those found in autism.

Interestingly, increased levels, which are found amongst approximately 30 per cent of people with autism, are said to cause an increase in the levels of brain endorphins while a decrease of serotonin causes a corresponding reduction in these endorphins.

Tryptophan, vitamin B6 and lithium are essential for the production of serotonin.

Night terrors. Occur during the transitionary phase when we move from deep sleep into a lighter sleep which precedes **REM** sleep: REM is the period during which we dream (or have nightmares), so called because rapid eye movements are observed. It is during the transitional stage that bed-wetting, sleep-walking/talking and night terrors occur. During the latter the person will sit up, scream hysterically with an expression of real fear and may breathe and sweat heavily. He will be very difficult to arouse but will usually fall asleep again after about ten minutes and, in contrast with the person who has a nightmare, will generally have no recollection of events.

Phenolic food compounds. The aromatic food compounds which colour, flavour and preserve our food. For simplicity they are generally referred to as **phenolics** in the text.

Polydipsia. A term used to describe excessive drinking. Note that excessive thirst is also sign of a deficiency of essential fatty acids (often found in boys with ADHD).

Appendix B The Brain

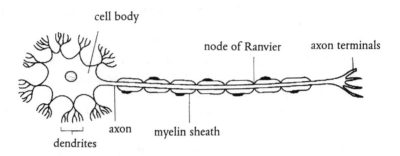

Figure B.1 A neuron

Figure B.1 A neuron

Axons pass impulses to other cells where they are received by dendrites. When the impulse reaches the synapse it triggers the release of a neurotransmitter which links the axon and the dendrite, allowing the impulse to cross between the two before the neurotransmitter is reabsorbed or destroyed by a particular enzyme. One of the most important enzymes used in this process is **monoamine oxidase (MAO)** which breaks down serotonin, dopamine and norepinephrine. If these enzymes are faulty and the neurotransmitter is not removed properly once it has fulfilled its task the neuron will continue to fire impulses across the gap. This would cause problems as in the case of a reflex action where the action would continue to be carried out repetitively for some time.

Glia cells are packed between the neurons and 'glue' the brain together. They are involved in nearly every aspect of neuronal activity, insulating and nourishing the neurons, receiving and passing messages from and to the neuron and also removing waste products – especially the neurotransmitters and other chemicals released into the synaptic gap.

The cell bodies of the neurons are found in the spinal cord. The brain is not generally involved in the reflex process unless the receptor is nearer to the brain than the spinal cord – for example, most visual stimuli would pass directly through the brain.

The **reticular activating system** (or **reticular formation**) takes its name from the Latin 'reticulus' which means 'little net' and is situated within the **reptilian complex**. It acts as an alarm and arousal system by sieving all incoming sensory information. It will then either discard messages or, if they are novel or important enough, pass them on for the brain to deal with. This network grows with experience, learning to filter out things which might initially have aroused it – which is why we can gradually adapt to sleeping even when in noisy situations. Its function can be summed up by Figure B.2.

External world	Reticular activating system	Brain
Important sensory input	————————————————————————————→	
Unimportant sensory input	——————————→	

Figure B.2 The reticular activating system

It also contains the **brainstem** (which is connected to the **spinal cord**), **midbrain** and the **basal ganglia (caudate and putamen)** as shown in Figure B.3.

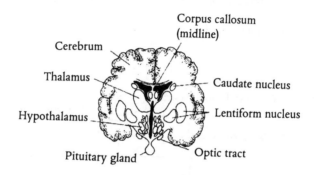

Figure B.3 Frontal section of the brain

The **basal ganglia (neostriatum)** act as a relay station which regulates/integrates sensory, emotional and voluntary inputs to motor activities. This controls muscle movement and integrates motor functions to produce complex behaviours. These control instinctive stereotyped behaviours which, once triggered by environmental cues, are played out to completion. Such behaviours require no thought and have therefore been linked with the obsessive or compulsive behaviours found amongst some people with Tourette's syndrome.

Figure B.4 shows the **fore-brain** or **cerebrum** which consists of two **cerebral hemispheres** which are joined by a bridge of white nervous tissue called the **corpus callosum (midline)**. The fore-brain is connected to the **cerebellum** by the **brain stem**, which consists of the **medulla oblongata, pons** and **mid-brain** plus the **hypothalamus** and **thalamus**.

The cerebellum maintains co-ordination and balance and also acts as a sensory modulator or volume control. It is related to unconscious co-ordination of muscular movements and also affects sensory reception. If it is damaged a person will make jerky movements or suffer from tremors and have difficulty in co-ordinating muscle

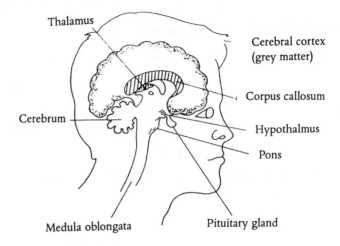

Figure B.4. Side section of the brain

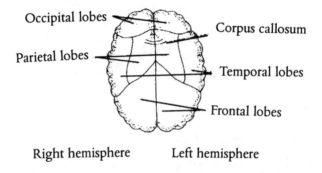

Figure B.5 Section of the brain showing the right and left hemispheres

movements as in walking or speaking. It is interesting to note, though, that people born without a cerebellum seem to manage reasonably well without it.

The hypothalamus is the regulator of instinctive behaviour, including hunger and thirst. It is also concerned with the emotions and the secretions of the pituitary gland.

Figure B.5 is a section of the brain showing the right and left hemispheres. The **frontal lobes** contain sensory and motor strips which control various parts of the body and are associated with foresight. The frontal and **temporal lobes** deal with speech and memory and the **parietal lobe** deals with relationships between the body and mind.

The **prefrontal lobes** form the central processor for information from the senses. Together with the limbic system they make plans for action to be passed on to the motor areas. When they do not work properly the ability to pay attention and make or change plans are affected. Reactions become thoughtless and impulsive and the person shows little motivation or concentration.

The prefrontal lobes are not fully mature until the child is four to seven years old. Myelination in this area and that of the inferior parietal area also occurs much later than in other areas and therefore minor damage or problems in this area may not become apparent until after the onset of puberty.

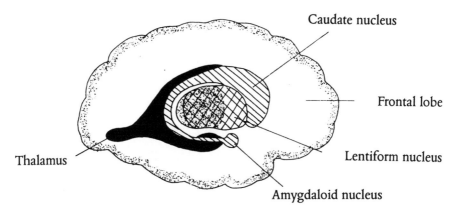

Figure B.6 The limbic system

The **limbic system** is a wishbone-like structure which borders various other structures as shown in Figure B.6. It participates in any form of structured brain work a person can do when awake: perception, voluntary action, thinking, remembering, calculating, reading, discriminating and speaking. It is connected with memory and:

- expresses emotional aspects of behaviour such as pleasure, affection, pain, or rage;
- controls the vital inner urges related to survival, such as hunger and thirst.

It is also involved with everything pertaining to movement, controlling the limbs, muscles and organs, and can be damaged by stress, thereby disrupting the ability to learn and remember.

The **amygdala** is a small almond-shaped structure lying at the base of the brain near the base of the limbic system. It is thought to be one of the oldest parts of the brain and is central to the processing of our emotions. It is this organ which stores our emotional memories.

Research by Joseph LeDoux from the Centre for Neural Science at New York University (Goleman 1995) shows that the amygdala can receive sensory signals from the ears and eyes and react to them before they reach the cortex, which gives a slower but more informed response. Thus sometimes we are thrust into action before we have had time to make a considered response.

The amygdala is particularly important in relation to fear for, by enabling us to assess each situation and perception so rapidly, it can invoke a flight or fight response immediately. Certain connections between nerve cells in the amygdala are strengthened whenever someone learns to fear something and thus fear actually leaves a physical imprint on the wiring in the brain. Damage to the amygdala will result in an inability to read the emotional content of situations and the loss of personal meanings, so that the person's emotional life becomes blunted or absent.

Appendix C: The Digestive System

The **pancreas** produces the pancreatic juices (enzymes used in digestion) from the **exocrine** section. The **endocrine** system is involved in carbohydrate metabolism, secreting insulin and glucagon which help to control the blood sugar.

Problems with the pancreas can cause reactive hypoglycaemia or diabetes. They can also deplete vitamin B12 and cause a malabsorption of essential fatty acids and vitamin A; the latter two being implicated in visual abnormalities and changes in the retina.

The **intestines** form part of the alimentary canal between the stomach and the anus. The small intestine is the longest part (the duodenum being the first part of it) and it is here that digestion is completed. The large intestine then extracts moisture from the food residue which is later excreted as faeces. Under certain adverse conditions the lining of the intestines can become porous and this may cause problems as particles of food which are not fully digested may enter the body and can then affect the functioning of the brain.

The **liver** is the largest and most complex organ in the body and plays an extremely important part in several vital metabolic functions. These include the formation, breakdown and storage of fats, proteins and carbohydrates. It also releases glucose, plasma proteins and cholesterol into the bloodstream in order to maintain a constant level and releases other compounds such as vitamins when the body requires them.

Of most importance here is the detoxification system. This transports waste to the kidneys or via the gall bladder into the intestines to be excreted – a complicated process known as **biotransformation**. This process involves two specific phases.

Phase I reactions are catalysed by a superfamily of enzymes involving at least 71 genes. These are known as the **cytochrome P450** or mixed-function oxygenase system. In the first stage, oxygen is introduced into the toxins in the blood. Once the process is completed these will be excreted as acids via the urine. Initially, though, the addition of oxygen creates other more toxic products – similar in effect to tranquillizers – which are controlled by antioxidant nutrients and enzymes. In some people (known as pathological detoxifiers) this phase is overactive and can cause a build-up of toxins.

Phase II converts fat-soluble toxins into more water-soluble substances ready for excretion using several different processes including:

- **Acetylation**. This is the main pathway for histamine, serotonin and other compounds which contain aromatic amines. It requires pantothenic acid (vitamin B5) to function.

- o **Sulphation**. This is the primary route of detoxification for neurotransmitters, certain drugs and some phenolics in addition to other compounds.

- o **Methylation**. This is involved in detoxifying phenolics, noradrenalin, adrenaline, dopamine, serotonin and melatonin amongst others. The process is dependent on magnesium.

If problems occur in the liver's detoxification process the normal nutritional metabolism will be disturbed and the toxins will affect other areas of the body. Studies into several diseases like Alzheimer's, Parkinson's and Crohn's have led to the suggestion that some part of this process does not function properly (sulphation being linked to the first two). This would then cause a progression of symptoms from chemical/food sensitivity to a depletion of nutrients and finally to a particular named disease.

Digestion

There are several stages in the digestive process. First is thinking about and anticipating food. This causes the body to begin to secrete digestive enzymes and hydrochloric acid in the stomach, which will help the digestion of the meal once it arrives. This process can be hampered by stress and anxiety which then causes digestive problems such as malabsorption.

The food then travels to the stomach for the second (gastric) stage, during which it becomes acidic. Specific hormones are released which begin the enzyme breakdown of the food – one of the most important being gastrin. This, in turn, causes the secretion of hydrochloric acid which is essential for full digestion. Amino acids such as phenylalanine and tryptophan stimulate the release of pepsin. Poor digestion will arise if the meal is too low in protein as it will not then stimulate gastrin.

The food remains in the stomach for some time before being pushed into the duodenum (the first part of the small intestine) for the next phase. This is where the major breakdown of protein, carbohydrates and fats occurs using digestive enzymes secreted from the exocrine portion of the pancreas. These vary according to the type of food which is being processed. The production of these enzymes is stimulated by two hormones called secretin and cholecystokinin which come from the duodenum, their release being triggered by the acidity of the food. Thus secretin is essential for effective nutrient absorption.

Digestive problems can arise from:

- o an underacid stomach which produces an overacid small intestine;

- o a lack of or reduction of secretin the secretion of which can, in some people, reduce with age.

The **adrenal glands** respond to stress by producing adrenaline and a group of hormones known as the cortiscosteroids – including cortisol. Cortisol depletes the immune system and is often found at high levels in those with stress-related problems.

Appendix D: Hearing and Sound

The **ear** is a complex system concerned with both balance and hearing. It consists of three parts: the outer, middle and inner ears. Sound waves are directed through the auditory canal to the eardrum causing it to vibrate. These are then passed to the middle ear. Infection of this area (which then fills with fluid) is common, especially in young children and until remedied can cause deafness and ear-ache. If the fluid is infected it becomes thick and gluey – hence the description 'glue ear' (otitis media).

The sound vibrations are then passed on to the fluid-filled inner ear which contains two parts:

- the **cochlea**, which passes the sound message to the temporal lobe in the brain where conscious perception of sound occurs;
- the **vestibular system**, which is involved with equilibrium. It is made up of the semicircular canals (which are sensitive to head movements) and the **utriculus** and **sacculus** (which are sensitive to the position of the head when it is not in motion).

The speech centre is located in the left brain and consists of two areas: **Broca's area**, which is concerned with speech, and **Wernicke's area**, which deals with the comprehension of language.

Sound travels through the air as **sound waves**, which have two characteristics:

1. **Frequency.** This is experienced as pitch ranging from deep to high. It refers to and is recorded as the number of vibrations per second, known as hertz (Hz). The audible frequencies (as heard by most humans) fall in the range 15 Hz to 20,000 Hz (usually written as 20kHz or 20 kilohertz). Vibrations below this are known as infrasound whilst those above (such as a 'silent' dog whistle) are referred to as ultrasound.

2. **Amplitude.** This refers to the loudness of the soundwaves and is measured in decibels (dB). A rock band might play at over 120 dB whilst a whisper would be heard at approximately 30 dB. Hearing is often described as good or bad according to the level of decibels the person can hear.

   Normally the ear can hear extremely quiet sounds – between 0 and 20 dB – and can also tolerate very loud sounds (up to 110 dB) without discomfort.

Central auditory processing disorder (CAPD) is a condition in which the person can hear perfectly well but is unable to process or sort the information correctly. He will be unable to differentiate or discriminate between irrelevant and important sounds and can be highly auditorily distractible.

Hyperacusis is hypersensitivity to certain sounds. This is now recognized as a possible factor in tinnitus and also often seems to occur in people with autism and some related conditions.

A similar condition affects people whose hearing is deteriorating, so that even with a hearing loss they still find that some noises seem intolerably loud. This is called **recruitment** – when the ability to grade different intensities of sound is impaired so that some sounds are heard as more loud than they really are. Someone with this condition might be unable to hear sounds (especially those of high frequency) below 50 dB but will find that sounds over 80 dB are uncomfortable and may seem distorted.

Appendix E: Vision

The **eye** has a dual purpose, sending visual stimuli to the visual cortex via a complex system and also passing light via the hypothalamus to the pineal gland which produces melatonin.

The amount of light which enters the eye is controlled by the muscles of the iris, which determine the diameter of the pupil; the sharpest image normally is formed in bright light with a small aperture.

The light rays are refracted (bent) as they pass through the eye. The amount of refraction depends on the shape of the **lens**, which alters in order to focus on near or distant objects.

The **retina** contains two different types of cells: the **rods**, which give black and white vision; and the **cones**, which enable us to see colours – although these only function in the light.

There are two major pathways in the visual system.

- One system is composed of large (**magno**) cells which carry out the fast processes used in seeing motion, position, depth, shape and low contrast.

- The other consists of smaller (**parvo**) cells which carry out the slower processes and enables us to identify colour, still images, detail and high contrasts.

The overlap in the field of vision between our two eyes – which each see slightly different images – gives us **binocular vision**. This allows us to see in three dimensions and also enables us to judge distances.

A **lack of convergence** between the eyes, when the eyes do not work in conjunction with each other, will initially cause the person to see double. Generally, if uncorrected, one eye will generally become dominant and the other ceases to function. Thus the child will become effectively blind in one eye, which leads to a consequent loss of depth perception.

The **visual field** describes the distance within which you can see with your head still and looking to each side whilst covering first one eye and then the other. In some people the visual field is small and this reduces the amount of visual information which they can take in, thereby creating a condition similar to tunnel vision (something you would not be aware of if born with this condition). **Peripheral vision** is the ability to see out of the side of the eye.

A lack of essential fatty acids has been implicated in problems with the development of the eye, in particular in the cells needed to see in dim light, peripheral vision and visual acuity.

Appendix F: Heredity

Each cell in the human body is made up of 46 **chromosomes** which occur in pairs and are inherited in equal measure from each parent. Each cell contains 22 pairs of chromosomes with the remaining two being known as either X or Y. These are the chromosomes which determine the baby's sex: two matching XX chromosomes develop into a female while an X and a Y will be male.

Chromosomes consist of a long string of **deoxyribonucleic acid (DNA)** with associated molecules. Some inherited problems are caused by a fault on a chromosome, as with Down's syndrome for example. It was once thought that Down's syndrome was caused by problems in the transfer of vitamin A from the mother to the foetus but it is now thought to be an inherited problem due to a fault in chromosome 21. However, research suggests that the two theories are not incompatible as chromosome anomalies can be induced by a vitamin deficiency (Jennings 1972, p.131).

A gene is an extremely minute segment of the DNA. Genes aid our development by regulating the production of proteins, which affect the chemical reactions which take place within the body thereby determining our characteristics such as eye colour.

If the child receives two identical genes (one from each parent) he will be born with a particular characteristic e.g. brown eyes. Alternatively if the genes are different one will take dominance over the other (recessive) gene e.g. one brown eye (dominant) gene combined with a blue eye (recessive) gene will give rise to brown eyes.

The dominant characteristic always takes precedence over the recessive feature but the recessive gene stays in the cell and may be passed on to future generations. Thus a particular feature may remain in a family but not appear for several generations.

Unfortunately, genes can mutate or be damaged and the resulting weakness can be passed from parent to child. While the causes of such structural changes may, in many cases, never be known, a variety of factors have been identified as potentially hazardous to the healthy gene. These range from nutritional deficiencies to exposure to certain chemicals.

Appendix G: Prenatal development and birth: potential problems

According to World Health Organization figures Britain currently (reported in March 1998) has the highest proportion of underweight babies (under 5 lb or 2.5 kg) in the European Union, above that of Latvia or Albania. Low birth-weight can lead to an increased risk of the child dying within the first month and also increases the risk of epilepsy, cerebral palsy, mental handicap or autism.

While specialists blame this on social inequalities it is interesting to note that studies (Jennings 1972) show that maternal nutrition, particularly at or about the time of conception, is an extremely important factor in the development of the embryo. Poor nutrition can affect the growth of the foetus and contribute to a low birth-weight. This can lead to the baby being born with a nutrient deficiency thereby leaving him at greater risk of neurodevelopmental disorders (problems affecting the development of the brain) than other children.

Premature babies are also in the high risk category as they are born with immature defence systems which put them at risk from various disorders. Hence it is important to breast-feed such children as, unlike other feeding regimes, human milk supplies the nutrients needed to build the immune system and correct deficits.

Several other things can affect the development of the foetus, which is particularly vulnerable during the first three months. Beside the well documented factors such as illness, smoking, drinking, toxaemia (poison in the blood supply) and anoxia (lack of oxygen during birth), there is, interestingly, severe stress. This is obviously not the kind of short-lived minor stress that happens to most expectant mothers during pregnancy, but refers rather to serious, repeated or prolonged anxiety which may at times be related to overwork. This affects the embryo by bringing adrenalin and other substances into the bloodstream, which are then conveyed to the baby via the umbilical cord. The end result of the mother's anxiety may be seen in a baby who is 'addicted' to higher levels of adrenalin than he should be and, consequently, is more than normally irritable and easily upset.

Breech birth describes the situation in which the baby is bottom down at birth.

Placenta praevia is a major cause of bleeding in the twentieth week and haemorrhage in the final two months. Although the cause is unknown it occurs when the placenta is implanted in the lower part of the uterus where it creates an obstacle when the baby is born – the baby cannot pass down the birth canal without dislodging the placenta and cutting off its own blood supply.

Appendix H: Development

Piaget divided development into various stages, giving examples of the behaviour and general characteristics displayed at each stage:

- ○ **0–2 years**. The young child initially uses only reflex actions but then gradually develops the ability to make various directed movements. She may then begin to symbolize actions – for example, opening her mouth to symbolize the opening of a box.

- ○ **2–4 years**. At first she uses elementary but generalized forms of speech – for example, all men may be 'Daddy'. During this period she gradually begins to use pronouns and generally starts referring to herself as 'I' by the age of three. The use of symbols continues to develop. The child sees no distinction between herself and the rest of the world – for example, she regards objects as alive or aware and believes every event has a cause, so that the table is 'naughty' if she bangs her head on it.

- ○ **4–7 years**. During this stage she gradually develops the ability to reason. Initially her reasoning is based on appearances – for instance, the same amount of liquid in a short wide jar will appear less than in a tall narrow jar – and her thinking is limited by the difficulty of understanding more than one concept at a time so that a set of red wooden beads is either red or wooden. Uses symbolic thinking.

- ○ **7–12 years**. This stage sees increased flexibility and the ability to see another person's point of view. There is development in understanding and reasoning about time, number, weight and size.

- ○ **12 years – adulthood**. Thinking is flexible, sophisticated and symbolic. The child is able to reason about abstract ideas and can formulate general principles, hypotheses, etc.

It is important to note that the ability of many children is in advance of the stages noted above whilst the transition from one stage to another is a more gradual, continuous process than Piaget described.

The beginning of self-awareness can be seen at approximately eighteen months of age, although it takes time to develop fully.

Appendix I: Vitamins and Minerals

Our health is dependent on various vitamins, minerals, fatty acids and amino acids, all of which are needed for many of the chemical reactions taking place within our bodies. These are vital to the body, enabling it to carry out necessary physical repairs and contributing to our emotional behaviour and mental well-being. It is thought that a large percentage of the population may lack sufficient quantities of many of these vitamins and minerals – for example, 75 per cent of Americans have a magnesium deficiency – although perhaps given modern life styles this is not such a surprise.

Whilst prolonged and/or severe deficiency of some of these will eventually cause severe physical symptoms such as scurvy, the road to such severe collapse is often a long one with many other 'lesser' (?) effects being found along the way.

So, Table I.1 gives a brief guide to some of the vitamins and minerals and to the potential effects of certain deficiencies which may be relevant to this book.

Table I.1 Guide to vitamins and minerals

Vitamin/ mineral	Deficiency contributes to:
A	Various visual problems including blurred vision and an inability to adapt to light. Hearing problems
B vitamins	*are found together and therefore a lack of one indicates a deficiency in the others. They are involved in a variety of functions, for example fat and carbohydrate metabolism; regulating the blood sugar balance/boosting the effectiveness of insulin; and in our vision and hearing*
B1 (Thiamine)	Apathy, backache, depression, headaches, insomnia, lack of concentration, low blood pressure, palpitations, dizziness, nausea, vomiting. Visual problems including burning/dry eyes, double vision and involuntary eye movements, sensitivity to light, decreased visual acuity
B2 (Riboflavin)	Depression, hysteria, decreased hand grip, lethargy, hypersensitivity to light
B3 (Niacin)	A multiplicity of symptoms similar to those of anxiety states and phobias. Like those listed under B1 they also include many visual or auditory problems – for example, a misperception of distance, distorted shapes or a 'fog' or even the 'hearing' of (non-existent) voices
B6 (Pyrodoxine)	Migraine, depression, irritability and some physical symptoms. A severe deficiency can cause convulsions in infants plus depression, skin disease and anaemia in adults

B12	Symptoms are variable but may include mild mood disturbance, lack of concentration or, when more severe, agitation, paranoia or depression
Vitamin C (Ascorbic acid)	Bruising, pain (aching limbs/back pain), lethargy, depression, irritability, withdrawal, visual problems, cataracts, anorexia
Vitamins D and E	*are antioxidants which help protect the body against a number of diseases*
Calcium	Nervousness
Folic acid	Affective disorders, depression. (Excess supplementation can reduce the level of vitamin B12)
Iron	Abnormalities of behaviour and mental performance, fearful, less responsive
Magnesium	Muscle weakness and hypersensitivity to sound and touch
Potassium Selenium	Muscle weakness and sensitivity to touch
Zinc	Altered taste – everything tastes awful or has no taste at all. Digestive problems, growth problems, urinary tract problems, hypersensitivity to smell, problems in ridding the body of excess toxins

Appendix J: Tourette's syndrome – genes

Comings can provide much more detailed information, but for those interested in such genetic aspects the genes that have been identified to date (Comings, Comings and Muhleman 1991) are:

1. **The dopamine D receptor gene (DRD2).** The DRD2 appears to be involved in producing a serotonin–dopamine imbalance which affects the function of dopamine. The Taq I A1 allele, a variant of the DRD2 gene (D_2A1) which is carried by one-fifth of the population, has now been found in a substantial proportion of people with Tourette's syndrome and is said to be unusually common in people with autism.

2. **Dopamine B–hydroxylase (DβH) chromosome 9q34.** This is one of the major enzymes for dopamine metabolism catalysing the conversion of dopamine into norepinephrine. Animal experiments suggest that a deficit of DBH results in the excessive production of dopamine which is associated with hyperactivity, self stimulation, stereotypic movements and aggression – all of which may be found in TS. The Taq B allele of DβH (DβH B1) has now also been implicated in TS.

3. **Dopamine transporter (DAT1) on chromosome 5p15.3.** This directs the re-uptake of dopamine from the synapse back into the presynaptic neuron from which it was released. It is the 10/10 genotype of DAT1 which has been implicated both in TS and also in autism.

This is obviously not the end of the research for Comings feels that other genes are yet to be identified. However, whether any of these will link in with the results of the current genetic research into autism remains to be seen.

Appendix K: Treatment of ADHD

Such problems often respond to dietary measures or to supplements of vitamins, essential fatty acids and/or iron but in recent years there has been an increase in the use of medication, particularly Ritalin (a stimulant). Although it may seem strange to use a stimulant to treat people with hyperactivity, such problems stem from an underactive nervous system and it is this which the medication aims to correct.

Peter Bennett, who carried out a study for the QED programme 'Little Monsters' (see main text) now jointly runs the Behavioural Health Partnership which approaches problem behaviours from a nutritional angle. He dislikes the increased use of medication, suggesting instead that Vitamin B6 can be used as an alternative to Ritalin: an idea that has the support of many.

One other treatment for this condition has been brought to my attention recently. This is a product called beCALM'd which was developed by Terry Naher and is based on a combination of amino acids, vitamins and minerals. One trial (as yet unpublished) found that it proved effective in alleviating the symptoms of ADHD in 62 per cent of patients who had previously been on Ritalin and indicated that by the third month there was little difference between this group of ADHD patients and the general population.

Useful Addresses

These are listed alphabetically in five sections:

1. Contact groups for people with autism and Asperger's syndrome
2. Organizations which provide treatment, support etc.
3. Other addresses/organizations
4. Suppliers of vitamins, minerals etc.
5. Respite care/recreational facilities

Contact groups for people with autism and Asperger's syndrome

Autism Network International

PO Box 448
Syracuse
New York 13210 0448
USA

A self-help and advocacy organization run by people with autism for people with autism and related disorders. It is open to people of all ages and abilities throughout the world. It offers a penpal directory, an Internet discussion list and a speaker referral service. It also publishes a quarterly magazine, Our Voice.

Patrick Frey

Oberer Promenadenweg 4
CH-3110 Munsingen
Switzerland
+41 31 7219026

Martijn Dekker

email: martjin@inlv.demon.nl
A self-advocacy group within the Independent Living Movement. Martin Dekker is based in Holland.

Organizations which provide treatment, support etc

Alternative Approaches to Autism

see Centre for Sensory Disorders

Allergy induced Autism (AiA)

8 Hollie Lucas Road
Birmingham B13 0QL
0121 444 6450

Offers support for families and research scientists. Organizes conferences.

Asperger's Partner Support

Brenda Wall
15 Belmont Road
Parkstone
Poole
Dorset BH14 0BD

Autism Research Institute

Dr Bernard Rimland
4182 Adams Avenue
San Diego
California 92116
USA
619 281 7165
Fax 619 563 6840

Has a large data bank of research and publishes information on a variety of subjects, including various approaches to autism – vitamins / minerals, AIT etc. ARRI also publish the Autism Research Review quarterly which details the latest developments in research and treatment.

Autism Research Unit

Dr Paul Shattock or Paul Whiteley
Sunderland Polytechnic
Sunderland SR2 7EE
0191 510 8922

Have done a great deal of research into the metabolic causes of autism. Can provide urine tests to determine whether the person is intolerant of wheat or milk.

Centre for Brain Injury Rehabilitation and Development (BIRD)

5 Lower Brook Street
Ipswich
Suffolk IP4 1AG
01473 219505
Fax 01473 219707

Provides treatment for aberrant reflexes.

Centre for Social and Communication Disorders

Dr Lorna Wing and Dr Judith Gould
Elliot House
113 Masons Hill
Bromley
Kent BR2 9HT
0181 466 0098

Centre for Sensory Disorders

Stella Waterhouse
3 Platt Close
Beadon Park
Salcombe
Devon TQ8 8NZ
01548 843860

Incorporates Alternative Approaches to Autism. Provides advice, help and support plus auditory training and treatment for visual problems.

Centre for the Study of Complementary Medicine

14 Harley House
Upper Harley St
London NW1 4PR
0171 935 7848

or

51 Bedford Place
Southampton
Hampshire SO15 2DT
01703 334752

or

Dr Dankzak
IBH Victoria Hospital
Victoria Park
Daisy Bank Road
Manchester MI4 15QH
0161 257 2233

Some of the doctors in this practice already have experience of treating children and adults with autism.

Colorimeter –
Specific Learning Difficulties Clinic
Dr Bruce Evans
The Institute of Optometry
56–62 Newington Causeway
London SE1 6DS
0171 407 1479
The clinic can also supply a list of optometrists throughout the country who use the colorimeter and provide tinted lenses.

Communications Options
5 Ingham Road
London NW6 1DG
Anne Emerson 0181 964 9307
Trudi Scrivener 0171 433 1146
Information on facilitated communication in Britain.

Communication Therapies
Rosemarie Mason
58 Brisbane Road
Ilford
Essex IG1 4SL
0181 554 6522

Delacato UK
151 Camberton Rd
Leighton Buzzard
Bedfordshire LU7 7UW
01525 853337

Delacato and Delacato
Consultants In Learning
Thomas Rd At Northwestern
Linslade Avenue
Philadelphia
Pennsylvania 19118
USA
610 828 4881
Evaluates and prescribes home treatment programmes for brain-injured children.

Developmental Centre

Steve Clarke
PO Box 32
Manchester M24 6SW
0161 654 4104

Division of Special Education and Rehabilitation

Douglas Biklen
School of Education
Syracuse University
805 S Crouse Avenue
Syracuse
New York 13244 2280
USA
315 443 2693
Information on facilitated communication in the USA.

Geneva Centre

111 Merton Street
4th Floor
Toronto
Ontario M4S 3A7
Canada
416 322 7877
Fax 416 322 5894

Georgiana Organization

690 Finchley Road
London NW11 7NN
0181 455 5107 or 0181 458 2496
or
PO Box 2607
Westport CT06 880
USA
203 454 1221
Information on AIT and local practitioners who use Bérard's method.

Giant Steps

PO Box 23547
227 Vodden Street East
Brampton
Ontario L6V 1N2
Canada
416 499 6218

Offers a programme of intensive therapies, education and support services.

HACS (Hillingdon Autistic Care and Support)

22 Cherry Grove
Hillingdon
Middlesex UB8 3ET

This group, founded by Anna and Sean Kennedy, established a school for children with autism in 1999.

Higashi School

2618 Massachusetts Avenue
Rexington
MA 02173
USA
617 862 7222

For details of a possible British school contact:

British Higashi Hope Foundation

Secretary Mrs Rita Murray
71 Heath Park Road
Romford
Essex RM2 5UL
01708 449286

Information on schools for children with special educational needs can be found in Special Schools in Britain *available from Network Publishing, 01572 834400.*

International Autistic Research Organization

49 Orchard Avenue
Shirley
Croydon CR0 7NE
0181 777 0095

Irlen Institute

5380 Village Road
Long Beach
California 90808
310 496 2550

This also has centres throughout Britain, Ireland and many other countries.

For the address of the centre in Britain nearest you contact:

Irlen South West

Patricia Clayton
123 High Street
Chard
Somerset TA20 1QT
0146 065555

or

Irlen Centre

Ann Wright
9 Orme Court
London W2 4RL
0171 229 8810

Institutes for the Achievement of Human Potential

8801 Stenton Avenue
Wyndmoor
PA 19038
USA
+1 215 233 2050

Offers assessment and home treatment programmes for brain-injured children.

Institute of Neuro-Physiological Psychology (INPP)

Sally Goddard Blythe and Peter Blythe
Warwick House
4 Stanley Place
Chester CH1 2LU
01244 311414

Treatment for aberrant reflexes. Available from practitioners throughout the country and abroad.

JABS (Justice, Awareness and Basic Support)

1 Gawsworth Road
Golbourne
Nr Warrington
Cheshire WA3 3RF
01942 713565 or 01204 796433 or 0191 258 1466
The latest information re vaccine damage.

Light and Sound Therapy Centre

90 Queen Elizabeth Walk
London N16 5UQ
0181 880 1269 or 0181 802 1616
Fax 0181 809 4303
Offers AIT, light therapy, facilitated communication etc.

MAAP

PO Box 524
Crown Point
IN 46307
USA
A positive international newsletter network for parents and professionals.

National Autistic Society

393 City Road
London EC1V 1NE
0171 833 2299
Provides day and residential centres for the care and education of children with autism plus some facilities for adults with autism. Supplies information to parents and professionals and can provide contact names for local support groups. Publishes a quarterly magazine. Also runs an Asperger's syndrome support group and can give the names of local contacts.

Option Institute and Fellowship

2080 South Undermountain Road
Sheffield
MA 01257
USA

Option Trust for Autism

Mr and Mrs P.M. Hamilton-Ely
Orchard House
Moor Hill
Fovant
Salisbury
Wiltshire SP3 5LB

Parents and Professionals and Autism (PAPA)

Resource Centre
Knockbraken Healthcare Park
Saintfield Road
Belfast BT8 8BH
01232 401729

PRO Autism

85 Colleton Drive
Twyford
Reading RG10 0AX
Parental contact / support group. They are active fundraisers and have now set up a Respite Care Facility at 77 Russell Street, Reading.

Scottish Society for Autistic Children

Hilton House
Alloa Business Park
Whins Road
Aloa
SK10 3SA
01259 720044
Provides day and residential centres for the care and education of children with autism. Puts parents in touch with one another. Gives information and advice.

Sound Learning Centre

Pauline Allen
12 The Rise
London N13 5LE
0181 882 1060

Other addresses/organizations

Behavioural Health Partnership

Peter Bennett
Outalong
Lower Broad Oak Road
West Hill
Ottery St Mary
Devon EX11 1XH
0171 827 6536

For children with behavioural problems (not autism). Provides a behavioural health assessment, detoxification programme, etc.

Educational Kinesiology UK Foundation (Brain Gym)

12 Golders Rise
London NW4 2HR
0181 202 3141

British Epilepsy Association

National Information Centre
40 Hanover Square
Leeds
LS3 1BE
01532 439393 or Helpline 01345 089599 (charged at local rates)

British Tuberous Sclerosis Association

Janet Medcalfe
Little Barnsley Farm
Catshill
Bromsgrove
Worcestershire B61 0NQ
01527 71898

Feldenkrais Guild UK

PO Box 370
London N10 3XA
0700 785 5006

Foresight

Mrs Peter Barnes
28 The Paddock
Godalming
Surrey GU7 1XD
For information on healthy pregnancy.

The National Society for Phenylketonuria (UK) Ltd

7 Southfield Close
Willen
Milton Keynes MK15 9LL
01908 691653

Sense

11 Clifton Terrace
London N4 3SR
0171 272 7774

Society of Homeopaths

2 Artizan Road
Northampton NN1 4HU
01604 21400

Tourette Syndrome Association

Mr Roy Hillard
169 Wickham Way
Welling
Kent
or
42–40 Bell Boulevard
Bayside
NY 11361 2857
USA
718 224 2599

UK Rett Syndrome Association

113 Friern Barnet Road
London N11 3EU
0181 361 5161
Information for parents and details of all organizations offering help with particular handicaps.

Suppliers of vitamins, minerals, etc.

Health Concern Ltd

28 Durley Road
London N16 5JS.
0171 502 0134

Sells vitamins and minerals specifically for people with ADD, ADHD, autism, hyperactivity, Down's syndrome, etc.

Efamol Ltd

Weyvern House
Weyvern Park
Portsmouth Road
Peasmarch
Surrey GU3 1NA
0870 6060128 or Freephone 0800 318545

Nutri Ltd

Buxton Road
New Mills
High Peak SK22 3JU
01663 746794

Will provide the name of a nutritional practitioner in your area or give advice on Ultra Clear and other products.

Ms Heidi Wagner

14666 Beacon Drive
Minnetonka
MN 55345
USA
612 931 9914

Respite care/recreational facilities

Aid for Autism
Christine Bertolucci
Grangewood School
Fore Street
Pinner HA5 2JQ
01895 625811 or 0181 429 3772

An out-of-school centre for children with autism and social and communication disorders.

Camp Mohawk

Wargrave on Thames
Berkshire RG10 8PU
0118 940 4045

A holiday camp specifically for children with autism which runs for a few weeks in the summer. Facilities include an all-weather swimming pool, jacuzzi, three multi-sensory rooms and an on-site hospital which also offers AIT.

Bibliography

Ahuja, A. (1999) *The Times*, 9.3.99.

American Psychiatric Association (1987) *Diagnostic and Statistical Manual of Mental Disorders, 3rd Edition* (revised). Washington: American Psychiatric Association.

Asperger, H. (1944) 'Die autistischen Psychopathen im Kindersalter.' *Archiv für Psychiatrie und Nervenkrankheit 117*, 76–136.

Bailey, A., Luthbert, P. and Dean, A. (1998) 'A full genome screen for autism with evidence for linkage to a region on chromosome 7q.' *Human Molecular Genetics 7*, 3.

Baron-Cohen, S., Leslie, A.M. and Frith, U. (1985) 'Does the autistic child have a "theory of mind"?' *Cognition 21*, 1, 37–46.

Baron-Cohen, S., Allen, J. and Gillberg, C. (1992) 'Can autism be detected at 18 months? The needle, the haystack and the CHAT.' *British Journal of Psychiatry 161*, 839–843.

Bauman, M.L. and Kemper, T.L. (1985) 'Histoanatomic observations of the brain in early infantile autism.' *Neurology 35*, 6, 866–874.

Baxter, L.R., Schwartz, J.M. and Bergman, K.S. (1992) 'Caudate glucose metabolism rate changes with both drug and behaviour therapy for obsessive-compulsive disorder.' *Archives Of General Psychiatry 49*.

Bemporad, J.R. (1979) 'Adult recollections of a formerly autistic child.' *Journal of Autism and Developmental Disorders 9*, 2, 179–198.

Bender, L. (1959) 'Autism in children with mental deficiency.' *American Journal of Mental Deficiency 63*, 81–86.

Ber, A. (1983) 'Neutralization of phenolic aromatic food compounds in a holistic general practice.' *Journal of Orthomolecular Psychiatry 12*, 4, 283–291.

Bérard, G. *Hearing Equals Behaviour.* New Canaan, Connecticut: Keats Publishing.

Bettleheim, B. (1967) *The Empty Fortress: Infantile Autism and the Birth of the Self.* New York: The Free Press.

Biklen, D. and Cardinal, D.N. (eds) (1997) *Contested Words Contested Science.* New York: Teachers College Press.

Birnbeck Hill, G. (ed) (1966) *Johnsonian Miscellanies, Volume 2.* London: Constable.

Blakeslee, S. (1991) 'Study ties dyslexia to brain flaw affecting vision and other senses'. *New York Times,* 15.9.91.

Bland, J. (1983) *Digestive Enzymes.* New Canaan, Connecticut: Keats Publishing.

Boswell, J. (1969) *Life of Johnson.* London: Oxford University Press.

Boyle, J. (1984) *The Pain of Confinement.* Cannongate Publishing.

Brazelton, T.B. (1993) *Touchpoints.* London: Penguin.

Carter, R. (1998) *Mapping the Mind.* London: Weidenfeld and Nicholson.

Clare, J. (1998) 'They don't make fun of you… children with learning difficulties need special attention.' *Daily Telegraph*, 15.4.1998.

Coccaro, E.F. and Murphy, D.L. (eds) (1990) *Serotonin in Major Psychiatric Disorders.* Washington, DC: The American Psychiatric Press.

Comings, D.E. (1981) *Tourette's Syndrome and Human Behaviour.* Duarte CA: Hope City Press.

Comings, D.E., Comings, B.G. and Muhleman, D. (1991) 'The dopamine DZ receptor locus as a modifying gene in neuropsychiatric disorders.' *Journal of the American Medical Association 266*, 13, 1793–1800.

Cook, E.H., Charak, D.A. and Arida, J. (1994) 'Depressive and obsessive compulsive symptoms in hyperserotonic parents of children with an autistic disorder.' *Psychiatry Research, 52,* 25–33.

Cook, E.H. and Leventhal, B.L. (1996) 'The serotonin system in autism.' *Current Opinion in Pediatrics 8*, 348–354.

Corchesne, E., Eyre, and Watson (1994) 'More evidence links autism, cerebellar defects.' *Autism Research Review 8*, 2,1–7.

Coren, S. (1992) *The Left Hander Syndrome.* London: John Murray.

Coward, A. (1998) *Daily Telegraph*, 15.4.98.

Creak, M. (1961) 'The schizophrenic syndrome in childhood.' *British Medical Journal 2.*

Crossley, R. and McDonald A. (1980) *Annie's Coming Out.* London: Penguin.

Dabiri, L.M., Pasta, D., Darby, J. and Mosbacher, D. (1994) 'Effectiveness of vitamin E for the treatment of long term tardive dyskinesia.' *American Journal of Psychiatry 151*, 6, 925–926.

Darwin, C. (1904) *The Expression of Emotion in Man and Animals.* London: John Murray.

Datlow Smith, M. (19 90) *Autism and Life in the Community.* Baltimore, MD: Paul H. Brookes Publishing Co.

Delacato, C. (1974) *The Ultimate Stranger.* New York: Doubleday.

Dennison, P. (1981) *Switching On.* Ventura, California: Edu-Kinesthetics Inc.

Docker Drysdale, B. (1993) *Therapy and Consultation in Child Care.* London: Free Association Books.

Doman, G. (1990) *What to Do about your Brain Injured Child.* Philadelphia: The Better Baby Press.

Donnellan, A.M. and Leary, M.R. (1995) *Movement Differences and Diversity in Autism/Mental Retardation.* Madison: DRI Press.

Doyle, C. (1998) 'Letting light into a shuttered world.' *Daily Telegraph*, 1.12.98.

Doyle Haynes, C., Giddens, D.A., King, G.D. and Dempsey, R.L. (1979) 'The improvement of cognition and personality after Cartoid endarterectomy.' *Surgery 80*, 6, 699–704.

Eastham, D. (1989) *Understand.* Ottawa: Oliver Pate.

Ehlers, S. and Gillberg, C. (1993) 'The epidemiology of Asperger Syndrome. A total population study.' *Journal of Child Psychology and Psychiatry, 34*, 8, 1327–1350.

Feldenkrais, M. (1949) *Body and Mature Behaviour*. London: Routledge and Kegan Paul.

Fisch, G. (1992) 'Is autism associated with fragile X syndrome?' *American Journal of Medical Genetics 43*.

Fisher, M. (1987) 'Letter to the Editor.' *Communication 21*,1.

Frith, U. (1989) *Autism: Explaining the Enigma*. Oxford: Basil Blackwell.

George M.S., Costa, D.C. and Kouris, K. (1992) 'Cerebral blood flow abnormalities in adults with infantile autism.' *Journal of Nervous and Mental Diseases 180*, 7, 413–417.

Gerland, G. (1997) *A Real Person – Life on the Outside*. Translated by J.Tate. London: Souvenir Press.

Gillingham, G. (1991) 'Autism: disability or superability.' Sunderland: *Collected Papers: Therapeutic Approaches to Autism. Research and Practice*.

Goddard Blythe, S. (1990) *A Developmental Basis for Learning Difficulties and Language Disorders*. INNP Monograph Series 1.

Goddard Blythe, S. (1991) *Personal Correspondence*.

Goddard Blythe, S. (1996) *A Teacher's Window into the Child's Mind*. Eugene, Oregon: Fern Ridge Press – Contact INNP for copies.

Gold, S. (1986) *When Children Invite Child Abuse*. Eugene, Oregon:Fern Ridge Press.

Goleman, D. (1995) *Emotional Intelligence*. London: Bloomsbury Publishing Co.

Gould, J. Rigg, M. and Bignall, L. (1991) *The Higashi Experience*. London: National Autistic Society Publication.

Grandin, T. and Scariano, M.M. (1986) *Emergence Labeled Autistic*. Arena Press.

Grandin, T. (1989) 'An autistic person's view of holding therapy.' *Communication 23*, 3.

Grove, T. (1988) 'Barnaby Rudge: A case study in autism.' *Communication 22*, 1, 12–16.

Hashimoto, T., Tatama, M. and Miyazaki, M. (1992) 'Reduced brainstem size in children with autism.' *Brain and Development 14*, 2, 94–97.

Herault, J., Perrot, A. and Barthelemy, C. (1992) 'Genetic abnormalities associated with infantile autism.' Presented at the Association Francaise de Psychiatrie Biologique.

Highfield, R. '"Shyness may lie in the genes," says Harvard Professor.' *Daily Telegraph*, 20.3.91.

Highfield, R. and Berry, A. 'Eccentric dons may be autistic.' *Daily Telegraph*, 29.8.91.

Hocking, B. (1990) *Little Boy Lost*. London: Bloomsbury Publishing.

Hornsby, B. (1984) *Overcoming Dyslexia*. London: Martin Dunitz.

Hundley, J.M. (1971) *The Small Outsider*. London: Angus and Robertson.

Itard, J.M.G. and Humphrey, M. (1962) *The Wild Boy of Averyon*. (English Translation) New York: Appleton-Century-Crofts.

Irlen, H. (1991) *Reading by the Colors*. New York: Avery Publishing Group.

James, O. (1997) *Britain on the Couch*. London: Century.

Jennings, I. (1972) *Vitamins in Endocrine Metabolism*. Reproduced for Foresight by William Heinemann Medical Press.

Jordan, I. (1998) *Visual Dyslexia.* Scunthorpe: Desktop Publications.

Kagan, J.J., Reznick, S. and Snidman, M. (1988) 'Biological bases of childhood shyness.' *Science 240,* 167–171.

Kanner, L. (1943) 'Autistic disturbances of affective contact.' *Nervous Child 2,* 217–250.

Kanner, L. (1946) 'Irrelevant and metaphorical language in early infantile autism.' *American Journal of Psychiatry 103,* 242–246.

Kanner, L. and Eisenberg, L. (1956) 'Early infantile autism.' *American Journal of Orthopsychiatry 26,* 556–566.

Kanner, L. and Lesser, L.I. (1958) 'Early infantile autism.' *Paediatric Clinics of North America 5,* 711–730.

Keenan, B. (1992) *An Evil Cradling.* London: Hutchinson.

Kiernan, V. (1997) 'Noise pollution robs kids of language skills.' *New Scientist 2081.*

Kurlan, R. (1993) *Handbook of Tourette's Syndrome and Related Tic and Behavioural Disorders.* New York: Martin Dekker.

Le Fanu, J. (1999) 'The art of seeing through yellow-tinted spectacles.' *Sunday Telegraph,* 7.2.99.

Lewine, J.D., Irlen, H. and Orrison, W.W. (1999) 'Visual evoked magnetic fields in scotopic sensitivity syndrome.' Irlen fact sheet.

Lipowski, Z.J. (1975) 'Sensory and information inputs overload: Behavioural effects.' *Comprehensive Psychiatry 16,* 3,199-221.

MacDonald, V. 'Measles jabs suspected in autism cases.' *Daily Telegraph,* 24.11.96.

Marriage, J. and Barnes, N.M. (1995) 'Is central hyperacusis a symptom of 5-hydroxytrytamine (5-HT) dysfunction?' *Journal of Laryngology and Otology 109,* 915-921.

Maurice, C. (1993) *Let Me Hear Your Voice.* New York: Ballantine.

Mayell, M. (1995) *Off the Shelf Natural Health.* London: Boxtree Ltd.

McClelland, R.J. *et al.* (1992) 'Central conduction time in childhood autism.' *British Journal of Psychiatry 160,* 659–663.

McDougle, C.J., Naylor, S.T. and Goodman, W.K. (1993) 'Acute tryptophan depletion in autistic disorder: A controlled case study.' *Biological Psychiatry 33,* 547–550.

McInnes, J.A. and Treffry, J.M. (1982) *Deaf-Blind Infants and Children.* Buckingham: Open University Press.

McLean, T. (1985) *Mental Jam.* London: Hodder and Stoughton.

Menage, G., Thibault, G. and Barthelemy, G. (1992) 'CD4+ CD45RA+ T Lymphocyte deficiency in autistic children: effect of a pyridoxine-magnesium treatment.' *Brain dysfunction 5,* 326–333.

Miedzianik, D. (1986) *My Autobiography.* c/o Dr Elizabeth Newson, Child Development Research Unit, University of Nottingham.

Minderaa, V.R.B., Volkmar, F.R. and Hansen, C.R. (1985) 'Snout and visual rooting reflexes in infantile autism.' *Journal of Autism and Developmental Disorders 15,* 4.

National Autistic Society (1997) *Statistics Sheet 1,* 3rd Edition, June.

Newson, E. (1977) 'Diagnosis and early problems of autistic children.' *Communication XI.*

Newson, E. (1979) *Making Sense of Autism: An Overview.* From a collection of conference papers published by the NAS and Inge Wakehurst Trust. 1–24.

Nony. (1993) 'Speculation on light sensitivity.' *Our Voice 3,* 1.

O'Gorman, G. (1967) *The Nature of Childhood Autism.* London: Butterworth.

O'Neill, J.L. (1999) *Through the Eyes of Aliens.* London: Jessica Kingsley Publishers.

Ornitz, E.M., Guthrie, D. and Farley, A.J. (1977) 'The early development of autistic children.' *Journal of Autism and Childhood Schizophrenia 7,* 207–230.

Panksepp, J. (1979) 'A neurochemical theory of autism.' *Trends in Neuro Science 2,* 174–177.

Park, C.C. (1982) *The Siege, 2nd Edition.* New York: Little, Brown and Company.

Pascoe, E.J. (1991) 'Can autism be cured?' *Woman's Day Magazine,* May.

Peltola, H., Patja, A. and Leinikki, P. (1998) 'No evidence for measles, mumps and rubella vaccine-associated inflammatory bowel disease or autism in a 14-year prospective study.' *The Lancet 351,* 9112, 1327–1328.

Rapoport, J. (1990) *The Boy Who Couldn't Stop Washing.* London: Fontana/Collins.

Reiss and Freund, L. (1992) 'Behavioural phenotype of fragile X Syndrome: DSM-111-R autistic behaviour in male children.' *American Journal of Medical Genetics 43.*

Rimland, B. (1964) *Infantile Autism.* New York: Appleton-Century-Crofts.

Rimland, B. (1989) 'GTC vitamin and mineral formula.' Institute For Child Behaviour Research.

Russell, P. (1979) *The Brain Book.* London: Routledge and Kegan Paul.

Rutter, M. (1978) *Diagnosis and Definition In Autism: A Reappraisal of Concepts and Treatment.* New York: Plenum Press.

Sacks, O. (1986) *The Man Who Mistook His Wife for a Hat.* London: Picador.

Sacks, O. (1987) 'The autist artist.' *Communication 21,* 2, 12-18.

Sanchez, L.E., Campbell, M. and Small, A.M. (1996) 'A pilot study of clomipramine in young autistic children.' *Journal of the American Academy of Child and Adolescent Psychiatry 35,* 4, 537–544.

Scott, C. (1998) 'Damage limitation.' *Sunday Times Magazine,* 28.6.98.

Shattock, P. (1991) 'Proteins, peptides and problems in autism.' Sunderland: *Collected Papers: Therapeutic Approaches to Autism: Research and Practice.*

Shattock, P. and Savery, D. (1997) *Autism as a Metabolic Disorder.* Sunderland: Autism Research Unit.

Sinclair, J. (1992) 'Bridging the gaps: an inside-out view of autism.' In E. Schopler and G.B. Mesibov (eds) *High Functioning Individuals with Autism.* New York: Plenum.

Singh, V., Warran, R.P. and Odell, D.J. (1993) 'Antibodies to myelin basic protein in children with autistic behaviour.' *Autism Research Review 7,* 1, 6.

Smits, T. (1997) *The Post Vaccination Syndrome.* Netherlands: Waalre.

Spencer, Pulaski, M.A. (1980) *Understanding Piaget.* New York: Harper Row.

Stehli, A. (1990) *The Sound of a Miracle.* New York: Doubleday.

Stehli, A. (ed) (1995) *Dancing in the Rain.* USA: The Georgiana Organization Inc.

Stuttaford, T. (1992) 'Life looks up for mad professors.' *The Times,* 3 July.

Tinbergen, A.N. and E. (1983) *Autistic Children: New Hope for a Cure.* London: George Allen and Unwin.

Tradowsky, P. (1997) *Kasper Hauser: The Struggle for the Spirit.* London: Temple Lodge.

Tuormaa, T.E. (1991) *An Alternative to Psychiatry.* Lewes: The Book Guild.

Upton, G. (1992) 'Two hours in the Musashino Higashi Gakuen.' *Communication 26,* 1.

Volkmar, F.R. and Cohen, D.J. (1985) 'The experience of infantile autism: A first person account by Tony W.' *Journal of Autism and Developmental Disorders 15,* 1, 45–54.

Waite, T. (1993) *Taken on Trust.* London: Hodder and Stoughton.

Wakefield A.J. *et al.* (1998) 'Ileal-lymphoid-nodular hyperplasia, non-specific colitis, and pervasive developmental disorder in children.' *The Lancet 351,* 9103, 637–641.

Welch, M. (1988) *Holding Time.* London: Century.

White, B.B. and White, M.S. (1987) 'Autism from the inside.' *Medical Hypotheses 24.*

Wilkins, A. (1995) *Visual Stress.* Oxford: Oxford Science Publications.

Wilkins, A., Milroy, R. and Nimmo-Smith, I. (1992) *Preliminary Observations Concerning Treatment of Visual Discomfort and Associated Perceptual Distortion.* Oxford: Butterworth-Heinemann.

Williams, D. (1992) *Nobody Nowhere.* New York: Doubleday (Republished 1999, London: Jessica Kingsley Publishers).

Williams, D. (1996) *Autism – An Inside-Out Approach.* London: Jessica Kingsley Publishers.

Williams, D. (1996) *Like Color to the Blind.* New York: Times Books–Random House (Republished 1999, London: Jessica Kingsley Publishers).

Williams, D. (1998) *Autism and Sensing.* London: Jessica Kingsley Publishers.

Wilson, I. (1989) *Superself.* London: Sidgwick and Jackson.

Wiltshire, S. (1987) *Drawings: Selected and with an Introduction by Sir Hugh Casson.* London: Dent.

Wing, L. (1980) *Autistic Children – A Guide for Parents, 2nd edition.* London: Constable.

Wing, L. and Gould, J. (1979) 'Severe impairments of social interaction and associated abnormalities in children: epidemiology and classification.' *Journal of Autism and Developmental Disorders,* 9, 11–29.

Wolff, S. (1995) *Loners: The Life Path of Unusual Children.* London: Routledge.

Wood, M. (1984) *Living with a Hyperactive Child.* London: Souvenir Press.

Zohar, J., Murphy, D.L., and Zohar-Kadanch (1990) 'Serotonin in obsessive compulsive disorders.' In E. Coccaro and D.L. Murphy (eds) *Serotonin in Major Psychiatric Disorders.* Washington: The American Psychiatric Press.

Subject index

abuse
  child 127, 217–19,
    227–8
accommodation anomalies
  168
acetylation 340
acetylcholine 331
adrenaline 119
adulthood, choices in
    314–18
  for the client 317–18
  for the parent 314–17
alcohol addiction 101
abstract ideas, inability to
    think in 38–9
addiction 92–3, 101, 203
adrenal glands 341
adrenaline 332
aggression 108, 117
agoraphobia 62
Aid for Autism 364
AIT *see* Auditory Integration
    Treatment
albinism 60
alexithymia 54–6, 133,
    190–1
allergies 100, 109, 114,
    201, 225
  and metabolic disorders
    74–82, 201
Allergy-induced Autism
    Support and Self-Help
    Group (AiA) 75–6, 77,
    103, 161, 163, 167,
    320, 353
Alternative Approaches to
    Autism 244–5, 264,
    352
  Consultancy 242
Alzheimer's disease 152
American Psychiatric
    Association 18, 96
amplitude 342
amygdala 337–8
amino acids 330

andrenoleukodystrophy 196
anger 16, 41
anxiety 16, 42, 88–94, 121,
    127, 131, 135–6, 140,
    199, 204, 205, 207–8
  acute, excessive 185, 193
  and OCD behaviours
    175–85
aphasia 108, 330
'archipelago' child 124
architectural drawings
    (Wiltshire) 15
ARRI 262
art therapy 303
AS *see* Asperger's syndrome
Asperger's Partner Support
    353
Asperger's syndrome (AS)
    11, 16, 18, 19, 53, 101,
    119, 121, 156, 160,
    171–5, 192, 199–208,
    227, 319, 327
asymmetrical tonic neck
    reflex (ATNR) 156, 208
attachment *see* bonding
attention deficit disorder
    hyperactivity disorder
    (ADD/ADHD) 82–7, 100,
    119, 159, 162, 163,
    166, 167, 171, 173,
    192, 195, 199, 201,
    210, 214, 216, 223,
    227, 248, 300
  treatment of 351
attention problems 108
auditory dyslaterality 65
Auditory Integration
    Treatment (AIT) 63, 71,
    243, 244, 245, 260–4,
    267
auditory problems 63–71,
    235
  hypersensitivity 48–50,
    63–71d
*Autism – An Inside–Out
    Approach* (Williams) 46,
    264

Autism as a Metabolic Disorder
    (Shattock and Savery)
    247
Autism Network
    International 352
Autism – New Hope for a Cure
    (Tinbergens) 29
Autism Research Institute
    (ARI) 250, 353
Autism Research Unit,
    Sunderland 69, 353
autisms 144
Autistic Artist, The (Sacks) 17
Autistic Children (Wing) 31
Autism Research Review
    International 114
'autos' 114
awareness 16
Awareness through
    Movement 297
axons 334

babies
  abnormal response to
    stimuli in 45–6
  'background of serious
    retardation' (in Creak's
    list of criteria) 16,
    186–90
Barnaby Rudge (Dickens) 11
basal ganglia (caudate and
    putamen) 335
breech birth 346
behaviour
  modification 271–7
  unusual 16, 41–2
Behavioural Health
    Partnership 361
Bethlehem Royal Asylum
    (Bedlam) 11
binocular system 344
biotransformation 340
birth
  breech 346
  and human development
    20–1
  inbuilt fragility at 90
  NDD indicator 234
  potential problems 346
  premature 201

Author index